CASE STUDIES IN

CULTURAL ANTHROPOLOGY

SERIES EDITORS

George and Louise Spindler

STANFORD UNIVERSITY

THE MI'KMAQ
Resistance, Accommodation, and
Cultural Survival

THE MI'KMAQ
Resistance, Accommodation, and Cultural Survival

HARALD E. L. PRINS

Kansas State University

HARCOURT BRACE COLLEGE PUBLISHERS

Fort Worth   Philadelphia   San Diego   New York   Orlando   Austin   San Antonio
Toronto   Montreal   London   Sydney   Tokyo

Publisher	Ted Buchholz
Editor in Chief	Christopher P. Klein
Senior Acquisitions Editor	Stephen T. Jordan
Developmental Editor	Margaret McAndrew Beasley
Project Editor	Laura J. Hanna
Production Manager	Diane Gray
Art Directors	Jim Dodson, Burl Sloan
Composition	Graphic Express

Cover photo courtesy of the History Collection, Nova Scotia Museum, Halifax. Pictured are (l-r) Mrs. Catherine Sack Maloney, Judge Christopher Paul, Mrs. Mary Jeremy Sadis, and Chief Peter Paul in Shubenacadie, N.S., 1905.

ISBN 0-03-053427-5

Library of Congress Catalog Card Number: 95-79475

Address for Editorial Correspondence: Harcourt Brace College Publishers, 301 Commerce Street, Suite 3700, Fort Worth, TX 76102.

Address for Orders: Harcourt Brace & Company, 6277 Sea Harbor Drive, Orlando, FL 32887-6777. 1-800-782-4479, or 1-800-433-0001 (in Florida).

Printed in the United States of America

5 6 7 8 9 0 1 2 3 4   066   0 9 8 7 6 5 4 3 2 1

To Bunny McBride

For the blessings of her companionship

Foreword

ABOUT THE SERIES

These case studies in cultural anthropology are designed for students in beginning and intermediate courses in the social sciences, to bring them insights into the richness and complexity of human life as it is lived in different ways, in different places. The authors are men and women who have lived in the societies they write about and who are professionally trained as observers and interpreters of human behavior. Also, the authors are teachers; in their writing, the needs of the student reader remain foremost. It is our belief that when an understanding of ways of life very different from one's own is gained, abstractions and generalizations about the human condition become meaningful.

The scope and character of the series have changed constantly since we published the first case studies in 1960, in keeping with our intention to represent anthropology as it is. We are concerned with the ways in which human groups and communities are coping with the massive changes wrought in their physical and sociopolitical environments in recent decades. We are also concerned with the ways in which established cultures have solved life's problems. And we want to include representation of the various modes of communication and emphasis that are being formed and reformed as anthropology itself changes.

We think of this series as an instructional series, intended for use in the classroom. We, the editors, have always used case studies in our teaching, whether for beginning students or advanced graduate students. We start with case studies, whether from our own series or from elsewhere, and weave our way into theory, and then turn again to cases. For us, they are the grounding of our discipline.

ABOUT THE AUTHOR

Harald E. L. Prins (Ph.D., New School for Social Research, 1988) was born in the Netherlands in 1951 as one of an anthropologist's nine children. His interest in North American Indians began in childhood, but his first personal encounter did not take place until 1971, when he visited the Passamaquoddy in Maine. As a student, he traveled widely in Europe, the Middle East, Central and South America. After his doctoral (1976) at the University of Nijmegen, he joined its history department as research and teaching fellow. Two years later, he was elected List Fellow at the New School for Social Research in New York. This was followed by training in advanced 16-mm filmmaking and then a year of fieldwork in the Argentine pampas. Upon return to the United States, he was hired as director of research and development by the Association of Aroostook Indians (1981–1982). This led to a decade of work with the Mi'kmaq of northern Maine, which resulted in a successful federal recognition and land claims settlement case for the Aroostook Band of Micmacs. In addition to ethnohistorical research, grass-roots community organizing, and political activism, he also coproduced a documentary on Mi'kmaq basketmakers (*Our Lives in Our Hands,* 1985). In 1986 he accepted a visiting lectureship at Bowdoin College, followed by visiting teaching positions at Colby College and the University of Maine. In 1990, after testifying before Congress as expert witness on behalf of the Mi'kmaq, he joined the faculty of Kansas State University, where he serves as associate professor of cultural anthropology. In 1993 the university awarded him the Conoco Prize for Outstanding Undergraduate Teaching. He has published over sixty scholarly articles, book chapters, essays, and reviews, and coedited *American Beginnings: Exploration, Culture, and Cartography in the Land of Norumbega* (1995). Often collaborating with his wife, Bunny McBride, a writer, he now lives in the beautiful Flint Hills of Kansas.

ABOUT THIS CASE STUDY

The Mi'kmaq: Resistance, Accommodation, and Cultural Survival chronicles the endurance of a tribal nation—its ordeals in the face of colonialism and its current struggle for self-determination and cultural revitalization. Inhabiting the northern Atlantic seaboard, Mi'kmaqs were among the first Indians in North America to encounter Europeans, and this book details the historical dynamics that have marked their culture over the last 500 years.

Those who read these pages will glimpse the full nature of the calamities visited upon the Mi'kmaq by the coming of the Europeans. First came the epidemics of smallpox, measles, and influenza that decimated their populations by as much as 90 percent. But the epidemics were just the beginning. As the country of the Mi'kmaq began to fill with Europeans, the relations of the Mi'kmaq to their own land and the relations to their animal kin (as they conceived of them) were profoundly disturbed. Exploitation of fur-bearing creatures broke all customary restraints on the taking of animal life, so that whole areas were "cleaned out" of fur-bearing animals. Mi'kmaq dependency upon imported European goods, including brandy, grew apace, and the Mi'kmaq were increasingly alienated from their lands as European settlement continued.

The "Europeans" who landed on America's shores were not a homogeneous people. The most important division was between the French and the English. In their struggle against the more numerous English, the French found the Mi'kmaq and other tribes to be most useful allies. They courted the Mi'kmaq with presents and privileges to retain their support. In contrast to the English, they forged a relationship with the Mi'kmaq that was often mutually beneficial. Further, French attitudes toward Indians in general were more acceptant. At any rate, as a consequence of the colonial wars, the fate of the Mi'kmaq was decided by treaties made in Europe.

One can scarcely comprehend the disasters that Europeans wrought upon the Mi'kmaq and other indigenous peoples of the eastern seaboard (and elsewhere in the Americas). Once the Europeans established a foothold, much of what followed seems inevitable, given the cultural and sociopolitical gulf between Indians and Europeans and European power. But conditions were exacerbated by the fundamental racism and ethnocentrism of all Europeans, particularly the English. They regarded everything native as brutish, foolish, or immoral. This attitude is deep in Anglo-Saxon culture and remains a powerful factor in mainstream-Indian relations in Canada and the United States—where Mi'kmaqs still exist. Most now live in small population clusters on scattered reserves, some as small as a few acres.

Reaching beyond historical chronology, this book describes how the cultural consciousness of contemporary Mi'kmaqs is shaped not only by their own oral traditions but also by knowledge of the past as documented by twenty generations of European observers. Representing opposite sides of the encounter, the text offers many direct quotations from Mi'kmaqs and outsiders, enabling the reader to appreciate the different, sometimes conflicting, points of view.

The author is an ethnohistorian and action anthropologist who spent ten years working on a successful native rights case, helping one Mi'kmaq group gain federal recognition and a financial settlement to establish a land base in northern Maine. Like other tribal nations trying to free themselves from the shackles of internal colonialism, Mi'kmaqs have come to appreciate the practical significance of historical information. Until recently, they quarried their past for great stories, which provided them with a mental escape and emotional comfort in troubled times. Today, they seek knowledge about what happened in their past as a source of cultural identity and as an instrument of justice.

It seems a miracle that the Mi'kmaq should survive this long-term apocalypse, but survive they did. They are currently enjoying both a burst in population and a revitalization of their culture as well as their sociopolitical status.

This case study is essential reading for anyone interested in the history of North America or in Indian-white relations.

George and Louise Spindler
Series Editors
Ethnographics, Box 38
Calistoga, CA 94515

Acknowledgments

Special thanks must go to my numerous Mi'kmaq friends in northern Maine. It has been a privilege to work with them for a noble cause. With pleasure I recall their generosity and hospitality. They not only tell great stories but are also a terrific audience. Indeed, I fondly remember their uproarious jokes and bursts of laughter. No doubt, in reading this book some of them will recognize subjects we talked about during our Mi'kmaq history seminars in the Aroostook Micmac Council's band offices in Presque Isle. While I cannot mention all, I would like to express special respect for Tom Battiste, a Mi'kmaq who helped found the Association of Aroostook Indians in 1969 before moving on to earn a master's at Harvard University and pursue a career in serving native peoples throughout the United States. Another Mi'kmaq whom I greatly admire is Donald Sanipass, a *meski'k mkamlamun* ("Great-heart"). Perhaps more than any other Mi'kmaq I know, he possesses the natural qualities of a traditional chieftain. Of course, others have aided my understanding—Abraham Harquail, Harold Lafford, Sarah Jacobs Lund, Marguerite Basque McNeal, Beatrice Paul, Frank Paul, Betsy Lafford Phillips, Paul Phillips, Wilfred Sanipass, Mary Lafford Sanipass, Marlene Sanipass, David Sanipass, Richard Silliboy, Tilly Pictou West, and so many others. Likewise, I have benefited enormously from some Maliseet friends, in particular Louis Paul and Dr. Peter Paul, both of Woodstock Reserve.

Certainly, my indebtedness to Maine's Pine Tree Legal Assistance, Inc., is great. Without the support of astute and highly motivated attorneys such as Nan Heald, Patrick Ende, and Eric Nelson, all three of whom remain dedicated to alleviating the harsh injustices of American society, my decade of community activism and native rights research on behalf of the Aroostook Band of Micmacs would not have resulted in federal recognition and a land claims settlement for the band.

Several great teachers have contributed to my theoretical understanding of how Mi'kmaq culture is historically articulated within the dynamic context of a wider field of force. Of special note are Eric Wolf and Ton Lemaire. Their encompassing knowledge and moral integrity continue to inspire me. Among those who share my intellectual interest in Mi'kmaq culture, I particularly thank my colleagues, Ms. Ruth Whitehead of the Nova Scotia Museum and Dr. Charles Martijn of Québec's Ministère des Affaires Culturelles, as well as Dr. Peter Christmas of the Micmac Institute for Cultural Studies. I would be remiss if I did not acknowledge also the competent assistance from the Maine State Library's reference specialists and the warm ambiance of the Hubbard Free Library in Hallowell.

Of course, I express my gratitude to my mother, P. A. C. Prins-Poorter, and my father, Dr. A. H. J. Prins, emeritus professor of cultural anthropology at the Rijksuniversiteit Groningen, who nourished my early fascination with America's indigenous cultures.

Finally, my wife and collaborator, Bunny McBride, deserves more praise than anyone else. It was she who first brought the Mi'kmaqs of northern Maine to my attention. In the past fifteen years, we have shared labor and love. Without her unswerving support and editing skills, this book could not have been written.

Contents

1 / Introduction: Quest for Cultural Survival

Numbering about 25,000, the Mi'kmaq are the largest of the surviving Algonquian-speaking groups in northeast America. Along with the closely related St. Francis Abenaki, Maliseet, Passamaquoddy, and Penobscot, they belong to a cluster of eastern Algonquians known as the Wabanaki ("Dawnland") Indians.

Most Mi'kmaqs hold membership in one of 29 communities known as bands. Only one, the Aroostook Band of Micmacs, is situated in the United States (northern Maine). The others are linked to reserves in Newfoundland (one), Quebec (three), and Canada's Maritime Provinces (Nova Scotia, thirteen; New Brunswick, nine; Prince Edward Island, two). Mi'kmaqs share certain fundamental cultural characteristics and values that identify them ethnically as members of the same tribe or nation, called the *Mi'kmaq Nationimow*. For instance, many still speak their ancestral tongue, which belongs to the eastern Algonquian language family, once spoken from Labrador down to North Carolina.

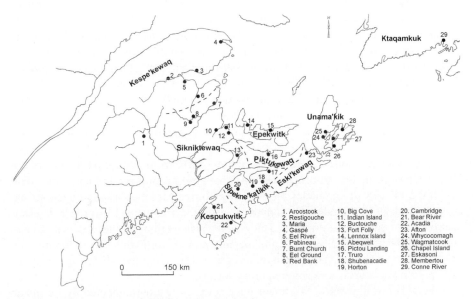

1. Aroostook	10. Big Cove	20. Cambridge
2. Restigouche	11. Indian Island	21. Bear River
3. Maria	12. Buctouche	22. Acadia
4. Gaspé	13. Fort Folly	23. Afton
5. Eel River	14. Lennox Island	24. Whycocomagh
6. Pabineau	15. Abeqweit	25. Wagmatcook
7. Burnt Church	16. Pictou Landing	26. Chapel Island
8. Eel Ground	17. Truro	27. Eskasoni
9. Red Bank	18. Shubenacadie	28. Membertou
	19. Horton	29. Conne River

Mi'kmaq Country: traditional districts and modern bands.

1

Traditionally Mi'kmaqs called themselves *L'nu'k* (or *Ulnoo*), meaning "humans" or "people" (Rand 1888:143). Today this Mi'kmaq word connotes native people in general. Early colonial records referred to Mi'kmaqs by an assortment of names (Souriquois, Gaspesiens, Miskoutins, Acadiens, Tarentines, Cape Sables, etc.), a practice that has caused some confusion among scholars. The name Mi'kmaq, itself, variously spelled, took precedence in European records in the late seventeenth century. Most accepted among various etymologies for the name is the belief that it derives from *nikmaq,* a greeting that translates as "my kin friends" (Lescarbot 1:79; Whitehead 1987:20).[1]

The Mi'kmaqs' geographic position on the northern Atlantic seaboard singled them out for the dubious honor of being among the very first indigenous peoples in northeast America to encounter the European vanguard. First they met Breton fishermen, who began frequenting the coasts of Mi'kmaq country in 1504. In 1525, a group of Portuguese men founded a short-lived colony at Cape Breton Island. Soon afterward, European fishermen began offering Mi'kmaqs a variety of commodities in exchange for furs, opening the door to a massive international fur trade. By 1600, the majority of Mi'kmaqs had died of diseases born of contact with Europeans, and survivors were transforming from seacoast foragers into market hunters and middlemen in the fur trade. By this time, some had acquired Basque sailing boats, which enabled them to range with relative ease from Newfoundland to Cape Cod. A few years later they obtained their first firearms, becoming one of the earliest American Indian groups to use this new weaponry. Meanwhile, some adventurous Mi'kmaqs even explored Europe. A chieftain named Messamoet, for instance, sailed across the Atlantic in the 1570s and lived in southern France for two years before returning to Nova Scotia.

European fishers and traders led the way to a full-scale colonization competition, between France and England in particular. For two centuries these newcomers battled for Mi'kmaq trade, land, and souls. When the smoke cleared, Mi'kmaqs and other Indian groups along the Atlantic seaboard found themselves landless or confined to small reservations. In the years that followed, they emerged as an impoverished and powerless underclass of artisans and seasonal laborers.

Today, Mi'kmaqs represent a tiny portion (about 0.6 percent) of the population inhabiting their ancestral domains. And their reservations comprise but a fraction (0.25 percent) of their original 40,000-square-mile territory—just a few acres per individual.

This book provides a concise description of Mi'kmaq culture on the eve of the European invasion and traces the changes that have taken place in that culture over the last 500 years. It chronicles the endurance of the Mi'kmaq as an indigenous nation, its ordeals in the face of colonialism, and its current struggle for self-determination and cultural revitalization. These pages also explore indigenous reactions to Europe's "New World discovery" and the cultural transformations it set into motion, revealing the complex historical dynamics that resulted in the Mi'kmaqs' remarkable, if tenuous, survival in contemporary society.

As this text illustrates, Mi'kmaqs have not been just outnumbered by European newcomers or overwhelmed by their powerful technology. They have also become victims of a European ideology that condemned indigenous nations in North America as inferior. A principal component of this colonial ideology is the construct of "history" as the progressive development of humanity in stages of gradual growth. As far as Europeans were concerned, there was no doubt that they were in the lead. Envisioning themselves as having reached the most advanced stage of human development, they presumed that cultures that most radically differed from their own were the most behind. Situated on the extreme end of an imaginary time line, the Europeans represented their own cultures as highly developed civilizations in contrast to the primitive lifeways of wild savages. Using the concept of "progress," they conjured up the idea that indigenous peoples such as the Mi'kmaq were ignorant. Stuck at an inferior stage of human development, as if they were children, the Mi'kmaq were seen as quaint or backward folks who required "improvement." If they refused to change their primitive ways, they were considered obstinate and in need of discipline. Europeans saw themselves as the chosen improvers and disciplinarians and called their task the "white man's burden." In fact, the real burden—subjection to domination—belonged not to the colonizers, but to the colonized.

Closely tied to this hierarchical construct of history is the European idea of "prehistory." Referring to the Western Hemisphere as the "New World," they have taken their own "discovery" of America as a chronological baseline. This event,

Aroostook Mi'kmaq tribal elder Donald Sanipass, the "Great Heart" (meski'k mkamlamun), and the author; Chapman, Maine, Summer 1992.

some five hundred years ago, has become accepted as the moment for American history to actually begin. It is as if it took a white man to push the magic button of the historical chronometer. Once the clock began to tick, local events were recorded as historical "facts" to be placed on a worldwide time scale. Events that took place before the arrival of Europeans were dubbed "prehistory" and viewed as nebulous and static, despite the vivid and dynamic pictures hinted at in native myths and legends.

These ideological constructs enabled European newcomers to Mi'kmaq country to legitimize conquest, rationalize political domination, justify cultural repression, and, finally, to excuse our ignorance of what really happened in the past. Today, however, Mi'kmaqs are keenly aware of the ideological significance of historical information and employ this knowledge as a political instrument in their ongoing struggle for native rights. Aware that voiding their past represses their prospects as a tribal nation with a viable future, Mi'kmaqs refuse to be omitted from texts that describe what happened in history. This new awareness is illustrated by the following incident. In 1984, three years after I began working on a native rights case with the Mi'kmaqs in northern Maine, their cry for justice was still ignored by federal and state authorities, and the general public remained unaware of the band's precarious survival as off-reservation Indians. Working out of the band's headquarters in the center of Presque Isle, I was midway through collecting the historical documentation needed for their case when a historical booklet celebrating the city's 125th anniversary (1859–1984) was published. Remarkably, the booklet's "Chronology of Historical Events" noted absurdly incidental events, such as the 1982 visit of the rock band Dr. Hook, but did not include a single word about the still-existing aboriginal inhabitants of the area. When I asked one of the authors why the Mi'kmaq had not been even mentioned in the booklet, he responded that "Indians were prehistorical [and] don't form part of history." In reaction, local Mi'kmaq leaders Paul Phillips and Richard Silliboy published a letter of protest in the regional newspaper: "Apparently the facts that we maintain an office in Presque Isle, that our fellow tribespeople performed stoop labor in the potato fields, and above all, that Indian people were the original proprietors of all the lands in Aroostook County, including Presque Isle, were not sufficient proof of our place in history" (*The Presque Isle Star Herald* 12 Dec. 1984).

It is ironic that Europeans who were responsible for diminishing Mi'kmaq life documented much of what they were destroying—in explorers' logs, trade records, missionary letters, colonial records, and so forth. Equally ironic is the fact that present-day Mi'kmaqs seeking to understand their cultural identity turn to these exogenic records as a key resource. On one hand, such chronicles do not objectively reflect what really happened in Mi'kmaq history. They are profoundly colored by the author's ideological lenses, and they touch upon Mi'kmaq life primarily as it intersected with European activities. Yet they often provide the only direct view of past Mi'kmaq life, and therefore influence the way the contemporary Mi'kmaqs understand and act upon their own history.

This given, the current cultural consciousness of Mi'kmaqs is shaped not only by their own oral traditions but also by knowledge of their past written by twenty generations of European observers. A survey of these "external" sources, coupled with the tribe's "inside" tradition, provides us with a rare opportunity to develop valuable insights into the dynamics of culture change. Also, it allows us to reflect critically on the cognitive dimension of hegemony.[2]

To truly comprehend the impact of written history on the culture of Mi'kmaqs today, we must become critically aware of the European in their consciousness. In other words, an in-depth understanding of European ideology is of crucial value in our effort to deconstruct European records concerning Mi'kmaqs. For this reason, beyond providing information about Mi'kmaq culture, I present the material in the context of a critical perspective, noting, where relevant, who wrote what, why, where, and when. Hopefully, this will alert readers to the underlying multivocality of history. Furthermore, I've aimed to sensitize readers to the concept of modern tribal cultures as ongoing, open-ended, historical processes. It is my hope that this book stirs our awareness of the continuing challenges of cultural preservation faced by the Mi'kmaq and other indigenous peoples—and, thereby, supports the struggle for native rights.

NOTES

1. Historically, the tribal name of the Mi'kmaq has been variously spelled. Although the most conventional spelling of their tribal name is Micmac, earlier forms include Miquemaque, Mukmacks, Migmag, and Mikemak. During the past few decades, Native linguists have proposed a more accurate rendition of their ethnonym. However, due to regional dialect variations and independently developed orthographic styles, some Quebec tribespeople prefer Migmag, whereas those of Nova Scotia favor Mi'kmaq. The latter appears to have become more popular. Consequently, unless it involves a quotation or a proper name, I have adopted the latter form in this text (the Smith/Francis System; see also Dickason, 1992:16).

2. In contrast to the English term "savage," which has an obvious pejorative meaning, the French word "sauvage" was historically used to describe American Indians. Because it does not have the same negative overtones as the English word, I have generally translated "sauvage" as Indian. This enables the reader to focus on the broader message of a particular French text pertinent to Mi'kmaq tribal history.

2 / Problems and Challenges: The Politics of History

I became acquainted with the Mi'kmaq nation in 1981 when I signed on as a researcher and community development specialist to work on a native rights case with the Aroostook Band of Micmacs in northern Maine. What did I find? A landless, impoverished scattered group of native people on the verge of disappearing in the melting pot of American society.

INTERNAL COLONIALISM AND DOMESTIC DEPENDENCY

Organized in bands, most Mi'kmaqs reside in villages or hamlets located on specially reserved tracts of land that were allocated primarily in the nineteenth century. Located in eastern Canada, these widely scattered reserves, carved from the Mi'kmaqs' once-formidable domains, are usually small in size and marginally situated. Rarely do they provide resident populations with adequate means of subsistence. After Euramericans usurped Mi'kmaq lands, Mi'kmaqs were gradually reduced to a state of dependency on the federal government. Denied their aboriginal right of self-determination, they were placed under the government's guardianship, and federal bureaucrats were appointed to oversee their affairs on the reserves. Powerless and impoverished, Mi'kmaqs were forced into a pattern of subordination, which one anthropologist has labeled "internal colonialism" (Cardoso, 1964). Typical for most indigenous peoples surviving in the modern world, internal colonialism refers to "a state where an independent country has, within its own boundaries, given special legal status to groups that differ culturally from the dominant group, and has created a distinct administrative machinery to handle such groups" (Colby and Van den Berghe, 3).

HEGEMONY AND ALIENATION: ENDANGERED HERITAGE

As an Indian nation, the Mi'kmaq, like other native groups in the Americas, are caught between two worlds—the indigenous realm of their forebears and the modern system dominated by white society. Their traditional culture has been systematically repressed by mainstream society (racist ideology, paternalistic bureaucracies, churches, schools, and labor markets) and caricatured by the popular media as backward, primitive, and inferior. Until very recently, in schools their history was ignored, their culture dismissed, and their language prohibited. Children were mocked as "bucks," "squaws" "chiefs," "redskins," and even "dirty savages." In some places, this continues to this day.

Such attitudes are reflected in the way Mi'kmaqs in Aroostook County, Maine, describe their position in the regional stratification of society: "Whites on top, of course, and next are the [few] Blacks. The Indians are at the bottom...[because] we figure that we've been defeated. Like in history we've always been losing." The words of a contemporary white Aroostook farmer who has hired Mi'kmaqs to work his potato fields illustrate a general ignorance about Mi'kmaqs: "They're an amusing group. . . . Money doesn't excite them. They just want enough to get by. It's been the same for years and always will be. [The problem with them is] they've no drive . . . no staying power. . . . Politicians might as well face it that these people don't want new houses like white people. It's not in their make-up."

What are the roots of these viewpoints? From early on, European newcomers were determined to "civilize" Mi'kmaqs. As a Jesuit priest noted upon his arrival in Mi'kmaq country in the early 1600s: "If they are savages, it is to domesticate and civilize them that we have come here..." (JR 1:183). Generally, French colonists were less concerned with civilizing Indians than with having them as trade and military allies against English rivals, but this was not the case with the English. After the British crown gained full control over northeast America, two ideas dominated its

Mi'kmaq home in northern Maine, Summer 1992. Until recent native rights gains, poverty was endemic among Aroostook's Indians.

administration of Indians: "that as a people they were disappearing, and that those who remained should either be removed to communities isolated from whites or else be assimilated. . . .'Civilization' was to be achieved by education . . . entrusted to missionaries" (Dickason, 1992:225; Fleras and Elliott, 73). In 1876, Canada's federal government issued the Indian Act, which set the course for a form of bureaucratic ethnocide or "civilized" destruction of indigenous culture. Almost succeeding in its assimilation objectives, this government policy remained in place until the early 1980s.

In 1958, Nova Scotia archaeologist J.S. Erskine wrote: "The Mi'kmaq is faced with the unenviable choice of going out into the white man's world where he may find a future but must lose his past, or of remaining in the reserve where he may keep his past but will have no future. Could we not have spared a little dignity to their sunset? Must every people enjoy only one crowded hour of glorious life and then end not with a bang but with a whimper?" (Erskine, 452). By the 1960s, at many reserves a majority of traditional customs were forgotten or no longer observed. An anthropologist working with Mi'kmaqs at that time gave this poignant illustration: "The conditions of life have changed so drastically at Restigouche [Mi'kmaq Reserve] during the last sixty years that almost all sense of cultural continuity has been lost. I showed the Wallises' historical ethnography of the Mi'kmaq to several informants: . . . one woman who glanced through the book accepted the descriptions as true, but commented, 'It's like reading about another world'" (Bock 1966:88). This same anthropologist noted that for many Mi'kmaqs the question of identity had become paramount:

Of all the questions asked during my time on the Reserve, the one most often repeated—sometimes defensively, sometimes pleadingly—was: "Can you tell me where the Indians came from?" I suspect that it is the inability to answer this question which accounts, in part, for the patterns of compulsive drinking... and for the restlessness which affects so many of the younger people. I answered the historical question with some mumbled phrases about land bridges and Bering Strait, but for the latent question I had no answer.

(Bock 1966:87)

Mi'kmaq myths and legends reflect this tribal nation's struggle to deal with the dramatic changes it faced, as well as its determination to survive as a people. These oral traditions, many of which were recorded by Baptist missionary Silas T. Rand between 1846 and 1889, show how the Mi'kmaq constructed their own interpretations of what happened in their history. Old storytellers, talking about legendary ancestors and strange happenings in the past, provided their listeners with a vital sense of what it meant to be a Mi'kmaq. These stories, passed down through generations, helped shape the historical consciousness of the Mi'kmaqs and enabled them to make sense of the complex and often-baffling processes of changing power relations that had left them politically and economically marginalized and culturally subordinated.

Striving to hold on to a sense of dignity and self-worth, Mi'kmaqs found cultural refuge in this dramatic repertoire, packed with magic power, superhuman strength, daring feats of bravery, and wily tricks. Cruel reality might stare them in the face, but they found joy in an imaginary world where their people won an upper hand against overwhelming odds. Given their history of hegemonic contact and colonial domination, it is not surprising that Mi'kmaq tales tell of *puowin* (sorcerers/shamans), *kinap* (magic-doing heroes), primordial giants, and mysterious little people. The most important character is their culture hero, Klu'skap. He is said to be a giant magician who came into being "when the world contained no other man, in flesh, but himself" (Nicolar, 7, 12), and his name is variously translated as "man out of nothing," "good man," or "the liar." As Klu'skap's children, the Mi'kmaqs inherited a natural landscape that still bears this ancient enchanter's mark. According to legend, he abandoned the Mi'kmaqs just before the European invasion.

Klu'skap legends came to the fore in the mid-1800s, when it appeared that Mi'kmaqs would become extinct as a people by the end of the century. About that time, Josiah Jeremy, a Mi'kmaq of Nova Scotia, told this story about Klu'skap's departure and promised return:

> Gluskap resided near the salt water, on a high bank, against which the deep sea dashed. When about to go away and leave the Indians, he called up a whale to carry him off on his back. . . .A huge whale answered the call, and laid himself alongside the bluff... and called, Noojeech, cogoowa pawotumun? ("Little grandson, what is your wish?") "Nikskamich (Grandfather), I wish you to take me across the water, to a distant land in the west."
>
> "Get on my back then," said the whale.
>
> So Gluskap descended, and sat upon the back of the huge monster, which then moved off with his burden. After proceeding some hours at a rapid pace, the whale inquired, "My grandson, does not the bowstring appear above the horizon?"— referring to the first sight of land....
>
> [Finally, reaching the faraway land, the whale dashed on the beach and was stranded high and dry.] Gluskap leaped off his back, . . . placed his bow against the whale's huge carcass, and gently pushed him off into deep water. "My little grandson," said the whale, "haven't you some piece of a broken pipe to give me?"
>
> "I have," said Gluskap; and forthwith he filled one with tobacco, lighted it, and placed it in the whale's mouth. The whale puffed out volumes of smoke at intervals as he swam off towards his distant home. Gluskap ascended a high hill to watch him as he went. . . .The two were then separated, to meet no more. Gluskap went on his way. The Mi'kmaqs expect his return in due time, and look for the end of their oppressions and troubles when he comes back.

(in Rand, 1894:228–29)

In 1982, when I began to hear firsthand stories about Klu'skap, some Mi'kmaqs identified him as the Indian Messiah. In the minds and tales of others, the old culture hero had somehow merged with Big Foot. Echoing timeworn Klu'skap legends, Wolf Sanipass, a Mi'kmaq woodsman in northern Maine told me, "Big Foot got his name because he put his feet between the Miramichi and St. John's River and thus divided the land. He lives in the woods, on a big hill. The cross is a sign of his presence and is evident everywhere." Illustrating this, Wolf pointed to a web of lines under his right eye and asked, "What do you see there?" "A cross," I said. Then, opening the palm of his hand, he pointed to another pair of crossed lines and asked, "Why do you think I see the sign of a cross all over when I walk in the woods? It is the mark of Big Foot. When the leaves of the trees flutter softly, even when there's no wind, that's the voice of Big Foot, his breath. . . . Big Foot will come to help the Red People."

THE MI'KMAQ AS ETHNIC GROUP

Although contemporary Mi'kmaqs recognize all too well the disintegration of their culture, they are also keenly aware of an intrinsic bond with one another. What binds them together? What does it mean to be a Mi'kmaq Indian? Obviously there are myriad individual differences between Mi'kmaqs, based on locale, personality, and circumstance. For instance, many reside in isolated reserve communities, while others live in ethnically mixed urban neighborhoods, and a handful live in suburbs. Moreover, ethnicity is not solid or constant. It changes with time. Qualities that elders might agree upon as essentially "Mi'kmaq" are not necessarily shared by their grandchildren. On top of this, not everyone has equal access to the available cultural repertoire of Mi'kmaq ethnicity.

Still, we can make some generalizations. First, Mi'kmaqs have a shared history and recognize an ancestral range or territory. A kin-ordered culture, they historically formed a tribal network of related bands. Today, their identity is often still determined by band affiliation. Traditionally, they shared a tongue that distinguished them from neighboring tribes. Many still speak their ancestral language, and those who cannot often feel obliged to apologize for their lack of verbal knowledge. The importance of speech as an ethnic marker is illustrated by this and by the fact that Mi'kmaqs speaking English or French typically throw in some native words to assert their ethnic identity.

Traditionally, Mi'kmaqs held a united worldview—common social values and spiritual beliefs, plus customs, rituals, and ceremonies that expressed their ideas about the world in which they lived. Today, most Mi'kmaqs are members of the Roman Catholic Church, but growing numbers declare interest in traditional "Indian" ways by participating in the sweat lodge ceremony or placing faith in Indian healing ("medicine") and medicine men.

Mi'kmaq ethnicity is also defined by certain livelihoods that are particularly common to the group, such as high steel construction, splint basketry, and migrant work in potato fields or blueberry barrens. In aboriginal times it was hunting and gathering, which gave way to market hunting, ethnic soldiering, and craft production after Europeans arrived on their shores.

Ethnicity involves self-ascription. Mi'kmaqs intentionally distinguish themselves from others—especially non-Indians. Taking a public stance as "Indian," they display themselves in contrast to ethnic "others," sometimes accentuating their identity by donning distinctive clothes, accessories, and hairstyles. Indeed, highlighting ethnic boundaries, they tend to stress sometimes-minor differences with these neighboring communities.

Last but not least, Mi'kmaq ethnicity is defined by members' unique political position in larger society. Like most other indigenous peoples in North America, they are often enrolled in formally recognized Indian bands. Band members possess

Indian "status," which entitles them to certain native rights that are guaranteed by federal law.

RECONSTRUCTING HISTORY

When I accepted the job with the Aroostook Band of Micmacs, I found myself in-volved not only in the band's legal battles but also in its members' efforts to revital-ize their culture. During our ten years of work together, the importance of history as a primary tool for political justice and culture reclamation was vividly clear.

In reconstructing the historical process of Mi'kmaq culture change we are de-pendent upon written as well as unwritten sources of information about the Mi'kmaq past. Because Mi'kmaqs, like other American Indians, were mostly nonliterate until about one hundred years ago, nearly all chronicles about them predating the late 1800s were penned by Europeans. Written from an outside point of view, these records do not always report what was really going on, but rather what European ob-servers *thought* was going on.

Beyond spontaneous errors, historical documents about Mi'kmaq culture in-clude data that were reforged, repressed, or deliberately concocted to mislead certain parties for political or economic reasons. Commenting on such historical disinfor-mation, French historian Fernand Braudel (1982:209) wrote: "Interpreting official figures inevitably brings mistakes. Merchants and officials spent all day telling lies to the government, and governments spent all day deceiving themselves."

Moreover, these writings reflect a historical consciousness that is not Mi'kmaq. As historian Robert Berkhofer (71) noted in *The White Man's Indian:* "The Indian of imagination and ideology has been as real, perhaps more real than the Native Amer-ican of actual existence or contact. As preconception became conception and con-ception became fact, the Indian was used for the ends of argument, art, and entertainment by White painters, philosophers, poets, novelists, and moviemakers among many." Certainly the views that European colonials held of Mi'kmaqs were "inextricably bound up with the evaluation of their own society and culture, [their] ambivalence . . . over the worth of their [own] customs and civiliza-tion. . ." (27). Vacillating between opposite ideas of "otherness," Europeans idealized American Indians as "noble savages" or maligned them as "ignoble savages."

As noble Indians they represented primitivism, which, in the words of a con-temporary historian, "postulated people dwelling in nature according to nature, ex-isting free of history's burdens and the social complexity felt by Europeans in the modern period, and offering hope to mankind at the same time that they constituted a powerful counter-example to existing European civilization" (Berkhofer, 72). This view is exemplified by the comments of an early French visitor in Mi'kmaq country, who wrote this about Mi'kmaqs in 1610:

> I consider all these poor Indians, whom we commiserate, to be very happy; for
> pale Envy doth not emaciate them, neither do they feel the inhumanity of those
> who serve God hypocritically, harassing their fellow-creatures under this mask;
> nor are they subject to the artifices of those, who, lacking virtue and goodness

wrap themselves up in a mantle of false piety to nourish their ambition. If they do not know God, at least they do not blaspheme him, as the greater number of Christians do. Nor do they understand the art of poisoning, or of corrupting chastity by develish artifice. There are no poor no beggars among them. All are rich, because all labor and live.

(JR 1:93)

In contrast to this positive configuration stands the Indian as ignoble savage, representing the crude backwardness of a brute in the wilderness. Evidence of this preconception shows up in many early European descriptions of encounters with the Mi'kmaq. Among the oldest surviving accounts is Giovanni da Verrazano's 1524 description of native hunters on the Maine coast as "Bad People" who were "full of uncouthness and vices" (in Hoffman, 1955:22–23). Verrazano's report influenced subsequent early voyagers, who described the Mi'kmaq with phrases such as "bad people, strong, and great bowmen" (in Sauer, 100) and "very stout and very malicious" (in Hoffman, 1961:139, 177). In 1611 a French Jesuit wrote about them in similar terms: "The nation is savage, wandering and full of bad habits. . . . They are, I say, savage, haunting the woods, ignorant, lawless, and rude. . . . as a people they have bad habits, are extremely lazy, gluttonous, profane, treacherous, cruel in their revenge, and given up to all kinds of lewdness, men and women alike. . ." (JR 1:173–74).

These conflicting images of the noble savage as nature's innocent child and of the ignoble savage as dangerous brute "persist from the era of Columbus up to the present without substantial modification or variation" (Berkhofer, 71). Should we be surprised to learn that when anthropologist Philip Bock (1966:88) showed a historical ethnography of the tribe to some Mi'kmaqs at Restigouche, "the young men charged that it was 'all made up'"?

Despite various problems with early European chronicles that describe Mi'kmaq life, Mi'kmaqs need such chronicles to piece together and safeguard their cultural heritage for future generations. With careful examination and analysis of the documents, it is possible to extract basic elements of historical truth and reconstruct a narrative that makes sense of the Mi'kmaqs' journey through the centuries to the present.

POLITICAL SIGNIFICANCE OF HISTORY

In the fall of 1989, fourteen Mi'kmaq moose hunters appeared in the provincial court at Sydney, Cape Breton, charged with 27 specific violations of a provincial law known as the Nova Scotia Wildlife Act. The *Micmac News,* a tribal paper, followed the ensuing trial, making sure the native perspective reached the public:

> Micmacs base their hunting rights on a covenant chain of 18th-century treaties and British proclamations, specifically the treaty of 1752, which guaranteed the tribe . . . "free liberty of hunting and fishing as usual. . . . for themselves, their heirs, and the heirs of their heirs forever." To the native community, such agreements were binding, political compacts between two independent and sovereign

nations which form the legal foundation of their self-determination and self-government.

(Douglas, MN Sept. 1989:3)

The prosecution countered with expert witness Dr. Stephen Patterson from the University of New Brunswick. Summarizing his testimony, the *Micmac News* reported,

> The Crown argues that the treaties do not apply to Cape Breton and that guarantees outlined in the treaties were terminated by hostilities shortly after they were signed. The Crown contends that many of the treaties were not applicable to Cape Breton Micmacs because the island was under French rule until the final siege of Louisbourg in 1758 when the British gained power. . . . the Royal Proclamation of 1763 does not guarantee the traditional way of life of Nova Scotia Micmacs, [as] it was initiated to solve "a western problem."

(MN Nov. 1989:6–7)

Dr. Patterson's interpretation of the 1763 Royal Proclamation was challenged by the Mi'kmaq Grand Council's legal advisor, who suggested that Patterson's representation was slanted because he relied on white historical records and ignored accounts of Mi'kmaq tribal culture and Mi'kmaq explanations of the treaty-making process: "'We're not hearing anything new. . . . We're simply dealing with an interpretation of 18th-century events which reflect a racist and colonial bias, inappropriate in an era of decolonization'" (MN Sept. 1989:2). Furthermore, he argued, "the proclamation confirms pre-existing rights, which include, among others, the Mi'kmaq right to hunt and fish." With respect to Cape Breton, the proclamation "would leave it a Mi'kmaq hunting ground with a diplomative relationship with the Government of Nova Scotia" (MN Feb. 1990:33).

Under a large headline, "History On Trial," the tribal paper quoted a Mi'kmaq leader as saying, "'What we're going into is a major war. . . . It's a war of survival for our people.'" The *Micmac News* reporter elaborated,

> The battlefield is no longer Fortress Louisbourg, Beauséjour or the Plains of Abraham. This modern warfare is being fought in a provincial courtroom in Sydney and government boardrooms in Halifax. The weapons are not guns, mortars and bombs, but thousands of pages of historical records and documents detailing British colonial affairs in the 18th century and the Micmac relationship with the British government. Today's combatants are not France and England fighting for supremacy in Europe and North America. It is the Nova Scotia government and the Micmac peoples fighting for control of the portion of Mikmakik territory now called Nova Scotia. . . . what's on trial is the historical fabric of Micmac tribal society, their land claims and self-determination. History is on trial.

(Douglas, MN Sept. 1989:3)

Some Mi'kmaqs were outraged by the trial, particularly by Dr. Patterson's testimony. Lawrence Paul, a former chief of Membertou Reserve and a veteran of World War II and the Korean War, was so "disgusted" by what he heard in the courtroom that he left. Outside the courtroom, he staged a personal protest, burned the Canadian flag and the Union Jack. Speaking to the *Micmac News* reporter, he fumed,

"'The Union Jack symbolizes colonialism and suppression. The Canadian flag represents a government that oppresses native people . . . I will never defend this country again'" (MN Sept. 1989:4–5, 21).

In January 1990, the provincial court judge ruled that the 1752 treaty, on which Mi'kmaqs had based their case, had been cancelled soon after it was signed due to a renewed outbreak of Anglo-Mi'kmaq fighting. Mi'kmaq reaction to the ruling was bitter. In the words of one band chief quoted in the *Micmac News,* "'I have not seen a shred of evidence . . . that our ancestors ceded title to our lands to the British. The evidence I've seen to date supports the theory that title was taken illegally, without any compensation whatsoever, and in total defiance of the Royal Proclamation of 1763" (MN Jan. 1990:9).

Two months later, thanks to a Nova Scotia Supreme Court appeal decision in a related fishing rights dispute, the moose hunters were acquitted. Their defense had cost them in excess of $200,000. Despite this stunning cost, Grand Chief Donald Marshall and other tribal leaders were pleased with the outcome. They viewed the decision as a major step on the long road to self-government and called upon the federal and provincial authorities to begin dealing with the Mi'kmaq as a sovereign nation (MN April 1990:4–5).

This story is emblematic. For generations, Mi'kmaqs who hunted, fished, and trapped in the ways of their grandfathers have faced arrest by provincial police or game wardens for breaking laws that were often unknown or unclear to them. Certainly they were not consulted in the creation of regulations that revoked their traditional freedom as the indigenous heirs to the lands of their ancestors. Violations resulted in fines, jail sentences, or both. Trials were carried out in front of white juries and judges, who typically had little knowledge, understanding, or interest in Mi'kmaq traditions.

In recent years, Mi'kmaqs have challenged their accusers and the laws they are accused of breaking. Like their oppressors, they have armed themselves with history. They have come to understand that libraries and archives are repositories of knowledge, "banks of cultural capital" whose meaning is subject to multiple interpretations, each with a potential for shaping a distinct political reality. They now know that in their struggle for cultural survival they must be able to locate themselves in the past in order to secure a more satisfying future for their people. Taking control over their own production of historical knowledge needed in the political arena, the Mi'kmaq have witnessed some dramatic reversals: No longer perpetual losers in the chambers of power, they have—in measure—reclaimed alienated lands, regained lost hunting and fishing rights, protected free trade and border-crossing rights, restored self-government, and secured federal recognition of their Indian status. In the process, they have turned history itself around.

In search of information about their past, Mi'kmaqs do more than comb through archives and libraries to find new data; they also reanalyze and reinterpret records already uncovered. Equally important, they record what the elders recall from their nation's collective memory. Both the Union of Nova Scotia Indians and the Confederacy of Mainland Micmacs have their own research departments, actively conducting historical research into Mi'kmaq land claims and treaties at the provincial archives in Halifax and at collections in many other places. As Mi'kmaq research director Don Julien explained in 1990: "We are constantly dealing with new findings and researching these through to completion" (MN Jan. 1990:9).

Actively engaged in revising and rewriting history, Mi'kmaqs have questioned the veracity of accepted accounts and challenged some as distortions or as lies. It is not surprising that in the emerging discourse of contesting histories, their own position is sometimes viewed in partisan terms as deliberate deception (Washburn 1987:95, 97; Prins 1988:117–19). It would be tragic if Mi'kmaqs and other historical revisionists, after exposing the ideological bias of establishment history, fell into the same trap of distortion. It would be equally tragic if the outcome of the Mi'kmaqs' quest for knowledge about their past were trivialized as "just another viewpoint." Historical exploration at its best is a process in which, from multiple vantage points, we circumnavigate events and peoples through time. In this process, not only are errors of fact and interpretation exposed, but also a fuller, more balanced picture of what "really" happened emerges. If revisionist Mi'kmaq history descends to the realm of unchecked subjective interpretation, its application would rob the native rights struggle of its source of moral energy.

In the United States, as well as in Canada, Mi'kmaqs have made native rights headway. This is certainly true of the Aroostook Band of Micmacs in northern Maine, with whom I have been most closely associated. When I began working with the band in 1981 the United States government did not acknowledge their Indian status, dismissing them as "Canadian Indians." My task was to do the ethnohistorical research necessary to find out if the aboriginal ties that they claimed to the area were

Grand Chief Donald Marshall signs a proclamation in 1986, declaring October 1 as Treaty Day and official public holiday. The date is the anniversary of the signing of the 1752 Treaty between the British and the Mi'kmaq.

substantiated. They were. After a decade of intensive research, community support building, political lobbying, and complex legal wrangling, the band gained federal recognition—which made it eligible for certain rights and benefits through the Bureau of Indian Affairs. Members also gained $900,000 to establish a five-thousand-acre land base in a region where their ancestors roamed. Clearly, knowledge is power, and in this case it brought justice in the form of rights and land.

In the following chapters we will step back five hundred years in Mi'kmaq history and walk forward to the present. En route we will witness staggering tribulations of the Mi'kmaqs, including the death of 90 percent of their people, the usurpation of more than 99 percent of their land, and the relentless erosion of their culture. We will also witness their remarkable will to persist—evident in their struggle from near extinction as a people to their emergence as one of the most revitalized tribal cultures in North America.

3 / Aboriginal Baseline: A Historical Ethnography

NATURAL HABITAT

Traditional Mi'kmaq country stretched from Cape Breton Island west to the St. John River and north to the Gaspé Peninsula. The region is characterized by a long, indented coastline of great bays, estuaries, sea creeks, capes, and little islands. It is famous for high tides, in particular at the Bay of Fundy, where the water rises seventy feet. The upland area, which comprises the drainage of various rivers, including the St. John, Restigouche, and Miramichi, reaches some 2,000 feet above sea level. Of the few mountains, highest is Mont Jacques-Cartier on Gaspé Peninsula (4,160 feet).

Climatic conditions in Mi'kmaq country are highly diverse. Beyond extreme seasonal fluctuations, there are significant regional contrasts. Northern and western areas are generally colder than the southern and eastern regions, and conditions are more temperate at the coast than inland. Air temperatures in the territory seldom surpass 90 degrees Fahrenheit. or drop much below 0 degrees Fahrenheit. Rainfall averages 35–60 inches per year. The frost-free season numbers just 90 days, and frost can occur as late as June and as early as September. Although snowfall in the coastal area is often light, it regularly exceeds 110 inches in northern Maine and New Brunswick. From December to mid-April, between one and two feet of snow covers most of the land, except some of the immediate Atlantic shores.

Historically, at least 90 percent of the Mi'kmaq habitat was woodland, comprised of a rich mosaic of trees. Expansive tracts of towering conifers (especially spruce, fir, and pine, as well as cedar and hemlock) dominated the scene, interspersed with mixed forests of deciduous hardwoods (maple, birch, beech, oak, elm, and ash). In addition to these now-diminished arboreal lands, the region features tracts of tidal mud flats, marsh, brushland, and rock barren. It is drained by a vast system of thousands of lakes, rivers, and streams. Some coastal lowlands, especially the saltwater marshes in the Bay of Fundy area, support grasses and associated herbaceous plants, while the poorly drained sandy or boggy soils of eastern New Brunswick host tamarack, jack pines, and white birches.

Wildlife has long thrived in this natural habitat: moose, caribou, and, to a lesser extent, white-tailed deer, as well as black bear, wolf, raccoon, red fox, lynx, bobcat, fisher, marten, otter, and skunk, and also porcupine, hare, beaver, and muskrat. Coastal waters harbor large sea mammals such as gray seals, walrus, porpoise, and whales, as well as lobsters, and various types of shellfish, including clams and oysters. Inland streams feature, at least seasonally, salmon, trout, sturgeon, bass, smelt, and alewife. Moreover, multitudes of aquatic birds breed and feed in the region, again mostly seasonally: loons, ducks, cormorants, geese, swans, and herons. Finally, raptors, such as eagles, hawks, and vultures, live here, as do pigeons, partridges, grouse, pheasants, and a host of smaller birds (Clark, 31–35, 39–41; Putnam, 83–84).

MI'KMAQ ORIGIN LEGENDS

In their myths Mi'kmaqs imagined the genesis of all life. Stories accounted for the elementary forces in nature—the sun, moon, stars, thunder, lightning, rain, snow. They envisioned the origins of lands, lakes, and rivers and gave reasons for the particular shapes of these elements. Myths explained why animals look and behave as they do. They also told how the Mi'kmaqs' ancestors—the first real humans or *L'nu'k*—came into being. As polygenetic creationists, Mi'kmaqs held that different peoples descended from different ultimate ancestors and that theirs had come into existence within the maritime territories.

Although there are several variations of the Mi'kmaq origin legend, the basic continuity of the tale is evidenced in two well-spaced accounts—one published in 1691, the other in 1955. The first, recorded by a French missionary who lived among the Mi'kmaq, noted: "They say that when the sun, which they have always recognized and worshipped as their God, created all this great universe, he divided the earth immediately into several parts, wholly separated from one another by great lakes: that in each part he caused to be born one man and one woman, and they multiplied and lived a very long time . . ." (LeClercq, 84–85).

The second legend, recorded two and one half centuries later by an anthropologist among Mi'kmaqs of the same region (Restigouche), goes like this:

> In old time, after he had made the whites across the sea, God landed in Gaspé and walked along the shore up to the mouth of the Restigouche River where there is a nice sandy beach. God molded a man in the sand and looked twice at what he had made. He gave him the breath of life and stood up. He did not say a word. He bent down again and made a squaw. He got up and said nothing. They were the first Indians. He made a little dog. He said nothing. The dog got its breath and wiggled around the trees. God said, "Get up. Tell the man something." The dog got up. The man looked at the dog, and language came to him. "Look," he said, meaning look at the dog. The dog said, "see that white bush." He named it and everything around them. "It's all your property, all the Gaspé and farther still. . . . The Lord went on to the next lake and here made another man and woman. He went all over Canada and at each lake he made a new tribe with a different language. When the people from these lakes met in the woods, they couldn't understand each other.

> (in Wallis and Wallis, 1955:482–83)

Perhaps some Mi'kmaqs still adhere to these timeworn interpretations of life's beginning. But most, after generations of European indoctrination, accept either the Judeo-Christian interpretation based on the biblical account in Genesis or the modern anthropological Bering Strait theory and its associated archaeological evidence of their distant origins in Eurasia or Africa.

KLU'SKAP AS CULTURE HERO

A prominent figure in the oral tradition of Mi'kmaqs (and other Wabanaki tribes) is a culture hero called Klu'skap, "a divine being, though in the form of a man" (Rand 1894:232). Originally Klu'skap tales served to make the universe of social action intelligible to Mi'kmaqs, who believed this supernatural giant put the earth into such a shape as to make it "a happy land for the people" (Nicolar, 5). Recounting his primeval exploits, traditional storytellers explained how mountains, islands, rivers, and lakes took their forms. As told by Stephen Hood—one of the last great Mi'kmaq hunters in Nova Scotia—Klu'skap came to Mi'kmaq country from the east, from far across the great sea. His canoe was a rock of granite:

> Gluskap was the friend and teacher of the Indians; all they knew of the arts he taught them. He taught them the names of the constellations and stars; he taught them how to hunt and fish, and cure what they took; how to cultivate the ground, as far as they were trained in husbandry. When he first came, he brought a woman [usually represented in animal form as the marten] with him, whom he ever addressed as Noogumich (Grandmother) a very general epithet for an old woman. She was not his wife, nor did he ever have a wife. He was always sober, grave, and good; all that the Indians knew of what was wise and good he taught them.

Explaining Klu'skap's role in the geological origins of the regional landscape that formed part of his traditional range as a hunter-fisher, Hood recounted in 1869:

> In former days, water covered the whole Annapolis and Cornwallis valley [in southwest Nova Scotia]. Gluskap cut out a passage at Cape Split and at Annapolis Gut, and thus drained off the pond and left the bottom dry; long after this the valley became dry land. Aylesford bog was a vast lake; in this lake there was a beaver-house; and hence the Indian name to this day,—Cobeetek (the beaver's home). Out of this beaver-house Gluskap drove a small beaver, and chased it down to the Bras d'Or lake in Cape Breton, pursuing it in a canoe all the way. There it ran into another beaver-house, but was killed; and the house was turned into a high-peaked island; Gluskap feasted the Indians there. A few years ago a heavy freshet tore up the earth in those regions, and laid bare the huge bones of the beaver upon which Gluskap and his guests had feasted,—monstrous thighbones, the joints being as big as a man's head, and teeth huge in proportion. In cutting open a beaver-dam at Cape Chignecto, a small portion of the earth floated away; and Gluskap changed it into a moose and set his dogs on it. The moose took to the bay and made off; whereupon Gluskap turned him back into land, made him an island,—the Isle of Holt,—and fixed him there. He changed the dogs into rocks, which may be seen to this day, seated on their haunches, with their tongues lolling out of their mouths; the plain is called Ooteel (his dogs). Spenser's Island is his [cooking] kettle turned over; and the scraps he shovelled out when trying out his oil still lie scattered around but turned into stone.

(in Rand, 1894:232–37)

THE PREHISTORIC PAST: ARCHAEOLOGICAL AND
LINGUISTIC EVIDENCE

It is not known precisely when Mi'kmaq-speaking peoples moved into the region that they now call their ancestral homeland (Bailey, 3). Although some native traditions hold that they have always lived in *Mi'kma'kik* ("Mi'kmaq land"), others recount that they originally hailed from the southwest. For instance, when collecting Mi'kmaq legends in the mid-nineteenth century, Silas Rand noted: "The tradition among the Mi'kmaqs is that their [ancestors] came from the Southwest; and the old people up to a very late date spoke of their home in the Southwest" (1894:110, n.2; cf. 136). Although much about their prehistoric past will remain forever mysterious, archaeological research has shed some important light on the question.

Linguistically, the Mi'kmaq form part of a large Algonquian block extending "within historic times from the foothills of the Rockies to Nova Scotia, and south, through New England, to the southern Atlantic states" (Bailey, 2). Until about 4,000 years ago, these peoples formed a single speech community now referred to as proto-Algonquian. This block was broken up when groups of northern Iroquoians branched off from the Cherokee and drove a wedge between the eastern Algonquian and the main body in the Great Lakes area. The process of internal divergence among the eastern Algonquian languages may have begun some 2,000 years ago (Goddard, 70; Snow 1980:27).

Although linguists offer revealing insights about long-forgotten relationships between Mi'kmaqs and their neighbors, they cannot tell us much about the ethnic identity of the earliest humans ranging through the Maritimes and adjacent territories. Were they ancestral to the Mi'kmaqs? What do we know about them? Although

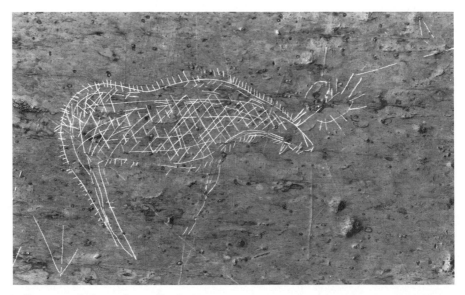

Mi'kmaq petroglyph at Lake Kejimkujik, Nova Scotia.

there are obvious limits to what can be inferred from material data such as stone artifacts or charcoal remains, archaeological research provides us with fascinating information about the prehistoric past. Generally, the time before European contact is divided in three major periods: PaleoIndian, Archaic, and Woodland.

PaleoIndian Period: About 20,000 years ago, perhaps even earlier, Ice Age ancestors of today's Indians, including the Mi'kmaq, first arrived in North America. Migrating from Siberia, they followed herds of mammoth, mastodon, giant bison, and saiga antelope that grazed the boggy steppe called "Beringia" (Dickason, 1992:21). With the warming of the climate some 14,000 years ago, the melting ice cap and glaciers made the sea levels rise. Gradually, the 1,200-mile-wide grassy plain of Beringia flooded, and this land bridge became what is now known as the Bering Strait. Moving southward, the hunting bands, now called PaleoIndians by anthropologists, migrated from Alaska until they reached the southern edge of the late Wisconsin glaciation. They fanned eastward into the Great Plains, where 12,000-year-old camps and mammoth and bison kill sites have been found. Among the artifacts they left behind are flint tools, including lanceolate bifaces known as Clovis or "fluted" points, used to tip hunting spears (J. Jennings, 82).

Some big game-hunting bands continued eastward, reaching the Atlantic seaboard as early as 11,000 years ago. Turning northward, they followed the retreating line of melting glaciers into present-day New England and the Maritimes of Canada. They were sustained by caribou and musk-ox, gregarious animals that roamed the tundra in herds of ten to fifty individuals and that could be ambushed by hunting bands who knew their trails (Snow 1980:46). Thousands of stone artifacts, including scores of Clovislike fluted points, have been found at kill sites and camps in the region. Ranging the still-cold tundra environment, PaleoIndian hunting bands returned to base camps at places such as Debert in western Nova Scotia. At this site, which dates to about 10,600 B.P., some four thousand fluted points, scrapers, gravers, awls, drills, charcoal, and other artifacts have been unearthed clustered around the hearths of eleven living areas (J. Jennings, 94).

Archaic Period: This period, extending from about 10,000 to 2,000 years ago, began as a gradual warming trend transformed the tundras into vast woodland habitat. Melting ice resulted in steadily rising sea levels reaching nearly two hundred feet above the early postglacial level in the Gulf of Maine and Bay of Fundy. Averaging a one-foot rise per hundred years, the sea soon flooded coastal plains. According to archaeologists, the emerging woodland, largely comprised of spruce, pine, birch, and alder, had a low carrying capacity for animals that were key to man's survival. This may account for "the relative scarcity of human remains between 10,000 and 5,000 years ago" (Sanger, 18, 26–27). During the final phase of the long Archaic Period, hardwoods (especially beech, maple, ash, and elm) gradually dominated conifers, forming a more productive forest attractive to moose and white-tail deer—and, in turn, to hunting and gathering humans (Sanger, 16–18).

In time, the human population increased and creatively adapted to the regional varieties of available resources. While some foraging groups focused on the interior woodlands, others targeted marine resources, in particular swordfish, porpoise, whales, harbor seals, and walrus: "The heavy woodworking tools which characterize the Maritime Archaic assemblages imply that large dugout canoes were used in these pursuits. Porpoise and whale effigies also attest to the importance of marine hunting" (Nietfeld, 124).

During the final phase of the Archaic (3500–2000 B.P.), the basic cultural pattern was established. Although there were some regional variations and periodic changes, the pattern prevailed until the European invasion. Typically, local bands made use of both coastal and interior resources, with seasonal movements to specific hunting, fishing, or gathering sites.

The maritime economy supported a relatively high population, which developed a culture complex of a type not generally associated with northern forest hunters— evidenced in the discovery of concentrated cemeteries containing over a hundred graves. These Maritime Archaic communities engaged in elaborate mortuary ceremonialism. They applied red ochre pigment to the deceased and bestowed burial gifts that included finely made slate bayonets and animal effigies (Tuck, 32–34). Ramah chert (flint) artifacts from northern Labrador were also among the offerings, suggesting a wide sphere of ritually structured communication (Nietfeld, 125–26).

Woodland Period: Beginning about 2,000 years ago, this final prehistoric phase lasted until the early 1500s, when European mariners began frequenting Mi'kmaq shores. During this era, some changes occurred, including the diffusion of ceramic traditions from the southwest and a shift from sea mammal hunting to shellfish gathering—evidenced in a rapid increase in the size and frequency of shell middens (Nietfeld, 141, 155). From fall through spring, Mi'kmaqs established their base camps near extensive shellfish beds of clams and mussels, located on flats along Maine's coast, in southern Nova Scotia bays, and on Northumberland Strait. From these settlements, they tapped other aquatic resources (fish, migrating birds, and sea mammals—seals in particular) as well as land mammals (primarily beaver, plus caribou, moose, deer, black bear, muskrat, porcupine, fox, and otter). In the summer, when shellfish could be poisonous or less desirable because of spawning, Mi'kmaqs turned to the sea for birds and sea mammals or to rivers for anadromous fish.

This subsistence and residence pattern did not exist in northeastern New Brunswick and parts of Nova Scotia where large shellfish beds are absent. In these regions a seasonal riverine settlement system existed with large campsites occurring at three types of locations, each offering particular resources: Sites near river mouths on protected bays offered flounder and smelt; positions along the middle courses of rivers provided spawning and migrating birds; and upstream spots supplied alewives and eels. Smaller sites were scattered in between, and areas not advantageous for fishing were avoided. Land mammals, hunted from these river base camps, were only a secondary consideration in site selection for Mi'kmaqs, for hunting was probably a dominant activity only in February and March (Nietfeld, 210–12).

PERSONAL APPEARANCES: DRESS, HAIRSTYLE, TATTOOS

In dress, hairstyle, and adornments, Mi'kmaqs expressed a sense of aesthetics that distinguished them from other tribes or ethnic groups. Moreover, these outward appearances could reflect social divisions within their own communities, such as gender, age, and personal status. How did Mi'kmaqs look on the eve of the European invasion? In height they resembled the newcomers, with adult men measuring up to six feet. Typically, both men and women were well-shaped, strong, and slender. Generally, the men were beardless and plucked out scant facial hair.

Mi'kmaqs often greased their faces, arms, and legs with seal oil or other animal fat as a protection against cold, rain, and gnats. During the cold winter period, they donned thick fur robes made of beaver, otter, raccoon, or even bear skins. In warmer seasons they usually wore a soft leather breechclout and leggings, with a coat of wild goose or turkey feathers or a mantle made of a smoothly dressed, white moose-hide or tanned deerskin. Women typically made these garments, dressing the hides by scraping and rubbing them with seabird oil, then decorating the hide with paint, colored moose hair, or flattened porcupine quills. White moose-hide coats were commonly embroidered in colored stripes and chevrons or studded with animal figures (JR 3:73–77; N. Denys, 411). Clothing and belts were also adorned with small red metal tubes, made from thin sheets of copper found in the Cap d'Or region of Nova Scotia (Whitehead and McGee, 31). For footwear, Mi'kmaqs preferred sealskins, but also used recycled moose-hide coats. Women embellished moccasins with pigments and dyed porcupine quills (N. Denys, 411, 413). Knee-high mukluks were often made from a long tube of skin peeled off whole from a moose leg and then sewn up across the toe (Whitehead and McGee, 28).

Mi'kmaq warriors tied their long hair in a knot at the crown or back of the head with leather thongs. Into these topknots they sometimes wove bird feathers, shell beads, dyed moose hair, or porcupine quills (Champlain 1:444–45; Lescarbot 3:133–34). Mi'kmaq boys fastened their long hair in two tufts, one on each side of the head. Some added ornaments of colored porcupine quills. Unmarried women also wore their hair long, gathering it into a tail at the back of the head. An early seventeenth-century French trader noted that traditionally the women beautified themselves by wearing

> ornamental pieces of the size of a foot or eight inches square, all embroidered with Porcupine quills of all colours. It is made on a frame, of which the warp is threads of leather from unborn Moose, a very delicate sort; the quills of Porcupine form the woof which they pass through these threads. . . . All around they make a fringe of the same threads, which are also encircled with these Porcupine quills in a medley of colours. In this fringe they place wampum, white and violet.

> (N. Denys, 414)

Mi'kmaqs also tattooed and painted their faces and bodies with various designs and colors. Some men, for example, whitened their eyebrows. Others reddened their faces and drew black or blue lines across the nose and forehead. Black could signal the mourning of a deceased relative. From pierced ears, they hung pendants of birds, beasts, and fishes, beautifully carved from bone, shells, and stone (N. Denys, 414). Finally, both men and women bedecked themselves with white and blue shell beadwork

Titled "Homme Acadien," this engraving shows a Mi'kmaq hunter with wampum headdress and various body tatoos. By J. Laroque, after J. Grasset de St. Sauveur.

("wampum") in the form of bracelets and long necklaces, some of which they obtained as gifts or by barter with distant groups (Lescarbot 3:157–58).

DEMOGRAPHICS

Although we can reconstruct the way Mi'kmaqs probably looked before the onslaught of European influence five hundred years ago, it is more difficult to establish their pre-contact population. We know for certain that they suffered a calamitous demographic decline due to alien pathogens carried by the newcomers (JR 1:177; N. Denys, 403). About one century after first contact, a Jesuit missionary who worked among the Mi'kmaq guessed that all told they "would not amount to two thousand." Later he upped the figure to 3,500, commenting, "and I believe it is the highest number" (JR 3:43). Because there is disagreement about epidemic mortality ratios, ranging as high as twenty to one between aboriginal populations at first contact with Europeans and those same populations at their subsequent low ebb (Snow 1980:34), pre-1600 population projections generally vacillate between a low of about 3,500 (Mooney) and a high of 35,000 (Miller). Envisioning themselves a once-great Indian nation, many Mi'kmaqs now believe that they must have numbered at least 100,000. My own educated guess is more modest.

Based on the size of their aboriginal territory (40,000 square miles), mode of production (foraging), and an estimated aboriginal population density of 10–20 persons per 40 square miles, I estimate a precontact population of about 10,000–20,000—or about 15,000 people (cf. Snow 1980:36; Nietfeld, 393). If we factor in the Jesuit's postepidemic population estimates (2,000–3,500), we find that Mi'kmaqs suffered a mortality rate of 75 to nearly 90 percent after one hundred years of direct contact. Although this population loss is dramatic, it is fairly typical among tribes in the Western Hemisphere who suffered epidemics born of European contact.

MODE OF PRODUCTION AT THE TIME OF CONTACT: SUBSISTENCE FORAGING

Ranging the Atlantic seaboard and the St. Lawrence Gulf coast, the Mi'kmaq developed a mainly maritime economy. As migratory hunters, fishers, and gatherers, they deftly exploited the ecological diversity of their territory, fitting their way of life to the growth cycles of vegetation and the seasonal behaviors of game animals and fish.

Severe winters and a short growing season (and low mean summer temperatures on the coast) thwarted the development of horticulture as a viable subsistence strategy in traditional Mi'kmaq country. Planting crops such as corn, beans, and squash would have been a risky undertaking. Tobacco, on the other hand, described as "a thing most precious with them," may have been cultivated (Lescarbot 3:252; Bock 1978:109).

Having developed a particular ecological niche, the Mi'kmaq organized themselves into highly mobile bands. Each of these loosely structured communities consisted of several related kin-groups who periodically assembled at certain favored campsites. Assuming that the average Mi'kmaq band counted about two hundred members, it is reasonable to suggest that there may have been some 75 distinct communities.

Moving seasonally between particular hunting districts and specific coastal fishing, clamming, fowling, and sealing sites, Mi'kmaqs harvested the natural resources in their habitat. Typically, they dispersed in small family groups of about 10–15 people during the fall and winter—their hunting seasons. It is not clear whether hunting districts were "owned" by individual families or were periodically allocated to the various kin-groups within each band. But it appears that these tracts averaged two hundred to three hundred square miles per family (Speck 1915:183, 194–95). In other words, Mi'kmaq country may have been divided into some 2,000 tracts. For hunting expeditions, Mi'kmaqs armed themselves with spears, bows and arrows, axes, knives, and other equipment, including traps. Often, dogs accompanied these parties. Spears and arrows were commonly used to kill big game, such as moose, caribou, or bear, while smaller creatures, including otter, beaver, muskrat, and rabbit, were taken in special traps. Although some animals were killed year-round, fur-bearing animals were typically hunted in the winter and spring only (N. Denys, 419, 421, 429).

In the spring, when abundant shellfish (in particular, clams) and spawning fish were easily accessible, families reconvened and assembled in bands of 200 or more. Different bands occasionally came together for special meetings. Although each family was for the most part self-sufficient, these larger gatherings served many social purposes—exchanging information, making new friendships and affirming old ones, finding spouses, offering gifts, and engaging in barter (Bock 1978:109; Biard 1612, in JR 3:79–83).

A Frenchman familiar with the Mi'kmaq way of life on the shores of the Bay of Fundy in 1606–1607 described the Mi'kmaqs' migratory subsistence pattern like this:

> When Spring comes, they [assemble] into bands upon the shores of the sea, until Winter; and as then the fish withdraw to the bottom of the great salt waters, they seek the lakes and the shades of the forests, where they catch Beavers, upon which they live, and other game as [moose], Caribou, Deer, and still smaller animals. And yet, sometimes even in Summer, they do not give up hunting: besides, there are an infinite number of birds on certain islands in the months of May, June, July, and August.

(JR 1:83–85)

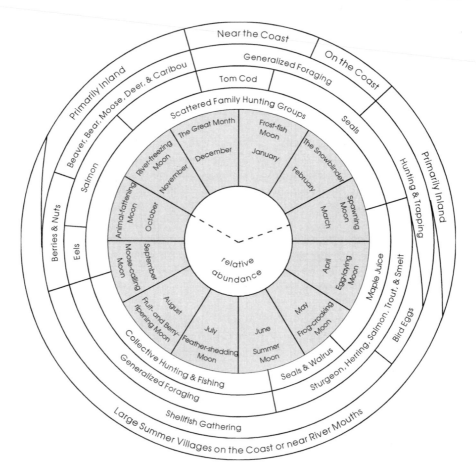

Annual cycle of Mi'kmaq subsistence activities.

Seventeenth-century documents suggest that for ten out of twelve months Mi'k-maqs oriented their economy toward maritime resources, which accounted for perhaps 90 percent of their diet (Nash and Miller, 47). The maritime habitat supplied them with an abundance and variety of fish (sturgeon, salmon, trout, bass, mackerel, alewife, smelt, herring, tomcod, eel, etc.). To preserve their catch, they cleaned, split and placed the fish on low wooden racks over a very smoky fire (Whitehead and McGee, 11–12). As one early French visitor commented, "Without Fish they would have to endure evil days, for they do not always have fresh or smoked meat to eat" (Diereville, 116). A French Jesuit who observed a Mi'kmaq band in southwest Nova Scotia in the early 1600s sketched this seasonal overview of Mi'kmaq fisheries:

> In the middle of March, fish begin to spawn, and to come up from the sea into cer-tain streams. . . . First smelt, then alewives, at the end of April. At the same time come the sturgeon, and salmon. . . . From the month of May up to the middle of September, they are free from all anxiety about their food; for the cod are upon the coast, and all kinds of fish and shell-fish. . . . Now our Indians in the middle of September withdraw from the sea . . . to the little rivers, where the eels spawn, of which they lay in a supply; they are good and fat . . . and then in December . . . comes a fish called by them ponamo [tomcod], which spawn under the ice.
>
> (Biard, in JR 3:79, 81–83)

For their fisheries, the Mi'kmaq employed various ingenious devices. To catch smelt, alewife, and shad, they constructed fish weirs called *nesakun* by driving wooden stakes side by side into the ground at the mouth of tidal streams or rivers. The fish swam over the wall at high tide and found themselves trapped at ebb tide when the water level dropped below the weir's top (Diereville, 113–15). Mi'kmaqs also used bag-nets woven from strips of basswood or hemp, described by a French-man who came to the region early in the seventeenth century:

> At the narrowest place of the rivers, where there is the least water, they make a fence of wood clear across the river to hinder the passage of the fish. In the middle of it they leave an opening in which they place a bag-net like those used in France, so arranged that it is inevitable the fish should run into them. These bag-nets, which are larger than ours, they raise two or three times a day, and they always find fish therein. It is in the spring that the fish ascend, and in autumn they descend and return to the sea. At that time they place the opening of their bag-net in the other direction.
>
> (N. Denys, 437)

To catch large salmon, trout, bass, and flounder, as well as lobster, Mi'kmaqs used a special fish spear, or leister—a long pole tipped with a bone or ivory point flanked by two wooden prongs. When the spear pierced a fish, the prongs closed around the prey and kept it from wriggling loose (Barratt, 7–15). Mi'kmaqs usually turned to spearfishing in the spring and early summer when the ice left the estuaries and pools, creating temporary havens for fish swimming to their spawning places upriver. Often they fished at night, using birch-bark torches as lures: "The Salmon or the Trout, seeing the fire which shines upon the water, come wheeling around the canoe. He who is standing up has in his hand a [leister]. So soon as he saw a fish passing he speared at it, and rarely missed. But sometimes the spear did not take hold, for want of catching on some bone; thus they lost their fish. This did not prevent them from taking a hundred and fifty to two hundred in a night" (N. Denys, 173, 436–37).

Perhaps even more spectacular than their spearing the savory salmon, which sometimes weighed up to 70 pounds (Hardy, 89), Mi'kmaq fishermen also preyed upon sturgeon, which could measure 8–12 feet in length. For this they relied on a harpoon,

> which is made like a barbed rod, of eight to ten inches long, pointed at one end, and with a hole at the other in which is attached a line. Then it is fastened at the end of a pole, so that it may be used as a dart.
>
> (N. Denys, 353–54)

The extensive muddy flats and banks along the coast of northern Nova Scotia all the way to Chaleur Bay harbored enormous quantities of shellfish—clams, mussels, and especially oysters, which were the major food in the region during the spring and a backup food in the winter (N. Denys, 171, 359).

Mi'kmaq hunters also depended upon sea mammals, including walrus and seals, which were speared or harpooned while resting on beaches and islands or swimming in the coastal waters. Seal was especially valued for its tasty flesh and soft hide, which was made into moccasins. Perhaps most important, however, was its precious oily fat: "All the oil they can yield is about their bladder-full, and in this the Indians place it after having melted it. This oil is good to eat fresh, and for frying fish. It is also good to burn for light. It has neither odour nor smoke, no more than olive oil. . . . The oil is to the Indians a relish at all the feasts they make among themselves. They use it also to grease their hair" (N. Denys, 349–50). The Mi'kmaq also feasted on stranded whales, savoring the blubber "of which they made good cheer" (N. Denys, 353–56, 403; Lescarbot 1612, in JR 2:185; LeClercq, 283).

Among the many types of berries, nuts, and other plant forms that sustained Mi'kmaqs, sugar maples are of special note. Each spring Mi'kmaqs tapped the sap in these trees by gashing the bark and inserting into it a hollowed elderberry twig through which the sweet juice dripped into a birch-bark container. They either drank the sap or boiled it into syrup.

Dining on nature's rich variety in game, fowl, fish, fruit, and nuts, Mi'kmaqs had an ample supply of protein and vitamins. In addition, as early French observers noted, they took care of their health "by the use of hot rooms and sweat boxes [sweat lodges], and by the bath. They also use massage, afterwards rubbing the whole body with seal oil [which allows them to] stand heat and cold better." Consequently, the French marveled, "You do not encounter a big-bellied, hunchbacked, or deformed person among them: those who are leprous, gouty, affected with gravel, or insane, are unknown to them" (JR 3:75, 117).

PORTABLE MATERIAL CULTURE

To accommodate their mobile lifestyle, the Mi'kmaq preferred a simple and lightweight material culture. Skillfully making use of available natural materials such as leather, stone, bone, horn, and wood, they fabricated their own tools and weapons, including long spears, wooden clubs, stone axes and adzes, bows and arrows, flint scrapers and knives, bone fishhooks, as well as traps, snares, nets, and baskets. Bows were made of maple wood, polished with oyster shells and strung with moose sinew. Young alders were used to make arrow shafts, tipped with bone or stone points and trimmed with eagle feathers to stabilize flight. To take large fish or sea mammals, they fashioned harpoons with barbed bone or ivory heads, as well as the special three-pronged fish and eel spears. Their beechwood lances were equipped with a sharply pointed moose bone. Engaging in armed conflict, warriors carried stone axes, wooden clubs, and large wooden shields (N. Denys, 409, 419–20; JR 3:41, 91).

When traveling on land, Mi'kmaqs used special carrying straps, or tumplines, to haul loads of meat, furs, hides, and other valuable goods. This leather strap was usually worn across the forehead or chest, binding the heavy burden onto the back (Whitehead and McGee, 40). For winter travel, they made snowshoes of ash or beechwood, corded with moose or caribou rawhide. They transported loads on sleds or toboggans, which were made of wide flat planks split from a large trunk of the rock maple tree. When waterways were ice-free, Mi'kmaqs traveled in lightweight birch-bark canoes (*kwitn*), made of bark sheets that were stitched together with split spruce root and bound to a wooden frame. Seams were caulked with spruce gum to make the boat waterproof. Typically, the smaller hunting canoe, used for navigating very small streams and for portaging, measured about 12 feet. A longer model, the so-called big-river canoe, ranged from 15–20 feet. Their largest canoe, used in open water for hunting seal and porpoise, could exceed 24 feet (Adney and Chapelle, 58). Special canoes made of moose hide instead of bark were called *mu'sul'k* (Rand 1894:197). Maple, as well as beech and ash, were used for paddles, sometimes decorated with special designs. It was not uncommon for Mi'kmaqs to equip their canoes with a sail made of bark or (more often) young moose hide, sometimes painted with game animals. With a favorable wind a sail helped a canoe travel as "swiftly as the throw of a stone" (N. Denys, 422; Lescarbot 4:310; Morton, 186).

Accomplished weavers, Mi'kmaq women used all kinds of bark, as well as leather straps, long strands of sweetgrass, reeds, and rushes. With these skins and fibers they fashioned baskets, bags, bowls, and boxes, which were used to store and carry food and valuables.

Although the Mi'kmaq often smoked their meat and fish, most foods were boiled by placing them with fire-heated stones in a "kettle" that had been painstakingly carved from a hardwood log. Too heavy and cumbersome to transport, kettles were left behind when it came time to move camp—but they provided an incentive to return to the same site at a later date. To make fire for cooking or smoking, Mi'kmaqs first gathered some tinder (usually dry moss or rotted wood, called punk). Then, striking a piece of iron pyrite with a piece of chert, they sparked fire in the punk. Often, when they moved camp, they carried hot coals from their last fire in a clamshell lined with clay and tied shut. Punk stuffed around the coals kept the embers fed until they were needed to kindle a new campfire (Whitehead and McGee, 15, 48–52).

The Mi'kmaq dwelled in a cone-shaped dwelling called *wikuom,* which suited their migratory way of life. A cluster of several wikuoms formed a typical Mi'kmaq settlement. Easy to set up, dismantle, and transport to another camping ground, a *wikuom* consisted of a frame made of about 10 long spruce poles lashed together at the top with spruce root. These roots were also used to stitch the *wikuom* cover, fabricated of long sheets of bark made supple with water and heat. Although they preferred such waterproof birch-bark coverings, Mi'kmaqs also used animal hides or tightly woven matting. They made a fireplace in the center of conical *wikuoms*. Sometimes Mi'kmaqs built larger A-frame dwellings, which could have a door and a fire at each end. And, as described by a Frenchman who came to Mi'kmaq country in the 17th century, during the warmer summer months, "the shape of their houses is changed; for then they are broad and long, that they may have more air." These lodges, which could shelter more than 30 people, were "well matted above and below." Mi'kmaqs covered the floors of their dwellings with hemlock twigs or balsam fir needles, topped with mats, hides, or "sealskins as soft as velvet" (JR 2:41; JR 3:77).

SOCIAL STRUCTURE: FAMILY, BAND, TRIBE

Traditionally, the basic social unit among the Mi'kmaq was a residential kin-group consisting of a headman (*saqmaw*), his nuclear family, and some of his married sons and daughters and their families. This extended family could also encompass various other individuals—widowed parents, unmarried brothers, cousins, and other kinfolk in both the matri- and patrilineal lines. Even nonrelated individuals, including orphans, could form part of this household. Also, because social power came through having many relatives, in particular many children, polygyny was not uncommon (JR 2:23). Polygyny not only gave successful males the advantage of several wives (valued for their labor and reproductive capacities), but also offered women protection and security necessary for their own survival and that of their offspring.

Extended families formed part of the larger kin-groups or bands who typically came together during times when resources were abundant enough to support large gatherings. Among the Mi'kmaq, bands were highly fluid, loosely organized communities, ranging in size from less than 30 individuals to more than 300. Because membership was based on voluntary association, band size could fluctuate considerably from year to year.

Alliances between bands were facilitated by exogamous marriage rules, which urged young men to choose their wives from other bands. This strengthened the Mi'kmaqs' collective identity as an ethnic group, fostering "interband reciprocity, feasting, seasonal regional councils composed of neighboring local chiefs, and the extension of mutual aid when faced by common enemies" (Nietfeld, 458). Brideservice, in which a prospective groom spent a probationary prenuptial year or so living and foraging with his bride's family, may have played a role in the making of alliances between bands. Once married, the new couple usually went to live with the groom's family (Biard 1612, in JR 2:205). Although such patrilocality was preferred, residence was often bilocal in practice. Likewise, Mi'kmaq kinship terminology suggests that they reckoned descent bilaterally. Bilocal residence and bilateral kinship linkages provided the social flexibility that Mi'kmaqs needed to continually readjust themselves to fit the shifting resource availability on which they built their economy (Nietfeld, 410–415).

SOCIAL DIVISION OF LABOR

Labor division among the Mi'kmaq was based primarily on sex, and every able-bodied person had a role. Men hunted, fished, fought as warriors, and took care of making and repairing most tools, weapons, and equipment (bows, arrows, lances, shields, war clubs, fish traps and weirs, snowshoe and canoe frames, tobacco pipes, etc.). The tasks of women were more multifarious and burdensome. As described by a Jesuit priest in 1612, Mi'kmaqs had

> no other artisans, agents, servants, purveyors or slaves than their women. . . . be-sides the onerous role of bearing and rearing the children, [they] also transport the game from where it has fallen; they are the hewers of wood and drawers of water; they make and repair the household utensils; they prepare food; they skin the game and prepare the hides like fullers; they sew garments; they catch fish and gather shellfish [, berries, and nuts] for food; often they even hunt; they make [coverings for] the canoes [and *wikuoms*]... out of bark; they set up the tents wherever and whenever they stop for the night—in short, the men concern themselves with nothing but the more laborious hunting and the waging of war. For this reason almost everyone has several wives.
>
> (Biard, in JR 2:23, 77)

POLITICAL ORGANIZATION: *SAQMAQ* AND *NIKMANAQ*

With the essential self-sufficiency of each family unit, low population pressure, and a general lack of resource specialization among the widely scattered and migratory Mi'kmaq, there was no place for a formal political hierarchy to organize labor and redistribute goods on a regular basis. Instead, traditional Mi'kmaq political patterns included a loosely structured social organization, participatory decision making, voluntary association, minimalized institutionalization, and situational (as-needed) political leadership based on consensus instead of coercion (JR 3:87).

Traditionally, the head of a residential kin-group was known as a *saqmaw*. This term was generally used to express a measure of respect for anyone who held status as a leader or who had "a command of men" (Levett, in Baxter, 117; cf. Maillard, 11–12). As described by an early 17th-century missionary in Mi'kmaq country, "There is the [saqmaw], who is the eldest son of some powerful family, and consequently also its chief and leader. All the young people of the family are at his table and in his retinue." In addition to providing leadership in times of warfare, it was the saqmaw's "duty to provide dogs for the chase, canoes for transportation, provisions and reserves for bad weather and expedition" (Biard, in JR 3:87). Followers typically maintained a large measure of autonomy and personal freedom, and chieftains were generally incapable of exercising any form of coercive control: "They have [*saqmaq*], that is, leaders in war; but their authority is most precarious, if, indeed, that may be called authority to which obedience is in no way obligatory. The Indians follow them through the persua-sion of example or of custom, or of ties of kindred and alliance" (JR 2:73). Another missionary described the situation like this: "The most prominent chief is followed by several young warriors and by several hunters. . . . But, in fact, all his power and au-thority are based only upon the goodwill of those in his nation, who execute his orders just in so far as it pleases them" (LeClercq, 234–38). In short, the ideal political leader among Mi'kmaqs was someone who inspired confidence, possessed superior insights and knowledge, acted courageously in warfare, and was a generous and outstanding provider. For the most part, Mi'kmaq families survived on their own ingenuity. In times of need, through an informal system of generalized reciprocity, they usually re-lied on other families in their band network. However, a saqmaw, "because of the pres-tige his position . . . afforded him and because of the debts to him his generosity created, did collect, in a small way, excess production. He redistributed this surplus by helping those in need, by providing food for social occasions such as feasts and cere-monies, and by supporting group-wide activities such as war parties" (Nietfeld, 505; cf. Biard, in JR 3:87; LeClercq, 235–36).

Periodically Mi'kmaq leaders gathered for councils on band and regional levels. Councils dealt with both internal and external affairs. Held as the need arose, they settled internal disputes and decided on participation in wars (Nietfeld, 431–32). At local councils family headmen and other elders discussed issues such as vital natural resources and their distribution. According to a 17th-century missionary: "It is the right of the head of the nation. . . . to distribute the places of hunting to each individ-ual. It is not permitted to any Indian to overstep the bounds and limits of the region which shall have been assigned him in the assemblies of the elders. These are held in autumn and spring expressly to make this assignment" (LeClercq, 237). In addition to allocating hunting territories, the band council also "sent orphans and widows who were unable to support their children or be supported by them to live with the best hunters (Nietfeld, 432; LeClercq, 117).

Another missionary described the councils this way:

It is principally in Summer that they pay visits and hold their State Councils;
I mean that several [saqmaws] come together and consult among themselves
about peace and war, treaties of friendship and treaties for the common good. It
is only these [saqmaws] who have a voice in the discussion and who make the
speeches. . . . Now in these assemblies, if there is some news of importance, as that
their neighbors wish to make war upon them, or that they have killed some one, or
that they must renew the alliance, etc., then messengers fly from all parts to make
up the more general assembly, that they may avail themselves of all the confeder-
ates, which they call *Ricmanen,** who are generally those of the same language.
Nevertheless the confederation often extends farther than the language does, and
war sometimes arises against those who have the same language. In these assemblies so general, they resolve upon peace, truce, war, or nothing at all, as often happens in the councils where there are several chiefs, without order or subordination,
whence they frequently depart more confused and disunited than when they came.

(JR 3:87–91)

---

*The word *Ricmanen* appears to refer to *nikmanen,* also spelled *niqmanen,* which means "our friend" or "our ally"; *nikmanaq* means "our allies." (personal communication Mildred Milliea and Bernie Francis).

GRAND CHIEF AND DISTRICT CHIEFS

As migratory hunters, fishers, and gatherers, the Mi'kmaq appear to have formed a highly egalitarian society. Yet, as I will discuss in Chapter 12, many Mi'kmaqs today argue that their political system used to be more hierarchical, involving a centralized system of leadership. They maintain that when the Europeans first arrived on their shores, the Mi'kmaq nation was organized in seven major districts, each headed by a regional band chief, honored as first among equals. Because it is the seat of the "grand chief," Cape Breton is said to have been the traditional "head district." But as stated earlier, historical documentation for such a Mi'kmaq chiefdom or state remains inconclusive.

Although it remains unclear to what extent the Mi'kmaqs developed a national political structure, the district chiefs may have paid homage to one renowned leader, whose function as grand chief was unlikely to have been more than ceremonial. One such grand chief may have been Membertou, "the greatest, most renowned and most formidable Indian within the memory of man, of splendid physique, taller and larger-limbed than is usual among them; bearded like a Frenchman, although scarcely any of the others have hair upon the chin; grave and reserved; feeling a proper sense of dignity for his position as commander" (JR 2:23). As band chief in the Bay of Fundy area, he had an encampment that consisted of eight wikuoms. In addition to being a chief, Membertou was a shaman. One early missionary wrote of him: "He has done [divination] so well that his reputation is far above that of all the other [saqmaws] of the country, he having been since his youth a great Captain, and also having exercised the offices of Soothsayer and Medicine-man" (JR 1:74–77). However, it remains unclear to what extent other Mi'kmaq bands acknowledged this local saqmaw as a "grand chief." Is it possible that this title was bestowed upon him by the French, in honor of his allegiance to the newcomers and his subsequent baptism as a Roman Catholic convert? A Frenchman personally familiar with Membertou described him as "the great [saqmaw], [who] exhorts every one of the Indians to become Christians." In 1610, the same Frenchman provided these details about Membertou: "At Port Royal, the name of the Captain or [saqmaw] of the place is Membertou. He is at least a hundred years old. . . . He has under him a number of families whom he rules, not with so much authority as does our King over his subjects, but with sufficient power to harangue, advise, and lead them to war, to render justice to one who has a grievance, and like matters" (JR 2:182–83).

IDEOLOGY: WORLDVIEW, DREAMS, GUARDIAN SPIRITS, AND SHAMANISM

Living in the "happy land" (Nicolar, 5) created by their culture hero Klu'skap, the Mi'kmaq developed a worldview not unlike that of other hunting peoples. It grew from a profound knowledge about their natural environment, including its fauna and flora. Their place-names often convey vital elements of ecological understanding, revealing a locality's distinctive geographic features, dangers, or natural resources (Cronon, 65). On their journeys, moving swiftly in lightweight birch-bark canoes,

Mi'kmaqs were guided by such toponyms—verbal signposts that told them which fork to take, where to portage to a connecting travel route, and where to expect swift currents, dangerous rapids, or gravel bars. Many place-names in the region still contain ancient verbal clues, such as *sipu* (river), *meniku* (island), *wnikn* (portage), *sipaqn* (passage), *matawe'k* (confluent), and so forth.

Although there are no indications that the Mi'kmaq kept permanent cartographic collections, there is evidence that they made maps for temporary needs. If, for instance, a local scout encountered tribesmen from an enemy village secretly roaming in the area, he would scratch on a piece of bark a picture of the place, indicating the streams, points, and other landmarks. Sometimes, he would leave incisions in the bark of a tree near the stream where his friends would follow him by canoe, or place sticks on the trail, indicating that a message in hieroglyphics was hidden nearby. Commenting on this use of picture-writing, a French missionary noted: "They have much ingenuity in drawing upon bark a kind of map which marks exactly all the rivers and streams of a country of which they wish to make a representation. They mark all the places thereon exactly and so well that they make use of them successfully, and an Indian who possesses one makes long voyages without going astray" (LeClercq, 136).

The Mi'kmaq worldview was not one that allowed for a clear-cut divide between the natural and supernatural. Perceiving both spheres as interlinked, perhaps as one and the same, they believed that all of creation was pregnant with a spiritual force known as *mntu* (also spelled *mindu* or *manitou*). Mntu referred to the impersonal, preternatural power of the universe. Shrouded in mystery, it could be found in certain objects, plants, or animal beings. Most of all, Mi'kmaqs honored the sun, *niskam,* as a powerful spirit force. At dawn they came out from their wikuoms "to salute the sun when it began to dart its first morning rays, and they did the same also without fail at its setting. . . . [They] asked that it would grant their needs: that it would guard their wives and their children: that it would give them the power to vanquish and overcome their enemies: that it would grant them a hunt rich in moose, beavers, martens, and otters, with a great catch of all kinds of fishes: finally they asked the preservation of their lives for a great number of years, and a long line of posterity" (LeClercq, 144).

Mi'kmaqs attached great significance to visions. They believed that on special occasions, during sleeping dreams or in a trance, they entered a nonordinary world of spirit powers. In those moments of dreamlike consciousness, a special *ntio'ml* ("animal spiritual helper") might contact them. As a guardian spirit, the ntio'ml offered support and protection against danger, especially invisible threats. With its help, one could gain knowledge about otherwise unknown or secret things. For instance, it enabled Mi'kmaqs to interpret certain omens. Moreover, it offered advice on how to prevent mishap or how to make good things happen. Failure to listen could lead to bad luck, illness, even death. Because Mi'kmaqs regarded dream experiences to be as real as waking events, they greatly respected (and sometimes feared) individuals who were believed to possess special spiritual power. These individuals demonstrated their "psychic" powers, which included clairvoyance and telepathy, by extraordinary feats. For instance, they were said to be able to forecast weather, locate game and fish, predict enemy raids, heal the sick, and use magic to harm, even kill, opponents. The Mi'kmaq called such a spirit-endowed person, or shaman, a *puowin,* a term that may be translated as "mystery person" or "magic-doing person" (JR 2:45; LeClercq, 215–18; Johnson, 59).

Although much about puowins remains unclear, it appears that someone born as the seventh son or seventh daughter was destined to possess supernatural powers. Moreover, certain families were known for their psychic abilities, which apparently could be passed from one generation to the next. In general, however, a man or woman could become a puowin through a metaphysical experience such as having a vision or a revelation in a dream. Such experiences were sometimes induced. According to one account: "The novice must keep his object a secret while camping alone in the woods with an outfit for two, the other, an invisible companion. A being will finally appear, it is thought, who will give him the gift of magic, the power to assume animal shapes, to walk through fire unharmed, through water without being drowned, to translate himself through the air with the quickness of thought, to control the elements, to walk on the water and the like" (Hagar, 172).

In shamanic practice, a puowin employed special fetish objects, which could include small carvings of animal bone or wood, a piece of leather or bark, a pebble, or any other object. These charms were carried in a leather pouch called *puowinuti* ("mystery bag"). Although medicine pouches varied, one has been described as "made of the skin of an entire head of a moose, with the exception of the ears, which were removed." It held several animal fetishes, including a bark figure of a little wolverine adorned with blue and white wampum beads. Moreover, it contained a miniature bow and arrow, as well as "a fragment of bark, wrapped in a delicate and very thin skin, on which were represented some little children, birds, bears, beavers, and moose. Against these the [puowin], using his little bow, shot his arrow at pleasure, in order to cause the death of the children or of some other thing of which the figure is represented on this bit of bark." Also among the contents was

> a stick, a good foot in length, adorned with white and red porcupine quills; at its end were attached several straps of a half-foot in length, and two dozen dew-claws of moose. It is with this stick that [the puowin] makes a develish noise, using these dew-claws as sounders. . . . Finally, the last article in the bag was a wooden bird, which they carry with them when they go hunting, with the idea that it will enable them to kill waterfowl in abundance.

> (LeClercq, 221–22)

Without the magic power, spiritual guidance, and healing skills of their puowins, the Mi'kmaq feared for their survival. Accordingly, at least one puowin lived in each community. When he helped or healed people, they expressed their gratitude with special gifts such as precious otter or beaver skins or other valuables (JR 1:75–77).

SOCIAL NICHE: MI'KMAQS AND THEIR NEIGHBORS

Ranging a vast coastal territory, the Mi'kmaq rarely confronted strangers. But they knew the tribal boundaries of other Indian peoples. Just beyond the range of their immediate neighbors, the Maliseet and Passamaquoddy, were other Algonquian-speaking

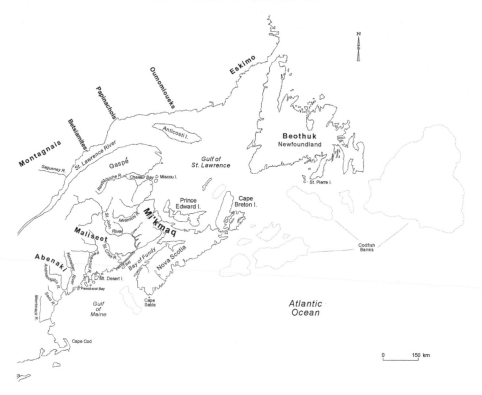

Aboriginal northeast America: the Mi'kmaq and their neighbors.

groups—Abenaki, Montagnais, and Algonkin. Farther away lived the Pennacook, Sokoki, Massachusetts, and Wampanoag, as well as a host of other New England Algonquians. West of the Hudson sprawled the homeland of the Mohawk and other Iroquois, who could be reached by traveling up the St. Lawrence River. Montagnais (Innu) ranged on the north side of this river, and across the St. Lawrence Gulf lived the Beothuk of Newfoundland and the Inuit (Eskimo) of Labrador.

Although the Mi'kmaq possess a distinct language, they could (and can) somewhat understand neighboring Algonquian-speaking peoples. Also, bilingualism or even multilingualism was (and is) not uncommon, in part because Mi'kmaqs (like other tribes) sometimes recruited foreigners into their bands. This occurred through marriage, such as with Maliseet, Montagnais, or Abenaki. It also took place through capturing enemies, some of whom were adopted as kin to replace dead relatives.

Commenting on their relationship with the Maliseet, Mi'kmaq claim that these neighbors are a breakaway tribe from the Mi'kmaq. This explains why Mi'kmaqs can still, to a degree, understand Maliseet speakers in contrast to unrelated groups such as the Mohawks, whom they called "cannibals." Stories of this fission survive to this day. One version, recorded in 1907, goes as follows:

> Before the whites came, the Micmac held a pow-wow and a feast at Prince Edward Island. Two dogs fought over some bones. The master of one dog struck the other dog. The second dog's owner said, "You and your dog are one," and hit the first

man. The followers of the two men now joined the two fighting men. The van-
quished party were pushed off the island. From that time onward they were so
afraid of the other Micmac that they changed their speech so that they could not be
understood. Maliseet means "corrupted speech."

(Watson, 160–62)

INTERTRIBAL CONFLICTS

With an abundance of natural resources available in their spacious habitat, Mi'kmaqs
had no need to fight for more territory. However, their warriors did sometimes
raid neighboring populations in order to increase their own numbers with captives.
Women and, in particular, children were usually adopted to replace deceased kinfolk. Revenge for the killing of a fellow Mi'kmaq, especially a kinsman, also
prompted warfare, as did the need to repel intruders. And there were other reasons—
including dreams. For instance, if someone dreamed about a spirit being, such as a
deceased ancestor who wanted a certain wrong to be revenged, a war party might be
assembled to actualize the dream (Lescarbot 3:263–64; JR 47:223).

Mi'kmaqs also fought to avenge insult. In a speech following a successful campaign against the Maliseet, a Mi'kmaq orator pointed out that they had not waged the
war because the Maliseets had "deprived us of the means of hunting for our maintenance and cloathing; they have not cut off the free passage of our canoes, on the
lakes and rivers of this country; but they have done worse. . . . They have defloured
[ravaged] our principal maidens" (Maillard, 24).

Because of its potential to devastate, Mi'kmaqs viewed war as something very
sacred, and not lightly to be undertaken" (de la Varenne, 101). As a French missionary living among them noted: "War is never declared except by advice of the old
men, who alone decide, in the last resort, the affairs of the country. They prescribe
the order which must be followed in the execution of their military undertakings."
Aid from their allies was requested "if they cannot themselves settle their quarrels;
and they send ambassadors, with collars of wampum, to invite these to take up the
hatchet against the enemies of the nation" (LeClercq, 269). These allies, "which they
call [nikmanaq], . . . are generally those of the same language. Nevertheless the confederation often extends farther than the language does, and war sometimes arises
against those who have the same language" (JR 3:91).

Once the final preparations were completed, the old chieftains would "fix the
day of departure; and they assemble the young warriors to the war feast. These come
there with their usual arms [spear, bow and arrow, hatchet, and knife, coupled with a
wooden shield]" (LeClercq, 269). At the feast, enjoying boiled dog flesh dipped in
seal oil or moose grease, warriors listened to songs and speeches. Finally, before taking off on the warpath, they painted their faces red. It might be months before they
were expected to return from the battlefield (Maillard, 6, 30–32).

Typically, Mi'kmaqs engaged in a type of guerrilla warfare, ambushing enemies
at a strategic point where they were known to pass "to hunt, or provide bark for
making their canoes. It was commonly in these passes, or defiles, that the bloodiest
encounters or engagements happened" (Maillard, 32; cf. JR 3:91). However,

although it is true that stealth and surprise played an important role in their strategy, the Mi'kmaq sometimes issued a formal declaration of war. In these instances, they dispatched some scouts toward the enemy: "When they draw near the village, they give the earth several strokes with their hatchets . . . and shoot two of their best arrows at the village, and retire with the utmost expedition." Having been targeted for attack, the people in the village were forced to make a choice, namely, "whether they shall maintain their ground by staying in their village, and fortifying it. . . . or look out for a place of greater safety, or go directly in quest of the enemy" (Maillard, 30–31). Once the war had been kindled in earnest, Mi'kmaqs tried to pursue it "with the utmost rigor by way of terror" in an effort to end the fighting as quickly as possible (de la Varenne, 101).

As in other tribal societies, powerful reputations were built on success in warfare. An old Mi'kmaq explained that young warriors might go off to war in quest for trophies "that they might achieve the reward, honor, and renown annexed to the acquisition of them" (Maillard, 17). As an early French missionary noted: "They are always boasting, and do all they can to be renowned and to have the name of 'Greatheart'. . . . [This title] is the crowning virtue" (JR 3:91). High status, in turn, allowed a man to attract a personal following as a headman. Moreover, renown brought more wives into his household and therefore increased his ability to play host and have more children.

Mi'kmaqs enjoyed discussing heroic feats carried out in their wars against enemy tribes. Although Mi'kmaqs liked to portray all their ancestors as courageous, they saved their special admiration for magic-doing warriors known as *kinaps*. Some Mi'kmaq legends recount long-standing wars with the *Kwetej* (the now-extinct St. Lawrence River Iroquois and later the Mohawk), hostile encounters with the Abenaki, and bitter feuds with Maliseet neighbors. Mi'kmaqs also fought against the Montagnais, Beothuk, and Eskimo. There are many historical accounts that tell of long-distance raiding parties, in which Mi'kmaq warriors ventured far north to Newfoundland and Labrador, south to Massachusetts, and west to Lake Champlain and even beyond.

How did the Mi'kmaqs conclude their wars? Sometimes enemies were annihilated. As a French missionary noted: "Whole nations have been known to destroy one another, with such an exterminating rage on both sides, that few have been left alive on either" (Maillard, 32). In one legend, Mi'kmaqs recall that they destroyed a Kwetej village, "with the exception of three or four warriors; these were marked on their naked legs . . . by cutting the skin in several stripes up and down the leg, and peeling the skin down about half-way from the knee to the ankle, and letting it hang. They were let go without any further cruelties, and told to go on to the next village and tell their friends what beautiful leggins had been made for them" (in Rand 1894:218).

Sometimes Mi'kmaqs forced an enemy to withdraw and seek refuge in distant territories. According to Mi'kmaq legend, the Kwetej (Iroquois) once lived on the banks of the Restigouche River and occupied Gaspé Peninsula, but due to a violent conflict with their Mi'kmaq neighbors were forced to abandon this area (Rand 1894:200–06).

Finally, enemy chieftains could conclude a peace and stage a special ceremony, exchanging valuable presents with each other (JR 30:139–40; Rand 1894:181–82). During the colonial period, Mi'kmaqs engaged in a peacemaking ritual, in which both parties buried their weapons in a grave. It appears that this ceremony originated among the Iroquois. From there it spread throughout the rest of eastern North America.

CONCLUSION

As described in this chapter, long before contact with Europeans the Mi'kmaq had reached a level of cultural development in their habitat that satisfied their needs and gave them pleasure. They enjoyed their culture not only because it provided them with a time-tested know-how of survival in a sometimes-dangerous environment, but also because it contained the accumulated experience of their ancestors. For generations, Mi'kmaqs were aided by an oral tradition of learning that allowed them to tap into a trove of wisdom. After many centuries of relative calm, they were swept up in a tidal wave of historical change. Brought on by European newcomers arriving on their shores, this "breaker" revolutionized the world that had been so familiar to Mi'kmaqs for so long. The pages ahead trace the stunning changes that have taken place in Mi'kmaq country since the dawn of the European invasion nearly five hundred years ago. Keeping in mind the aboriginal baseline described in this chapter will shed light on this radical cultural transformation.

4 / First Contact: Europe's Advent and Klu'skap's Exit

EUROPEAN CULTURE ON THE EVE OF THE INVASION

Stimulated by intellectual revolutions and an aggressive mercantile expansionism born of a quick series of major technological innovations, 16th- and 17th-century Europe rode high on the glorious wave of the Renaissance. Although most Europeans remained shrouded in poverty, struggling to survive as rural peasants and laborers, some lived in the luxurious ease of kings, princes, barons, and rich merchants. The elite were an enterprising, arrogant, and supremely confident lot, ready to push back the limits of their traditional worlds to seek wealth and glory in faraway lands. No longer believing that the earth was flat, nor that it was the center of the universe, they were dazzled by a desire to discover all that the wide world had to offer. In the words of one historian, "Everything intrigued them . . . unknown plants, unknown animals . . . . men . . . with strange customs and strange religions" (Febvre, 41).

Mobility was one of the great social features of the day in Europe. Nobles, merchants, and commoners—on horseback, in litters, and often on foot—traveled muddy highways fraught with potholes and robbers. They journeyed to political centers, marketplaces, and religious shrines, seeking power, wealth, salvation, and adventure. Pilgrims made their way to Jerusalem, Rome, Santiago de Compostela, or Our Lady of Loretto (Mandrou, 213) Merchants ventured by ship to far-flung emporiums, such as Alexandria, Egypt, where they could buy spices and silks from Asia and ivory and rare woods from Africa—all of which could be resold at exorbitant prices in Europe (Denieul-Courmier, 181). And, after Columbus's notorious 1492 voyage, transatlantic destinations were quickly added to the itineraries of Europeans from many walks of life—explorers, inspired by the prospect of discovering new worlds; sailors, excited by the dangers of the sea; entrepreneurs, thrilled by the prospect of new profit-making ventures; and missionaries, fired by new flocks of heathens needing salvation. By travel standards of the day, it did not take long to cross the Atlantic Ocean. If all went well it took only about twenty days to reach Newfoundland, and a few days more to Nova Scotia.

WENUJ: STRANGERS ON THE COAST

Thinking themselves to be the easternmost people on earth, Mi'kmaqs were unaware of human beings across the great salt water until 1504, when they first sighted European sailing ships approaching their shores. The story of their first encounter was put to memory and retold among Mi'kmaqs for many generations:

> When there were no people in this country but Indians [*L'nu'k*], and before any others were known, a young woman . . . . dreamed that a whole island came floating in towards the land, with tall trees on it, and living beings,—among them was a man dressed in rabbit-skin garments. . . . It was the custom in those days, when anyone had a remarkable dream, to consult the wise men, and especially the [puowin or shamans]. These pondered over the girl's dream, but could make nothing of it. The next day an event occurred that explained all. Getting up in the morning, what should they see but a singular little island . . . which had drifted near to the land and become stationary there! There were trees on it and branches on the trees, on which a number of bears . . . were crawling about. They all seized their bows, arrows, and spears, and rushed down to the shore, intending to shoot the bears. What was their surprise to find that these supposed bears were men, and that some of them were lowering down into the water a [strange] canoe, into which several of them jumped and paddled ashore. Among them was a man dressed in white, a priest with his white stole on, who came towards them making signs of friendship, raising his hand towards heaven, and addressing them in an earnest manner, but in a language which they could not understand.

(in Rand 1894:152–153)

Little did they know then that the newcomers on the floating island with trees (a ship with masts) posed a dangerous threat to their existence as heirs to an ancient culture. Initially amazed to see bearded mariners, Mi'kmaqs (according to one French chronicler of the day) "could not get over their wonder as they gazed at our customs, our clothing, our arms, our equipment" (Lescarbot 3:21). Their surprise is reflected in their name for the alien-looking invaders from across the eastern sea: *Wenuj* ("Stranger")—derived from their word for "who is that?" The fact that these foreigners came from the direction of the rising sun had a particular significance for the Mi'kmaq, because *niskam,* the divine being they worshipped, comes up in the east.

The first newcomers, French Breton fishermen, came to exploit the bountiful fisheries (especially cod) in the Gulf of St. Lawrence—as did those who followed them: Normans and Basques from France, and other fishers from England, northwest Spain, and Portugal. They practiced two types of commercial fishery: "wet" (in which the cod was salted and barreled on board and taken directly to Europe in special transport ships), and "dry" (in which the catch was dried on land before being transported to Europe). They came to the Gulf in the spring and sailed back to Europe in the fall. By the 1520s hundreds of fishermen were summering on the shores of Newfoundland, Cape Breton, and Labrador. Their seasonal voyages more or less coincided with the migratory movements of Mi'kmaq family bands who each spring returned to the coast from their winter trapping grounds. Mi'kmaqs and Europeans were quick to recognize the value of one another's possessions. Fishermen began bartering with native hunters, who offered them beavers and other precious furs in exchange for hatchets, knives, and other metal tools. From early on furs were added to the cargoes of fish being carried to southern Europe's port cities.

THE PORTUGUESE OF CAPE BRETON: A LOST COLONY (1525)

In 1525, navigator João Alvarez Fagundes and some entrepreneurs from the port city of Viana, Portugal, formed an expedition to found a colony on Cape Breton Island—at the edge of Mi'kmaq country. Commissioned by Portugal's king, their "large ship and a caravel" sailed to the Azores Islands just west of Portugal (where ten families of settlers came on board), then crossed the Atlantic to the Bahamas, and coasted north until reaching Cape Breton. It seems they established their settlement somewhere on the island's north side, at Glace Bay or St. Anne Bay, "where there are many people and goods of much value and many nuts . . . whereby it is clear the soil is rich" (Souza 1570, in Biggar 1911:195–97).

That same year a Portuguese mariner named Estevan Gomez guided *La Anunciada,* a 50-ton Spanish caravel, from the Spanish port of Corunna to Cape Breton—instructed by Emperor Charles V of Spain to search for the northwest passage to China. Unable to find this fabled western gateway to the wealth of the Orient, Gomez "filled his ship with innocent people of both sexes, half naked, and shipped them back to Spain as slaves" (Sauer, 48–51). Because his slave raid broke a newly proclaimed Spanish law, Gomez had to set his captives free—in Spain. We can only guess what happened to these unfortunate, uprooted Indians.

Were Gomez's victims Mi'kmaqs? If so, this would have spelled disaster for Cape Breton's fledgling colony. According to a report penned by a French pilot in 1559, "the natives [Mi'kmaqs] of [Cape Breton] put an end to the [settlers'] attempt and killed all of those who came there" (in Ganong, 157). Some fifty years after this report, French explorer Samuel de Champlain noted that "the rigour of the season and the cold made [the Portuguese] abandon their settlement" (Champlain 1:467–68). However it ended, this early European foothold in coastal North America was short-lived. Were there no survivors? Or, as was common practice among the Mi'kmaq, were some Portuguese women and children allowed to live and perhaps adopted? This raises the intriguing possibility that the thickly bearded Mi'kmaq chief Membertou, later encountered by French colonists at Port Royal in 1605, may have had an ancestry traceable, in part, to Portugal's Azores Islands.

CARTIER'S EXPLORATIONS ON THE MI'KMAQ COAST (1534–1536)

In 1534 French explorer Jacques Cartier, commissioned by King Francis I to explore the new lands across the Atlantic and to seek the northwest passage to China, left his home port at St. Malo and sailed toward Mi'kmaq country. Following the route well known to the Portuguese, Spanish, Basque, Breton, and Norman fishermen, he commanded three small vessels and 61 men. They reached Newfoundland in about three weeks, which was fairly typical at that time (Cartier, 3).

Coasting down the Strait of Belle Isle into the Gulf of St. Lawrence, Cartier encountered various French fishing vessels (Cartier, 9, 30–31). After passing the Isles de la Madeleine (where he saw "a great many" walrus) (Cartier, 14), he came to Prince Edward Island. Anchoring off its north coast, he and some of his crew explored the shore in their shallops (or longboats) and "caught some sight of some Indians in their canoes" (Cartier, 17). After scouting the island's western tip (and catching a glimpse of one other "savage"), Cartier led his ships across the mouth of Northumberland Strait to the coast of present-day New Brunswick and followed it northward to Chaleur Bay, which he hoped was a passage to China (Cartier, 19). Reaching the bay's north shore, he found a harbor, where he anchored for a week. Exploring the area in one of his shallops, Cartier encountered a group of Mi'kmaqs near Paspebiac Point. Clearly, they were eager and experienced traders:

> We caught sight of two fleets of Indian canoes that were crossing [Chaleur Bay from the southern shore], which numbered in all some forty or fifty canoes. Upon one of the fleets reaching this point, there sprang out and landed a large number of people, who set up a great clamour and made frequent signs to us to come on shore, holding up to us some skins on sticks. But as we were only one boat we did not care to go, so we rowed towards the other fleet which was on the water. And they [on shore], seeing we were rowing away, made ready two of their largest canoes in order to follow us. These were joined by five more of those that were coming in from the sea, and all came after our [shallop], dancing and showing many signs of joy, and of their desire to be friends, saying to us in their language: *Napou tou daman asurtat,* and other words we did not understand.
>
> (Cartier, 20, my italics)

Unaware that these Mi'kmaqs had already encountered European mariners who were interested in their furs, Cartier did not recognize that they addressed him in a pidgin (trade language) with some Portuguese and Mi'kmaq words: *Napew tu dameu a cierto!,* which translates as "Man [cock], give me something!" (Prins and Whitehead n.p.; cf. Lescarbot 2:45; Bakker). However, now surrounded by seven canoes, Cartier and his crew felt threatened, and they

> waved them to go back [and then] shot off over their heads two small cannon. On this they began to return towards the point, and set up a marvellously loud shout, after which they proceeded to come on again as before. And when they had come alongside our [shallop], we shot off two fire-lances which scattered among them and frightened them so much that they began to paddle off in very great haste, and did not follow us any more. The next day some of these Indians came in nine canoes to the point at the mouth of the cove, where we lay anchored with our ships . . . . they had come to barter with us; and held up some skins of small value, with which they clothe themselves. We likewise made signs to them that we wished them no harm, and sent two men on shore, to offer them some knives and other iron goods, and a red cap to give to their chief. Seeing this, they sent on shore part of their people with some of their skins; and the two parties traded together. They showed marvellously great pleasure in possessing and obtaining these iron wares and other commodities, dancing and going through many ceremonies, and throwing salt water over their heads with their hands. They bartered all they had to such

an extent that all went back naked without anything on them; and they made signs
to us that they would return on the morrow with more skins.

(Cartier, 21)

The next day Cartier sailed by shallop to explore the mouth of Restigouche
River. Returning to his north shore anchorage, he "caught sight of the Indians [at
Tracadigash Point], who were making many fires that smoked. We rowed over to the
spot." There, he noted, the Mi'kmaqs

> brought us some strips of cooked seal, which they placed on bits of wood and then
> withdrew, making signs to us that they were making us a present with them. We
> sent two men on shore with hatchets, knives, beads and other wares, at which they
> showed great pleasure. And at once they came over in a crowd in their canoes to
> the side [of the lagoon] where we were, bringing skins and whatever else they pos-
> sessed, in order to obtain some of our wares. They numbered, both men, women
> and children, more than 300 persons. Some of their women, who did not come
> over, danced and sang, standing in the water up to their knees. The other women,
> who had come over to the side where we were, advanced freely towards us and
> rubbed our arms with their hands. Then they joined their hands together and raised
> them to heaven, exhibiting many signs of joy. And so much at ease did they feel in
> our presence, that at length we bartered with them, hand to hand, for everything
> they possessed, so that nothing was left to them but their naked bodies; for they of-
> fered us everything that they owned, which was, all told, of little value.

(Cartier, 22)

A week later, "being certain that there was no passage through [Chaleur] bay,"
Cartier sailed onward to Gaspé Bay. There he encountered a band of two hundred
Iroquoians from Stadacona (Quebec) "who had come to . . . fish for mackerel,
of which there is great abundance." He distinguished them from the Mi'kmaq:
"They are not at all of the same race or language as the first we met. They have their
hair shaved all around in circles, except for a tuft on the top of the head, which they
leave long like a horse's tail. This they do up upon their heads and tie in a knot with
leather thongs" (Cartier, 24–25). As will be discussed in a later chapter, these
Iroquoian Indians soon became fierce enemies of the Mi'kmaq, who referred to them
as *Kwetej*.

COD FISHERS AND FUR TRADERS

By 1578 the Newfoundland fisheries numbered at least 350 ships, which, on average, carried home cargoes of 100,000 fish apiece. Among the vessels, 150 were
French (chiefly Breton), 50 were Portuguese, and more than 100 were Spanish
(Wright, 1965:77–81; JR 1:3). In total the cod fisheries of the day involved nearly
twenty-thousand men (Nietfeld, 286–98; Sauer, 241). Many crews returned to the
same fishing grounds annually. For instance, from the 1560s onward (each year for
more than forty years), a Basque fisherman named Savalet from St. Jean-de-Luz
steered his 80-ton, 16-man vessel across the Atlantic to Canso Harbor on the northeast coast of Nova Scotia (Lescarbot, in Murdoch 1:37).

At this time there were also numerous Spanish and Basque whale and walrus hunters active in the St. Lawrence Gulf. In 1578 a Bristol merchant noted that there were "twenty or thirty [vessels] that come from Biscay [Basque country] to kill whale for train [oil]," which was used for soap, lamp fuel, and lubricant. Commenting on the region's value, one French observer of the day wrote: "There is a great traffic in Europe of the oil of the Newfoundland fish. And for this cause many go to fish for the whale, and for the river-horse, or [walrus], as they call the beast with the great tooth . . . . our Frenchmen, especially the Basques, go every year to the [mouth of the] great river of Canada [St. Lawrence] for the whale" (Lescarbot 6:241).

According to Champlain (2:151–153),

> The cleverest men at this fishing [whaling] are the Basques, who, in order to carry it on, place their vessels in a safe port, or near the spot where they judge there are many whales, and then they man with stout sailors a number of shallops, and equip them with lines. . . . They have also many halberds, half a pike long, armed with an iron blade, six inches wide, and others a foot and a half or two long and very sharp. In each shallop there is a harpooner. . . . From the quantity of water thrown up [by the whale] one estimates the amount of oil which the whale will produce. . . .
> [After harpooning and killing the whale, they] tow it ashore to the place where they do the curing, that is to say where they melt the fat of the whale, in order to obtain the oil.

In the course of the sixteenth century, fishing vessels returned to Europe with more and more pelts in their cargo holds. Beginning in 1581, French merchants from St. Malo, Rouen, and Dieppe organized voyages specifically to trade for furs. Others followed suit. In 1584 St. Malo merchants arranged a five-ship expedition to the St. Lawrence. The ships returned so heavily laden with furs that the merchants prepared a fleet of ten ships for the following year (Biggar 1937:32; Trudel, 56–58). Although furs were long in demand for luxury coats and blankets in Europe, it was a sweeping beaver hat fashion craze toward the end of the century that really ignited the transatlantic fur trade (Innis, 8–9). Mi'kmaqs and other Indians inhabiting the North Atlantic seaboard and the St. Lawrence Gulf and River region vigorously pursued the exchange of furs for a growing array of European commodities: iron tools and weapons, copper kettles, glass beads, biscuits and flour, woolen cloth and blankets—and alcohol.

By the late 1500s the English also became increasingly interested in the region, not only for its codfish, but also for whales, walrus, and seals, which provided oils that were "rich commodities for England" (Brereton, 1602, in CMaHS III/8:97). So it was that an English expedition under the command of Richard Strong sailed to the gulf and landed at Cape Breton in 1593. There, Strong reported, he and his crew encountered and clashed with a group of Mi'kmaq "savages." The commander's comment on this encounter suggests that Mi'kmaqs were accustomed to European aggression: "We bestowed halfe a dousen Musket Shotte upon them, which they avoyded by falling flatte to the earth" (in Hakluyt 8:159).

Four years after Strong's visit, Charles Leigh and fellow Englishmen also sailed to Cape Breton and encountered several Mi'kmaqs:

> This day . . . we tooke a Savages boat which our men pursued: but all the savages ran away into the woods, and our men brought their boat on boord . . . . In the

evening three of the Savages, whose boat we had, came unto us for their boat: to whom we gave coats and knives, and restored them their boat againe. The next day being the first of July, was their King, whose name was Itarey, and their Queene, to whom also we gave coats and knives, and other trifles. These savages called the harborow Cibo [*sipu* is Mi'kmaq for "river"]. (in Hakluyt 8:173–74)

MI'KMAQS AS FUR TRADE MIDDLEMEN

Because Mi'kmaqs were among the first Indians of northeast America to have contact with Europeans, they had early access to European goods. This, coupled with their strategic coastal position, seafaring skills, and early acquisition of small sailing boats (shallops), placed some Mi'kmaq chieftains in the position to become middlemen in the fur trade. With a cache of European trade goods in their shallops, they ventured to more remote Indian villages on the coast of New England to obtain skins, which were later resold to European merchants and mariners on their shores. Although the value of furs was not constant, these ventures were worth the trouble. Even in the 1630s, when furs glutted the European market, one beaver sold for about twenty iron knives. In addition to supplying European commodities in exchange for furs, Mi'kmaqs also bartered to get corn, squash, beans, and wampum (white and blue quahog shell-beads) from the Abenaki and other southern neighbors (Champlain 1:333). Before the French and English began settling the Gulf of Maine in the early 17th century, Mi'kmaq mariners briefly monopolized the coastal fur trade.

Numerous early 17th-century European reports mention native-manned shallops sailing in the Gulf of Maine on trading expeditions (Lescarbot 2:309–10, 3:81–82; JR 1:153). The following description of a 1607 encounter between an English vessel and a Mi'kmaq shallop represents what seems to have become a fairly common scene. The English ship, passing from Plymouth to the Maine coast, carried an Abenaki guide who had been kidnapped two years before. Near southwest Nova Scotia, then under control of the famous Mi'kmaq chieftain Messamoet, who had traveled to France before 1580, a Mi'kmaq shallop carrying eight men and a little boy approached the English vessel and "rowed about" it. Then, in the words of one of the Englishmen,

> They cam near unto us & spoke unto us in thear Language. & we makinge Seignes to them that they should com abord of us showinge unto them knyues glasses beads & throwinge into their bottt Som bisket but for all this they wold nott com abord of us. . . . The next daye the Sam Salvages wth three Salvage wemen . . . retorned unto us bringinge wth them som feow skines of bever in an other bisken shallop & propheringe thear skines [many beavers] to trook [trade] wth us [for knives and beads]. But they demanded ouer muche for them and we Seemed to make Lyght of them. . . . & So they dep[ar]ted [. It] Seemth that the french hath trad wth them for they use many french words.

(Griffith 1607, in Thayer, 42–44)

In 1609, French ships from St. Malo were anchored at the St. John River, where Breton sailors were active in the fur trade with the regional Indians (JR 2:27–29, 3:211–13). That summer, the Dutch vessel *De Halve Maen*, en route from Amsterdam to the Hudson River, ran into some French fishing vessels and Mi'kmaq shallops. Anchoring at Penobscot River, the Dutch crew "espeid two French shallops full of [Indians] come into the harbour. . . . They brought many beaver skinnes and other fine furres, which they would have changed for redde gowns. For the French trade with them for red cassockes [coats], knives, hatchets, copper kettles, [iron pots], beades, and other trifles" (Hudson 1609, in M. Hamilton, 21).

MI'KMAQS DISCOVER EUROPE

During the contact period a significant number of American Indians traveled to Europe, beginning with a group of Taino Indians who sailed from Haiti to Spain in Columbus's caravels in 1493. Records from 55 transatlantic journeys show that about 2,000 Indians, traveling in European ships, had landed in Portugal, France, Spain, and England by the time Pilgrims sailing on the Mayflower landed on Massachusetts shores in 1620. Two thirds went as unwilling captives and were usually sold as slaves. But the balance went for other reasons—as guides, envoys, sightseers or entrepreneurs, as well as performers or curiosities on parade. Of these, some went voluntarily, while others were kidnapped or coerced (Prins 1993).

Perhaps the earliest Indians to go to Europe from the North Atlantic region were sixty Beothuks, captured in Newfoundland by Portuguese navigator Gaspar Corte-Real and taken to Lisbon in 1501. With cunning admiration the Venetian ambassador to Lisbon described these unwilling travelers as "tall, well-built" natives who "will make the best slaves I have ever seen" (in Abbott, 24, n2). The next year Beothuks were taken as curiosities to meet King Henry VII at his royal palace in England. The fact that they had dyed their skin scarlet with vegetable

Mi'kmaqs carrying a birch-bark canoe on a portage route between the St. Lawrence River and the Gulf of Maine. Detail on a French 1678 map, Carte pour servir a l'eclaircissement du Papier Terrier de la Nouvelle France, *by J. B. L. Franquelin.*

juice is said to have prompted the description "Red Indian" (Carrington, in Porter, 209). In 1509 another group of painted Beothuks (dressed in loincloths, adorned with feathers, and carrying bows, arrows, and a birch-bark canoe) paraded through the streets of Rouen "to the wonder and applause of France" (Biard 1616, in JR 3:39).

Not long thereafter, some other Mi'kmaq neighbors also took an unplanned trip abroad. In 1534, when Kwetej Chief Donnacona and three of his sons sidled up to Cartier's ship in their canoe to harangue the French explorer for erecting a large wooden cross on the coast without their permission, they were forced to come on board. Cartier gave them gifts, food, and drink, along with assurances that no harm would befall them. Eventually Donnacona and one of his sons were allowed to go ashore, but Cartier kept the chief's two other sons to serve as guides. They traveled with him to St. Malo, France, learned French, and told their host that the St. Lawrence was not the strait to China, but instead a route to a country named Canada, which—so they led Cartier to believe—contained the gold he was seeking. The next year they recrossed the Atlantic and directed Cartier up the St. Lawrence. In 1536 they again journeyed to France with Cartier, who managed to press their father, Donnacona, and several other leading Stadaconans to come along (Cartier, 217). Not one of these Stadaconans ever returned to Canada. When Cartier set out on his next voyage in 1541, intending to establish a colony in their homeland, all lay in their graves, including Donnacona, "who died in France as a good Christian, speaking French, for he had lived there four years" (Thevet 1558, cited in Hoffman 1961:156).

We possess quite a few records of Indians who voluntarily made the passage to Europe for reasons related to the fur trade. Both Indians and Europeans had a vested interest in enhancing trade partnerships, and an Indian's willingness to travel abroad often helped to strengthen these relationships. European entrepreneurs sponsored such friendship exchange trips. Typically, come autumn, Indian visitors would freely board a fishing vessel loaded with dried codfish and skins and make the voyage across the Atlantic. After wintering over in Europe, they usually returned home the following spring. Among the most fascinating of such travelers was Messamoet, a Mi'kmaq chieftain in Nova Scotia. Probably sailing on a Basque fishing ship, and likely clad in a beaver or otter robe and moose-hide moccasins and leggings, he went to France around 1578. For two years he lived as the guest of the governor of Bayonne, a Basque seaport north of the Pyrenees Mountains. Clearly the Mi'kmaq and the Basque were useful links for each other in the lucrative fur trade. After Messamoet's trip abroad, he prospered as a middleman, sailing his own Basque shallop, negotiating deals in pidgin French or Basque. Messamoet may well have been the Mi'kmaq commander encountered by an English crew at Cape Neddick (southern Maine) in 1602: In a party of Mi'kmaqs sailing in a Basque shallop "the commander wore a waistcoat of black work [serge], a pair of breeches, cloth stockings, shoes, hat and band, [and] with a piece of chalk described the coasts thereabouts and could name Placentia [Plaisance] of the Newfoundland; they spoke divers Christian words, and seemed to understand much more than we" (Archer 1602, 73–74; Brereton, in Wright, 1965: 137–38). Messamoet later guided French explorer Samuel de Champlain on his first journeys along the Maine coast in 1604, and 1606.

Messamoet was by no means the only Mi'kmaq to venture abroad. Among the others was Chief Cacagous, who also went to France. When this chieftain returned to Nova Scotia in 1610, he met a Jesuit priest who later noted: "[Cacagous] told me he had been baptized in Bayonne, relating his story to me as one tells about going to a ball out of friendship" (JR 1:165). This attitude seems typical among the many Indians who allowed themselves to be baptized while visiting Europe. To most, the ritual probably had more to do with business and friendship than religion. (See Chapter 6 for a detailed discussion.)

What did these men and others like them think when they came in sight of a French harbor and port city? What did they make of cities such as Paris? The experience seems to have generated some mixed emotions. Certainly, they were impressed by the immense size of the population. Returning from a visit to France, Mi'kmaqs would point to the hairs on their heads and the leaves of the trees "to indicate to their fellow-country-men the great number of people whom they had seen" (LeClercq, 137). Most, including two Indians who sailed from Tadoussac to St. Malo in 1603, probably came home and, perhaps a bit overwhelmed, "reckoned up the faire Castels, Palaces, Houses, and people which they had seen, and our manner of living" (Champlain 2:157). One Mi'kmaq who ventured to Paris was particularly impressed to see where a trade item of special value to Mi'kmaqs was made: "Passing by the Rue Aubry-bouché where there were many coppersmiths, he asked of his interpreter if they were not relatives of the King, and if this was not the trade of the grandest Seigneurs of the Kingdom" (N. Denys, 441). Others who journeyed to Europe, however, appear to have been less impressed. One Mi'kmaq story, still told in the 19th century, recounts how not long after the French first arrived in Mi'kmaq country, a tribesman named Silmoodawa returned with them to visit France:

> Among other curious adventures, he was prevailed upon to exhibit the Indian mode of killing and curing game. A fat ox or deer was brought over out of a beautiful park and handed over to the Indian; he was provided with all the necessary implements, and placed within an enclosure of ropes, through which no person was allowed to pass, but around which multitudes were gathered to witness the butchering operations of the Indian. He shot the animal with a bow, bled him, skinned and dressed him, sliced up the meat, and spread it out on flakes to dry; he then cooked a portion and ate it, in order to exhibit the whole process, and then [to] take a mischieveous revenge upon them for making an exhibition of him, he went into a far corner of the yard and eased himself before them all.

(Rand 1894: 279)

MI'KMAQ PERCEPTIONS AND ATTITUDES TOWARD WHITE NEWCOMERS

Initially, Indians did not differentiate between the various nationalities of Europeans coming to their shores (JR 24:61–63). The Montagnais and Algonkin of the St. Lawrence River referred to them as *Mistigoches*—"Builders of Ships" (Champlain

2:121, 125; LaHontan, 738). The Narragansett of Rhode Island called them "Coat-men," or "Sword-men" (JR 24:61–63; Williams, 81, 89). And, as was noted earlier in this chapter, the Mi'kmaq dubbed them *Wenuj* ("Stranger"). In time, of course, this changed. For instance, after almost a century of contact, Mi'kmaqs carefully distinguished between Normans ("Nortmandia"), Bretons ("Samaricois"—in reference to the port city of St. Malo), and Basques ("Bascua") (JR 1:163, 165).

Chroniclers of Indian interactions with and attitudes toward Europeans noted a curious mix of awe, admiration, and disdain. Notwithstanding their high regard for European technology, Mi'kmaqs and their neighbors typically rated the strangers "as physically inferior, as weak and unfitted to stand up to the rigours of arduous canoe journeys, hunting expeditions, and forest warfare." Often looking down upon the Europeans, they "found them ugly, especially because of their excessive hairiness, and their frequent deformities and infirmities" (Jaenen, 271–72; JR 3:22, 75). Furthermore, commented one writer, "[Mi'kmaqs] are proud as can be . . . . [and] consider the French less intelligent than they" (JR 4:199).

According to a Jesuit who lived in Mi'kmaq country in the early 17th century, Mi'kmaqs

> conclude generally that they are superior to all Christians. . . . They regard themselves as much richer than we are, although they are poor and wretched in the extreme. . . . They consider themselves better than the French; "For," they say, "you are always fighting and quarreling among yourselves; we live peaceably. You are envious and are all the time slandering each other; you are thieves and deceivers; you are covetous, and are neither generous nor kind; as for us, if we have a morsel of bread we share it with our neighbor." They are saying these and like things continually.

> (Biard 1611, in JR 1:175)

THE "GREAT DYING": EPIDEMICS ON THE MI'KMAQ COAST

The real price for the many useful trade goods brought by Europeans to Mi'kmaq Country was far higher than shiploads of furs. In many cases interaction with Europeans cost Indians their lives. And, if not their lives, their lifeways. The newcomers introduced alien viruses and bacteria against which Indians had no immunity, causing several waves of epidemics and a devastating population decline during the first century of contact. In 1611, a Jesuit who missionized among the remnant Indian communities, including Mi'kmaqs, noted that a Mi'kmaq chief who was more than one hundred years old told him that in his youth "he had seen *chimonutz* [native people] . . . as thickly planted there as the hairs upon his head." But now, the priest commented, "They are astonished and often complain that, since the French mingle with them and carry on trade with them, they are dying fast, and the population is thinning out. For they assert that, before this association and intercourse, all their countries were very populous and they tell how one by one the different coasts, according as they have begun to traffic with us, have been more reduced with disease" (Biard 1611, in JR 1:177–79; 1616, in JR 3:105–07).

It seems that the old Mi'kmaq chief witnessed a holocaust in which minimally 75 percent of some 15,000 Mi'kmaqs died, primarily of foreign diseases (smallpox, measles, cholera, bubonic plague, whooping cough) during the first century of contact with Europeans. The tragedy continued well into the 17th century. A priest in Mi'kmaq country noted in 1611, "During this year alone 60 have died at Cap de la Hève, which is the great part of those who lived there" (JR 1:177–79). Another epidemic wave hit the region between 1616 and 1618. Before the century's end, Mi'kmaqs declined to a demographic nadir of two thousand.

Europeans saw the epidemics as God's good providence. For instance, an English chronicler commenting on the pestilence of 1616–1618 noted that now "the greater part of that land was left desert, without any to disturb or oppose our free and peaceable possession thereof" (Gorges, 90). Recurrent epidemics made it increasingly difficult for the survivors to resist actively the intrusion on their lands by Europeans who, in the 17th century, began an all-out colonization effort.

There were many side effects of the Great Dying. No doubt it made Indians more susceptible to alcoholism and missionization (detailed in Chapters 6 and 8). Ironically, because the stunning losses unhinged the traditional economic and social interdependencies of Mi'kmaqs and other tribal groups in the region, survivors came to depend on the very newcomers who brought on their devastation. Responding to European demands for furs, many became market hunters, ever more dependent on goods available at the European trading posts that burgeoned during the seventeenth century. Game depletion followed, and, in turn, competition over hunting territories exacerbated traditional conflicts and led to violent intertribal wars. When hunting and trapping yields were meager, many purchased essentials on credit at the posts and fell into debt. A French missionary active among the Mi'kmaqs of Chaleur Bay from 1675 to 1687 lamented that the Mi'kmaqs had "been almost totally destroyed, as much by the war which they have waged with the Iroquois as by maladies which have infected this land, and which, in three or four visitations, have caused the deaths of a very great number" (LeClercq, 151–52, 189–90).

Ultimately, as detailed in the following chapters, contact with Europeans affected Mi'kmaq aboriginal culture in virtually every respect—their subsistence patterns, social and political relations, values and beliefs. Miraculously, the Mi'kmaq survived as a people. Many tribal groups did not.

5 / Moving In: European Colonists in Mi'kmaq Country

Throughout the 1500s, Europeans occupied only summer base camps on North America's northeastern shores, primarily to facilitate the fur trade and fishing industry. As the French, Dutch, and English emerged as major trading nations, they took increasingly active interest in revenues generated through overseas trading. Eventually, the demand for wood products, such as masts and planks, increased the economic incentives for taking territorial control of the region. France and England made particularly grandiose claims of sovereign title to Indian lands in northeast America. Some of their colonial claims overlapped. Very roughly speaking, the French asserted their rights to Canada (Newfoundland plus the territory stretching from the Great Lakes to the mouth of the St. Lawrence) and Acadia (Gaspé Peninsula plus the land extending from Penobscot Bay to Cape Breton and westward to the northern Appalachian Mountains). The English declared that they possessed the entire Atlantic seaboard from Newfoundland down. For two centuries, these conflicting and ill-defined claims on Indian domains were asserted in Europe's courts and North American combat zones.

By the early 17th century both French and English crowns had decided to effect their claims and establish permanent settlements to seize fully North America's economic opportunities. By this time epidemics had diminished the Mi'kmaq population from about 15,000 to 3,500, and they found themselves seasonally outnumbered by European fishermen camping on their coasts. In the next century they would be reduced to a year-round minority.

Mi'kmaqs who had survived the onslaught of European diseases were now forced to deal with the fact that the intricate interdependencies of their traditional way of life had been dismantled by the huge death toll. Unable to fathom the extent to which contact, trade, and colonization would unravel the fabric of their traditional culture, they carried on by responding creatively to the expectations and challenges hurled at them by Europeans. They allied themselves with the French, the major European presence in Mi'kmaq country. This relationship bought them partial protection and many useful gifts.

Mi'kmaqs often camped near French settlements, especially during the height of the fur-trading season from late spring through summer. In the course of time, these two distinct peoples developed a system of closely associated linkages: economic (trade partnerships), military (mutual armed support), religious (common ceremonials), and social (kinship through intermarriage and fictive kinship through baptism with French godparents). New cultural forms emerged as timeworn Mi'kmaq traditions meshed with French customs. In this process of culture change, Mi'kmaqs were not simply passive victims of imposed new world order. They seized useful foreign technologies and, to a degree, accommodated the newcomers, but they never surrendered their freedom and autonomy. Certainly they rejected all efforts to settle them permanently, held on to their ancestral tongue, and preserved many other features of their cultural heritage. In short, they refused to become assimilated.

INTERNATIONAL LINKAGES

After 1600 the fur trade expanded dramatically. Within a few decades, it extended from the St. Lawrence and its tributaries to the Great Lakes and its vast hinterland. Yet, however valuable as a resource for Europeans, furs were economically less important than the cod fisheries. At the time there was a huge demand for fish in southern Europe's Roman Catholic countries (especially France, Spain, and Portugal), where religious rulings had multiplied the number of fast (meat-free) days to 166, including Lent. Coupled with income from whale oils, cod generated triple the revenues of furs in French Canada (Champlain 2:342–43). Not counting Basques and others fishing on Mi'kmaq coasts, the numbers of Frenchmen involved in the cod fisheries were enormous. Each year about 250 fishing boats sailed from mainly French Norman ports to the Great Banks north of Nova Scotia. Manned by 15–50 crew members, each vessel could transport a cargo of 20,000–200,000 fish. Barrels of "green" cod (gutted and packed with salt on shipboard) were destined for the market in Paris. In addition to 4,000 green cod fishermen, some 2,500 men worked in the "dry" cod fisheries, drying the cod on shore stages before shipping it to Europe (N. Denys, 258–270).

In contrast to fisheries, which depended almost exclusively on imported manpower, the fur trade involved native trappers. Each spring hunting families quit their trap lines in the interior woodlands, loaded their birch-bark canoes with beaver and other furs, and paddled to the coast to await European captains at designated rendezvous sites. Activity at these seasonal trading grounds could be hectic, with as many as 20 ships riding at anchor at the same time (JR 4:207).

Competing European ship captains and merchants drove fur prices up so much that they began to suffer losses. Seeing the value of their furs climb, Indians got the hang of free trade and became shrewd deal makers (Champlain 2:146). Trying to regain the upper hand, French entrepreneurs appealed to the French Crown to control the market by limiting the right to do business with Indians in its colony. Initially, trading monopolies were granted to various private companies or wealthy entrepreneurs. This had mixed success. In 1618 the Crown granted "exclusive trade in peltries" in Canada to the Company of New France. This company, in turn, gave a limited number of merchants the right to frequent officially designated trading stations. For instance, at Tadoussac on the north bank of the St. Lawrence, only two merchants had grants under the new policy. Consequently, two ships rather than twenty would come,

> and that only once a year, about the beginning of the month of June. These two ships bring all the merchandise which [the company] use in trading with the Indians; that is to say, the cloaks, 5 blankets, nightcaps, hats, shirts, sheets, hatchets, iron arrowheads, bodkins, swords, picks to break the ice in winter, knives, [awls,] kettles, prunes, raisins, Indian corn [maize], peas, crackers or sea biscuits, and [Brazilian] tobacco . . . in exchange for these they carry back hides of the [caribou, seal,] moose, lynx, fox, otter . . . martens, badgers, and muskrats; but they deal principally in beavers, in which they find their greatest profit . . . during one year they carried back as many as 22,000 the usual number for one year is 15,000 or 12,000 at one pistole [a small gold coin] each, which is not doing badly.

> (JR 4:207)

Ships packed with furs crossed the Atlantic to French seaports, where Dutch merchants purchased many of the best furs and shipped them to large warehouses in Amsterdam. As a Dutch report noted in 1624, "A large quantity of otter skins was received here in Amsterdam from France, finer than had ever been seen in this country, sold by those of Canada . . ." (in Jameson, 76–77). From Holland, merchants exported beaver fur to Russia for further processing. This "international network of re-exports often prevented gluts on European markets, . . . and kept prices steady throughout the international system" (Wolf, 159).

COLONIZATION AND THE SEIGNEURIAL SYSTEM IN MI'KMAQ COUNTRY

The French Crown aimed to structure its colonial political economy according to the time-tested seigneurial system. Originated in the Middle Ages, this feudal system had substantial impact on Mi'kmaq culture. It redefined Mi'kmaqs' territorial arrangements, focused their economic activities, influenced their seasonal movements, determined their village sites, designated their trading partners, and, indirectly, imposed religious beliefs and customs. Underlying the colony's seigneurial system was a European legal fiction known as the Doctrine of First Discovery. According to this doctrine, the French Crown possessed sovereign title over the vast wilderness of northeast America that it called New France. That these lands had been inhabited since time immemorial by Mi'kmaqs and other indigenous peoples was deemed irrelevant, in part (so the reasoning went) because the natives existed outside the Christian world order. In the context of this legal construct, there was no room for the idea of "aboriginal title." This given, French colonial authorities did not engage in treaty-signing with Mi'kmaqs or other Indians in North America. (See Chapter 10 for a more detailed discussion of French views on aboriginal title.)

Once the French had established the fiction of sovereign title, they introduced a medieval political principle asserting that no land could be held without a lord. Thus the Crown divided the colony by distributing large tracts to individuals or companies that were obliged to "improve" these tracts at their own expense. Persons who received such land grants were called *seigneurs,* and the domains were known as *seigneuries.* Seigneurs did not actually own their estates, but they were entitled to profit from the revenues the estates generated. Land grants authorized seigneurs to exact tribute payments in the form of rents or labor services. As feudal lords, they exercised considerable power over the tenant farmers they imported to settle their holdings in the colonies (Trigger, 329).

Land grants also stipulated a seigneur's obligations to the king, and nonfulfillment could result in revocation. Beyond being responsible for the development of his estate, a seigneur was obliged to promote actively the conversion of Indians to Christianity, and the French Crown often required him to support a Catholic mission on his land. These stipulations demanded considerable capital outlay from the entrepreneur, who aimed to get back his investment and turn a profit. Toward this end, some chose to raise livestock or to cultivate the land. Others tried to capitalize on the fur trade or fisheries by building a trading post or fishing station. Whatever the business, a seigneury could not become productive without hands to perform the work. Hence, seigneurs were always trying to draw settlers to their estates.

In addition to procuring colonists from Europe, seigneurs tried to lure Indian bands or families to their domains "and thus carry on a good trade in beaver" (JR 35:57, 59). Colonial estates that centered on the fur trade became known as Indian seigneuries (*seigneuries sauvages*).

What did a typical seigneury in Mi'kmaq country look like? Each frontier estate had its own peculiarities, but based on a composite, the following is fairly representative. First we have the trading post, usually made of heavy logs, although stone was also used. Dependent on supplies that had to be shipped in from overseas, the trading post was strategically located on the bank of a major river, usually at its mouth or upriver near the first rapids or falls. As there was always danger lurking, these posts were usually palisaded. In each corner of the palisade rose a wooden bastion, equipped with several small cannon. Inside stood a storehouse for valuable trade goods, plus a French-style dwelling for the seigneur's family, some retainers, and servants. Near the manor were barns, a vegetable garden, an orchard (apples and pears), as well as a few clearings for crop cultivation (wheat and peas) and pasture for livestock (cattle, swine, and poultry). At larger estates could also be found a chapel and cottages for a blacksmith (to repair tools and weapons) and a few tenant farmers. Nearby the manor, it was not unusual to find a cluster of Mi'kmaq wikuoms.

Interestingly, the French treated local Mi'kmaq chieftains more or less as seigneurs in their own right (Cadillac, 81). Returning from their woodland hunting territories in the late spring, Mi'kmaq families reassembled under their chieftains and descended upon a seigneurial trading post in canoes loaded with furs and hides. Their coming was anxiously awaited, and according to records of the day, "In order to satisfy them . . . sometimes the guns, and even the cannon, are fired on their arrival. The leader himself assembles all the canoes near his own and ranges them in good order before landing, in order to await the salute which is given him, and which all the Indians return to the French by the discharge of their guns" (LeClercq, 246). Thus welcomed by the seigneur and his men, the Mi'kmaqs beached their canoes, unloaded packs of fur, and set up their wigwams near the post. Sometimes, noted one

Frenchman, "The leader and chiefs are invited for a meal in order to show to all the Indians of the nation that they are esteemed and honoured. Rather frequently they are even given something like a fine coat, in order to distinguish them from the commonality. For such things as this they have a particular esteem, especially if the article has been in use by the commander of the French" (Ibid.). After selling their furs and purchasing fresh supplies from the storehouse, they would stay for a few days, sometimes weeks or even months, only to withdraw to their vast woodland hunting grounds for the rest of the year.

THE EARLY COLONIZERS

In 1603, after some aborted colonial settlements at Quebec (1541–1543), Sable Island (1598–1603), and Tadoussac (1600–1601)—with settlers comprised mostly of conscripts, convicts, and vagabonds—the French king commissioned Pierre Du Gua, the Sieur de Monts, to settle Mi'kmaq country with colonists. Appointed lieutenant general of the region called Acadia, de Monts obtained a financially lucrative 10-year monopoly over the fur trade in exchange for promising to settle one hundred French colonists each year. They were expected to be self-sufficient (Reid, 14–15).

The first of de Monts's settlers arrived in 1604. With Samuel de Champlain as navigator, this expedition of 79 men (there were no women) sailed into the Bay of Fundy and settled on a small island. Surprised by the severity of their first winter, almost half died of scurvy and other diseases (Champlain 1:304). The following spring, guided by a Mi'kmaq trader, the French found a better location across the bay at a strategic site on the north bank of Annapolis River. Here they founded the settlement of Port Royal. The newcomers befriended the local Mi'kmaq chieftain, Membertou, who had his seasonal camping ground nearby. As Champlain (1:384) recalled in his memoirs, this "captain of Indians . . . promised to look after them [the French], and they should be no more unhappy than if they were his own children." Champlain and 45 surviving cohorts began building a French Norman-style establishment—a large dwelling in a closed quadrangle protected by a gun platform armed with four cannon. Outside the fort they cleared land for gardens (Trudel, 88). That same summer, leaving most of the settlers behind, de Monts sailed back to France to report to his king. The next year, additional men arrived at Port Royal, including Jean de Biencourt, Sieur de Poutrincourt, who had received the place as his personal land grant, or seigneury, from de Monts. Also among the newcomers was Marc Lescarbot, a young lawyer who later published an important description of the Mi'kmaq.

In addition to seeds for the principal field crops of northwestern Europe (wheat, rye, barley, and oats and garden vegetables such as beans and peas), which were sown that same spring, Poutrincourt brought one sheep, several swine, "which multiplied abundantly," and some "hens and pigeons, which failed not to yield the accustomed tribute, and to multiply abundantly" (Lescarbot 2:226; Clark, 86). For the Mi'kmaq, these foreign animals must have been a fascinating sight. Soon the settlement, fields, and valley were linked by a web of paths, and the village had a lime kiln, smithy, and water-powered gristmill. Settlers tended to their fields and

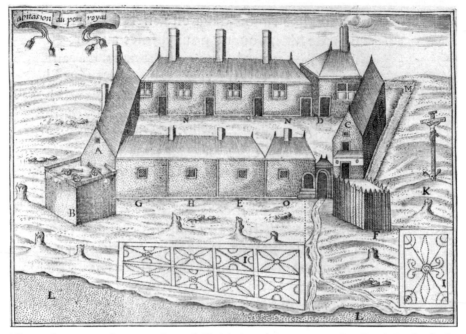

The French Norman-style seigneurial stronghold of the Sieur de Poutrincourt at Port Royal, Acadia. Built in 1605–1606, the manor was left in the care of Mi'kmaq Chief Membertou for two-and-one-half years. In 1613, it was looted and destroyed by English raiders. Located near the water in front are the gardens. Also outside is a large cross, marking the cemetery. Upon entering the gate, the trading store is on the right; next come the seigneur's offices. Immediately to the left are the blacksmith's workplace and the bake shop, followed by the communal quarters and the chapel (upper left corner).

trades and devoted considerable time to fishing, hunting, and gathering shellfish (Clark, 79).

With a friendly European stronghold so close to his village, Membertou gained a measure of security against traditional enemy raiders such as the Abenaki from southern Maine. According to Lescarbot, the chief "was well content to keep close to the French, in order to live in safety" (Lescarbot 3:355; cf. Champlain 2:44–50). Beyond military advantage, he enjoyed direct access to valuable trade goods, including steel knives, copper kettles, textiles, Brazilian tobacco, and even French wine and bread (Lescarbot 3:505–06). His proximity also benefitted the French, who could purchase valuable furs and garner precious information about the lay of the land from local Mi'kmaqs. Commenting on their relationship, Lescarbot (2:343–44) wrote, "Bread was given them gratis as one would do to the poor. But as for the Sagamos [chieftain] Membertou, and other chiefs, who came from time to time, they sat at the table, eating and drinking like ourselves. . . . sometimes we had half-a-dozen sturgeon at once, which the Indians brought us, part of which we bought, and allowed them to sell the remainder publicly and to barter it for bread, of which our men had abundance."

In the summer of 1607 the Port Royal community received bad news: Due to sharp complaints from rich merchants in Rouen and St. Malo, the French Crown had revoked de Monts's trading privileges, and the colonists were to abandon the successful settlement. Poutrincourt delayed "departure until samples of grain were available for exhibits at home," then left the manor and storehouse, along with 10 barrels of flour, to the care of Chief Membertou: "We had found him a good Indian all the time we were there" (Champlain 1:384). Before departing, Poutrincourt also presented his Mi'kmaq friends with iron arrowheads and some muskets (Trudel, 91).

That same spring de Monts assigned Champlain as commander of a French colonizing expedition to the St. Lawrence River, which led to the building of a new fortified settlement at Quebec in the summer of 1608. Meanwhile, French and other fur traders were active on the coasts of what are now Nova Scotia, New Brunswick, Maine, and beyond.

Concerned about the increased competition for beaver and other furs in Acadia, Poutrincourt arranged to reclaim his domain at Port Royal. In 1610 he returned to the abandoned site with 20 "honest men and artisans" (JR 1:69). Membertou had carefully guarded the place during Poutrincourt's three-year absence: "When Sieur de Poutrincourt arrived, he found his buildings entire, the savages (as these people have been called up to the present) not having touched them in any way, even the furniture remaining as we left it . . ." (JR 1:69). A few weeks later, Membertou and his family allowed the French to baptize them, each receiving "the name of some illustrious or notable personage here in France" (JR 1:77). Subsequently, Poutrincourt "[took] the trouble . . . to have them taught by his eldest son . . . who understands and speaks the native language very well" (JR 1:69).

Supplied by a successful fall harvest, Poutrincourt and some 40 men wintered at Port Royal. His eldest son, Charles de Biencourt, sailed to France with a shipload of furs and returned to Port Royal the next year, accompanied by his mother, some additional men, and two Jesuits—Fathers Pierre Biard and Enemond Massé. Learning that rival traders had set up on the St. John River nearby (Clark, 81), Poutrincourt went to France seeking the financial backing needed to gain an edge in the competition. In Paris, he won the support and partnership of Madame de Guercheville, lady-in-waiting to the queen mother. Soon afterward, de Monts conceded all of Acadia to her, except Poutrincourt's estate at Port Royal.

Meanwhile, Chief Membertou died, and discord erupted between Biencourt and the Jesuits. Dissatisfied with the situation, de Guercheville decided to finance a new settlement along the Maine coast, where the Jesuits could establish a mission well outside Poutrincourt's domain. René Le Cocq, the Sieur de La Saussaye, led the expedition. Sailing from Honfleur with two other Jesuits and a group of settlers in the spring of 1613, he landed briefly at Port Royal to take Fathers Biard and Massé aboard, then continued toward the Maine coast. In May they anchored by Mount Desert Island, where the Jesuits founded their mission, naming it St. Sauveur. They were accompanied by some 30 colonists, plus livestock and supplies. Immediately, the men were put to work cultivating the land (Biard 1612, in JR 3:211–13; Lescarbot 3:52–56).

Unfortunately, St. Sauveur was located in a contested territory claimed by the English and the French. That summer an English raider from Virginia sailed into the Gulf of Maine with orders to "plunder and demolish all the fortifications and settlements of the French . . . along the entire coast as far as Cape Breton" (JR 4:35). The raider attacked St. Sauveur, killing several Frenchmen and taking Father Biard and others prisoner. Father Massé and some companions managed to escape by boat and join a group of Frenchmen fishing off Nova Scotia. The English raider proceeded to Port Royal and destroyed it, but Poutrincourt's son Biencourt and the settlers managed to escape into the woods and find refuge among their Mi'kmaq friends (JR 3:11). They associated closely with Mi'kmaqs in the region, trading with them and living like them on fish, game, and wild berries (Clark, 82). After his father's death in 1615 the young Biencourt became the local French commander in Nova Scotia. He maintained occasional contact with French merchants, selling them furs and dried fish. Although he contributed to the record 25,000 pelts collected from all over Acadia in 1616 (Clark, 82), other harbors eclipsed Port Royal as centers of French activity in the region for the time being (Reid, 19).

In 1620, unbeknownst to the Mi'kmaq and their French partners, the English Crown granted Acadia to the newly incorporated Council for New England as part of a vast coastal tract that stretched from present-day New Jersey up to Chaleur Bay. In 1621 the council conferred a portion of this territory to Sir William Alexander, Lord of Stirling. This Scottish gentleman entrepreneur eyed Mi'kmaq country as a place to "disburden" overpopulated Scotland and named it Nova Scotia after his own country (Reid, 21–22).

When Biencourt died in 1623 he and his cohorts were probably still unaware of Lord Stirling's plans. One of Biencourt's companions, Charles Turgis de Saint-Étienne et de La Tour, succeeded him as commander of Acadia and established a small coastal stronghold at the southwest tip of Nova Scotia. There, Mi'kmaqs periodically stopped by, swapping furs for goods that La Tour purchased from passing merchant ships or fishing vessels (Reid, 29).

In 1627 war broke out between the English and French over their conflicting claims to Acadia. Writing from his small stronghold, La Tour complained to French King Louis XIII that he "was constrained by the bad treatment that we have received from Englishmen to live like the natives and be dressed like them, hunt animals, and fish." Accompanied by a "small band of Frenchmen with three medium-sized barques," he requested a formal commission to protect the Acadian coast (author's translation, in Reid, 29–30).

In 1628 Lord Stirling's fleet sailed from the Scottish port of Dumbarton to establish two new settlements. One, consisting of about 70 colonists on the coast of northern Cape Breton, had barely gotten started when a French captain en route to Quebec learned of this encroachment from French fishermen on the coast. Aided by about 60 sailors and a group of local Mi'kmaq warriors, he took the Scots by surprise, raiding the fort and taking prisoners to France (Reid, 31—32). The other Scottish settlement, established near the deserted site at Port Royal, lasted a bit longer. A handful of French settlers who had remained in the area were agreeable to Scottish allegiance, and the local Mi'kmaqs, too, seemed eager to trade with the Scots. About this time a Mi'kmaq chief named Segipt, along with his family, traveled to England to visit King Charles I at Whitehall Palace near London "and to submit his kingdom to him" (Anon. 1630, in Reid, 32). During Segipt's sojourn, 30 Scottish settlers at Port Royal died of illness. Soon thereafter, in the 1632 Treaty of Saint-Germain-en-Laye, the English king consented that Mi'kmaq country would be left to the French

Crown and agreed to evacuate the surviving Scots from Port Royal. Only one or two families remained (Reid, 38–39; Clark, 91).

THE COMPANY OF NEW FRANCE AS FEUDAL OVERLORD
(1627–1663)

In 1627, just before the Scots attempted to settle in Mi'kmaq country, the French king granted all of Canada and Acadia as feudal territory to the Company of New France. Headquartered in Paris, this new enterprise represented 100 business associates—powerful aristocrats and rich merchants. In return for exemption from customs duties, exclusive rights to the fur trade, and a monopoly on all other commerce except the fishery, the company agreed to ship 4,000 settlers to the colonies by the year 1643. Further, it agreed to support French Catholic religious orders in their efforts to convert the native "heathens." To raise the necessary capital it was allowed to subcontract with individual entrepreneurs or smaller companies (Reid, 25).

In the next few decades, the company granted many seigneuries in the St. Lawrence Valley and a few large seigneuries in Acadia for both economic and political reasons. For example, concerned about the rapidly growing colonies of New England, it granted several large seigneuries to a French nobleman named Isaac de Razilly in 1632. Razilly, a famous naval commander and a Knight of Malta, was also the king's new lieutenant general for New France and governor of Acadia. He sailed to Mi'kmaq country in a fully equipped warship, accompanied by two other vessels. In addition to soldiers, he traveled with 300 colonists—farmers, laborers, craftsmen, a dozen women, some children, and a few Franciscan (Capuchin) priests (Clark, 94–95). After founding a small habitation at Canso on the Atlantic coast, Razilly made his principal settlement at La Hève further south, where he founded an offshore fishery. In 1635, after Razilly's sudden death, his successor, Charles de Menou d'Aulney, relocated most of the La Hève settlers to Port Royal. There they established themselves on fertile marshlands opposite Poutrincourt's original site (Reid, 41). Some colonists, apparently those who had taken Mi'kmaq wives, remained in La Hève, which became a settlement of *métis* (mixed-blood) families (Clark, 95).

During the next 15 years, through reproduction and continued emigration from Touraine and Britanny in France, the population at Acadia's Port Royal headquarters grew. As in La Hève, intermarriage between the mostly single French males and local Mi'kmaq women was not uncommon, and a French-Mi'kmaq métis population began to emerge in the region. Gradually, the settlement extended beyond a cluster of houses around the fort (Reid, 41). Ignoring Governor d'Aulney's demand to clear and cultivate wooded areas in the interior, settlers expanded their farming activities by diking tidal flats all along the Bay of Fundy coast (Clark, 73, 90). Treeless and covered by dense rich grasses, these marshlands comprised thousands of acres. They were not very important to the economy of the local Mi'kmaq, but they proved vital to the colonists, who found them suitable for hay, pasture, or grain crops (Reid, 8; Clark, 24, 27). Thanks to the great fertility of these diked fields, French Acadia gained a reputation for rich soil (Clark, 54).

Back at La Hève, Nicolas Denys, (who, like d'Aulney, had come to Acadia under Razilly's command), began a logging operation with a small labor force of 12 men. He also established a partnership with his brother, Simon Denys, and set up a sedentary fishery plant nearby, manned by 40 men (Reid, 45). During the next four decades, Nicolas Denys greatly expanded his seigneurial domains on the north shore of Mi'kmaq country. (Briefly called Gaspesia by the French, this northern Acadia region stretched from Gaspé Peninsula to Cape Breton Island.) In addition to owning smaller boats, Denys operated a 500-ton sailing vessel (N. Denys, 206). In 1645, while engaging in the fur trade with Mi'kmaqs in the Chaleur Bay region, he also acquired a concession for the fisheries at Miscou from the Company of New France (Reid, 43). A few years later, he established residence at Cape Breton. Located at an important Mi'kmaq portage route between Bras d'Or Lake and the sea, he named his fortified trading post St. Peter. As stipulated by contract, Denys sustained several Franciscan (Capuchin) missionaries, who tended to the French fishermen and Mi'kmaq trappers frequenting his establishments (Leger, 34). Next, he founded several other fishing stations and trading posts in the Chaleur Bay area, including one at Nepisiguit (1651). In 1653, the Company of New France granted him the fur-trade monopoly in all of Gaspesia. By that time, however, the commercial value of fur began to decline. In contrast, the cod fisheries remained highly significant (LeClercq, 1, 12, 61; Murdoch 1:171).

During this period, Sieur de La Tour acquired two seigneuries, one at Cape Sable in southern Nova Scotia, and another at the St. John River. He, too, tried to attract settlers and managed to hire some Scottish soldiers, perhaps some drifters from Port Royal (CSP 5:596). In 1651, La Tour resettled at the St. John River and subgranted his Nova Scotia domain to another seigneur.

Rivalry between French seigneurs and their retainers could be as intense as the rivalry between France and England. In 1650 Governor d'Aulney died, deeply indebted to the French merchant banker Emmanuel LeBorgne, who claimed the deceased governor's Acadian domains (Clark, 119–20). In 1654, after several years of bitter feuding between the region's seigneurs, English forces attacked the small garrisons at Port Royal and some other French settlements in the area. Proving no match, the French troops surrendered quickly. As far as the Mi'maq hunters, and even the French Acadian peasants, were concerned, the changing of the guards meant little. With southern Acadia in English hands, the French king appointed Nicolas Denys as governor of northern Mi'kmaq country (Gaspesia). Continuing his fishing and trading activities, he became known among the local tribespeople as "Big Beard." A few years later, he opened a trading post at Miramichi River (1658), soon followed by another station at Chedabucto (Canso) (c. 1660), outfitting both "with cannon and swivels" (Charlevoix 3:136–37). After his Cape Breton headquarters at St. Peter burned down in 1668–1669, Denys relocated to Nepisiguit on Chaleur Bay. Here, in the dangerously competitive area, he built a house "flanked by four little bastions with a palisade, of which the stakes are eighteen feet in height, with six pieces of cannon in batteries" (N. Denys, 213–14). At this residence he planted apple and pear trees and cultivated wheat and peas. Then, thousands of miles from his homeland, the old colonial entrepreneur began to write his now famous memoirs titled *The Description and Natural History of the Coasts of North America (Acadia),* published in France in 1672.

THE FRENCH CROWN TAKES OVER SEIGNEURIES FROM NEW FRANCE COMPANY

Compared to English colonization efforts in North America, the Company of New France performed poorly. Its profit margin, largely dependent on fur-trade revenues, dwindled as countless native trappers died due to epidemics and Iroquois raids. By colonization standards, the French population was undersized and maldistributed. By 1663 only some 3,000 French settlers resided in Canada and just 500 in Acadia. The majority subsisted as farmers in the area around Quebec, and most of the 69 seigneuries allocated by the company were situated in this region (Trigger, 329–30; Reid, 28). In contrast, the rapidly growing Protestant colonies in New England already numbered 50,000 settlers living in more than 100 villages and towns. Boston alone had more than 14,000 inhabitants. Collectively, the New Englanders could easily raise 8,000 troops, compared to New France's 700 soldiers and 2,000 colonists who were "capable of bearing arms" (CSP 3:532; PD 1:61). New France seemed "on the brink of economic and military ruin" (Trigger, 339–40). Advising King Louis XIV that his colony was in dire straits, Minister Colbert accused the company of having "scandalously" evaded its obligations to the Crown. Aiming to centralize power in the realm, the Crown revoked the company's feudal rights to all property and assumed direct control over the colony's seigneuries (Trigger, 339–40; Murdoch 1:136).

SEIGNEURIES IN ACADIA AND GASPESIA

In 1667, 13 years after losing Acadia to the English, the French Crown regained title to the territory by the Treaty of Breda. Three years later the English formally surrendered control of the colony to the newly appointed French governor Hector d'Andigné, Chevalier de Grandfontaine. The governor's jurisdiction, home to a mere 500 French settlers (plus a large seasonal influx of fishermen and traders), was hardly impressive. Port Royal, with its 350 inhabitants, was by far the largest settlement. Some outlying establishments in various harbors on the region's southern and southwestern coasts hosted fewer than a handful of French souls apiece (Clark, 121). In an effort to get a stronger grip on the colony, the French Crown awarded its army officers and naval commanders generous land grants.

Although some seigneuries had been created in Acadia before the French lost control over the region in 1654, most were granted between 1670 and 1710, especially in the fertile St. John Valley, but also around the Bay of Fundy. The exact number of seigneurial grants in Mi'kmaq country is not known, but about 55 have been identified between Gaspé and the Penobscot River in Maine (Clark, 115). However, many failed to develop beyond the paperwork that established them, and information about the others is scarce. We do know that grants were poorly described and often overlapped, thereby fueling the region's turmoil with confusion (Clark, 114–16).

ACADIA'S INDIAN SEIGNEURIES

As noted earlier, some French seigneurs tried to turn a profit not by settling their estates with immigrant tenant farmers, but instead by drawing Indian hunting families to their trading posts. Records indicate two major clusters of seigneuries sauvages, each controlled by a French colonial family. The d'Amours family ran a series of trading posts in the St. John River valley, where they did business with Mi'kmaq, Maliseet, and Abenaki fur trappers from the early 1670s onward. Mathieu d'Amours, the first in this family to receive a concession in the valley, ran a fishing station as well as a trading post on his seigneury on Gaspé Peninsula and operated another seigneury nearby. His three sons acquired several seigneuries in the valley and an additional one on the Richibucto (P.D. 1:122, 124; Murdoch 1:163, 182, 198–99; MacBeath, 1969:166; Grenier, 245; Thwaites in Lahontan, 324–25, n.3; Webster, 171).

Perhaps even more important were several seigneuries operated by the Denys family in "Gaspesia" (the territory from Cape Breton to Gaspé Peninsula). The fur trade in this vast tract of northern Acadia had been monopolized for about two decades by Nicolas Denys. In the early 1670s, however, he had lost title to some of his domains in the region "through non fulfillment of the conditions as to settlement" (CNBHS III/1:20–21). He did hold on to several seigneuries, including those at Restigouche, Nepisiguit, Miramichi, and Cape Breton. His son Richard, born at Cape Breton in 1655, succeeded him. Richard Denys had grown up at his father's residence in the seigneury of Nepisiguit at Chaleur Bay. As he himself later noted, he had been raised among the Mi'kmaqs and learned their language "perfectly" (Raymond, 48). About 1680 he built his own stronghold, Fort de Fronsac, in his seigneury at Miramichi, where he possessed exclusive rights on the fur trade, and collected "rentals" from the French residents in his domain. He also sustained a Catholic mission post for the region's Mi'kmaq. A 1689 report notes that he had

> seated two villages of Indians near his establishments, one in the Baye des Chaleurs of 60 families and about 400 souls, the other at Miramichy of 80 wigwams or families of 500 souls. Thus his concession is peopled by 103 French and 900 Indians, to whom he furnishes all necessities temporal and spiritual, having always maintained monks or priests at his own expense . . . [having] a storehouse from which the Indians and French get their supplies. (CNBHS III/1:37–40)

Two of young Denys's close relatives possessed seigneuries across Chaleur Bay. His cousin Pierre Denys, Sieur de la Ronde, based at Gaspé Point, ran a fishing station and trading post and supported a small Catholic mission post for French fishermen and Mi'kmaq Indians. His nephew, Simon-Pierre Denys, Sieur de Bonaventure, operated a fishing station at nearby Bonaventure Island, where the Franciscans (Recollets) founded a church with St. Claire as patron saint (LeClercq, 75). Richard Denys's older sister married a powerful colonist named Michel Leneuf de La Vallière, who possessed a seigneury at Beaubassin on the Isthmus of Chignecto. This had been granted to him as a reward for service that he (and Richard Denys) had provided the French Crown: Cruising the Acadian coast in search of Dutch privateers. La Valliere tried to settle his estate with French Canadian tenants. In 1679 he was appointed commander of Acadia (Reid, 171–72).

In 1690, two years after the outbreak of the Anglo-French colonial war known as King William's War, English privateers from New York attacked and burned the French seigneuries of Acadia and Gaspesia, including Fort de Fronsac and its chapel for the Mi'kmaq converts of Miramichi, and the Franciscan mission churches and establishments at Miscou, Nepisiguit, Bonaventure, and Isle Percée. The following year, 36-year-old Richard Denys perished at sea, leaving behind two French-Mi'kmaq children, the ten-year-old Marie-Anne and her younger brother Nicolas. What became of them is not recorded, but it is likely that they were adopted by their Mi'kmaq relatives (LeClercq, 160, n.2).

MI'KMAQ-ACADIAN INTERMARRIAGES

Although the idea of "blood" has acquired social significance in contemporary claims of ethnic identity, it appears that 17th-century Mi'kmaqs were not interested in "racial" issues. Organized in bands, they attached more importance to social ties of kin and friendship. To establish a widespread social network Mi'kmaq bands relied on marriage exchanges with neighboring groups. Seeing very few women in the early French settlements, visiting tribesmen may have recognized the plight of their new neighbors. The French, unlike their Protestant neighbors in New England, did not frown upon having sexual liaisons with Indian women. Cases of miscegenation were many and varied, spawned by love, lust, convenience, alliance building, economic opportunism—or some combination of these. Many of the latter 17th-century French seigneurs who were born and raised in the colonies with Indian neighbors had sexual liaisons with native women. Often, as in Richard Denys's case, these relationships led to marriage. However, records also noted, "there are married men who, in addition to their own wives, keep Squaws" (PD 3:278–79). From early on, French colonial authorities encouraged intermarriages in order to produce a colonial hybrid population—"a complete fusion of the two races by bringing them into perfect contact" (Shea, in LeClercq, 33).

The history of French-Indian relations in colonial North America reveals interesting contrasts between the French and English. From early on English Protestants aggressively pursued a racial segregation policy, condemning Indian-white sexual relationships. For instance, the New England Commonwealth Laws of 1646 ruled: "An English woman suffering an Indian to have carnal knowledge of her, had an Indian cut out exactly in red cloth sewed upon her right Arm, and injoyned to wear it twelve moneths" (Josselyn, in CMaHS III/3:330).

Mixed marriages occurred among the most prominent French families in the colonies and were often formalized by the Catholic church. Most resulted in children who were baptized and given Christian names. According to one scholar, "Just how much intermarrying or interbreeding there was is uncertain. . . . It is likely that liaisons, on both sides of the blanket, continued throughout the Acadian period,

chiefly between young Acadian men and Indian girls during the winter hunting period, and that some of the offspring may have been accepted in time into the Acadian
communities, but most métis children of the first generation were brought up in their
mother's homes as Indians" (Clark, 377).

Given the social interaction between Mi'kmaq communities and French settlers
in Acadia, both of which were relatively small in size, the result of this early miscegenation process was that few of the local Mi'kmaq and French Acadians belonging
to long-established regional families would have been "full-bloods" by the mid-
1700s. Some examples follow.

About 1610 a young French fur trader took off with the wife of a Maliseet chieftain on the lower St. John. After the chief complained to the seigneur of Port Royal
about the affair, the youth was arrested—but soon escaped "in a shallop, and went
off with the Indians" (JR 1:67). On another occasion, in the Bay of Fundy region, a
Frenchman "debauched" a chieftain's daughter. This "was highly resented by her father . . . [and] the injury was finally compensated by the marrying of the parties"
(Sullivan, 89). Certainly there were "libertines" among seigneurs as well as among
common French fur traders. Among them was the Sieur de Bonaventure, who was
accused of misconduct with Indian women in Acadia. His sexual escapades were so
notorious that "the Indians are said to have made songs on the subject, which they
sing in the woods" (in Murdoch 1:258).

Among the first church-confirmed Mi'kmaq-French marriages was that of Sieur
de La Tour, who came to Nova Scotia as a 17-year-old in 1610. La Tour was among
the Frenchmen who escaped the English raid on Port Royal in 1613. Retreating into
the woods, he found refuge among the Mi'kmaq. In 1626, he married a Mi'kmaq
woman whose name is no longer known, by whom he had three daughters, the oldest being "the first métis child mentioned" in the history of this region (Trudel, 155).
He established a small fort at the southwest tip of Nova Scotia and later moved to the
mouth of the St. John River, where he built Fort St. Marie. One of his métis daughters, christened Jeanne, married the Basque colonist Martin d'Aprendestiguy, who
later became the Sieur de Martignon and also had a fort at the mouth of the St. John
after 1672 (Baudry, 63; MacBeath, 1966:595–96; Bourgeois, 66–67).

And, as already noted, Richard Denys, living on his extensive seigneury at Miramichi, married a Mi'kmaq woman named Anne Patarabego, with whom he had
two children (Raymond, 45, 48; Leger, 104).

About 1676 a 24-year-old surgeon named Philippe Enault came to Nepisiguit in
the employ of Richard Denys. Soon after his arrival, he married a Mi'kmaq woman,
and they had several children. By 1679 he had obtained a grant of his own. A priest
who visited him that year noted that he "cultivates the soil there with success, and
harvests wheat more than sufficient for the support of his [Mi'kmaq wife and chil-
dren]" (LeClercq, 163). There were three other resident Frenchmen at Nepisiguit,
two of whom were also married to Indian women (CNBHS III/1:34–40). Nearby
was a seasonal encampment of Mi'kmaq converts (LeClercq, 163–64, 192–93). Following Enault's death, sometime after 1690, his métis offspring appear to have scattered among the Mi'kmaqs (LeClercq, 160–61, n.2).

Although most métis children were raised as Mi'kmaqs, in some instances
Franco-Mi'kmaq family clusters formed unique métis communities. For instance,

the mixed offspring of French colonists and Mi'kmaq women at La Hève formed their own distinct community on Nova Scotia's east coast from the early 1630s onward. Later that century they were said to live "like Europeans" and "numbered seventy-five or more" (Clark, 128–29). The occasional suggestions of Indian agriculture seem to stem chiefly from these mixed families (Clark, 377). Similar métis communities developed elsewhere in the region.

Interestingly, it was the Jesuits who pressed for ethnic separation, observing that close association with French communities led to alcoholism and other problems that hampered their missionary efforts. Beginning around 1668, the French Crown endeavored to change the Jesuit policy in this respect, inducing seigneurs to draw Indians "into the Canadian population by encouraging intermarriage and seeing that the children of whites and [Indians] received a common education" (Leger, 53–54). This attitude continued through the next few decades. In 1681 the king's intendant in Canada, Jacques Duchesneau, encouraged the French settlers "to rear Indians" and recommended that the king set aside "a small fund for the Indian girls who quit the Ursulines, on being educated, to fit them out and marry them, and establish Christian families through their means" (PD 1:150).

CONCLUSION

As indicated by historical evidence, Mi'kmaqs and French Acadians formed a symbiotic relationship during the colonial period. Recognizing the social benefits of sexuality, both groups participated in building cross-cultural channels of communication and reliance by forging intimate linkages. In the process they developed vested interests in one another's survival. Although intermarriages were to some degree the result of friendships, these bonds also served to enhance this French-Mi'kmaq symbiosis, in which each group occupied its own particular cultural niche. The migratory Mi'k-maqs specialized as market hunters and could count on the French for crops, manufactured goods, and arms. The sedentary French Acadians focused on their farms, the fisheries, or the fur trade; they relied on Mi'kmaqs for furs and eventually turned to Mi'kmaq warriors as valued allies during the colonial wars. Generally speaking, the two abided side by side without threatening each other's efforts to make a living. Yet, as described in the following chapters, Mi'kmaq associations with Europeans were by no means always beneficial. The colonial path was full of difficult encounters.

6 / Christianizing the Mi'kmaq: "Black Robes" and "Bare Feet"

Traditionally Mi'kmaqs saw all of creation as imbued with a spiritual force they called *mntu*. The greatest spirit force of all was *niskam*, the sun, which they saluted at its rising and setting. Aiming to convert Mi'kmaqs to Christianity, French missionaries began referring to the Christian god in terms of niskam. Gradually the word became equated with the idea of God. In the words of a 17th-century Mi'kmaq: "'Niscaminou' means 'Our sun, or our God'" (JR 3:133; cf. LeClercq, 84, 143). From the early 1600s onward, traditional Mi'kmaq sun worship waned. As noted by a priest active among the Mi'kmaq in the 1670s: "Such is the custom I have seen observed by a certain aged man of that nation, who, in dying, took with him, as it seemed to me, all that was left of superstition and false worship in a religion badly enough observed" (LeClercq, 144; cf. Biard in JR 3:133). (In recent years some Mi'kmaqs, apparently ignoring this spiritual tradition in their own culture, have embraced the Plains Indian Sun Dance ceremony, as noted in Chapter 13.)

Although sun worship became something of the past, Mi'kmaq shamanism was more difficult to repress or subvert. Putting a disdainful spin on his observations, a French priest observed in 1691: "In fact these Indians imagine that certain jugglers [shamans] among them have communication with the Devil, from whom they hope to learn that which they wish to know, or to obtain that which they ask. [The Mi'kmaq] have so much esteem for their jugglers that, when in trouble, they seek those who pass for the most famous (just as among us the sick in their ills have recourse to the most clever physicians). They are convinced also that these frauds can surely cure their ills" (LeClercq, 217).

Yet making sense of the epidemic scourges that claimed the lives of the vast majority of Mi'kmaqs in the first century of contact with Europeans stretched Mi'kmaq religious beliefs to the breaking point—and kindled Mi'kmaq curiosity about French spiritual leaders, those long-robed priests who remained celibate and had knowledge of "holy mysteries" (LeClercq, 225). Seeing these "white sorcerers" and their followers survive measles, plague, influenza, and smallpox epidemics (due to acquired immunity) while their own shamans seemed powerless in the face of these foreign diseases, Mi'kmaqs began to lose faith in their own guardian spirits and customary means of solving problems.

Traditionally the Mi'kmaq believed that some of the most powerful "medicine" came in visions induced by some difficult ordeal. In their view dreams were as real as the events of waking life, relaying the actions of the soul or spiritual counterpart of the dreamer. Dreams predicted the future and also demanded the fulfillment of the events that took place in them. Initially French missionaries saw the power of dreams as a great obstacle to their efforts to convert Indians. Later, however, they used them as a chief means of conversion. They discovered that when Mi'kmaqs were exposed to Christian indoctrination, vivid images formed in their minds and began to occur in their dreams. For instance, some parents dreamed that the spirits of their dead children visited them and told them to embrace Christianity. Utilizing this discovery, some priests actually staged little theatrical dramas to frighten Indians into accepting the new faith— portraying the soul of an unbeliever undergoing horrible torments at the hands of demons. Such enactments could induce spectators to have frightening dreams of hell (JR 18:87).

So it is no wonder that the Mi'kmaqs, in a time of great emotional affliction and cultural confusion, adopted some of the magic ceremonies of the newcomers. Catholic religious objects—rosaries, crucifixes, and sacred books—were especially intriguing to them, as were ritual gestures. Mi'kmaqs began making the sign of the cross and wearing wooden, brass, or even silver crucifixes around their necks. Some said grace before eating (Diereville, 150–151). Perhaps most fascinating to them was the use of holy water in a ritual called baptism, which promised eternal life in heaven (JR 20:49; see also Bailey, 80–82).

FRENCH CATHOLIC MISSIONS

Throughout the colonial period, Catholic missionaries were active among the Mi'kmaqs. Often in cooperation with colonial authorities, who assigned them their specific mission fields, the French priests initially established their headquarters near trading stations. This allowed them to reach out to the hundreds of tribespeople who assembled at these seasonal meeting points to barter furs and to hold communal celebrations. Sometimes these mission posts attracted large numbers of Indian refugees from distant regions because missions provided access to trade goods and protection against enemies. In return, the hunters brought in large quantities of furs and sometimes offered their armed services as frontier guerrillas.

Typically, early mission sites in Mi'kmaq country were only seasonally occupied and were visited by itinerant missionaries who traveled to reach their migratory constituencies. It was not unusual to see tribespeople from different ethnic groups frequenting the same trading stations and mission villages. For instance, the Jesuit mission at Mount Desert Island was destined for Mi'kmaqs, Maliseets, and Abenakis, while the mission at Rivière-du-Loup catered to both Mi'kmaqs and Maliseets, and Tadoussac was frequented by Montagnais as well as Mi'kmaqs, Algonkins, Maliseets, and even Hurons. Indeed, cross-cultural interaction was the hallmark of the colonial frontier.

JESUIT PRIESTS AND FRANCISCAN RECOLLETS: MISSIONARY PERSPECTIVES AND POLICIES

Of all French clergy, Jesuits and Franciscans, especially Recollets (a Reformed order), were most directly involved with the Mi'kmaqs, and the two developed highly contrasting policies. According to the Recollet priest Chrestien LeClercq (111): "To civilize them [the Indians] it was necessary first that the French should mingle with them and habituate them among us [and] to make the Indians sedentary, without which nothing can be done for the salvation of these heathens." Initially, the Jesuits expressed a similar view, evident in Father Pierre Biard's early comments about Mi'kmaqs camping near the French settlement at Port Royal:

> The nation is savage, wandering and full of bad habits; the people are few and isolated. They are, I say, savage, haunting the woods, ignorant, lawless and rude; they are wanderers, with nothing to attach them to a place, neither homes nor relationships, neither possessions nor love of country. . . . If they are savages, it is to domesticate and civilize them that we have come here; if they are rude, that is no reason that we should be idle; if they have until now profited little, it is no wonder, for it would be too much to expect fruit from this grafting, and to demand reason and beard [maturity] from a child.

> (JR 1:173, 183)

Soon, however, Jesuits became less ethnocentric. Unlike the Franciscans, they rejected the idea that Indians had to become "civilized" before they could be Christianized. In 1622 the order officially adopted a foreign mission policy based on the Doctrine of Adaptivity. Its guidelines held that: "There is no stronger cause for alienation [of heathen peoples] than an attack on local customs, especially when these go back to a venerable antiquity. Do not draw invidious contrasts between the customs of these peoples and those of Europe; do your utmost to adapt yourself to them" (in Mitchell, 145).

Commenting on this ideological difference between the two Roman Catholic orders, Baron de Lahontan wrote in 1703:

> The [Franciscan] Recollets brand the Indians for stupid, gross and rustick Persons, uncapable of Thought or Reflection: But the Jesuits give them other sort of Language, for they intitle them to good Sense, to a tenacious Memory, and to a quick Apprehension season'd with a solid Judgment.

> (Lahontan 2:411–14)

THE ARRIVAL OF "BLACK ROBES" IN MI'KMAQ COUNTRY (1611–1613)

Although individual priests had served on French vessels bound for Mi'kmaq country before, Jesuits were the first religious order to focus exclusively on the missionary practice. In 1611, authorized by the French Crown to convert these Indians to Christianity and to assimilate them into French colonial society, they established a mission at the small Acadian settlement of Port Royal, headed by the Sieur de

Poutrincourt. Since 1610, his entourage had included a secular priest, Jessé Fleche, called the "patriarch" by the Mi'kmaqs. Although "he did not know the language," Father Fleche had baptized local Mi'kmaqs. These Mi'kmaqs, as well as Maliseets from the St. John River, attended weekly church services at Port Royal. Among the Maliseets was a man named Chkoudon, who, according to Lescarbot, "loved the French, and . . . admired our civilization . . . to such an extent, that being present sometimes at the Christian admonitions, which were given every Sunday to our French people, he listened attentively, although he did not understand a word; and moreover wore the sign of the Cross upon his bossom, which he also had his servants wear . . ." (JR 1:79).

In 1611 Jesuits Pierre Biard and Enemond Massé succeeded Father Fleche. Not unlike Mi'kmaq shamans, the Jesuits treasured their own magic charms. For instance, Father Biard mentioned that when he and Father Massé left France for Acadia they were given "a bone taken from the precious relics of the glorified Saint Lawrence, Archbishop of Dublin in Ireland . . . for our protection during the voyage to these lands" (JR 2:19).

From Port Royal, Biard mailed detailed reports (known as "relations") to his superiors in Paris, describing the conditions in Acadia, its indigenous inhabitants, their way of life, and, of course, the commercial opportunities of the fur trade and the fisheries. In 1612 he reported: "They stay over night among us; we rove about with them, and hunt with them and live among them without arms and without fear; and, as has thus far appeared, without danger" (JR 2:71).

In 1613 Biard and Massé, known as *mak maqtawe'kji'j* ("little black ones," or "Black Robes") among Mi'kmaqs, relocated and founded the Mission of St. Sauveur on Mount Desert Island in the Gulf of Maine. Within a month this mission was destroyed by English raiders from Virginia, who then sailed on to sack Port Royal. This brought Jesuit missionary activity in Mi'kmaq country to a halt for two decades.

THE "BARE FEET" SPREAD THEIR GOSPEL (1619–1624)

In 1619 Franciscan Recollets arrived in Acadia, extending their mission field from the St. Lawrence Valley in Canada, where they had been active for about four years. Financially supported by a French merchant company, they set up a mission for French fishermen, Mi'kmaqs and other Indians at the mouth of the St. John River. Because Recollets wore open sandals, Mi'kmaqs called them *sesaki'kewey* ("Bare Feet"). In 1620 these priests expanded their activities to the Chaleur Bay area, founding small temporary mission posts at Nepisiguit, Miscou Island, and even at the Miramichi. But within four years they were instructed to terminate their religious venture in Mi'kmaq country and to focus on the St. Lawrence Valley, where they had five missions, from Tadoussac to Carhagouha in Ontario. In Quebec, which then consisted of only a cluster of buildings protected by Fort St. Louis, they possessed a small convent. In 1629, when the French colony surrendered to the English, the Recollets returned to France (see also Trigger, 200–203).

In 1632 the French retook Canada, and the Jesuit order managed to gain exclusive missionary rights to the colony. After three years they founded a college for Indian boys at Quebec. Four years later, they invited the Ursulines, a religious teaching order of nuns, who opened a school for Indian girls. Decades later a French priest active among the Mi'kmaq at Chaleur Bay in the 1670s and 1680s noted: "I have met, in my mission [at Restigouche], two daughters of our [Mi'kmaqs] who knew how to read and write, because they had lived with the Ursulines of Quebec, who, sacredly animated by that all-fiery zeal which they exhibit for the glory of God and the salvation of souls, receive among them the little daughters of the Indians, whom they teach with piety and devotion not only how to read and write, but also how to perform other tasks suited to their condition of life" (LeClercq, 125). About the same time that the Ursulines arrived in Quebec, a group of Hospital Nuns from Dieppe began a hospital there. In 1657 Sulpiciens, members of a newly founded French order, arrived to train young men for future service in the church.

In 1669, 40 years after evacuating Canada, the Recollets were allowed to return to the colony and join the growing number of French clergy. In the years that followed, many more missionaries came, representing various other religious orders.

CAPUCHINS: OTHER "BARE FEET" PRIESTS IN MI'KMAQ COUNTRY (1632–1654)

In 1632, when the English Crown returned Acadia to the French, the territory was assigned another branch of the Franciscan order known as the Capuchins. By order of Cardinal de Richelieu, six priests accompanied Sieur de Razilly when he repossessed Acadia in the name of the French Crown. As chaplains, they had the task of saving the French colonial population from "the power of darkness." Moreover, they were instructed to open, at the king's expense, a college or seminary at Port Royal. By 1643 the number of Capuchins had doubled. Besides Port Royal, they served Fort Pentagoet at Penobscot Bay, Fort St. John at the mouth of the St. John River, Fort La Tour at Cape Sable, Fort St. Peter at Cape Breton, and Nepisiguit at Chaleur Bay (Leger, 34). Although their primary purpose was to serve French settlers, fishers, traders, administrators, and military personnel, their work included providing spiritual care to Mi'kmaqs and other Indians who came to visit French settlements and posts. Mi'kmaqs referred to them as Sesaki'kewey ("Bare Feet")—the same term they used for Recollets, who were also part of the besandaled Franciscan order. In 1654, when a small English fleet sailing from Boston captured the French forts in Acadia, the Capuchin activity in the region came to an end (Reid, 164; Leger, 34–35).

"BLACK ROBES" RETURN TO MI'KMAQ COUNTRY

A year after France's 1632 reclamation of Acadia and Canada, the French came back. Champlain returned to Fort St. Louis (Quebec), his major stronghold in the St. Lawrence Valley. Jesuits accompanied him and soon founded a mission at the nearby seigneury of Sillery, serving mainly Montagnais and Algonkins. Next, Jesuits established a post for Hurons living upriver (JR 38:229), then one for Mi'kmaqs at Cape

Breton near a French fishing station on the island's north shore. In 1635 they started a fourth mission, this one for Mi'kmaqs frequenting a French trading post at Miscou Island at the entrance of Chaleur Bay (JR 7:263). French laborers were hired to build the residence and warehouse on this small island. When many of these laborers fell ill and died that winter, Indians (probably Mi'kmaqs) tried to plunder the warehouse. Subsequently, the Company of New France banished the Indians from the island, and the Jesuits relocated their mission to the mainland "to which a part of the natives might retire" (JR 32:37). By 1640 there were 13 Jesuits active at six missions, all under the command of a superior residing in Quebec (JR 20:93). From these widely dispersed posts, the Black Robes traveled to the seaside camps of French fishermen, the hamlets of Acadian peasants, and campsites of Indian hunting bands (LeClercq, 383–84). However, contact between these missions was sporadic. As one priest reported: "Now, as the vessels which go to Cape Breton and to Miscou do not go up as far as Kebec [Quebec], it thus happens that we have no communication with our [Jesuit] Fathers who are in the Residences of Sainte Anne [Cape Breton] and of Saint Charles [Miscou], except by way of France" (LeJeune 1635, in Kenton 1:95).

Only one "relation" (1634–1635) about the Cape Breton mission has been preserved. In this report the local Jesuit priest commented that the Mi'kmaqs were "well-formed men, good-looking, of the figures, strong and powerful. . . . As to their intelligence, if we may judge from their conduct and from their way of dealing with the French they are not at a great disadvantage. They are indeed so clever, that in order to disguise their language, they add to every word a syllable, which only serves to confuse the minds of those by whom they do not wish to be understood" (in Kenton 1:122). In 1641, closing the mission post at Cape Breton, the two resident Jesuit priests were reassigned to the Mi'kmaq mission at Miscou. The following year, visiting Mi'kmaqs informed the priests that they wished "to be converted, and to settle down to till the soil, in imitation of our [new Algonkin converts at the Jesuit mission of Sillery]" (JR 22:238–39). Moreover, the Mi'kmaqs planned "to have workmen brought out from France, to help them build small dwellings, and that they would pay for their work in furs" (JR 22:241). In 1643 the Jesuits reported: "They have since erected little houses in the French fashion, in order to lodge some families who have been instructed and baptized" (JR 32:41; JR 30:129).

The mission at mainland Miscou was of great significance. Mi'kmaqs hailing from as far away as the Bay of Fundy and Cape Breton came to be baptized by the Jesuits, who had learned to speak the native language well (JR 32:147). For instance, when a group of Mi'kmaqs from Nova Scotia visited the Jesuit chapel at Miscou, they joined the converted Mi'kmaqs of Chaleur Bay in prayer. Hearing Father Richard addressing them in Mi'kmaq, they exclaimed: "We have so long frequented the French settlements on our shores, and we have never been taught in that fashion. We know not what it is to pray, at least in our own language" (JR 28:35). Even Montagnais Indians frequented Miscou in those years. Likewise, Mi'kmaqs showed up at the Jesuit mission at Tadoussac on the north bank of the St. Lawrence, which served mainly Montagnais (JR 32:145, 147).

In 1643 Jesuits from Miscou started a mission at nearby Nepisiguit, a campsite frequented by many of the region's Mi'kmaqs (JR 24:41, 153). Dedicating their new residence to "Our Lady of Consolation," they founded a small mission village there

(LeClercq, 383–84). It began with a band of 25 Mi'kmaqs, residing in three cabins near the Jesuit residence. The number soon dwindled to only two Mi'kmaq families (15 people), and by 1648 they and, in turn, the Jesuits had abandoned the mission (JR 28:213). The mission at Miscou, however, continued for many more years and was still in operation in 1663 (Leger, 153). Serving some 40 Mi'kmaq families (about 200 people), it was described as "the most populous and the best disposed, and contains the most Christians [compared to Cape Breton and Richibucto]. It contains the Indians of Gaspé, Miramichy, and of Nepigigouit [Nepisiguit]" (JR 45:59).

Despite some success, by the mid-1660s all Jesuit missions among the Mi'kmaq had been closed. Why? By that time many Mi'kmaqs had become addicted to alcohol (supplied by merchants and fishermen) and had no interest in priestly preachings about their misbehavior (Leger, 53–54). Also, after more than 100 years of hectic business in the Gulf of St. Lawrence, the fur trade had started to decline in the mid-17th century—and the harvest of souls was closely linked to furs. The priests recognized that beavers "are the best money of the country" (LeJeune 1640, in Kenton 1:427). At Sillery, for instance, the order had maintained a large warehouse where it stored furs and hides until they were ready for shipment to France (JR 30:187). When French merchants no longer found it profitable to anchor at their customary rendezvous, these sites lost their appeal for Mi'kmaq hunting bands who were searching for traders to do business with. When Frenchmen and Mi'kmaqs failed to show up to trade each spring and summer, missionaries were left with empty chapels. Moreover, some Jesuit missions could not function without revenues from the fur trade. After the 1660s the Mi'kmaq were rarely visited by Black Robes. With the exception of the Mission of the Good Shepherd, a short-lived (1676–1679) Jesuit post for Mi'kmaqs and Maliseets in the seigneury of Rivière-du-Loup, east of Quebec, Jesuits focused most of their attention on saving Indian souls in the interior (JR 60:264–65; Dragon, 110–12).

RECOLLET MISSION AT GASPÉ (1673–1690)

After evacuating Canada in 1629, Franciscan Recollets were not invited to return until 1669, when French officials felt that the Recollets were needed to offset the increasing power and growing unpopularity of the Jesuit order. Soon there were about 16 Recollets in Canada—four at colonial headquarters in Quebec, the others scattered among various outlying missions, including those on the northern coast of Mi'kmaq country (LeClercq, 203, 404–05). Louis de Buade, the Count of Frontenac, Canada's new governor, directed two priests to stay at the seigneury of Pierre Denys, who had just been granted the exclusive rights to operate a trading post and fishing station at Isle Percée off the eastern tip of Gaspé Peninsula. One priest attended primarily to the spiritual needs of the local French community and the seasonal fishermen at Isle Percée, while the other took care of the Mi'kmaq mission. The latter, Chrestien LeClercq, was a 45-year-old monk from the Recollet monastery at Arras. Arriving in 1675, he stayed the winter of 1676 at Pierre Denys's mainland residence, trying to learn the Mi'kmaq language. That spring he went to a nearby seasonal Mi'kmaq campsite. In time, as Father LeClercq later wrote in his memoirs, he was adopted by a Mi'kmaq family, whose headman "called himself my father" (LeClercq, 321). Apparently this family had ties to Restigouche at the head of Chaleur Bay, and there LeClercq spent the summer. Aware that Indians in this region had been exposed to earlier missionary activity, the priest was not surprised to find that quite a few Mi'kmaqs had already been baptized (LeClercq, 92).

That autumn LeClercq left Restigouche and arrived at Nepisiguit, "one of the most charming places in all the great Bay" (LeClercq, 161). Although the seigneury belonged to Pierre Denys's cousin, Richard Denys, the estate was taken care of by Philippe Enault, who "cultivates the soil there with success, and harvests wheat more than sufficient for the support of his [Mi'kmaq wife and children]" (LeClercq, 163). Near the French house stood a Mi'kmaq winter camp that included some who had become Christians. Noting that the local chapel, dedicated to the Holy Virgin, had been built by earlier Jesuit missionaries, LeClercq reflected: "It is true that a number of our [Mi'kmaqs] wish at present to be instructed, asking Baptism; and they even seem on the surface to be pretty good Christians after having been baptized. They are zealous for the usual morning and evening prayers, modest in the churches, and given to confessing their sins in order to approach worthily the Holy Communion. But it can be said that the number is very small of those who live according to the rules of Christianity [that is, are "civilized"], and who do not fall back into the irregularities of a brutal and wild life" (LeClercq, 193).

Father LeClercq remained at Nepisiguit until early winter, then decided to visit Richard Denys at his Fort de Fronsac on the bank of the Miramichi river, some 50 miles due south. Before he left, the local Mi'kmaqs "assisted devoutly at the prayers, which we offered in the early morning to invoke the aid of the Guardian Angels of this country, and to ask of God the conversion of the [Miramichi Mi'kmaqs] to whom I was going, for the first time, to proclaim the truths of our holy religion" (LeClercq, 163–64).

Guided by a 55-five-year-old Mi'kmaq named Ejougouloumouet and his wife, Father LeClercq and Enault walked through the vast icy forest to Fort de Fronsac. During his stay at this heavily fortified trading post, hosted by Denys and (if already married) his Mi'kmaq wife, Anne Patarabego, LeClercq had ample opportunity to meet with Mi'kmaq trappers who came to the fort to sell their furs. Then, in the early summer of 1677, he decided to visit Quebec, where his order maintained a residence.

That year LeClercq decided to establish his new mission headquarters at Restigouche, building a chapel (no doubt a modest bark structure) "which they called the Wigwam of Jesus" (LeClercq, 129, 134). But during the next few years, keeping up with his migratory flock, he continued his wanderings in the Chaleur Bay region, alternating between Mi'kmaq encampments, periodic stays with French seigneurs, visits with other missionaries at fishing stations, and sojourns to Quebec, where he resided at the convent to recover from his labors. Reading his memoirs, one becomes aware of the challenges he faced in trying to convert the Mi'kmaqs to Christianity. Often depressed, complaining about "their indifference, superstition, and drunkenness," he seriously "questioned whether it was worth his while to waste his strength longer in so fruitless a field" (Ganong, in LeClercq, 5–6).

After a missionary stopover at Miramichi in 1679 LeClercq concluded that he needed to change his approach:

Mi'kmaqs arrive at the Miramichi River mission, where a Franciscan priest officiates at the Holy Mass. Note the "rough water" style of Mi'kmaq canoes. This ink drawing was probably made by Father Chrestien LeClercq as an illustration for his 1691 book on the "Gaspesians" (Mi'kmaqs).

The wandering and vagabond life of these [Mi'kmaq] peoples being unquestionably one of the chief obstacles to their conversion, I solicited Monsieur Denys de Fronsac to grant us [Recollets] a tract of land at Nipisiguit suitable for the cultivation of the soil, in order that we might render the Indians sedentary, settle them down, and civilize them among us. This Seigneur, who desired passionately to see Christianity established in that vast extent of country which he possessed, favoured the idea with pleasure. He had made the principal persons of our Indians accept the proposal, and form the resolution to do it.

(LeClercq, 205)

Because Mi'kmaqs remained committed to their free-ranging lifestyle, it is hardly surprising that Father LeClercq's hopes did not come to fruition. For several years, it seems, he continued his wanderings between Mi'kmaq camps and French settlements. Meanwhile, the fellow Recollet who had come to Acadia with LeClercq in 1675 had remained at the seigneury of Pierre Denys, attending to the spiritual needs of the local French community and seasonal fishermen at the eastern tip of Gaspé Peninsula, including Isle Percée. He left this post in 1683, and soon thereafter LeClercq went there. In 1686, visiting Denys's fishing station at Isle Percée, he dedicated the island's first church to St. Peter: "The Church of this Mission was dedicated to the Prince of the

Apostles, and the ceremony that was performed for that purpose came near costing me my life. For in order to render the ceremony more notable, more formal, and more magnificent, I had embarked in a canoe, with three or four Indians, for the purpose of taking to the church everything which I could find in the way of ornaments, when bad weather surprised [and capsized] us." LeClercq and his cohorts were saved by Mi'kmaqs who had witnessed their mishap from a shore campsite. The rescuers were duly rewarded: "Our French captains were pleased to recognise by their feasts, and by the presents which they bestowed generously upon all of these Indians, the good services which the latter had just rendered to their missionaries" (LeClercq, 73–74).

The next year LeClercq left Mi'kmaq country for good, returning to France to become superior of a Franciscan monastery (LeClercq, 9). There he penned a detailed memoir of his experiences among the Mi'kmaqs, entitled *New Relation of Gaspesia: With the Customs and Religion of the Gaspesian Indians.* A year before the 1691 publication of this book, Dutch and English privateers attacked French settlements from Cape Breton to Gaspé Peninsula, destroying the churches, chapels, houses, trading posts, and fishing stations (LeClercq, 13, 71, n.l). One Recollet priest witnessed and described the rampage of these Protestant raiders:

> They robbed, ravaged, and burnt the houses of the residents, who number at least eight to ten families . . . our church, . . . they used as a guard-house and as a place of debauchery. Animated by the same spirit as the iconoclasts, they shattered our images, trampled them under foot, and hurled against them a thousand imprecations with curses and insults, as if they had been living beings. The pictures of the Holy Virgin and of Saint Peter were not exempt from their fury, nor from their passion, for both of these were riddled with more than a hundred and fifty gun shots. . . . Not a cross escaped their fury . . . . these heretics [then] drank from our chalices their bumpers to the health of the Prince of Orange [King William III of England and Stadtholder of the Dutch Republic].
>
> (LeClercq, 69–71)

After the French Catholic missions in northern Mi'kmaq country were destroyed, the priest who wrote the above description boarded a ship homeward bound—only to be attacked at sea by a Dutch privateer (LeClercq, 66). These were dangerous times for all.

BAPTISM AS ALLIANCE RITUAL

Among the first French settlers of Port Royal was the young lawyer Marc Lescarbot, who described in detail what happened in the fledgling colony. From his writings (1610, 1612), as well as other sources, we know that it was fairly common for Mi'kmaqs involved in the fur trade to be known by European names—usually bestowed by their European trading partners. The names were not always flattering. For instance, the eldest son of Chief Membertou, whose band camped seasonally near Port Royal, was called Judas (JR 1:109). Many of the names were Christian, and Lescarbot (and others), perhaps out of piety, disapproved of the casual way the French were giving Christian names to Mi'kmaq "infidels" (Lescarbot 3:81 82).

With the arrival of Catholic priests in Mi'kmaq country, the French tried to regulate name-giving by linking it to baptism. As far as Christians in Europe were concerned, this ceremony was (and is) highly significant: Water that has been blessed is sprinkled over one's head as a symbol of spiritual purification and admission into the church. Assuming responsibility for a child's faith, or that of an adult convert, a respected church member serves as sponsor and is designated a godparent. As a token of new Christian identity, the baptized person is given a new name, often the sponsor's name or the name of that particular day's patron saint.

Although several Mi'kmaqs who ventured to France aboard French vessels in the 16th and 17th centuries had been subjected to baptism while abroad, Chief Membertou was probably the first Mi'kmaq to undergo it at home (JR 1:77). On the day of St. John the Baptist, 24 June 1610, he and his relatives were baptized by Father Fleche in the small chapel at Port Royal. Commander Poutrincourt named the old Mi'kmaq chieftain Henri, after the French king. Membertou's wife, sponsored by Poutrincourt "in the name of the Queen, was named Marie, after her." Next in line came their oldest son Membertoucoichis, alias Judas, who was named after French Crown Prince Louis. Then came Actaudin, Membertou's second son, named Paul after the pope in Rome, followed by Membertou's grandchildren: A 13-year-old girl named Christine after the oldest princess, an 11-year-old girl named Elizabeth after the younger princess, a 5-year-old boy named Jean after Poutrincourt himself, another little girl named Claude in honor of his wife, a fourth named Catherine after his mother, a fifth named Jeanne after one of his daughters, and a sixth named Charlotte after a French lady. In total, 21 Mi'kmaqs were baptized that day: "And thus to each one was given the name of some illustrious or notable personage here in France" (JR 1:77, 108–13). Called "the Patriarch," Father Fleche baptized in total about 80 Indians that year (JR 3:147, 165).

What did Mi'kmaqs make of this colorful ceremony? Because the French had "not yet succeeded in translating into the native language the common creed or symbol, the Lord's prayer, the commandments of God, the Sacraments, and other principles quite necessary to the making of a Christian," and because Father Fleche had "not been able to instruct them as he would have wished, because he did not know the language, and had nothing with which to support them," the answer is obvious: The Mi'kmaqs had no clue about the ceremony's religious significance (JR 1:161–63). Moreover, because they had no concept of sin (in the sense of violating a Christian law or moral principle), the idea of washing sin away was utterly meaningless.

Meanwhile, some orthodox Catholics in France condemned news of this "wholesale baptism" of the Mi'kmaqs as "profanation" (JR 1:311). When Poutrincourt's son, Charles de Biencourt, arrived in Port Royal from France in 1611, his ship carried two Jesuit priests, Pierre Biard and Enemond Massé. After visiting some of the newly baptized Mi'kmaqs, Biard belittled the secular priest's accomplishments. Despite baptism, he noted, the Indians "keep up the same manners and traditions and mode of life, the same dances and rites and songs and sorcery; in fact all their previous customs" (JR 2:89). The Jesuit found it "rather amusing that, when I asked them if they were Christians, they did not know what I meant; when I asked them if they had been baptized, they answered . . . 'Yes, the Patriarch has made us like the [French]'" (JR 1:161–63).

This is not to say that the Mi'kmaqs viewed baptism as a meaningless ritual, but rather they attached their own significations to this cultural construct. To them, baptism was an exotic kin-making custom, a dramatic spectacle in which they obtained a French partner, someone to call upon in times of need. Belonging to a kin-ordered society, they appreciated the idea of turning potentially dangerous strangers into relatives. In other words, such fictive kinship ties represented an exciting opportunity to expand their personal network across the ethnic divide. The French were certainly aware of this. Reporting to his superiors in France, Biard wrote: "They accepted baptism as a sort of sacred pledge of friendship and alliance with the French" (JR 2:89).

Whatever its significance, baptism became popular among the Mi'kmaq and neighboring tribes as well. As a ritual, it not only confirmed their friendship with the French, but it also reinforced their trade relations and, ideally, secured armed support against enemies. Through baptism and renaming ceremonies, new corporate identities were constructed. For instance, when a Huron Indian came to Quebec to be baptized, Canada's Governor Charles de Montmagny, a Knight of Malta, served as his godfather. Thanking the French nobleman for having given him his name, the warrior spoke: "The name you have given me is a rich present, it is an obligation that is peculiar to me, and which I shall feel all my life. This gun which you have added will make a great talk in our country" (JR 20:221). After the ceremony, an Algonkin headman at the Catholic mission village at Sillery told the newly named Charles: "My brother, all the [Indians] whom thou seest around thee are Christians. . . . Yes, thou art now so, we have henceforth but one Father, who is God, and but one common Mother, which is the Church; behold, then, thy Brothers who declare to thee, that thy friends are their friends, and that thy enemies are their enemies" (JR 20:221).

Beyond kin recruitment, baptism was seen as a magic ritual. Impressed that the French were much less likely to catch their death from disease, Mi'kmaqs conjectured that the French holy water ritual might offer protection. As a Jesuit reported from Miscou in 1644: "The principal men among them [Mi'kmaqs at Chaleur Bay and Miramichi River] . . . although they are infidels, are anxious to procure Baptism for their sick; they promptly inform us as soon as they see anyone in danger [of dying], and beg us to go and baptize them" (JR 28:31).

As alliance ritual, baptism became of particular importance during the intertribal conflicts known as the Beaver Wars (see Chapter 8). In this period, Christianized Mi'kmaqs could link up to a much wider network of Catholic missions and tap into a far-flung support system that bound all "French Indians" together in a common league. Occasional calls to native encampments by French missionaries and the founding of Indian mission villages with a resident priest cemented relations even further. Threatened by this united front, New England Protestants bitterly accused the French of religious exploitation, saying that the Indians were told that Jesus Christ "was a Frenchman and that the English murdered Him" (Cotton Mather, in Silverman, 238).

CULTURAL RESISTANCE: PERSISTENCE OF SHAMANIC BELIEFS

Spiritually and economically vulnerable in the vast wake of the Great Dying, Mi'kmaqs did adopt some of the new magic ceremonies and ritual objects and incorporate many Christian ritual elements into their culture. Still, the French missionaries ran into many obstacles in their conversion efforts. Beyond disregard or indifference, they sometimes faced active resistance. Typically the priests attributed Mi'kmaq obstinacy to the devil, but they also placed ample blame on their own compatriots for fostering alcohol abuse and other vices. In particular, they denounced French sailors and fishermen for their moral turpitude and "their bad example in the execrable blasphemies which they launched against Him whom the angels adore in Heaven" (LeClercq, 252–53).

Priests noticed that many Mi'kmaqs viewed French claims of spiritual primacy critically: "Our [Mi'kmaqs] have enough malice to say to the missionaries that these have not much sense to disapprove of their blowing on their sick, because the missionaries themselves make breathings when they baptize children, and that if the patriarchs have the intention of chasing out the Devil, or sin, by their breathings and their exorcisms, the Indians have also no other design than to chase out the germ, or the Devil, from the body of the sick man" (LeClercq, 220).

It was not unusual for Mi'kmaqs to merge the new and the old, developing a form of religious syncretism. When Mi'kmaq shamanic tradition blended with French Catholicism, the sun was thought of as the Father in Heaven, and Grandmother Moon had become associated with the Virgin Mary. Later in time some began to equate the culture hero Klu'skap with the Messiah, the Christian redeemer. In other cases, Klu'skap became associated with the biblical patriarch Noah, who built the ark to survive the flood, sending out a white dove that returned to him colored black, as a raven. Father LeClercq (229) discussed aspects of such religious hybridization in his writings:

> As our [Mi'kmaq] Indians perceive that much honour is accorded to the missionaries, and that they have given themselves in respect and reverence the title of Patriarch, some of these barbarians have often been seen meddling with, and affecting to perform, the office and functions of missionary, even to hearing confession, like us, from their fellow countrymen. So therefore, when persons of this kind wish to give authority to that which they say, and to set themselves up as patriarch, they make our Gaspesians [Mi'kmaqs] believe that they have received some particular gift from heaven. . . . It is a surprising thing that this ambition to act the patriarch does not only prevail among the men, but even the women meddle therewith.
> These, in usurping the quality and name of religieuses, say certain prayers in their own fashion, and affect a manner of living more reserved than that of the commonality of Indians, who allow themselves to be dazzled by the glamour of a false and ridiculous devotion. They look upon these women as extraordinary persons, whom they believe to hold. . .communication with the sun, which they have all adored as their divinity.

The priest went on to provide an example of a particular Mi'kmaq woman:

> Not long ago, we had a famous one of them who, by her extravagant superstitions, encouraged the same in these poor Indians. . . . This aged woman [born about 1560 and residing in the Miramichi region], who counted more than a hundred and fourteen years since her birth, had as the basis for all her ridiculous and superstitious devotions, some beads of jet, which were the remains of an unthreaded rosary. These she carefully preserved, and gave them only to those who were her friends,

protesting to them, meanwhile, that the gift which she gave them had come originally from heaven . . . "I have only, then," said she to them, "to hold up my hand and to open it, in order to bring down from heaven these mysterious beads, which have the power and the property not only of succouring the Indians in their sicknesses and all their most pressing necessities, but also of preserving them from surprise, from persecution, and from the fury of their enemies." . . . Some of our French, who had been in the [wikuom] of this aged [Mi'kmaq] woman, assured me that she held also in singular veneration a King of Hearts, the foot of a glass, and a kind of medal, and that she worshipped these trifles with so much respect that she prostrated herself before them as before her divinities . . . [Within her wikuom she had reserved a special place for a cross,] which she had beautified with beadwork, wampum, painting, and porcupine quills. The pleasing mixture thereof represented several and separate figures of everything which was in her devotions. She placed it usually between her and the French, obliging them to make their prayers before her cross, whilst from her side she made her own prayers, according to her custom, before her King of Hearts and her other divinities. These the Indians buried with her after her death, convinced as they were that she would go to be a patriarch in . . . the Land of Souls.

(LeClercq, 229–30, 232–33)

CULTURAL ACCOMMODATION: FROM GUARDIAN SPIRIT TO PATRON SAINT

In the battle for souls, the priests competed against the shamans for spiritual dominance and constantly undermined their rivals by ridiculing them as sorcerers, witches, charlatans, frauds, or jugglers. They also discredited native beliefs in traditional guardian spirits and spiritual forces, including *mntu,* which they depicted as a demon or evil spirit. Yet by renaming and reinterpreting native spiritual concepts, missionaries absorbed them into French Catholic religion. Gradually, open resistance to the Black Robes and Bare Feet wore away (JR 35:228–29, 231, 241). Mi'kmaqs began to consecrate their marriages according to Catholic ritual. As a French physician familiar with the Mi'kmaq observed about 1700: "They are now well-enough instructed in their duty to know that, without this ceremony, the marriage has no validity, & I have even seen some who have come from a great distance in order to receive this Sacrament from the Curé [parish priest] of Port Royal, & I have even seen those who had been married in the Indian fashion renew their vows before our Altars" (Diereville, 143–44).

In the process of replacing native shaman-chiefs, French priests not only took on their social role as spiritual guides and healers, but they also transformed guardian spirits into patron saints. According to Catholic doctrine, saints are persons living in heaven. They are asked to pray to God for a favor sought. The chief saint is the Virgin Mary. Next in importance are the angels, as well as Mary's mother Anne, Mary's husband, Joseph, and the apostles. In addition, there are the numerous Christian martyrs who have been declared saints in the course of time. According to French Catholic tradition, each member of the church has at least one patron saint from baptism, and another may be adopted at confirmation. These patron saints have a mutual relation of affection with their earthly clients, who may turn to them for help. Typically, a saint is commemorated on a special day ("saint's day") when his or her intercession is sought. A pilgrimage and annual celebration may be organized to honor a patron saint (Bridgwater and Sherwood, 1731).

Seeking divine blessings, seventeenth-century priests typically dedicated their particular mission post, chapel, or church to a specific patron saint whose special protection and divine intervention were sought. For instance, the first Jesuit mission for the Mi'kmaqs, established on Mount Desert Island in 1613, was named and dedicated to the Holy Savior (St. Sauveur). Twenty years later, when Jesuits established a mission on Cape Breton Island, they honored their patroness, Anne of Austria, queen mother of France, by dedicating their chapel to her patron, St. Anne. Because this island was named for the Breton fishermen who first ventured there a century earlier, the decision to honor Queen Anne, who was also the patroness of French Britanny, made all the more sense. In this historic moment lies the original St. Anne's Mission, an annual ceremony still celebrated at Cape Breton among Mi'kmaqs today.

St. Anne's was soon followed by another mission at Miscou Island, dedicated to St. Charles, and one at Nepisiguit, dedicated to St. Mary, the Holy Virgin (Wallis and Wallis 1955:183). That same century, Franciscans dedicated their church at Isle Percée to St. Peter. Others honored St. Louis, and so forth. These examples represent just a handful of the patron saints once honored by the French in Mi'kmaq country.

Converted to Catholicism, Mi'kmaqs originally participated in the devotions to the patron saint of a particular mission, chapel, or church they attended, thus honoring St. Charles, St. Louis, St. Peter, and so forth. Although St. Anne was of particular significance to Mi'kmaq converts at Cape Breton, it appears that she did not have such a venerated position in southern Nova Scotia, the Miramichi Valley or Chaleur Bay. Indeed, there is no evidence that this patron saint was of any particular significance to Mi'kmaqs in general before the 1700s. This changed during the mid-18th century, when St. Anne emerged as the major patron saint of all Catholic Mi'kmaqs. Her feast day is still celebrated 26 July, when Mi'kmaqs make pilgrimages to shrines that honor her. Kneeling before this "grandmother" saint, typically portrayed with a golden crown on her head and the child Mary cradled in her right arm, Indian pilgrims pray for her intercession on behalf of themselves and their loved ones.

MI'KMAQ HIEROGLYPHS: WRITING AS RELIGIOUS AGENCY

As an oral culture, Mi'kmaqs did not develop literacy until the 17th century, when a hieroglyphic system emerged, dealing primarily with the teachings of Christianity. Although it remains unclear who devised the system, which appears to be based on indigenous practice, Father LeClercq was the first to document this form of picture-writing among the Mi'kmaq of Restigouche (see also Schmidt, 1993). In his 1691 memoirs the priest explained:

> Our Lord inspired me with the idea of them the second year of my mission [1677], when, being much embarrassed as to the method by which I should teach the Indians

to pray to God, I noticed that some children were making marks with charcoal upon birch-bark, and were counting these with the finger very accurately at each word of the prayers which they pronounced. This made me believe that by giving them some formulary, which would aid their memory by definite characters, I should advance much more quickly. (131; cf. 126, 130)

Whereas Mi'kmaqs had been reluctant to learn conventional French orthography, they demonstrated no such opposition toward these word pictures, which they still call *komqwejvikasik* or *abutalvikasik* ("it is written with curves"; Wilfred Prosper, p.c.). According to LeClercq (126–27):

They have so much readiness in understanding [these leaflets], which they call . . . Kateguenne [*Wi'katikn,* Mi'kmaq for "book"]. They preserve these instructive papers with so much care . . . that they keep them very neatly in little cases of birch-bark bedecked with wampum, with beadwork, and with porcupine quills. They hold them between their hands, as we do our prayerbooks, during the Holy Mass, after which they shut them up again in their cases. . . . Admiration has often and justly been expressed in our monastery at Quebec for a little [Mi'kmaq] child about seven years of age, who read distinctly in his book the prayers that I had taught him.

French missionary teaching Mi'kmaqs their catechism by means of hieroglyphs. This ink drawing was probably made by Father Chrestien LeClercq as an illustration for his 1691 book on the "Gaspesians" (Mi'kmaqs).

Because these leaflets contained "the prayer of Jesus," Christian Mi'kmaqs regarded the hieroglyphs on each page as sacred. As LeClercq (133) noted, "Our [Mi'kmaqs] have so much veneration and respect for these characters that they scruple [hesitate] to throw them into the fire. When these are torn or spoiled they bring the fragments to me."

The priest commented on how the Mi'kmaqs quickly adopted this religious picture script:

> How agreeably I was surprised . . . when, wishing to present some of my [instructional religious] papers to certain Indians who had come from a long distance on purpose to be instructed [at Restigouche], I found that they could already decipher the characters with as much ease as if they had always lived among us. This was because some whom I had formerly instructed had returned to their homes and had taught the others, thus performing, in regard to them, the office of missionary. . . . It is easy then, from this, to judge the utility of these characters for a missionary who wishes to garner much fruit in a little time through all the extent of his district.
>
> (LeClercq, 130)

For the next three centuries the Catholic church remained a major force in Mi'kmaq life, and its ceremonies are now enmeshed with Mi'kmaq culture. Yet the church's role has been an ambiguous one—helping to undermine traditional Mi'kmaq beliefs and customs while providing the Mi'kmaq with a new religious foundation that enabled them to cope with the changing political-economic order in their world.

7 / Accommodation and Resistance: Mi'kmaq Life in the Colonial Period

COMMERCIAL FISHERIES

Throughout the colonial period Mi'kmaqs continued to be in regular contact with European mariners who annually crossed the Atlantic to fish at the banks off Newfoundland, Nova Scotia, and Maine. Thousands of commercial fishermen, coming in hundreds of vessels from many European harbors, worked along the Mi'kmaq coast between March and October. Until well into the 18th century, fishermen outnumbered not only the Mi'kmaq, but also French Acadian settlers (in AN 1:180–81). Although few Mi'kmaqs participated directly in the fishing industry, many were personally familiar with the crews, as fishers commonly bartered for furs on the side. Typically, Mi'kmaq hunters paddled out to the vessels riding at anchor or dropped in at the fishing stations to trade furs for food, cloth, steel tools and weapons, and, if possible, firearms. More often than not, the hard-drinking fishermen also offered beer, wine, brandy, gin or rum for trade. Although these activities were rarely documented, it is obvious that, given their numbers and their early and ongoing visits to Mi'kmaq country, fishermen played a highly significant role in the cultural changes and social upheavals that took place among Mi'kmaqs.

"Dry" fisheries (in which the catch was taken ashore and dried before being transported to Europe) had a more direct impact on the Mi'kmaq way of life because they were operated from a shore base and required larger crews than "wet" fisheries (in which the catch was salted on board and taken directly back to Europe). Usually two or three dry fishery ships anchored in a single bay or cove, although there were often many more (N. Denys, 222). Upon arriving each spring and anchoring ship, crews rowed ashore in small shallops and "set to work at the lodging for the fishermen, which is like a hall covered with a ship's sail. The sides at the bottom all around are lined with branches of Fir, interlaced into pickets or stakes of four to five feet driven into the ground" (N. Denys, 280). From the mid-1600s onward, the more established shore fisheries had sprawling infrastructures on the beaches of the mainland and adjacent islands—housing for seasonal shoremen; buildings to store gear, supplies, and fish; dozens of stages for loading or unloading vessels, and acres of flakes for drying them (Clark, 228). From these coastal stations, crews sailed to the offshore banks, where they dropped and hauled their lines and cleaned and salted the fish. Then they sailed back toward shore, unloaded the catch, and laid the fish out to dry on a clean gravel beach or on the roughly constructed stagings known as flakes. For several weeks a "rather elaborate process of repiling and respreading went on until the fish were completely hardened and cured" (Clark, 22). The number of fishermen in one place was often considerable—and their trade goods could attract sizeable Indian communities. For instance, records show that some 200 French Breton and Basque fishermen summered regularly near a band of 300 Indians at one of the Isles de la Madeleine fishing stations (Hakluyt 8:169; Martijn, 163–174).

During the fishing season, special transport ("sack") ships came from Europe, bringing the fishermen new supplies, including salt. In return, they carried cargoes of cured fish, often directly to major markets in France, Spain and Portugal. From the mid-1600s onward, New England fishing vessels ("ketches") also frequented the banks. For Massachusetts Colony, the cod fishery quickly became a staple. By 1664, its fleet had grown to 1,300 fishing vessels, and about 300 merchant ships. The colony exported fish, a cheap source of animal protein, not only to southern Europe, but also to the Caribbean, where poor quality cod and mackerel were sold as food for plantation slaves (CSP 3:532).

French "dry" cod fishers like these were stationed on the Mi'kmaq coast since the sixteenth century. Detail from a 1698 map by Nicholas de Fer.

MI'KMAQ-FRENCH SYMBIOSIS: A DUAL SOCIETY IN
COLONIAL ACADIA

In 1679 French settlers numbered about 9,400 in Canada and 515 in Acadia—not counting the many thousands of seasonal fishermen discussed earlier. During the next decade the French colonial population in Acadia doubled (PD 1:136). While the French grew in number, the Mi'kmaq declined, reaching a demographic nadir of about 2,000 by the end of the 1600s (Bock 1978:117). By that time French Acadians probably outnumbered the Mi'kmaqs in Nova Scotia, and during the next fifty years they increased tenfold.

Mi'kmaq losses due to diseases and violence forced the scattered clusters of survivors to regroup and form new composite bands that were about one quarter the size of their precontact kin-groups. Typically, these new bands averaged less than 50 individuals. They fluctuated in size according to season and opportunity, ranging from only a dozen members to about 500. For example, in the Nova Scotia region at this time some 438 Mi'kmaqs were divided into twelve small groups, each with a modest number of warriors:

Bands	Warriors	Totals
Isle St. Pierre (off Newfoundland)	25	77
Cape Breton Island	12	52
Canso (northeast tip of mainland Nova Scotia)	3	13
Chedabucto (Guysborough)	12	52
Chebucto (Halifax Harbour)	7	33
La Hève (La Have)	10	48
Mirliguech (Lunenburg Bay)	4	11
Port Rochelois (near Cape Negro)	6	21
Cape Sable (southern tip of Nova Scotia)	6	24
Port Royal (Annapolis)	9	36
Minas (upper Bay of Fundy)	15	50
Chignecto (at the Isthmus)	4	21
Totals	113	438

(Gargas, 1688, in AN 1:143–60)

As these low numbers indicate, the political power of Mi'kmaqs in their ancestral domain was tenuous at best. At times bands camped in the vicinity of a French farming village, seigneurial estate, fur trading post, or fishing station. For strategic reasons, political as well as military, French colonial authorities tried to consolidate these diffused and wide-ranging bands into permanent settlements centered around a mission post (PD 3:278–79; cf, PD 1:150). For example, in 1689 Richard Denys reported from his seigneury at Miramichi that he had "seated two villages of Indians near his establishments, one in the Baye des Chaleurs [Restigouche] of 60 families and about 400 souls, the other at Miramichy of 80 wigwams or families of 500 souls" (CNBHS III/1:37–40). However, these two "villages" were large summer settlements at best, occupied for little more than a few weeks. Clearly, Mi'kmaqs preferred their customary way of life and resisted outside control.

Most of the colonists who came from France to Mi'kmaq country settled down as small-scale farmers. Known as "Acadians," they built their homesteads near tidally flooded lands that were of little importance to the Mi'kmaq. In addition to cultivating wheat, rye, barley, oats, peas, and cabbage, they kept some livestock—pigs, sheep, goats, and chickens (and later horses and cows). As was the custom in rural France, they supplemented these farming activities with occasional hunting and fishing. Furthermore, they sometimes bartered goods and services with Mi'kmaqs. Village blacksmiths repaired the Mi'kmaqs' broken muskets or sharpened their knives and axes, and farmers gave them some surplus produce—in exchange for beavers and other furs, moose hides, smoked meat and fish, bags of feathers and down, or services as guides and long-distance messengers. For the hardscrabble Acadians, many of whom lived "in the most abject misery," bartering with Mi'kmaq trappers was vital to survival. Furs were the only trade items they had access to that had international exchange value. Without furs, these French peasants had little to offer merchants from abroad, whose trade goods they needed to get by (PD 1:165–66).

The Mi'kmaq, in turn, needed the Acadians. Although there can be little doubt that Mi'kmaqs would have preferred their traditional autonomy, their survival after the stunning socioeconomic shift caused by the Great Dying required accommodations to the influx of Europeans on their shores (Clark, 361). A symbiotic relationship emerged. As one historian noted: "European artifacts, if not European technology, became very important to the Indians, and in dozens of ways the Acadians learned from the Mi'kmaq— in hunting, fishing, and fowling, in the making and use of canoes, the fabrication of clothing, especially footgear, from fur and skin, and the use of native plants for food, herbal remedies, and dyes" (Clark, 377). Indeed, with each succeeding year Mi'kmaqs found themselves more intricately connected to their new French Acadian neighbors— connected by geography, trade interests, missionary activities, blood ties born of intermarriage, and the mutual need for protection against outside enemies (Clark, 361).

CULTURAL MÉLANGE: BLENDING THE NEW WITH THE OLD

As they had done for centuries, after the arrival of Europeans Mi'kmaqs hunted moose, deer, seals, ducks, and geese, fished for salmon, and harvested berries, roots, and nuts. But in addition to subsistence foraging, many turned to commercial trapping (especially fur-bearing animals) to obtain trade goods. Some men specialized as seal and walrus hunters, selling oil, hides, and ivory to European merchants. Only a few became active in European fisheries, and fewer still felt attracted to tilling the soil. Obeying bosses and staying in one place to farm were hardly the occupational dreams of Mi'kmaqs. Toward the end of the 17th century many turned to ethnic soldiering, fighting against the English with the French. Sometimes they earned bounties for taking prisoners or scalps. (This controversial issue is discussed in Chapter 9) Other times they received commodities simply for refusing to oppose French troops or for resisting English efforts to win them over as allies.

Although the French government made repeated efforts to settle them in permanent villages, Mi'kmaqs continued to be highly mobile. They still traveled rivers and coastlines in birch-bark canoes—with their hunting dogs aboard, plus spruce gum, strands of spruce root, and rolls of birch bark to repair the boats. But now, instead of skin or birch-bark sails, they sometimes hoisted sails made of European blankets or canvas. And, at open sea, they now preferred small sailing sloops or *shallops,* first acquired from Europeans in the late 1500s (Grace, 27, 30). As a French fur trader long active among the Mi'kmaq explained, "These they sometimes buy from the Captains who are about to leave after having completed their fishery; but the greater part they take from the places in which the Captains have had them hidden on the coast or in the ponds, in order to make use of them on another voyage" (N. Denys, 196–97; cf. JR 47:213). Convenient at open sea and carrying more freight than birch-bark canoes, shallops ranged in size (length, 18–30 ft.; breadth, 6–8 ft.; depth, 2–4 ft.; capacity, 2–10 tons). Akin to Basque whaleboats, Mi'kmaq shallops carried a single square sail made of moose hide or canvas on a mast stepped about amidships. With a crew of up to 15, they could also be rowed with oars. Shallops became so common among Mi'kmaqs that Nicolas Denys (196–97) remarked in 1672, "All have boats [shallops] for the sea." Indeed, there seems to have been no shortage of these small boats, for Mi'kmaqs occasionally sold them to New England fishermen (Winthrop 2:377). Several Frenchmen, witnessing Mi'kmaq mariners sailing shallops, commented on their seamanship. In the words of one: "They handle them as skillfully as our most courageous and active Sailors of France" (JR 47:213). According to another: "It is wonderful how these Indian mariners navigate so far in little shallops, crossing vast seas without compass, and often without sight of the Sun, trusting their instinct for their guidance" (JR 45:65). It was even said that Mi'kmaqs outsailed the French Bretons, navigating enormous distances from the St. Lawrence River up to Newfoundland and down south from the Bay of Fundy into the Gulf of Maine and beyond (JR 30:137, 179; JR 4:244–45).

Mi'kmaqs continued to live in birch-bark wikuoms and to use fir boughs to cover the ground in these dwellings. But some now laid blankets instead of skins over the bough floor. Only a few favored French-style houses. In the early 1640s, for example, several native families residing near the Jesuit mission at Miscou Island hired French workmen "to help them build small dwellings," paying them "for their work in furs" (JR 22:241; JR 30:129; JR 32:41). But, given their migratory way of life, most saw these dwellings as impractical and confining. A priest familiar with the Mi'kmaqs in the Chaleur Bay area noted, "the Indians esteem their camps as much as, and even more than, they do the most superb and commodious of our houses." One Mi'kmaq chief, after listening patiently to a French exhortation that Indians should adopt European housing, responded,

> I am greatly astonished that the French have so little cleverness . . . [trying] to persuade us to convert our poles, our barks, and our [wikuoms] into those houses of stone and of wood which are tall and lofty. . . . [Why] do men of five to six feet in height need houses which are sixty to eighty? . . . My brother, hast thou as much ingenuity and cleverness as the Indians, who carry their houses and their [wikuoms] with them so that they may lodge wheresoever they please, independently of any seigneur whatsoever.
>
> (LeClercq, 103–04)

Given the extensive dealings that Mi'kmaqs had with European fishermen, merchants, settlers, and missionaries, it is not surprising that many of them were at least bilingual, some even multilingual. Often they were rather fluent in French, while quite a few also knew at least some English and Basque. In addition, many could understand neighboring Algonquian languages, such as Montagnais, Maliseet, and Abenaki. Some even had knowledge of Iroquoian tongues.

With Europeans on their shores, Mi'kmaqs had ample opportunity to purchase foreign commodities, shipped in not only from Western Europe, but also from the Caribbean, Brazil, and even India and China. In exchange for furs (beaver, otter, muskrat), hides (moose, caribou, deer), feathers (goose and eiderdown), oil (fish, seal, walrus, porpoise), and crafts (including beautiful porcupine quillwork), they acquired a wide variety of new and useful goods. As hunters and warriors, they were especially eager to get their hands on European weapons—knives, axes, hatchets, sabres, iron arrow tips, and sword blades that they fastened to their long wooden shafts. Even more significant, they acquired firearms—muskets and pistols, plus powder, ball, and shot. As noted in an earlier chapter, firearms first came into their hands in 1607, when French fur traders offered muskets to Mi'kmaq Chief Membertou (Lescarbot 3:504–06; JR 32:177; JR 24:297). In little more than a decade, neighboring Maliseet and Abenaki on the Maine coast had also gained firearms and could use them with deadly effectiveness.

New weaponry transformed not only the ways in which Mi'kmaqs hunted and waged war, but also their defense strategies. The same year that Chief Membertou acquired firearms, he restyled his residence. Probably using European axes, saws, and nails, and no doubt with the help of French carpenters from Port Royal, he built his lodge "in form of a town surrounded with high palisades" (Lescarbot 2:353–54). Not long after, other Indian warlords in the region followed suit (JR 35:107–11; N. Denys, 195–96).

In addition to arms, Mi'kmaqs purchased cloth, blankets, coats, shirts, and stockings, as well as scissors, needles, and thread, with which they made petticoats and jackets, etc. Of the tradecloth (*poitou serge*), two colors were in great demand— scarlet red and blue. Mi'kmaqs bought canvas to make sails or to pack their furs and other valuables. Sometimes canvas was even used to make trousers (Baxter 23:33–34; Whitehead 1991:179). They also bought cooking kettles (which they sometimes used for drums, stretching deerskins over the top), plus peas, bread, biscuits, butter, salt beef, corn (for a porridge known as *sagamité*), and flour (to make white fry bread known as *lusknikn*). High on their shopping lists were barrels of pork, apples, and molasses (concentrated sugar cane juice imported from the Caribbean) (Grace, 14, 16; Whitehead 1991:129). In addition, they purchased tin mirrors, big black beads, red penny-stones (flat round stones used for games), fine (red) vermillion pigment, alcohol (brandy, rum, wine, etc.), and Brazilian tobacco from French traders or Virginian tobacco from the English (PD 1:216–21). Instead of indigenous stone tobacco pipes, some used European pewter calumets or white clay pipes for smoking (JR 28:167).

Incorporating these imported commodities into their way of life, Mi'kmaqs creatively blended traditional and foreign customs. For instance, although many remained fur-clad, it was fairly typical for them to dress partially in European clothes. According to a French missionary who visited Mi'kmaq country in the early 1600s: "In Summer they often wear our capes, and in Winter our bed-blankets, which they improve with trimming and wear double. They are also quite willing to make use of our hats, shoes, caps, woollens and shirts, and our linen to clean their infants, for we trade them all these commodities for their furs" (JR 3:75–77). Sometimes, after raids against the English, warriors would return from battle in full English outfits, with colorful additions such as "a turban . . . adorned with an extravagant number of beads and feathers of various colours" (in Whitehead 1991:149). On ceremonial occasions, local chiefs or successful trappers could be dressed "for the most part in French style, a shirt of white Holland linen, a neckband of lace, and a scarlet coat" (JR 28:205). For example, when a chieftain from the trading post at Tadoussac visited the French in Quebec in 1636, he arrived "clothed in the French manner, in a very handsome dress under a scarlet overcoat. As he was about to speak he took off his hat, and bowed with much propriety after the French manner" (JR 9:227). Although some Mi'kmaqs adopted French apparel, they didn't discard their traditional clothing. And few, if any, favored French shoes or boots over moccasins when it came to getting about in the woods or in a canoe. Also, Mi'kmaqs continued tattooing their bodies, painting their faces (sometimes in red vermillion or with blue streaks), and smearing their skin and long black hair with seal oil (Maillard, 55; Whitehead 1991:81, 93).

In 1672, reflecting on a forty-year career as a French colonial entrepreneur on the Mi'kmaq coasts, Nicolas Denys (441–43) commented that European commodities had become an "indispensable necessity" to the Mi'kmaq—although they often used them to enhance their traditional lifeways:

> They have abandoned all their own utensils, whether because of the trouble they had as well to make as to use them, or because of the facility of obtaining from us, in exchange for skins which cost them almost nothing. . . . But they practice still all the same methods of hunting with this difference, however, that in place of arming their arrows and spears with the bones of animals, pointed and sharpened, they arm them to-day with iron, which is made of a sword fixed at the end of a shaft of seven to eight feet in length. These they use in winter, when there is snow, to spear the Moose, or for fishing Salmon, Trout and Beaver. They are also furnished with iron harpoon. . . . The musket is used by them more than all other weapons in their hunting in spring, summer, and autumn, both for animals and birds. With the arrow it was necessary to approach an animal closely; with the gun they kill the animal from a distance with a bullet or two. . . .
>
> Above everything the kettle has always seemed to them and seems still, the most valuable article they can obtain from us. . . . The axes, the kettles, the knives and everything that is supplied them, is much more convenient and portable than those which they had in former times, when they were obliged to go to camp near their grotesque [wooden] kettles in place of which today they are free to go and camp where they wish. One can say that in those times the immovable kettles were the chief regulators of their lives, since they were able to live only in places where these were.

THE FUR TRADE: MI'KMAQ MARKET HUNTING

Although fish formed the staple of the colonial economies from Cape Cod to Cape Breton Island, furs remained important. Pelts provided income for French seigneurs and merchants and much-needed revenues for the Crown. Mi'kmaqs, having become dependent on firearms and other trade goods, also had a strong vested interest in the fur trade. Commenting on the value of furs in the colonial economy, a French observer remarked that beaver "are the best money of the country" (in Kenton 1:427). But this vital element in their quest for survival proved to be volatile—subject to fluctuations in the natural environment and in the international market.

No longer self-sufficient, Mi'kmaqs gradually transformed into market hunters, producing pelts for export in exchange for imported commodities. At trading posts, garrisons, and fishing stations they could even get supplies and services on credit: "In each man's account is noted the cost of the work that has been done [in repairing guns and obtaining food and other trade goods]; and what the Indians pay either for the stock of the gun or for the mending," and so forth (Coquart, 439).

Mi'kmaq hunters did not like to incur debts, perhaps because debts pricked their pride as free men. Failure to even up the account suggested that they were inferior to merchants and subject to their control. Moreover, freedom from debt implied that one was a good hunter. As described by one French missionary:

> It is enough among their people to be a good hunter and to pay off one's debts well to merit the name of *virtuosus*, which is expressed in their language as *Tochechkouèg* [toqejkwe'k]. . . . It is just that, to their way of thinking, to be a good hunter and to be meticulous in paying one's debts is the greatest, finest and highest ideal. [They say] "He represents what is best among our people. . . . If we were all like our ancestors in this respect . . . how happy and peaceful the life of all Indians would be. We would never lack for food or clothing. And we would have enough furs to pay for all the supplies, materials, etc., we borrow every autumn. We would be better able to help those among us who can no longer range the forests or manage a canoe, either because of their old age or because of some other impediment."

> (Maillard's letter in Whitehead 1991:105; see also Les Soirées Canadiennes 3[1863]:297)

Yet good hunting skills did not guarantee breaking even with European traders, especially when the market fluctuated. For instance, a French fur trader among the Mi'kmaq noted in 1672 that although fine otter skins "are still much sought, [they are] no longer so dear" (N. Denys, 362). As for beaver, he reported: "Those skins have had formerly a great vogue when the beaver hats were popular, but they are not so much [in fashion] at present" (362–63). Consequently, hunters frequently made purchases that were greater than the value of their furs, and they accumulated significant debts. For example, in the spring of 1685, Captain Negascouet, a Mi'kmaq chieftain in northeast Nova Scotia, took his furs from "his usual residence" at Neguedchecouniedoche to Fort St. Louis, a trading post and fishing station at Chedabucto, to pay off what he owed the French: Seventy moose skins, sixty marten, six otter, and four beaver (Murdoch 1:165).

Mi'kmaq hunters well understood that the number of fur-bearing animals available for trapping was not constant. They also knew about quality and were keenly aware that thick winter pelts were typically the most valuable. Moreover, they did not find it difficult to comprehend why beavers were worth more than muskrats. What they did find puzzling, however, were price fluctuations on the international market. Merchants found it difficult, if not impossible, to explain to them "that the prices of goods were not fix'd, but would frequently change according to the circumstances of the trade" (Baxter 10:398–99). When prices for their furs dropped, and Mi'kmaqs found that they could not get the usual amount of goods, they felt cheated and complained angrily. Sometimes trading post agents received instructions on how to deal with disgruntled Indians: "You must shew them by your invoice that our goods are likewise fallen, especially rum (which is much lower in proportion than beaver . . ." (in Baxter 10:398–99). Commenting on the downside of market hunting, one French Jesuit noted: "These Indians, loaded with debt and despoiled by their creditors, who do not leave them even their guns, are often obliged to abandon the country and to go over to the English, despairing of being able to pay their debts" (in PD 7:882).

Trade dissatisfaction posed serious problems in the wider political arena where European powers elbowed for position. When French authorities tried to dictate where Mi'kmaqs could sell their, furs, they responded, "It is a free trade" and made it clear that they would do business with whomever they pleased (PD 1:144).

Since the early 1600s England increasingly had the edge over France (and the Netherlands) in transatlantic commerce for several reasons: It had more efficient manufacturing structures; it possessed the world's largest shipping fleet and an expansive trade network, which made it possible to transport a greater quantity and variety of goods; and, unlike French ships, which had only seasonal and circuitous access to the colonial headquarters at Quebec by way of the St. Lawrence River (which was frozen for months at a time), English ships had a year-round straight sail from England to Boston and New York.

This given, it is not surprising that records from 1680 show that English merchants offered about twice as much for beavers as their French counterparts did. Plus the French charged two and a half times more than the English for guns (five beavers for a gun), three times as much for lead (three beavers for 40 pounds), and four times as much for gunpowder (four beavers for eight pounds) (NYCD 4:407–08; cf. PD 1:144).

Not only did English merchants offer more attractive prices, but they also often provided higher quality merchandise. Moreover, their rum (made from fermented sugar cane juice) was much cheaper than French brandy (distilled from grapes), and so was their tobacco. Even French seigneurs were enticed by these incentives— hiring Indians or *coureurs de bois* ("forest rovers"—itinerant French or métis fur traders) to carry their fur cargoes to English trading posts or Dutch merchant vessels (PD 1:143–44, 165–66; PD 3:278; PD 6:798). As there were no well-defined boundaries between the colonies, native traders and coureurs de bois found it easy to avoid or bypass the few poorly guarded frontier posts or other checkpoints. Moreover, many vessels sailing the coastal waters carried fishermen or merchants who conducted trade without official licenses. Typically, they offered the Mi'kmaq a better price than licensed merchants, who were obliged to pay operating fees and import duties to French government officials (N. Denys, 172).

Not gaining enough revenues from furs, the French Crown complained that corruption and smuggling had "ruined" the trade (PD 1:155). Wanting to gain control over the fur trade and being increasingly aware of Acadia's strategic importance, colonial authorities cracked down on the large number of coureurs de bois ranging the forests, annulled land grants to "rascal" seigneurs, and revoked trading licenses

(PD 1:148–49). In 1679 the Crown appointed a new governor to administer Acadia from its center in Port Royal, protected by a garrison of soldiers. Still, the contraband continued unabated. Apparently, even the fort's commanding officer was dealing with foreign merchants from Boston (AN 1:176, 198).

DECLINE OF THE FUR TRADE: THE PROBLEM OF INDIAN ALLIANCES

By 1700, the economic magnitude of the transatlantic fur trade had waned dramatically. An English colonial official observed that beaver as a

> commodity is grown almost quite out of use, which is of ill consequence, for as it falls in price in England it must necessarily do so here. . . . The beaver trade here [in Albany] and at Boston is sunk to little or nothing, and the market is so low for beaver in England that 'tis scarce worth transporting. I have been told that in one year when [New York] Province was in the possession of the Dutch there were 66,000 beaver skins exported from this town [Albany], and this last year [1699] there was but 15,241 beaver skins exported hence.

This 75-percent decline, the official wrote, was "a mighty damp on that trade, and a great discouragement to our Indians" (in NYCD 4:789). But overall, given the fact that New England's fish, timber, oil, and tobacco trade was booming, the downturn was not catastrophic. But it was a different story for New France, which had a less diversified economy and still relied on the fur trade:

> The trade of Canada consists chiefly of beaver & some other furrs, which is managed by a Compa(ny), who are supplyed by the Indians and French hunters, as far as Messasippi River and some even from Hudsons Bay. . . . The value of the furrs exported from thence to France annually may be computed at sixty thousand pounds sterling; they also export to the French West Indies some flower [flour], pease, and lumber, to the value of about twenty thousand pounds sterling annually. If the furr trade of Canada should fail, the country would be but of little worth.

> (1718 Memorial to the Lords of Trade, in Baxter 10: 114)

Despite the diminished importance of fur to England's colonial economy, the English continued to rival the French in their fur-trade activities—primarily to gain an edge in alliance building with Indian tribes, which still relied on furs as a vital part of their economy.

French officials in Canada suggested that the Crown subsidize trade with Indians to "counterbalance the price of the Indian article, and then as our [gun]powder is better [than England's] we would thereby obtain the preference: become masters of the trade and maintain ourselves at peace; for it cannot be doubted that those who will be masters of the trade will also be masters of the Indians, and that these can be gained only in this way" (PD 7:774). Soon the French king furnished aid, consisting of annual presents (PD 7:941). Seeing the French build alliances with Indians in this way, one English official advised his government not to neglect the Indian trade, noting that: "The French thought it worth their while to gain those people to their interest, by yearly presents, which consisted chiefly in apparel of blue and red bayes or coarse serges, some arms and ammunition, to the value of 500 or 600 pounds" (in Murdoch 1:352). The English soon followed suit.

But gifts came erratically, and prices for furs continued to fluctuate and frustrate Indian trappers.

SEA MAMMAL HUNTING

In the early 1600s European merchants became interested in the commercial potential of seals, which were traditionally hunted by Mi'kmaqs, who relished seal oil and always knew where and when seal pods could be found. As with other trading concessions in the French colonies, authorities tried to avoid cutthroat competition in seal-hunting areas by granting exclusive rights to certain individual entrepreneurs or companies (JR 35:57, 59). Usually an operational base was founded within each concession.

Each February, after the mother seals birthed on the offshore island beaches, seigneurs dispatched crews to kill hundreds of these sea mammals, old and young alike. Butchering the animals, they cut off large chunks of blubber, boiled them, and poured the resulting oil into barrels for export. Commenting on the value of seal oil, a French seigneur wrote: "Fully three or four young ones are needed to make one barrel of oil, which is good to eat when fresh, and as good for burning as olive oil. . . . It has not [the smoke or] the odour in burning of other fish oils, which are always full of thick dregs or of settlings at the bottom of the barrels; but this is always clear" (N. Denys, 130–31). "If one were to bring it to Paris, it would sell there very well" (Ibid., 350).

Recognizing that local Indians were expert seal hunters, French Jesuits reported that "The French can make a great deal of oil from the seals that the Indians kill" (JR 59:59). Indeed, from about 1700 onward, especially in areas where fur-bearing animals had been depleted or fur trade was no longer profitable, market seal hunting offered new economic opportunities for local bands. Soon enough Mi'kmaqs and other coastal Indians became active as commercial seal hunters. Some hunting expeditions were remarkably large scale. For instance, in 1724 Wabanakis captured two English schooners at Penobscot Bay on the Maine coast and fitted these vessels out for a seal-hunting expedition to Grand Manan Island and the Bay of Fundy (Baxter 10:289). By this time Indians visiting trading posts on the lower St. Lawrence brought very few furs. According to one Jesuit, "The Principal occupation of this post [at Tadoussac] is hunting of the seal which is carried on from the month of December to the end of March." Sealskin, "which when dressed is like morocco [fine goatskin leather] . . . is used for making Indian shoes and clothes, and for covering boxes" (JR 68:85). More important, seal oil was in demand "for light in this country, and for dressing hides in Europe" (JR 68–83). Tadoussac alone provided some 80–90 casks of oil a year: "The Seals killed for 90 Casks of oil would naturally produce from 900 to 1,000 sealskins; yet hardly 5[00] to 600 are obtained, because the Indians keep many of them to make shoes and to clothe their children, without counting the skins lost by lack of care" (Coquart, 435).

In the Gulf of St. Lawrence and lower St. Lawrence River, Indian seal hunters also traded with other Indians. As one chronicler of the day noted, "The Indians of

Tadoussac and of the [Jeremie] islets trade their oil for the beaver; five pots of oil for one, and a cask for 22; one large sealskin for a beaver; and so on, in the same proportion" (Coquart, 448).

Like fur-trapping bands, sea-mammal hunters attached themselves to particular concessions, but the boundaries tended to be imprecise or overlapping. The entrepreneurs who controlled the concessions were often rivals and used all means possible, including brandy, to "steal each other's [seal-hunting] Indians" (Coquart, 441, 446–47).

Relentless hunting nearly wiped out the seal population in some areas. This actually did happen with the walrus, which could be found in the coastal waters of Mi'kmaq country until the late 18th century. In the 1730s Mi'kmaq hunting parties from Cape Breton Island frequented the Isles de la Madeleine, concentrating their efforts on the walrus hunt, clearly for commercial reasons. Mi'kmaqs traded the long and thick walrus tusks with European merchants and neighboring tribes, including the Penobscot (Coquart, 350–51; Speck 1940:109–10; Martijn, 46, n.93). The hides and tusks, plus walrus oil, were traded at European settlements (Martijn, 20, 36, 48). As commercial products, walrus and seal oil were used by Europeans and New World colonists for illumination, for frying food, for tanning leather, and later for the lubrication of machinery. In addition, walrus hides could be boiled into glue.

Beyond seals and walrus, European merchants were interested in porpoises, which "yield plenty of oil, almost a barrel to each one" (N. Denys, 351). Although European fishermen had targeted porpoises since the 1600s, native people in the St. Lawrence Gulf area did not start hunting them until the early 1700s—probably in response to the drop in demand and prices for furs. Chasing these sea mammals from early May to mid-August, the Montagnais at Tadoussac may have been the first to do so, soon followed by their Mi'kmaq neighbors (Leighton, 410; Nietfeld, 313).

MI'KMAQ CRITIQUES OF EUROPEANS

As noted in Chapter 4, some Mi'kmaqs had the opportunity to view the French on both sides of the Atlantic in the 16th century. During the colonial period, others ventured to France aboard French fishing, merchant, and military vessels. Not all their voyages ended in good cheer. Some Mi'kmaq travelers became sick and died in a strange city or perished at sea. If they didn't return with the fleet the following spring, they were sorely missed by their kinfolk, who may have discouraged others from making the long and dangerous voyage. As one chronicler of the day noted: "When the question is raised of asking them for some of their children . . . in order to bring them into France, and show it to them, they will not give them; and if any one of them yields, presents, and great promises must be made him, or hostages given" (Lescarbot 3:87; cf. 2:360).

Still, a fair number made the journey. Father LeClercq (97–98) described the humorous confusion that a group of Mi'kmaqs experienced when they visited the French royal court at Versailles:

Our Indians, who some time ago came to France, have not been able to hear without breaking into laughter, the raillery of certain ladies who took them for masqueraders, because they made their appearance at Court painted in the Indian fashion. "They have no sense," said these Indians to their interpreter, "and their reproach is unjust, because they themselves have their own faces all mottled with black, like our Indians, from which it appears that they are always in mourning, judging by their manner of painting themselves."

It is, of course, true that Mi'kmaqs making the voyage to western Europe mingled less often with aristocratic ladies and gentlemen or members of the clergy than with common sailors and dockworkers. Exposed to the seamy side of French "civility" in seaside boarding houses and taverns, these Mi'kmaqs returned home with tales about the European underside. Nicolas Denys (451) commented on the negative impact of these associations:

> [Drunkenness and thievery are] the return of all that which they have learned. And the Indians whom the fishermen have taken to France have contributed still more to it through consorting there with blasphemers, in pot-houses [taverns] and vile places, to which they have been taken. Then [there are] the wars which the French have made among themselves to dispossess one another, through their ambition and desire to possess everything; these things the Indians know well, and, when one represents to them that they ought not to rob and pillage vessels, they say in prompt answer that we do the same thing among ourselves.

Indeed, French fishermen on both sides of the ocean had a more profound impact on Mi'kmaqs than did the upper layers of French society. Certainly, self-admiring French gentry who believed that exposing their Mi'kmaq guests to European "civility" would make the visitors give up their traditional customs were often mistaken. A French priest lamented in the early 1600s: "Some [Mi'kmaqs] . . . were occasionally brought to France and baptized there, but . . . as soon as they returned to these shores, immediately resumed their former habits and traditions" (JR 2:87). "For all your arguments, and you can bring on a thousand of them if you wish, are annihilated by this single shaft which they always have at hand, *Aoti Chabaya*, (they say) 'That is the Indian way of doing it. You can have your way and we will have ours . . .'" (JR 3:123). Elsewhere, he complained: ". . . once they have gotten their fill they go off, mocking the French and everybody else at a distance and secretly laughing at everything, even the religion which they have received" (JR 2:79). Furthermore, bemoaned another priest, "They mock openly at our bowings, at our compliments, and at our embracings. They never remove their hats when they enter our dwellings; this ceremony seems to them too troublesome" (LeClercq, 252).

Also, although fascinated by seeing the French read and write, Mi'kmaqs were reticent to pick up these skills. One priest surmised, "They suppose that there is some enchantment or jugglery [magic] in them, or that this letter has a mind, because, say they, it has the virtue of telling to him who receives it everything which is said and everything which is done, even the most hidden and most secret" (LeClercq, 135). Yet, he continued, "they all have the false and ridiculous belief that they would not live long if they were as learned as the French" (LeClercq, 125).

After nearly two centuries of direct contact with Europeans, Mi'kmaqs had become thoroughly familiar with the foreigners on their shores. While trying to make sense of their own losses, they had watched the newcomers become ever more imposing in numbers, possessions, and technology. Even as they reached out to deal with them, they seem to have recognized that something essential was being lost through their dealings with these immigrants. This is evident in the comments that a Mi'kmaq made to a French sea captain at Chaleur Bay in the 1680s:

> It is true that we have not always had the use of bread and of wine which your
> France produces; but, in fact, before the arrival of the French in these parts, did not
> the [Mi'kmaq] live much longer than now? And if we have not any longer among
> us any of these old men of a hundred and thirty to forty years, it is only because we
> are gradually adopting your manner of living, for experience is making it very
> plain that those of us live longest who, despising your bread, your wine, and your
> brandy, are content with their natural food of beaver, of moose, of waterfowl, and
> fish, in accord with the custom of our ancestors and of all the [Mi'kmaq] nation.

(in LeClercq, 106)

By the end of the 17th century, European colonization of northeast America had already disempowered or destroyed many native populations, and Mi'kmaq numbers were at an all-time low. As Mi'kmaqs sorted out the contradictory consequences of interactions with the newcomers, it is not surprising that their attitudes toward Europeans were at times tinged with indignation, reflected in the following speech given to the French by a Mi'kmaq Indian chieftain:

> You say of us also that we are most miserable and most unhappy of all men, living
> without religion, without manners, without honour, without social order, in a word,
> without any rules, like the beasts in our woods and our forests, lacking bread,
> wine, and a thousand other comforts which you have in superfluity in Europe.
> Well, my brother, if you do not yet know the real feelings which our Indians have
> toward your country and toward all your nation, it is proper that I inform you at
> once. I beg you now to believe that all miserable as we seem in your eyes, we con-
> sider ourselves nevertheless much happier than you in this, that we are content
> with the little that we have; and believe also, once for all, I pray, that you deceive
> yourself greatly if you think to persuade us that your country is better than ours.
> For if France, as you say, is a little terrestrial paradise, are you sensible to leave it?

(in LeClercq, 104)

Having barely survived the 17th century, Mi'kmaqs had few choices left. Being unable to drive out the Europeans and unwilling to forsake their cultural heritage, they could endure as a people only by swaying between accommodation and resistance. This they did.

8 / Cultural Stress: Alcoholic Rage and Beaver Wars

ALCOHOL: AGENT OF SELF-DESTRUCTION

From early on, Europeans were drinkers of wine, beer, or hard cider. Flowing copiously from the taverns, these beverages provided not only cheap calories but also a welcome escape from the burdens of everyday life. Polish peasants drank up to three liters of beer a day, whereas the French consumed on average some 120 liters of wine per year. However, as French historian Fernand Braudel (1981: 241) noted, "The great innovation, the revolution in Europe was the appearance of brandy and spirits made from grain—in a word: alcohol. The 16th century created it; the 17th consolidated it; the 18th popularized it." From the 1600s public drunkenness increased everywhere in Europe. Especially the Dutch and English were notorious for their excessive drinking (Boxer, 208–209). Consumption of brandy, gin, rum, and other alcoholic drinks "increased by leaps and bounds. It soon became the custom to give alcohol to soldiers before battle" (Braudel, 1981: 244).

As noted in earlier chapters, Europeans also exported vices to the Americas, where indigenous peoples became addicted to the bottle. Alcoholism among Mi'kmaqs, surely fueled by the social, economic, and spiritual upheaval wrought by the Great Dying, had become a significant problem in Mi'kmaq country by the early 1600s. Throughout the colonial period French authorities and missionaries repeatedly mentioned the destructive effects of alcohol on Mi'kmaqs. At the time, Mi'kmaqs could "get a pint of brandy for a beaver" (PD 1:216–20). Calling drunkenness their "predominant vice," Father LeClercq (254) lamented in the late 17th century: "These barbarians, who formerly mistook wine for blood, and brandy for poison, and who fled with horror from the French who would give them these liquors, are to-day so enamoured with these kinds of drinks that they make it a principle of honour to gorge themselves therewith like beasts; and they only drink, properly speaking, in order to get drunk." LeClercq (250–51) described Mi'kmaq women as "very modest, chaste, and continent." Yet, the missionary added, "one does see among them some girls and women who are libertines and who live in dishonour. But indeed it is a fact that the drinking of brandy and drunkenness causes these lapses." LeClercq (255) blamed such conduct on European traders who used brandy "to abuse the Indian women, who yield themselves readily during their drunkenness to all kinds of indecency, although at other times . . . they would be more likely to give a box [slap] on the ears than a kiss to whomsoever wished to engage them to evil." Furthermore, he complained, French traders gave alcohol to Mi'kmaq hunters to "make them drunk quite on purpose, in order to deprive these poor barbarians of the use of reason, so that the traders can deceive them more easily, and obtain for almost nothing their furs, which they would not sell except for a just and reasonable price if they were in their right minds" (LeClercq, 254).

When using alcohol as a trade commodity, Europeans cheated Indians by thinning it with water, thus, according to LeClercq (255), "rendering themselves, by this miserable kind of trading, the masters not only of the furs of the Indians, but also of their blankets, guns, axes, kettles, &c., which the traders have sold them at a very dear rate." In sum, the priest anguished, the ill effects of alcohol were horrific and manifold: "Injuries, quarrels, homicides, murders, parricides are to this day the sad consequences of the trade in brandy; and one sees with grief Indians dying in their drunkenness."

When French authorities tried to curb the alcohol trade in their colonies, Indian middlemen filled the void. In 1642 a French priest complained that Mi'kmaq traders from Chaleur Bay "brought barrels full of brandy to [a large intertribal rendezvous at] Tadoussac; from Tadoussac they have come to Kebec, and this year have caused the greatest disorder among the Indians" (JR 22:241–43). Indeed, brandy had become a highly profitable commodity: Three times the value of wine, one barrel of brandy equalled 140 small axes or ninety "large Biscay axes" (PD 1:36–37).

In 1690 French Colonial Governor Denonville wrote that he had "witnessed the evils caused by that liquor [brandy] among the Indians. It is the horror of horrors." In his estimation, "Remedies are impossible as long as every one is permitted to sell and traffic in ardent spirits." And, he added, "Those who allege that the Indians will remove to the English if brandy is not furnished them, do not state the truth; for it is a fact that they do not care about drinking as long as they do not see brandy; and the most reasonable would wish there never had been any such thing; for they set their entrails on fire and beggar themselves by giving their peltries and clothes for drink" (in PD 4:441–42).

The problem was tenacious. Repeatedly, French missionaries complained that smugglers created havoc among the Mi'kmaqs and other Indians by selling them rum and other hard liquors, such as brandy. Colonial officers described Indians as "being out of Temper" because they were "overcome with Rum and Strong Drink . . . . by many fishing Vessels and Traders which Drink makes the Indians Distracted and very Abusive in their behaviour and Inclinable to Mischief to the Hazard of their [own] lives and the lives of others" (Baxter 23: 84).

Sometimes, after buying rum from ship captains riding at anchor, Indians climbed back into their canoes and immediately began drinking, only to capsize and drown (Baxter 9:448). In the early 18th century rum was described as "the greatest reason of all the disturbances" among Indians on the Maine coast (in Baxter, 9:446). By that time, according to a French missionary, several northeastern tribes had been "almost wholly destroyed by brandy" (in PD 7: 882–83).

GAME DEPLETION

The European invasion had other dire consequences. The dramatic population decline among Mi'kmaqs and their native neighbors, caused by alien pathogens, initially eased pressure on the region's natural resources, in particular game animals
such as moose and caribou. But this respite was brief, given the rapidly growing European demand for beaver and other furs, which transformed the way local hunters
related to their environment. Pelts gave Mi'kmaqs access to European trade goods,
and their dependency on these goods grew swiftly. After they acquired firearms, they
had an ongoing need for ammunition and repairs (usually paid for in beaver skins).
Regional chieftains found that the distribution of imported goods at feasts (again, acquired with pelts) won them the loyalty and admiration of their followers. Such display also gave them a leg up in the competition for power and prestige between rival
chieftains. Further, Mi'kmaqs who had become dependent on alcohol needed skins
to buy the intoxicating drinks. Soon, instead of viewing animals as four-legged relations, Mi'kmaqs and other hunting tribes in the region began to see them as commodities to be harvested each winter and spring. One hunter best expressed the new
attitude toward their animal brothers: "The beaver does everything perfectly well, it
makes kettles, hatchets, swords, knives, bread: and, in short, it makes everything" (in
Kenton 1:151).

To fulfill their new needs Mi'kmaq hunters declared "war" on game animals and
soon faced the consequences of purely profit-oriented hunting practices. In some
areas, especially coastal regions, the reproduction rate of the animals could not keep
up with the kill rate of hunters, and some species became scarce, even extinct. This
depletion would have been interpreted by traditional Mi'kmaqs in terms of a "revenge" by game animals who were so offended by the greed of hunters that they
would refuse to offer themselves to be killed (Martin, 113–49).

Reliant on game for subsistence, hunting bands were then forced to abandon the
depleted region. As long as they had access to other territories where game was still
abundant, they could continue their subsistence strategy by moving—but this could
lead to conflicts with neighboring hunting bands.

Although we possess no written information about game depletions in the 16th
century, we have a few documents that chronicle 17th-century depletion. For instance, records note that in the early 1600s, Mi'kmaq hunting bands ranged the
northern woodlands of Cape Breton Island in pursuit of game during the winter and
traded the hides and skins with European fishermen and merchants during the spring
(Champlain 1:170). By 1620, intensive harvesting had taken its toll, and a Franciscan missionary noted, "This Cape Breton is an unproductive land, yet pleasant in
some parts, although as I am told, Indians are seldom seen there" (Sagard, 36). Two
decades later, the island's animal population seems to have replenished itself, at-
tracting Mi'kmaq hunters back into the region and, in turn, inspiring French merchants to invest in trading stations there. The resurgence lasted less than 20 years, for
in 1672 a French trader reported, "This island has also been esteemed for the hunting
of Moose. They were found formerly in great numbers, but at present there are no
more. The Indians have destroyed everything, and have abandoned the island, find-

ing there no longer the wherewithal for living" (N. Denys, 186–87). The cycle continued. According to a 1689 French census, a small band of 52 Mi'kmaqs reoccupied the area, which indicates game numbers had climbed again. The populations of animals and the humans who relied on them may have dropped once more, but French records show that moose were again abundant on the island in the 1730s (PD 10:6, 17–18).

A Frenchman who traded with Mi'kmaqs in the early 18th century made note of this adaptive pattern of shifting territoriality: "When they are in a district where Game and Wildfowl are to be found, they remain so long as there are any left; when almost all have been killed, & the pot is no longer as full as it should be, they go elsewhere in search for better hunting, & they are never well off except in places where they find a great deal to eat" (Diereville, 172).

As already noted, as Mi'kmaqs became increasingly enmeshed in the international capitalist system and transformed into market hunters, they gradually lost their self-sufficiency as subsistence foragers. Turning more and more to French trading posts for supplies and services and trading on credit when necessary, many built up debts (Coquart, 437–42). A missionary who lived among Mi'kmaqs for many years in the mid-1700s explained that his role was not only to save Indian souls but also "to engage and spur them on to the making of a copious chase, when the hunting-season comes in, that their debt to the dealers with them be paid, their wives and children be cloathed, and their credit supported" (Maillard, 2–3). Being confronted with old debts or aiming to ensure future credits, desperate Mi'kmaq hunters sometimes resorted to trapping very young fur-bearing animals, even in the summer, when their pelts were almost worthless (Coquart, 442). Learning from such mistakes, Mi'kmaqs later tried to manage their hunting territories in a sustainable fashion, practicing a form of fallow hunting whenever possible. Dividing the hunting grounds and streams between families, Mi'kmaqs applied a system not unlike that of their Penobscot neighbors, who "hunt every third year & kill 2/3 of the bevier [beaver], leving the other third part to breed and that their beviers were as much their stock for a leving as Englishmens cattel war his leving" (in Butler and Hadlock, 18).

"BEAVER WARS": INTERTRIBAL CONFLICTS

International trade exacerbated traditional intertribal conflicts. Competition over game-rich territories, intensified by the availability of muskets and other lethal European weapons, led to violence. Alcohol no doubt fueled the aggression, and each killing called for revenge. All of this triggered a cycle of bloody warfare commonly referred to as the "Beaver Wars," involving virtually all native groups from Cape Breton Island down to Chesapeake Bay and as far inland as the Great Lakes. These wars—periodic vicious outbursts—continued throughout much of the 17th century.

With the introduction and spread of firearms, Indians began to adjust their defensive strategies—beginning with the palisading of Chief Membertou's village near Port Royal in 1607 (Lescarbot 2:353–54). In the 1630s the Huron followed Jesuit advice "to make their palisade forts, not as hitherto, in a circular form, but rectangular, with small flanking towers at the corners for the arquebus-men [gunners]" (JR 35:107–11). By 1651 the Jesuit mission at Sillery was also fortified, as was a nearby Indian settlement (JR 36:193). Fifteen years later, Mohawk villages were described as "castles," one of which "had a triple palisade twenty feet high, with four bastions" (Charlevoix 3:91, n.3) Among fortified strongholds noted in the 1660s was also the residence of Mi'kmaq warlord Iariet (known as Captain Denis among the French), located at the mouth of the Richibucto River, probably on Indian Island (JR 28:23):

> He has upon the border of the basin of this river a rather large fort of stakes, with two kinds of bastions; inside is his lodge, and the other Indians are encamped around him. . . . From a watchtower, with a sentry, Captain Denis keeps a close watch on the coast and far out to sea. If any vessel or canoes are seen, he has his entire force brought under arms with their bows and arrows and their muskets, places a sentinel on the approach to ask what persons they are. . . . Before entering, it is required that they make a discharge of their guns, as a salute [and, no doubt, to empty their weapons!].

> (N. Denys, 195–96)

By 1685 the Abenaki Indian mission at the Chaudière River was fortified (Charlevoix 3: 308, n.2), and in 1686 French Governor Denonville reported that "redoubts and stockaded posts" were necessary in each seigneury for the defense of Canada against Iroquois and English—"for the security of the people, their grain and cattle" (PD 3:288).

Mi'kmaqs had several advantages in the fur-trade competition. They were skilled mariners who acquired and mastered seaworthy European sailing shallops by about 1600. And, positioned at the coast, they gained early access to European trade goods. These factors helped them emerge as middlemen in the coastal fur trade of northern New England in the early 17th century. For a time, this role helped them counter shortages born of game depletions and allowed them continued access to trade goods. Other tribal groups, seeking direct access to European merchandise, soon aimed to eliminate Mi'kmaq middlemen, who fought aggressively to maintain their position. Intertribal relations worsened, and conflicts flared into the "Beaver Wars."

Although each of the conflicts was triggered by its own unique events, they all were the result of a basic pattern of disruption in the balance between local tribal communities and their natural resources. But these wars cannot be explained only in political or economic terms. Some were the outcome of a spiral of revenge killings, so-called "mourning wars." Others may have had their origins in dark dreams about sickness, suffering, or death. For example, a missionary active among the Mi'kmaq noted that such ominous dreams "make them believe that their departed relatives will not rest in peace unless some human beings are sacrificed to them" (JR 47:213). Whatever the causes, records show that Mi'kmaqs were almost incessantly clashing with neighboring groups from the mid-1500s onward—first Stadaconans (St. Lawrence Iroquois), then Abenakis, Maliseets, Massachusetts, Montagnais, Inuits, and, most dangerous of all, Mohawks and their Iroquois allies.

MI'KMAQ-STADACONAN WAR

From early on Mi'kmaqs were involved in war against the St. Lawrence Iroquoians—specifically the Stadaconans, who ranged the lower river valley from Quebec to Gaspé Peninsula. During the 1530s Stadaconans camped and fished regularly at Gaspé, a Mi'kmaq border region, and in 1534 Mi'kmaqs killed some 200 of these tribespeople (Trigger, 147; cf. Biggar, 1924:178). Using the name they applied to all Iroquoian-speaking peoples—(*Kwetej*)—Mi'kmaq storytellers later recounted this ancient event in a legend about the origin of the war between the Mi'kmaqs and the Kwetej: "On the two opposite banks of the Restigouche [River], near its mouth, were two towns—one inhabited by Micmacs, and the other by the [Kwetej]. They were at peace with each other, and frequently attended each other's festivals." One day during a game, a Mi'kmaq child was killed. "It was passed over as an accident, but the circumstance was remembered." Not long after, the Mi'kmaq invited the Kwetej to a feast. After the feast, during a ball game, Mi'kmaq boys took revenge by killing two Kwetej children. "It was passed over as an accident, but the young folk laid it up in their hearts, and awaited an opportunity for revenge." Subsequently, the Kwetej ambushed a Mi'kmaq salmon-fishing party. This, in turn, provoked the Mi'kmaq to revenge. After a bloody battle, the victorious Mi'kmaq drove the Kwetej from their village to the upper St. Lawrence (Rand, 1894:200–206). By the late 16th century these Iroquoians had vanished from the region, their ultimate fate remaining somewhat of a puzzle.

MI'KMAQ-ABENAKI WAR

Fur trading became such a potentially dangerous occupation that one could never be certain what to expect when sailing into a bay or landing on a river bank. Surprise attacks, robbery, and even murder were always possible. The adventures of a young Mi'kmaq fur trader named Panoniac may serve as illustration.

In 1604, two French vessels entered the Gulf of Maine. The expedition's navigator, Samuel de Champlain, scouted the area for a suitable place to locate a new colony and fur trading post and initially established one on an island at the head of Passamaquoddy Bay. Guided by two local Indians, Champlain and 12 crewmen explored the coast (Champlain 1:280). One of the guides was the famous Mi'kmaq chieftain Messamoet of La Hève, who had taken a sojourn in France some 25 years earlier (Lescarbot 2:324) and now served as Champlain's interpreter. On his second exploration voyage along the coast from Passamaquoddy Bay to the Kennebec River in the summer of 1605, Champlain employed Panoniac, who was of Chief Membertou's band. With the help of Panoniac, who was married to an Abenaki woman from southern Maine (Champlain 1:311–15), the French began searching for a better settlement site. Panoniac took them across the Bay of Fundy to a place near one of his band's favorite seasonal camping grounds. Here the French established Port Royal. The following summer Messamoet accompanied Champlain again, this time sailing his own shallop in tandem with the Frenchman. They sailed from Passamaquoddy Bay south to Saco Bay, where Messamoet hoped "to make an alliance with those of that country by offering them sundry presents" (Champlain 1:394). At Saco, Messamoet negotiated with the local Abenaki chieftain, Olmechin. In return for trade goods "gained by barter with the French, which they came thither to sell—to wit, kettles, large, medium, and small, hatchets, knives, dresses, capes, red jackets, peas, beans, biscuits, and other such things," Messamoet received "a canoe laden with what [Olmechin's people] had, to wit, corn, tobacco, beans, and pumpkins [squash] . . ." (Lescarbot 2:324). To his great displeasure, he received no furs from his Abenaki hosts. That summer, already strained Mi'kmaq-Abenaki relations turned openly hostile when a party of Mi'kmaq warriors under Chief Iouaniscou killed some Abenakis on the Maine coast (Champlain 1:442). Unaware of the brutality committed by fellow tribesmen, Panoniac sailed with a cargo of French trade goods from Passamaquoddy Bay south to Penobscot. There, in revenge for their slain kinsmen, Abenakis killed the innocent Panoniac. His corpse was taken back to his Mi'kmaq home near Port Royal, where his relatives mourned his death. To wrap the body, Champlain gave Chief Membertou a fine red woolen blanket—a "catalogne" from Catalonia, Spain (Champlain 1:442–45; Lescarbot 6:273–74). Because Panoniac's killing could not be left unavenged, the old chief assembled a fighting force of about 40 Mi'kmaq and allied Maliseet warriors. Armed with spears, tomahawks, bows, and iron-tipped arrows and newly equipped with French muskets, the warriors boarded their shallops and sailed to Saco Bay, where they defeated the local Abenakis. They returned home knowing that sooner or later they would suffer an Abenaki counterattack.

MI'KMAQ-MALISEET WAR

Fur-trade competition also fueled hostilities between Mi'kmaqs and Maliseets (including Passamaquoddies) of the central Maine coast. Their powerful leader, Bashaba, lived in the Penobscot Valley and was even recognized as paramount chief by neighboring Abenakis. Maliseet relations with the Mi'kmaqs were already strained in 1604, when Champlain first sailed up the Penobscot River. Bashaba's followers told the French explorer that "they wished to live in peace with their enemies, in order that in future they might hunt the beaver more than they had done, and barter these beavers with us in exchange for things necessary for their usage" (Champlain 1:295–96). Unwilling to give up their privileged position as fur-trade middlemen, Mi'kmaqs tried to intimidate their neighbors, determined to get by raiding what they could not get by trading. From their Gulf of Maine stronghold at Mount Desert Island, sailing in shallops and armed with muskets, they staged lightning raids against coastal Maliseets unwilling to engage in barter.

In 1615 Mi'kmaq warriors "surprised the Bashaba, and slew him and all his people near about him, carrying away his women and such other matters as they thought of value" (Gorges, 90). With Bashaba and so many of his great warriors dead, the confederacy collapsed. The ongoing violence was disastrous for the native peoples involved. Soon "the surviving, great Sagamores [chieftains] fell at variance among themselves, spoiled and destroyed each other's people and provision, and famine took hold of many: which was seconded by a great and general plague, which so violently reigned for three years [1616–1619] together, that in a manner the greater part of that land was left desert" (Gorges, 90).

Until the 1630s, Mi'kmaqs occupied the Maine coast as far west as Penobscot Bay and launched raids against corn-growing coastal tribes inhabiting territories southwest of the Kennebec River (Smith, 1898:15, 18–19; Bradford, 126–30; Levett, 93; Prince, 32–34). Their victims, according to William Bradford, governor of Plymouth Colony, "were very much affraid of the [Mi'kmaqs], a people to the eastward which used to come in harvest time and take away their corne, & many times kill their persons" (Bradford, 126–30).

Some of the Maliseet and their southern allies who survived the epidemics and Mi'kmaq attacks went into hiding. In 1623 a French missionary noted that small numbers of these Indians were living in the barren mountains north of the St. Lawrence River, near Tadoussac. He reported that so many of their cohorts had been killed in various wars with the Mi'kmaq that they kept themselves hidden "and dare not show themselves" (Sagard, 149–50). For many decades thereafter, Mi'kmaqs and Maliseets remained on a hostile footing and engaged sometimes in vicious combat (JR 28:203–05). At the end of the 1620s, however, Mi'kmaqs lost their technological advantage when their Maliseet and Abenaki neighbors acquired firearms.

MI'KMAQ-MASSACHUSETTS WARS

The 1616–1619 pandemic reduced the strong Massachusetts Indian nations to impotent, small remnants barely able to defend themselves against Mi'kmaq raiders who ventured down to Massachusetts Bay. Once a great leader, Chief Chicataubut, had been weakened when virtually all his people died in the epidemics. The powerful Chief Nanapeshamet of northern Massachusetts lost his life in a war against the Mi'kmaq in 1619, leaving his widow, the "squaw sachem" in charge of the surviving tribespeople in the region (Salwen, 170). She, like Massasoit of the Wampanoags of northern Massachusetts, welcomed the English colonists as allies who could protect them against marauding Mi'kmaqs.

Mi'kmaqs continued to make annual forays, raiding the afflicted Indian villages south of the Kennebec River down to Massachusetts Bay. Their aggression prompted the tribes they targeted to seek colonial support. In 1629 the Penacook chieftain Passaconaway of the Merrimac River, together with three allied chieftains, asked the English to make an alliance with them and establish trade relations: "Whereas wee the Sagamors [chiefs] of Penecook, Pentucket, Squomsquot and Nuchanawack are Inclined to have the English Inhabit amongst us as they are amongst our Countreymen in the Massachusetts bay by which means we hope in time to be strengthened against our Enemys the [Mi'kmaqs] who year by year doth us Damage" (YD 8, folio 16).

In 1631 Mi'kmaqs attacked Saugus, halfway between Salem and Boston. After they "rifled" the wigwams of these Massachusetts Indians, taking "Nets, Biskets, &c.," they demanded ransom in the form of several "fathoms of Wompampeag [wampum beads] and Skins" (Prince, 32–34). That same year, according to Governor Winthrop of Boston, these Mi'kmaqs, "to the number of one hundred," came by boats in the night [and] assaulted the wigwam of the sagamore of Agawam [Ipswich], by Merrimack, and wounded John Sagamore, and James [sons of Nanapeshamet, who was killed by Mi'kmaqs in 1619], and some others [who later died], and rifled a wigwam where Mr. Caddock's men kept to catch sturgeon, took away their nets and biscuit, etc." (Winthrop, 71–72). But the aggression and bloodshed were not one-sided. Records note that John, the sagamore of Agawam, had "treacherously killed" the families of some of his Mi'kmaq attackers "and therefore was the less pitied by the English that were informed thereof'" (Hubbard, 145).

MI'KMAQ-MONTAGNAIS WAR

Generally, the Mi'kmaqs got along well with the Montagnais, who ranged the vast woodlands across the wide St. Lawrence River mouth. Indeed, the two were often allied in war against their common enemy, the Iroquois. However, some northern Montagnais groups, at the time known as Bersiamites and Papinachois, had provoked Mi'kmaq wrath and became targets of numerous seaborne raids from the 1620s onward. One such attack took place in 1644 when a Mi'kmaq war party from Nova Scotia under Chief Herout sailed to Labrador and raided the Bersiamites. As a resident missionary at Miscou Island observed, both tribes "bore each other a mortal hatred" (JR 30:138). Returning with seven scalps and about 13 captives, most of whom were children, they stopped at the Jesuit mission post at Nepisiguit at Chaleur Bay, where they celebrated their victory. As Father Richard observed: "[They] desired by these massacres to allay the grief and sorrow of all the Country, which is afflicted by the death of many persons who have died during the past few years. They threw on the shore, at landing, the scalps of the poor massacred people, and at the same time spread joy through the cabins. . . . The women vied with one another who should first seize these Trophies, and who should sing and dance the best" (JR 30:35–37). Captives could be tortured and their heads cleaved upon entering the Mi'kmaq villages (JR 45: 69; Charlevoix 3: 241). Typically, however, their destiny was servitude.

Three years after this raid Mi'kmaqs agreed to make peace with these Indians. They rendezvoused on Isle Percée, off the eastern tip of Gaspé Peninsula—near the winter hunting grounds used by the Montagnais at the time—and concluded a treaty.

Despite the peace, Bersiamites remained uneasy when Mi'kmaq warriors appeared on their coasts. In 1661, 30 Mi'kmaqs armed with arquebuses boarded two shallops and sailed westward, intending to strike against the Bersiamites and Papinachois. Because of a bad omen, however, the crew of one shallop aborted the raid and returned. The other continued and encountered a canoe carrying a family of four. Chasing them down, they killed the parents and one child and captured a boy (JR 47: 231). After 1662 we hear little about these northern Montagnais bands as they were nearly exterminated by epidemics (Charlevoix 3:40).

MI'KMAQ-INUIT WARS

In the 1630s Mi'kmaqs also did battle against Inuits (Eskimos) across the Gulf of St. Lawrence. Sometimes they took captives who were forced into servitude by their owners. For example, one Inuit boy, captured at age ten, was used as a moose hunter by his Mi'kmaq owners (JR 30:135). For the next several decades, Mi'kmaqs were repeatedly on the warpath against the Inuit (JR 47: 213).

MI'KMAQ-IROQUOIS WARS

More awesome than the Mi'kmaq in fighting power were the Iroquois, who lived in what is now upstate New York and were militant participants in the fur trade. In the 1620s warriors from the five nations that belonged to this confederacy (Mohawk, Oneida, Onondaga, Cayuga, and Seneca) began raiding the Mahican and other immediate neighbors in the Hudson Valley. Gradually, the Iroquois expanded and intensified their aggression, and in 1640 Algonkin and Montagnais envoys traveled to the Abenaki of Kennebec and other rivers to solicit allies in a league against the Iroquois. About this time the Iroquois secured firearms from Dutch merchants on the Hudson River, heightening their militancy. In 1643 a French Jesuit reported that they possessed "nearly three hundred arquebuses—they are skilled in handling them" (JR 24:297). Colonial authorities in Quebec, challenged by Iroquois warriors raiding French settlements, joined the emerging alliance. A key force in this political development was French missionaries, in particular the Jesuits, who were active throughout the region. One of their major headquarters was at Sillery, the Indian mission near Quebec that was inhabited primarily by recently converted Montagnais and Algonkins.

By this time the Iroquois (especially Mohawks) suffered the effects of game depletion in their hunting territories. Venturing beyond their traditional bounds they sought the much-desired furs elsewhere, launching raids against the Mahican, Sokoki, Huron, Algonkin, and others—forcing them to pay tribute in furs or wampum, retreat to remote countries, or face extermination through warfare.

Coming to the aid of their Algonkin and Montagnais allies, Mi'kmaq warriors repeatedly sailed in their shallops far up the St. Lawrence River to fight their traditional Iroquois enemies. From the Jesuit mission at Miscou, Father Richard reported in 1643: "A number of our [Mi'kmaq] Indians, not only from this Bay, but from all the coast, are going up to Tadoussac; some particularly of the youth, may proceed as far as Kebec, and beyond, in order to go to war against the Hiroquois" (JR 32:147). The following year, a Mi'kmaq war party returning from a victorious raid against the Bersiamites interrupted their feast at Nepisiguit (Chaleur Bay) upon the rumor that their Iroquois enemies had appeared, which "made them think of flight" (JR 28:33–37).

In 1647 the Huron also received firearms from their French allies. Nonetheless, two years later they were soundly defeated by invading Iroquois warriors who brutally destroyed their villages. Aided by French Jesuits, Huron survivors made wooden forts with bastions, built according to European "military rules" (JR 35:

Attack against Iroquois village.

83–85). In 1651, as noted earlier, the mission village at Sillery was also fortified "by a good and strong wall which is flanked at the four corners and can withstand the assault of the Iroquois" (JR 36: 193). Other tribes, including Mi'kmaqs, did the same with their own villages.

Afraid of being exterminated in these vicious wars, Algonquian groups in New England, including Abenakis from the Kennebec area, formed large coalitions that included the Mi'kmaqs. In 1656 Iroquois warriors took their canoes down the St. Lawrence River and attacked the Huron refugee village at Isle d'Orléans, near Quebec, and subsequently defeated the Algonkins near Three Rivers. The Algonkins induced a village of Montagnais from the Saguenay River (probably Tadoussac) to come to Sillery to support them. Mi'kmaqs of Acadia promised their aid, as did the Nepissings. Together they could form war parties numbering 400 or 500 men. Yet these allied tribes failed to beat back the Iroquois, and the wars continued for another decade (Blair 1:193–97). Meanwhile, the incessant Iroquois violence pressured many Algonkins from upper Canada into exile among the Abenaki in Maine (Prins, 1995a).

In 1662 Iroquois raiders penetrated deep into the lower St. Lawrence Valley, fanning out into Canada and Acadia. They reached as far as the Penobscot and St.

John rivers, where they clashed with Maliseets. Their war chief was "surnamed Nero" by the French "because of his notorious cruelty" (JR 48:99–105, 169–71). During this time, even Tadoussac, "where hitherto scarcely ever less than twelve hundred Indians were seen at the time of trade, began to be almost entirely abandoned" due to the crippling combination of Iroquois depredations and a new wave of epidemics (JR 47:107; cf. Charlevoix 3:153). In the words of one priest, Mohawks "made a desert of Tadoussac" (JR 47:107).

In 1663 Ojibways defeated an Iroquois war party near Lake Huron. Moreover, a smallpox epidemic "committed great ravages" among the Iroquois (Charlevoix 3:62–65), and the French Crown sent the colony its finest regiment of soldiers plus several hundred regular troops to subdue them. In 1667 the Mohawk and other allied Iroquois tribes finally concluded a peace with the French at Quebec. In 1670 the Ottawa also made peace with the Iroquois, followed by the Mahican in 1671. Yet south and west of the Iroquois, the Beaver Wars continued.

Despite peace treaties, the Iroquois continued to be a threat to their neighbors, and, as one missionary noted, many Indians "arrived from Acadia to join the French and their allies in Quebec, showing a furious passion to attack the Iroquois." Also, he added, "others have come from different parts, that is, some [Sokokis from the Connecticut River] and some Gaspessiens [Mi'kmaqs]" (Bigot, 35–38). By the 1680s Mi'kmaqs of the north shore were still intimidated by the Iroquois, on top of being plagued by a new wave of diseases. According to Father LeClercq, who visited the Miramichi Valley at the time, Mi'kmaqs in that district had "been almost wholly destroyed, as much by the war which they have waged with the Iroquois as by the maladies which have infected this land" (LeClercq, 150–51).

INTERTRIBAL DIPLOMACY AND PEACE

At special feasts, these nations formalized their political contracts. After orators, representing their respective nations, gave harangues, leaders exchanged strings of valuable wampum beads and other ceremonial gifts to seal their bond. When Mi'kmaqs concluded a treaty with their Bersiamite enemies at Isle Percée in 1647, the procedure went as follows: A Mi'kmaq Christian from the Miscou mission and a converted Montagnais chief from Tadoussac served as mediators. The peacemaking ritual involved an elaborate exchange of gifts. As the priest at Miscou reported:

> The Captain of the Indians of our [Nova Scotia and New Brunswick] coasts, together with Ignace Ouandagareau [of Miscou], loads a young man with a bag of wampum; two others carry on their shoulders two dozen new blankets; others, thirteen fine arquebuses, [gun]powder, lead, and some swords longer and broader than usual. Then they had everything carried into a great cabin, where many Indians—Montagnais, Algonkins, three of the nation of the Sorcerer, and two Bersiamites assembled; they assert that they have all banished . . . the former enmity, in confirmation whereof they offered all these presents.

(JR 30:141–43)

In return, the Bersiamite representatives and Montagnais chief "caused to be brought a goodly number of bundles of beaver skins." After this exchange, which settled the peace, there were several days of dancing and feasting (Ibid.).

Mi'kmaqs had long been allied with their Algonkin neighbors in the St. Lawrence Valley and had reestablished alliance with the Montagnais. They also made peace with other Algonquian-speaking groups in the region. In the 1670s they began to operate as French military allies and entered into an alliance with their Maliseet and various Abenaki neighbors, including the Penobscot. A Mi'kmaq oral history recorded in the early 1900s tells of a peace treaty between the Mi'kmaq and Penobscot:

> Dja'djaginwi't, a [Mi'kmaq] chief, fought the Penobscot. Later they made peace, and as a record painted with alder (red or brown) an eel and a turtle on one side of a bearskin. They crossed a tomahawk, spear, bow, and arrows, and buried them thus. Over this spot they erected a small birch-bark wigwam; and at the top of it put bearskin. This was at Peter Denys Point [Princeton], Maine. After this, [Mi'kmaq] and Penobscot intermarried. The [Mi'kmaq] told the Penobscot: "If you break this treaty, there is the Sun above you to see you. If you break it, you will be like salt on the ground when water is poured on it." (in Wallis and Wallis 1955:204)

Peace between the Iroquois and Mi'kmaq did not come until about 1700. Two centuries later Mi'kmaq oral tradition recounted how the war against the Mohawk (*Kwetej*) came to an end: "Residing at Lustegoocheehch—now called Miramichi in English—was a powerful chief named Mejelabegadasich, or Tied-in-a-hard-knot. He was not only a great warrior but also a mighty powwow [*puowin,* or shaman], and could divine with great correctness." During hand-to-hand combat against Wohooweha, the powerful Kwetej chieftain, he crushed Wohooweha's skull with one blow of the tomahawk. With their leader dead, the Kwetej were beaten in the ensuing battle. "The two parties now made peace for their two nations, and settled it upon so firm a basis that it has never since been broken" (Rand, 1984:212–15).

But while the Mi'kmaqs and their neighbors ceased to fight against each other, smallpox and other epidemics continued to thin their ranks, and untold numbers perished. Many communities vanished, leaving no trace in the historical records. The survivors forged new intertribal alliances. Nonetheless, the Northeast continued to be steeped in violence: As the next chapter illustrates, Mi'kmaqs were swept up in colonial warfare as French allies against the English.

9 / Colonial Wars and Alliances

In the late 17th century Mi'kmaqs became involved in a long series of colonial wars between the French and English. Before turning to a chronological discussion of these bloody contests, key components need to be introduced: The escalation of Anglo-French rivalries; factors that drew Mi'kmaqs and other Indians into the conflicts; the creation of the Wabanaki Confederacy (an alliance among Mi'kmaqs and other native peoples in the region); alliance ceremonial practices; the role of missionaries in warfare; and the introduction of commercial scalping.

MOUNTING ANGLO-FRENCH RIVALRIES

Anglo-French rivalry for domination of northeast America was part of a worldwide struggle for empire building. Europe's prosperity depended on huge merchant fleets that sailed all across the globe—from Japan and New Zealand to Brazil and Canada. To fend off or destroy competitors, those in power employed heavily armed warships and maintained fortified trading compounds in their far-flung colonies and trade centers, where they could refit their ships and replenish their stores.

Although local trade disputes in New England and New France sometimes led to violent conflicts, assaults on coastal strongholds and raids on settlements in the contested borderlands between these colonies were usually spin-offs of distant wars in Europe. There, in the scramble for greater wealth and glory, mighty leaders raised massive armies to gain the competitive edge. For reasons of state or trade, they stormed one another's fortified cities and fought pitched battles on open fields. Wars were also prompted by fierce religious dissension (especially between Protestants and Roman Catholics), as well as by inheritance disputes and dynastic marriage politics between royal families. Warfare on the European continent inevitably affected seaborne trade and colonial possessions. Thus we see that the wars in the American colonies known as King William's War, Queen Anne's War, King George's War, and the French and Indian War roughly correspond to the European War of the Grand Alliance (1688–1697), War of the Spanish Succession (1701–1713), War of the Austrian Succession (1740–1748), and the Seven Years War (1756–1763).

INDIAN INVOLVEMENT IN EUROPEAN RIVALRIES

Occupying strategically important lands subject to overlapping French and English claims, Mi'kmaqs found themselves in the thick of these colonial wars. Every time France faced troubles on its New England frontier, French officials called upon Mi'kmaq warriors, offering basic provisions and gifts in exchange for armed service. With the drastic decline of the fur trade, many Mi'kmaq families relied on such *ethnic soldiering* as a means of survival. But their willingness to fight alongside the French went beyond material remunerations. They, like their French and Indian neighbors, needed help holding back English expansionism.

Mi'kmaqs, reduced to a mere 2,000 souls by the end of the 17th century, could not have survived without alliances. Counting all males older than 12, the combined force of all Mi'kmaq bands was only about 400 warriors. By comparison, the five allied Iroquois nations, numbering nearly 20,000 people in the mid-1600s, could collectively field about 2,200 warriors (F. Jennings 1984:35–36). Although their population declined considerably during the second half of the 17th century, the Iroquois still greatly outnumbered the Mi'kmaq—and they were further strengthened by friendly ties with some 9,000 Dutch settlers living in the Hudson Valley. After 1664, when the English Crown took control over New Netherlands and renamed it New York, Iroquois connections only grew, extending to New England and its 80,000 settlers. Allied to Dutch and English Protestants, the fierce Iroquois represented a major political power on the colonial frontiers.

In contrast to the rapidly growing English colonies, New France (Canada and Acadia) still counted fewer than 10,000 settlers by 1680. Greatly troubled by the Anglo-Iroquois alliance, wondering if its own colonial experiment was doomed, the French Crown did much within its power to retain its Indian allies. These allies, together numbering perhaps as many as 20,000 individuals, included Mi'kmaqs and other Wabanakis in Acadia, plus many refugee Indians who had fled English and Iroquois aggression in their homelands and resettled among the French in Canada.

To put North America's political affairs somewhat into perspective, nearly six million people lived in England, and 25 million in France. Indeed, the entire Mi'kmaq population of 2,000 souls could have fit into a small rural town in either of these countries (Braudel, 1981:54, 482–83). Because European military officers had fought in armies of 100,000 men, they were not impressed by the small number of Mi'kmaq warriors. What they did find notable, however, was the Indians' ability to strike quickly. The English referred to their guerrilla style as the "sculking war." Expert archers and musketeers, Mi'kmaqs also wielded tomahawks, lances, and even swords with great skill. One Frenchman, describing their use of tomahawks, noted, "[They] are very dextrous in flinging these, so as to hit a Mark no bigger than a Crown-piece at thirty Yards distance, and by that Means it is a dangerous Weapon in a Skirmish" (Grace, 11). Indicative of their value on the battlefield, Mi'kmaq chiefs and outstanding warriors were sometimes awarded silver medals embossed with the French king's bust and were given honorary military titles such as captain, major, and even colonel (de la Varenne, 80–81).

THE WABANAKI CONFEDERACY

Facing the aggressive expansionism of New England's colonists backed by the powerful English royal army and Iroquois warriors, Mi'kmaqs allied themselves not only with the French but also with the Maliseet, Passamaquoddy, Penobscot, and more remote Abenaki communities. In the late 17th century, these Indians formed a *putu'swaqn* ("convention council") that became known as the Wabanaki Confederacy. The founding of this important alliance is recounted in several oral traditions. For instance, as told in a Passamaquoddy narrative:

> Long ago, the Indians were always fighting against each other. They struck one an-
> other bloodily. There were many men, women, and children who alike were tor-
> mented by these constant battles. . . . It seemed as if all were tired of how they had
> lived wrongly. The great chiefs said to the others, "Looking back from here the
> way we have come, we see that we have left bloody tracks. We see many wrongs.
> And as for these bloody hatchets, and bows, arrows, they must be buried forever."
> Then they all set about deciding to join with one another in a confederacy [literally,
> "be related to one another"].

(Leavitt and Francis, 38–39)

As "brothers" in the Wabanaki "family," the allied nations could call upon each other for aid against outside enemies (Speck 1915c:498). They reciprocated each other's military services or gave auxiliary warriors gifts, such as furs, in exchange for their help. Wabanaki leaders held regular conventions at their various "council fires" (seats of government).

ALLIANCE CEREMONIAL PRACTICES

The Wabanaki Confederacy was more than a political alliance. It was also a cultural agency, ritually bonding different and even formerly hostile groups. At special gatherings chieftains and ambassadors discussed common issues and forged agreements. Because everyone's future depended on a precise understanding of statements and promises, words were important. To prevent misinterpretation in these intertribal assemblies, leaders developed protocol, which included a stylized language of diplomacy, underlined by meaningful gestures and supported by the presentation of ritual objects.

Wampum: Wampum belts played an important role in Wabanaki diplomacy. Although the Mi'kmaqs had long prized these blue and white shell beads as adornment and as precious gifts, their function in political ceremonies was probably introduced by the Iroquois or Huron (Speck, 1919). Mi'kmaqs began using wampum belts in their diplomatic transactions after the mid-1600s. The Wabanaki Confederacy was represented by four white triangles on a blue background—one triangle for each of the allied nations. In times of need, envoys took this belt to invite the allies "to take up the hatchet against the enemies of the nation" (LeClercq, in Speck 1919:33; cf. JR 28:293).

Dog feast: About the same time that Mi'kmaqs adopted ceremonial use of wampum, they also acquired a new war-making ritual usually known as the dog feast. In this ceremony, which they may have borrowed from the Huron, war leaders from allied nations shared a ritual meal of boiled dog before going to battle against a common enemy. Typically hosted by a renowned chief or famous warrior, these feasts were attended by invited chiefs and warriors from several different villages. Holding a council of war, they discussed their options. If they agreed on battle, they devised a campaign strategy, elected a war chief, and ordered the young men to kill dogs for the feast. Those who ate were committed to fight (NEHGR 18 [1864]:163; CMeHS II/4:291). Sometimes French military officers hosted dog feasts. For example, in 1690 Canada's governor entertained Indian chiefs "at a grand feast consisting of two oxen, six large dogs, two barrels of wine, some prunes, and tobacco to smoke" (PD 4:479). The Wabanaki practiced this war-making ritual until French Canada fell into British hands in 1763. Among the Mi'kmaq, the last reported dog feast took place in the Miramichi area in 1761. As an English captive later reported: "We found the head of a dog smoaked whole, the hair singed off, but the teeth and tongue still standing—The Indians, when they make a great Feast, kill two or three dogs, which they hold as a high treat—at such times they have a great dance" (in Whitehead, 1991:165).

Smoking the calumet: This ceremonial practice, perhaps adopted from the Ottawa, signified the creation of "sacred kinship" and was sometimes referred to as "singing the calumet." (Today this ritual is better known as "smoking the peace pipe.") In 1671 a French fur trader also active in Mi'kmaq country noted that the pipe "compels the suspension of hostilities and secures the reception of deputies from hostile tribes who undertake to visit those whose people have been recently slain by theirs. It is, in one word, the calumet which had authority to confirm everything, and which renders solemn oaths binding" (in Blair 2, 182–86).

Burying the hatchet: This Iroquois ritual was another widespread peace ceremony adopted by the Wabanaki. One of the earliest references to this practice among Mi'k-maqs comes from a French observer, who noted in 1700: "When a war is ended, they bury the hatchet in the deepest hole they can dig, in order that it may not be found again; they wish thus to show . . . that peace is so sweet & so precious, that no one should ever disturb it" (Diereville, 172).

KINSHIP TERMINOLOGY AND ALLIANCE

Before the Wabanaki nations joined each other in the confederacy, each had formed strong ties of friendship and alliance with the French. They referred to the French as they did to one another—as "brothers" (Nicolar, 129). This use of kinship metaphor was not a unique cultural practice. For instance, nations in the Iroquois Confederacy also addressed each other as brothers.

Allowing for some ranking difference between an older and a younger "brother," this kin term generally expressed equal status. More complex is the term "father," which became an important concept in the political rhetoric of colonial diplomacy. In medieval Europe it was sometimes used to refer to a feudal lord or king: In exchange for the protecting care of his lord ("father"), a vassal ("son") pledged obedience. When the French colonized North America, they forged a new social order based on old ideas, some (such as the seigneurial system) stemming from feudal traditions. When the French Crown, disturbed about the disorder and lack of progress in the colony, appointed Count de Frontenac governor of Canada, the governor tried to turn the allied Indian nations into colonial subjects of the Crown (Charlevoix 3:260). Imagining himself as a feudal lord, Frontenac referred to himself as a "father," a symbolic expression of his suzerain authority. As Frontenac saw it, the Indians paid their respects "with all the proofs of submission that Children owe their Father" (PD 1:105).

However, because they did not share a feudal tradition, the Indians did not interpret the term "father" in the same way as the French. Among the Indians, "fathers had no power to command children, but among Europeans they did. [They] quickly came to understand this difference" (Jennings 1984:44–45). Whatever the problems in cross-cultural interpretation, the custom was picked up, and it became commonplace for French Indian allies to refer to the governor in Canada as their "father."

FRENCH MISSIONARIES AS WARRIOR-PRIESTS

Catholic missionaries, answerable to their religious superiors as well as to the French Crown, played an important role in northeast America's colonial wars. By the 1680s, after about 70 years of exposure to missionary activity, many Mi'kmaq Indians had been converted to Catholicism (although the degree to which they embraced Christian religious doctrine is uncertain). France, desperate to retain the alliance of Indians, especially those living on the New England frontier, banked on missionary influence to hold the Indians within its sphere of influence.

What made the missionaries so valuable as political agents and providers of military intelligence? Most important, they were ideologically committed to the French cause. As God's loyal servants on earth, they saw themselves as spiritual warriors against the "Antichrist." By founding Indian missions, they believed that they were building a Christian bulwark against the forces of evil, in particular English heretics who corrupted the "noble children of the forest" with Protestantism and liquor. Moreover, as participant observers in tribal communities, priests were familiar with native customs and language and were personally acquainted with the local leaders and their followers. Also, because they traveled often with hunting bands throughout the area, they knew the lay of the land, including English trading posts, fishing stations, and military strongholds. Typically keen and articulate, they were usually capable of providing French military officers with detailed and accurate information.

Financially supported by the French Crown, missionaries distributed gifts from the king, thus obliging the recipients to their "father." Their success as power brokers translated not only in political capital but also in added spiritual prestige. This, in turn, was used to convince Indians to abandon their traditional beliefs and become Christians. As far as the Indians were concerned, missionaries were valued because they offered direct access to French economic wealth, political power, and military aid (de la Varenne, 118). The remarkable success of these missionaries stirred resentment among old shaman-chiefs, whom they often replaced, and enraged New England's Protestant colonists. Protestants accused the priests of grossly misleading the Wabanaki Indians by telling them "that Jesus was a Frenchman, and his mother, the Virgin, a French lady; that the English had murdered him, and that the best way to gain his favor was to revenge his death" (Parkman, 395). Surely priests had something to do with the fact that the Mi'kmaq term for a Protestant person was *mu alasutmaq* ("he who does not pray").

THE INTRODUCTION OF COMMERCIAL SCALPING

In previous chapters references have been made to scalping by Mi'kmaqs and others. As a token of victory, a scalp offers gruesome evidence that its holder has triumphed in battle and killed his enemy: "The whorl of hair on the crown and especially male scalplocks, braided and decorated with jewelry, paint, and feathers, represented the person's 'soul' or living spirit" (Axtell, 214). Scalping was widely practiced by natives in North America before European contact, including Mi'kmaqs, who "cut off the scalps . . . , which they dry, or tan, and make trophies with. . . . they take them, and dance with them . . ." (Lescarbot, 3:271). Although scalping was not practiced in Europe, Europeans did take heads (or tongues, hands, or other body parts) for triumphant display. Furthermore, among Englishmen the practice of paying bounties for heads was well established. For instance, it was common during the wars in Ireland in the 13th and 14th centuries (Jennings 1976:167–68).

During the colonial wars in North America, Europeans began offering bounty for scalps, transforming the traditional trophy from a memento of valor into a commodity to be exchanged for cash or merchandise. Commercial scalping became common practice in the summer of 1689 when the Massachusetts government began recruiting Mohawk Indians from New York to take Wabanaki scalps (Baxter 6:491). In reaction, the French Crown offered payment for English scalps. Drawing a racial distinction between themselves and the "savages," the English protested that "setting a price upon Englishmen's heads [was] Unchristian and not agreeable to the custom of Nations" (in NEHGR 18 [1864]:162–63). Nonetheless, from 1693 onward, Wabanaki warriors regularly "brought in English Prisoners & Scalps," for which the French colonial government paid them good cash (Calloway, 95–96). Soon, the gruesome practice became commonplace, and anyone—Indian, French, or English—was eligible to scalp or be scalped.

In other words, although Europeans did not introduce scalping to North America, they did institute its commercialization, turning tribal warriors into colonial mercenaries. Illustrative of this frontier "business" is an official French request in 1695 that Wabanaki tribesmen hunt for English scalps instead of beaver pelts (NYCD 4:120). Scalp fees offered by colonial authorities were often quite astounding: 30 English pounds for each male scalp in 1689, 50 in the 1690s, 60 pounds in 1711, and one hundred in the 1740s—well over the entire yearly wage of a colonial coastguard in Massachusetts (Calloway, 95–96; NHSP 3, part 2:477; Baxter 23:296;

Murdoch 2:40; Swanson, 99). And warriors knew how to market their wares. As a French officer observed: "They know to make two or even three out of one" (Bougainville, 142).

Now that we have reviewed some major elements pertinent to colonial warfare let us turn to the series of wars which also involved Mi'kmaqs.

THE FIRST ANGLO-WABANAKI WAR (1676–1678)

The first Anglo-Wabanaki War came on the heels of a series of battles in southern New England (known as "King Philip's War," 1675–1676). In 1676, after the murder of Wampanoag Chief Metacomet (nicknamed "King Philip" by the English), many survivors fled to Canada, others to Maine. That same year English merchants kidnapped a small band of Wabanaki and shipped them with a cargo of dried fish to the Azores. Sold as slaves to the Portuguese, only two of them ever made it back home. In revenge, Mi'kmaqs and other Wabanaki warriors captured some 20 New England fishing ketches off Nova Scotia and several others on the Maine coast. Skirmishing continued in the borderlands until treaties formally ended the fighting in 1678 (Baxter 6:118–19, 180, 23:1; Hubbard, 94, 136, 151, 636; Beck, 31; Felt 2:212–13).

THE SECOND ANGLO-WABANAKI WAR (1688–1698)

The outbreak of the second Anglo-Wabanaki War was directly connected to an ongoing dynastic power struggle in Europe. In a nutshell, the following occurred: In the Glorious Revolution of 1688, the English Parliament ousted its Roman Catholic king, James II. His Protestant daughter, Mary, became queen, and her Dutch husband, William III (the Prince of Orange) became king. Their reign forged a Protestant coalition between the Netherlands and England. Trying to restore the toppled Catholic monarch to the throne, King Louis XIV of France offered James II refuge and support, declaring war on the English. Already at war with a coalition between the Netherlands, the Holy Roman (German) Empire, Sweden, and Spain (League of Augsburg), the French were surrounded by enemies during what became known as the War of the Grand Alliance. Because almost all of these warring European nations had rival mercantile and colonial interests in various corners of the globe, military confrontation could take place almost anywhere the French were active.

The particular event that ignited the second Anglo-Wabanaki War could well have remained an obscure local conflict between Sokokis and their English neighbors in northern Massachusetts. Knowing that these Algonquian-speaking Indians were close allies of Wabanakis in Maine, English officials decided to nip in the bud potential support by instructing military commanders on the Maine coast "to take and destroy all [Indians] in acts of hostility . . ." (Baxter 6:435–37). When innocent Abenakis were kidnapped and taken as hostages to a Boston prison, a small band of warriors retaliated by capturing some English settlers (Baxter 6:425–26).

Soon thereafter New England declared open war on the Wabanaki and in June 1689 began recruiting Mohawk mercenaries—offering them a bounty of 30 pounds for scalps belonging to native "murderers" and 20 "for any other men or enemies" (Baxter 6:491). New England also raised an army of English volunteers and "Friend Indians," in particular Wampanoags from Cape Cod and Mohegans from Connecticut, who "shall have the benefit of the captives, and all lawful plunder, and the reward of eight pounds per head, for every fighting man slain by them, over and above their stated wages" (Church, 13; Baxter 9: 4–7).

Meanwhile, prompted by news that their old Dutch allies had united with the English, and heartened by "a commitment of aid from New York," 1,500 Iroquois warriors surprised French settlers near Montreal, killing many and causing great suffering (Jennings 1984:195). About the same time, Mi'kmaqs and other Wabanaki warriors struck out against English fishing stations, settlements, and fortifications on the Maine coast. Sometimes missionaries accompanied them in battle, resulting in curious scenes: Ready to lay siege at an English stronghold at Pemaquid, several hundred warriors knelt in prayer before launching their assault. This particular English garrison, small and ill-equipped for defense, quickly surrendered. Attacking several other settlements and strongholds, the Wabanaki forced the English to vacate their holdings east of the Kennebec River, which the French Crown viewed as the colonial boundary between New England and New France (Sewall 5:184, 321; Gyles, 10–11). The English retaliated in the fall of 1689 (Baxter 4:464–65).

In the early months of 1690 the French launched a three-pronged attack against the English colonies. Headed by French military officers, each war party represented a combined force of French Canadian soldiers and Indian warriors, mainly Abenaki, but also Huron, Algonkin, and Sokoki. In reaction, New England decided to "forthwith undertake an expedition against the French at Port Royal, & places along shoar, that may give some check to their depredations" (in NEHGR 2 [1848]:150). Leaving Boston Harbor, "an English squadron, consisting of a forty-gun frigate, a vessel of sixteen, a third of eighteen guns, and four ketches," sailed to Port Royal. Although it was the largest French settlement in Acadia at the time, this garrison, with its 86 men and eighteen pieces of artillery, fell quickly in the face of England's military might (Gargas, 181). Taking the governor of Acadia prisoner, the fleet sailed on, destroying French fishing stations at La Hève and Chedabucto and sacking the various other small French establishments from Cape Breton to Gaspé Peninsula (Charlevoix 4:154–62).

With Acadia's governor captured and Port Royal surrendered, France placed Acadia under the command of a young captain named François de Villebon. Because the English now controlled Acadia's coastal area, Villebon moved his military headquarters to Fort Jemseg on the lower St. John River. This old wooden stronghold was in the domain of the Sieur de Chauffours, who also operated a fur trading post in his seigneury at the Richibucto River. At Jemseg Villebon had direct access to a large number of Mi'kmaq hunters who could be called into service as warriors for the French Crown.

In the fall of 1692, aiming to more effectively direct the guerrilla war against New England, Villebon relocated upriver to Nashwaak in another domain belonging to Chauffours. At this strategic point, at the confluence of the Nashwaak and St. John rivers, French Canadian workers began erecting the fort. Upon its completion in mid-April 1693, Villebon noted in his diary: "The fort is in a perfect condition. Besides the oak sheething on the inside, I had made, in the bastions and curtains, a terrace of good wattles, four and a half feet high by two in width . . . I have eight swivel-guns placed on the bastion . . . so that it will be possible to fire with accuracy in case the enemy have grenades. I had water brought from a spring into the fort by a wooden conduit under ground. . . . There is a barrack for the soldiers, 28 feet long" (in Webster, 48).

From this new military command post, Villebon controlled the St. John River traffic between the St. Lawrence Valley, Bay of Fundy, and the Miramichi River and distributed commodities, arms, and ammunition to the Mi'kmaq and their Wabanaki allies. About one mile from the fort the Mi'kmaq had their own fortified village, where warriors periodically "assembled to select chiefs and war-captains for the campaign" (Villebon, 105).

To feed his troops, plus the Wabanaki war parties who visited him at Fort Nashwaak, Villebon purchased barrels of peas and flour from French farmers at Minas and other Acadian villages, supplemented by foodstuffs shipped in from Europe (Villebon, 110). Villebon also needed gifts to reward the warriors for their services. These precious goods were brought from Europe aboard French warships, unloaded on the lower St. John, and transported in smaller boats to Nashwaak. When calling a war council, Villebon sent envoys as far as Cape Breton and the Androscoggin River, inviting the Mi'kmaq, Maliseet, and Abenaki to join in a military campaign against New England. Usually, the raiding season lasted only a few months, beginning in the late spring when the men returned from their winter hunting grounds.

To provision some 200 Wabanaki warriors for about two months, Villebon asked the French king to send 2,000 pounds of flour, 48 gallons of molasses, and 200 pounds of butter to flavor their sagamité (corn porridge). To arm them he also requested 60 guns, 2,000 pounds of gunpowder, 40 barrels of bullets, 10 barrels of swan shot, and 200 tomahawks. Among the gifts Villebon requested for his Wabanaki allies were 10 barrels (360 gallons) of brandy (without which it would be "impossible to prevail on them to act efficiently"), 400 pounds of Brazilian tobacco, 200 mulaix shirts, eight pounds of fine vermillion, and 200 tufts of white feathers. The feathers, Villebon explained, were "to be given to the Indians as a distinguishing mark in case of a night attack, [and should] be selected in Paris by [Simon-Pierre Denys, Sieur] de Bonaventure" (Villebon, 71; PD 5:577). Such presents, explained Villebon, "do much to preserve their alliance with the French; without the aid they receive from it they would be in no position to resist the English, and in consequence, [would] make peace with them" (in Webster, 141).

The Rise and Fall of New England's Fort Pemaquid (1692–1696)

In 1692, about the same time Villebon fortified himself at Nashwaak, the English returned to Pemaquid, where Wabanaki warriors had destroyed a small wooden fort three years earlier. Given Pemaquid's strategic location on New England's eastern frontier, the English now built a large stone fort there. The walls of this fort were over 100 feet long on each side and stood 10–22 feet in height. Its western bastion reached 29 feet. Outfitted with about twenty cannon and at least 60 militia (Bradley and Camp, 10), the stone fort seemed impregnable. Certainly it was the strongest garrison on the Atlantic seaboard, and it shifted the military balance even further in England's favor. Some Wabanaki leaders, perhaps foreseeing New England's supremacy on the Maine coast, sought peace with the English. According to the royal governor of Massachusetts: "The fort is strong enough to resist all the Indians in America and has so much discouraged them that they have laid down their arms and sent their sagamores [chieftains] to beg for an everlasting peace. I went to Pemaquid accordingly and concluded articles of peace [in August 1693]" (in Ibid.).

This concession caused friction within the Wabanaki Confederacy and greatly alarmed the French, who did everything they could to discredit the chiefs who signed the treaty and to stir into action those who opposed it. Among the Wabanaki leaders who opposed making peace with the English was Chief Hiarim of Richibucto, who repeatedly commanded Mi'kmaq war parties raiding the New England frontier. Another renowned war chief was Taxous, a Kennebec Abenaki. Villebon, probably on the advice of a French missionary familiar with Wabanaki concepts of making "sacred kinship," adopted Taxous as his ritual brother, sealing the ceremony with fine gifts (including his "best suit of clothes"). Taxous, in turn, assured Villebon that he would gather a large war party to raid the English (Villebon, 55).

Although guerrilla-style raiding was effective against unprotected frontier settlements of small palisaded wooden forts, the fortress at Pemaquid required a more radical strategy. Educated in France, where he had served in a dragoon regiment for about ten years, Villebon was familiar with siege warfare as it was practiced in Europe. Calculating that it was impossible to take the fort by land, he determined to take it by naval bombardment.

Certainly there was a role for Mi'kmaqs in this attack, given their seafighting skills. As we have seen, Mi'kmaqs were fully familiar with sailing European shallops and had successfully captured larger English fishing vessels on their shores. Moreover, many had journeyed to Europe aboard fishing boats, merchant vessels, or even warships. In all likelihood, some intrepid Mi'kmaqs had even sailed on pirate ships cruising the Atlantic coast from Newfoundland down to the Caribbean, perhaps beyond. And without doubt Mi'kmaq warriors served aboard the *Bretonne,* a French brigantine (warship) that sailed from France in April 1694 under the command of the Sieur de Bonaventure, a famous French Canadian seafighter. Bonaventure called on the harbor of St. John River with military supplies for Villebon, cruised along the Acadian coast, and visited Newfoundland. Then he convoyed a fleet of French fishing vessels back across the Atlantic (Webster, 164–65).

In the spring of 1695 Bonaventure returned to Fort Nashwaak with more military supplies, and the following spring he commanded one of two well-equipped frigates (small warships) sent by the French Crown to help Villebon capture Fort Pemaquid and destroy English fisheries and settlements in Newfoundland. An even more formidable French Canadian naval officer, Pierre LeMoyne, Sieur d'Iberville, commanded the other frigate. Father Jean Baudoin, a former musketeer of the King's Guards, sailed with them. This adventurous and hot-tempered priest had first come to New France in the 1680s, assigned to serve colonists at Port Royal. But he preferred ranging the woods with Mi'kmaqs (Webster, 163).

The frigates first went to Quebec to recruit more troops and then sailed to Cape Breton, where Father Baudoin said Mass for a group of Mi'kmaqs, took their confessions, baptized several infants, and married some couples. When the warships sailed on to the Bay of Fundy, about 30 Mi'kmaq warriors climbed on board. Ten days later they engaged three English warships and captured one of them. Continuing on to the mouth of the St. John River, the warships picked up another missionary and a band of Maliseet warriors. A French privateer, captaining his own ship, joined the group, and all went to Pentagoet at Penobscot Bay for a large Wabanaki rendezvous. At this place lived Baron de St. Castin, who had come to New France as a teenage ensign in an elite French regiment brought to subdue the Iroquois in 1665. In 1670 he was stationed at Fort Pentagoet near the mouth of the Penobscot River. Since then he had become a wealthy fur trader and married the daughter of a powerful Penobscot River chief named Madockawando. Thoroughly familiar with the Wabanaki, who recognized him as a chief, St. Castin was also well-informed about the military conditions at Fort Pemaquid just around the coastal corner.

The rendezvous at St. Castin's habitation included some 250 Wabanakis, including Mi'kmaqs. What did these warriors look like? Several wore a tuft of white feathers in their hair, some sported gray and black wigs, and others wore colored ones. (Wigs had become the height of fashion in France.) Those who were converts wore a brass or silver crucifix around the neck. All were well-armed with French muskets, waistbelts and cutlasses (short, thick curving swords favored by sailors), and most had a bayonet and pistol (see also Bradley and Camp, 8).

After a grand council of war and a lavish (dog?) feast, the Wabanaki warriors, under St. Castin's command, along with 25 French marines, set sail for Pemaquid in

Three seventeenth-century frigates. Mi'kmaq seafighters served on such warships from the late 1600s onward.

two warships. Not far from their destination, most of these troops disembarked and marched to the fortress, while the warships, under Iberville, anchored at Pemaquid's outer harbor (PD 5:658). Envoys rowed ashore waving a flag of truce and carrying a letter from Iberville calling for surrender. When the English commander refused, Iberville fired four bombs just outside the fort, then "summoned [the enemy] once more, threatening them to no longer give quarter if they compelled me to breach the ramparts at which time I would not be able to control the Indians" (in Bradley and Camp, 11). St. Castin, who also spoke English, handled the negotiations, which finally resulted in the English commander and his militia quitting the fort unarmed. In return they were given safe passage to Boston. Their artillery was taken aboard the French ships, their muskets were distributed among the Indian warriors, and the fort was burned (Casgrain, 188; Hutchinson 2:69; Webster, 16).

After this remarkable bloodless victory, Iberville sailed to Cape Breton, where most of the Mi'kmaqs went ashore. Father Baudoin and three warriors remained on board, joining Iberville's raid against the English fishing settlements at Newfoundland (Casgrain, 190–97; Webster, 163).

New England's Counterattack and Termination of War

In the summer of 1696 English Captain Benjamin Church commanded a naval expedition against French Acadia, ransacking the French and Indian settlements. His troops numbered 250 English volunteers and 150 Indians from Cape Cod (Massachusetts) (Church, 97–115; Villebon, 94–95). Raids and counterraids continued until events across the ocean called the colonial war to a halt. In 1697, signing the Treaty of Ryswick in the Netherlands, the French Crown finally recognized William of Orange as legitimate king of England, Scotland and Ireland, ending hostilities (for the time being) in Europe. However, it took until spring 1698 for the news to travel from Europe to the French stronghold in the St. John Valley. When the news arrived, messages were sent throughout the region with invitations to prominent Wabanakis to come to Fort Nashwaak. On 26 June 1698, Villebon (115–16) "gave a feast to the Chiefs and afterwards told them to cease all acts of hostility."

In 1699 chiefs representing the Wabanaki Confederacy signed a peace treaty with the English, but it was an uneasy peace. When envoys from Massachusetts referred to King William as "our common father," the Wabanaki protested, pointing out that the king of France was their "father." Because the French and English kings had made peace with each other as "brothers," the chiefs were willing to refer to him as "*Uncle* King William" and to express thanks that this "uncle" had accepted the Wabanaki into his "league of friendship" (Baxter 10:87–95).

As dependent as ever on a native buffer in the borderlands between New France and New England, the French Crown sought ways to maintain its influence among the Wabanaki. Beyond offering gifts, French governors began to confirm the election of Wabanaki chiefs by giving them the title of captain, a formal commission to command a particular district, and French flags to display in their villages and forts (in Upton, 46; PD 7:942; Murdoch 1:251). Soon it became custom for Wabanaki villages to fly the French flag. Likewise, when Indians came paddling or sailing to a French fort or trading post, they were to hoist the French flag. As far as the Indians were concerned, this was nothing more than a symbol of friendship. But in the European tradition flags indicated the power or jurisdiction of a lord or king over a certain place. So when the French asked Mi'kmaqs to hoist banners emblazoned with the royal *fleur-de-lis,* they aimed to impose French sovereignty over their allies. Not long afterwards the English Crown instituted the same policy within its colonial boundaries. In disputed borderlands, showing the wrong "colors" was a sure invitation for trouble (PD 8:1008–09; Baxter 9:275, 23:106).

And what about the powerful Iroquois? In 1699 they met their match when Ottawa River warriors, heavily armed by the French, delivered them a stunning blow near Lake Erie. After this encounter the Iroquois could field only about 1,200 warriors, barely more than the collective Wabanaki force. In 1700, greatly weakened, the Iroquois sent chiefs to Montreal to offer the French governor their wampum belts of peace (in Jennings 1984:209).

With the conclusion of King William's War, the Wabanaki hoped that they could return to trapping and trading as before. But the fur market had crashed. With the flow of furs from the Great Lakes no longer checked by Iroquois warfare, the supply rose. Meanwhile, the demand overseas had diminished greatly. Consequently, fur values dropped some 75 percent (in NYCD 4:789). Because the French depended on the Mi'kmaqs and other borderland tribes, they had little choice but to continue subsidizing their native allies.

Although the Mi'kmaq were harmed by the decline in fur prices, international competition for the cod fisheries on their shores proved even more damaging. Massachusetts merchants had their eyes on the abundant fish stocks off the Mi'kmaq coast—and knew full well that nothing but their French foes stopped them from capitalizing on this wealth of the sea (NYCD 4:790). And other natural resources attracted them to Mi'kmaq country: Rich deposits of "sea coal," valued as fuel, and great quantities of trees, prized for ship masts and fuel.

THE THIRD ANGLO-WABANAKI WAR (1703–1713)

Like the previous colonial war, this upheaval (known as Queen Anne's War) had European roots: The complex dynastic conflict known as the War of Spanish Succession (1702–1714). Once again, coalitions formed in Europe and battles were fought on many fronts. Catholic France and Protestant England remained in opposite camps. In the fall of 1702, following orders from the French Crown, Canada's governor declared war on the neighboring English colonists.

As in previous colonial conflicts, the French recognized that it was "highly necessary to embroil the [Wabanaki, who might otherwise] enter into arrangements with the English and be eventually opposed to us" (PD 6:743). Within the Wabanaki Confederacy many preferred neutrality, while others felt obliged to support their French brothers (K. Morrison, 1984:286–87) against New England's burgeoning population, now up to 150,000 (Murdoch 2:265). In the end, they fought. French missionaries, guided by a moral theology that justified a "holy war," once again played a crucial role in instigating Wabanaki involvement.

In August 1703 the French launched a surprise seaborne raid against English settlements on the Maine coast. Among the ranks were 200 Mi'kmaq warriors, two priests, three military officers, and 30 French soldiers (Pike, 50; Baxter 9:152;

NYCD 9:756). In response to this sudden attack, New England declared war on the Wabanaki and their allies and threatened to call in the Mohawks and other warriors. Encouraging settlers and mercenaries to kill Wabanakis, English authorities offered to "volunteers without pay" the formidable sum of 50 pounds per scalp, while the "regular forces under pay" received 10 pounds. Over and above scalp bounties, they were granted "the benefit of Plunder, & Captives of Women & Children under twelve Years of age . . ." (Penhallow, 47–49). Soon Wabanakis whose villages were exposed to English attack retreated to mission villages in Canada (Casgrain, 258–59).

In 1704 New England authorities launched a naval expedition that included three warships (one with 48 guns, one with 32, and one with 13) and twenty sloops. This force of 500 English volunteers from Massachusetts and 100 "Friend Indians" from Cape Cod coasted down east and systematically ransacked the deserted Wabanaki villages and attacked French hamlets (Church, 170; cf. Hutchinson 2:107; Penhallow, 27–30).

Losing the Fight for Acadia

To drive English vessels from French Acadia's coastal waters, Port Royal's governor commissioned French shipping captains as privateers. Individuals in this volunteer naval force (some hailing from as far south as the Caribbean) got to keep any enemy vessels (plus cargo) that they captured (Baxter 9:193, 212). Having already demonstrated their value as marines, Mi'kmaqs from Cape Breton were again recruited. Deployed on French warships and privateers, they raided English fishing settlements at Newfoundland in 1705–1709, ultimately ousting the English from the region. Although war inhibited access to vital trade goods, loot from these seaborne raids allowed the French to pay for some 70 Mi'kmaqs and other Wabanaki warriors, who had been promised that they would be rewarded according to merit (Murdoch 1:299–307).

In 1706, joining the Wabanakis in their raiding, a band of Hurons from the Canadian mission village of Lorette (near Quebec) attacked southern Maine's coastal frontier settlements. The next year the English assailed Acadia once again. Although the French lost vital control over the territorial waters in the Gulf of Maine and the Bay of Fundy, they still held Port Royal, seat of the colony's government. Four years later, however, New England troops, reinforced by English naval power, launched a final assault against Port Royal: An overwhelming force of 3,400 men and 36 ships laid siege to the town's ramshackle fort held by fewer than 300 French (Francis et al., a, 130). Launching out against the invaders, Wabanakis rallied to the support of their French allies but failed to break the siege. Many lost their lives, while others were captured and taken to Boston as hostages. With the loss of only 20 soldiers, the British took Port Royal, leaving behind a garrison of 270 troops to guard their newly captured stronghold in Acadia (PD 7:858–59; Murdoch 1:323, 325; Baxter 9:317–19).

Stationing another garrison at Canso to defend the fisheries, the English now controlled the entire Atlantic coast from Florida to northern Nova Scotia (PD 7:854). Defeated in Acadia, French troops withdrew to Cape Breton Island.

In 1711 New England authorities raised the bounty on Wabanakis to 60 pounds for a man, 30 for a woman, "and for every minor or *papoose* [child], fifteen" (in

NHSP 3, part 2:477). New England troops and their "Friend Indians" continued to raid all along the Gulf of Maine and the Nova Scotia coasts.

That summer the British planned the "Conquest of Canada." While one force marched through the woods to Montreal, over 5,350 men embarked on a fleet of 15 warships. En route from Boston to Quebec, nine vessels were shipwrecked, forcing the British command to call off the invasion (Penhallow, 67–73). About the same time, the French-Abenaki officer St. Castin, Penobscot Chief Simouret, and 150 Wabanaki warriors headed to Port Royal. Father Gaulin accompanied the force, which crossed the Bay of Fundy in bark canoes. They ambushed and killed 70 British troops who were en route from Port Royal to burn some French Acadian farms. The British military commander at Port Royal complained that "it is Impossible for us to prevent these skulking partys which so plague us but by a party of Indians who are equal to them in the woods." He requested a force of Iroquois, and in 1712 nearly 100 Mohawk warriors, accompanied by Major Livingston of Albany, New York, arrived at Port Royal, where a fort called the Mohawk House was built for them. Much as the French had used Mi'kmaqs to destroy English fishermen at Newfoundland, the British used Mohawk rangers to strike terror among the Mi'kmaq and their friends (Wallis and Wallis 1955:210–11; Murdoch 1:368–70).

TREATY OF UTRECHT (1713): MAKING PEACE AND DIVIDING WABANAKI LANDS

The third Anglo-Wabanaki War ended, as it had begun, in Europe. In 1713, after a decade of conflict, the various warring parties in Europe began peace negotiations in the Dutch city of Utrecht. The resulting treaty involved not only France and Great Britain, but also the Netherlands, Portugal, Russia, and Savoy. The war's cost had been stunning on all levels. Mi'kmaq and other Wabanaki warriors raiding all along the New England frontier had ravaged many English settlements, and the English had spent at least one thousand pounds for every Indian killed or captured (Penhallow, 48). But Wabanaki losses were proportionably far greater. Violence, diseases, and hunger had wiped out about one third of the total Wabanaki population (CMeHS II/4:291; Penhallow, 66).

To regain some of the territorial losses it suffered in Europe, the French Crown made concessions in its colonial possessions, ceding to Great Britain all claims to Newfoundland, except for fishing rights on its north shore. The king also gave up his claims on Hudson Bay and recognized British suzerainty over the Iroquois Confederacy. Furthermore, he surrendered control over most of Acadia (Francis et al., a, 110). Thus, with the stroke of a pen in Utrecht, the French Crown surrendered the lands of its Wabanaki allies. Port Royal's name was changed to Annapolis Royal, in honor of British Queen Anne. Some provisions were made concerning the French Acadians. They had the right to leave the area and resettle on lands still under French rule. However, having been granted "freedom of religion," most of these peasants stayed put and became known as the "neutral French" (PD 7:931).

10 / Colonial Wars: Losing the Armed Struggle for Independence

ABORIGINAL TITLE: FRENCH OPPORTUNISM IN ACADIA AFTER 1713

Informed of Anglo-French reconciliation, about 360 Wabanakis, including Mi'k-maqs, assembled at Casco Bay on the Maine coast, where they discussed the terms of peace with New England authorities. Speaking on behalf of the Wabanaki Confederacy, an orator addressed the British delegates from Boston: "It is well that the kings should be in peace. . . . It is not I that am striking you these past . . . years, it is the Frenchman who has availed himself of my arm to strike you. . . . Now the Frenchman tells me to lay [my tomahawk] down; I throw it very far, that no one may see any more the blood with which it is reddened. So, let us live in peace, I agree to it" (CMeHS II/4:293).

Then the British delegates announced to the Wabanakis that the French king had swapped their homeland and that the British Crown now claimed sovereign title over Acadia, from Penobscot to Gaspé, with the exception of Cape Breton and Isle St. Jean (Prince Edward Island). Moreover, the British expected the Wabanakis to submit themselves as loyal subjects. The Wabanakis demurred. Never having been conquered, they still considered themselves a free people. Although they had accepted the French governor in Canada (and by extension the French king) as "father," this had not entitled him to ownership of their territories (Dickason 1986:33). Denying that the French king had the right to give away their homeland, Wabanakis disavowed British title to Acadia. As their orator explained: "You say that the Frenchman has given you Plaisance [Newfoundland] and Portrait [Nova Scotia] which are in my neighborhood, with all the lands adjacent: He shall give you all that he will; for me I have my land which the Great Spirit has given me for living, as long as there shall be a child of my people, he will fight for its preservation" (CMeHS II/4:293). The Wabanaki agreed that the British could "forever enjoy all and Singular the Rights of Land and former [prewar] Settlements, Properties and Possessions," provided that the Wabanakis "own ground" would be saved and that their people would retain "free liberty of hunting, fishing, fowling, and all other lawful liberties and privileges" (in Penhallow, 79).

Although Wabanakis left this gathering satisfied with British assurances about their ancestral lands, they were indignant that their French allies had relinquished territory that was never given to them. They asked their missionaries: "By what right did the King of France dispose of [our] country?" (NYCD 9:879–80). Embarrassed, the missionaries appeased them by saying "that they had been deceived by an ambiguous expression, and that their country was not included in that which had been ceded . . ." (PD 7:878–79). Although there was indeed some confusion about the exact boundaries of Acadia, the fact is that Mi'kmaq sovereignty, native rights, and aboriginal title had played no role in France's negotiations with Great Britain. In fact, the French never considered the idea of aboriginal title until after they ceded Acadia to the British.

Because native sovereignty remains a bone of contention to this day, we need to consider this issue in a bit more detail. Although the French "took care to respect the territories of their allies," they "considered their [own] claim to sovereignty over lands preeminent to that of non-Christian [Indian] peoples" (Dickason 1986:33–34). In this respect, the French position differed from that of the Dutch and later the English, both of whom formally recognized the principle of aboriginal title, evidenced in the fact that they signed deeds of purchase or made formal claims based on victories in what they called "just wars." French policy toward aboriginal land rights was clearly established in 1618, when the Crown asserted that Indian territories were "free" and could be taken by the French king, "who will make himself master and lord" (Champlain 2:329–31). Over time, land confiscation rituals emerged. Usually, the French would invite the greatest possible number of Indian chiefs from the region to a strategic site for a great feast. When the feasting was done, French officials began the confiscation ceremony, typically turning up a chunk of sod, raising it three times, and crying "Long live the king!" The entire assembly, French and Indian alike, was pressed to repeat the cry. After several other symbolic acts, French officials erected their king's coat of arms (with the fleur-de-lis), signed a document in witness of the act, and asked the Indian chiefs to add their "hieroglyphic marks" (in PD 6:791). As with the raising of French flags in Wabanaki villages, it seems clear that French and Indian interpretations of these ceremonies differed. To the French, the ceremonies established sovereignty; to the Indians they confirmed friendship and mutual obligation. The two differing views did not result in conflicts primarily because the land was vast and the French were few.

Geopolitical self-interest, especially apprehension that the Wabanakis might turn their backs on them after the 1713 Treaty of Utrecht, caused the French to consider the concept of aboriginal title—at least as a convenient political strategy. Although they did not seriously accept the idea that Mi'kmaqs or other indigenous nations possessed territorial rights (Murdoch 1:352), they did employ the concept of aboriginal title "where it was useful for annoying the English" (Dickason 1986:33). One French official commented: "If we do not admit or pretend to admit their right to the country they occupy, they will never be induced to take a part in any war for the defence of this same country, which is the rampart of Canada" (PD 7:878–79).

Vulnerable without a Wabanaki buffer on their borders with New England, the French now argued that the Acadia that they had ceded in 1713 comprised only Nova Scotia peninsula and that the Wabanakis still retained aboriginal title to the region from the Saco River to Port Royal (PD 7: 904–05).

CAPE BRETON AS THE NEW FRENCH POLITICAL CENTER

In 1716 Massachusetts Colony alone counted over 90,000 settlers, while French Canada had less than 25,000. When the French Crown lost the St. Lawrence gateways of Acadia and Newfoundland, Cape Breton Island became of paramount importance—militarily for its strategic location and economically for its offshore cod fisheries. At this time, only 3,000 French inhabited Cape Breton, while several thousand more remained on the Nova Scotia peninsula now under British control. Gradually, new communities of French fishers and farmers emerged along Cape Breton's coast. In addition to farmsteads with gardens, hayfields, and livestock (cattle, horses, pigs, and fowl), French settlers established sawmills near the coast. For the most part, they left the island's interior to the Mi'kmaq.

Recognizing the need to defend the island against further British expansionism, the French Crown financed the construction of several strongholds. For example, near the site of Denys's old trading post, along the Mi'kmaq portage route to Bras d'Or Lake, they built Port Toulouse, which provided a good southern anchorage. And on the northeast coast they began constructing Fort Louisbourg, a 50-acre garrison town, surrounded with masonry and with an earth-packed wall about 1.8 miles in length. It would take more than 20 years to build the mighty citadel. By the time they finished, it would be a vital fishing port and commercial center for trade between France, Quebec, and the West Indies—the fourth-busiest port in colonial America, after Boston, New York City, and Charleston, S.C. (Francis et al., a:111–12).

FRENCH PROXY WARFARE: MI'KMAQ SEAFIGHTERS

Militarily restricted by the Treaty of Utrecht, the French now used the Wabanaki as proxy warriors. As long as the Crown offered them rewards, the Wabanaki were willing to help defend what was left of France's colonial holdings in northeast America (PD 7: 869). Of course, from their own perspective, the Wabanaki did not see themselves as mercenaries but as freedom fighters trying to liberate their homeland from the British intruders. As far as they were concerned, their French "father" was standing by them in this fateful time, showing his friendship by generously supporting them with gifts.

Each summer, to the resentment of the French, some 200 New England vessels fished off the Nova Scotia coast. From 1715 to 1722, Mi'kmaq seafighters harassed this fleet. Armed and encouraged by their French allies entrenched at Cape Breton, they formed an intrepid force of about 60 marines. Cruising along their coasts in shallops, or sometimes paddling their swift canoes, they searched for ketches and schooners hailing from distant ports. Especially when anchored in some cove, these British vessels were easy targets for surprise attack. Falling upon their prey, Mi'kmaqs would try to board the vessel and surprise the crew. Rather than killing the fishermen, the Mi'kmaq preferred to take them alive for ransom. Plundering whatever was deemed valuable, including the cargo of dried fish, they would bring their spoil to French settlements for sale.

Losing dozens of vessels every summer, the British condemned these Mi'kmaq raiders as pirates. In 1718 New England authorities dispatched a frigate and a man-of-war (combatant warship) to protect their fishing fleet in Nova Scotia—and to do some retaliatory damage to French fishing boats. But this did not stop the Mi'kmaq. Meanwhile, their Abenaki allies staged similar raids against New England fishermen on the Maine coast. Between 1715 and 1722 the British lost about 40 vessels. Later, Wabanaki seafighters seized many more (Baxter 9:432; Beck, 48–50; Dickason 1986:39; Hutchinson 2:180–1; Murdoch 1: 474–5; Upton, 40).

Each spring or fall, Mi'kmaqs assembled at some designated French rendezvous to receive rewards for their military exploits. For example, in the fall of 1716 many Mi'kmaqs congregated at Port Toulouse, the new French stronghold at southern Cape Breton. Some warriors were fresh from a campaign against English fishermen on their coasts (during which they had captured quite a few vessels). They came in the company of two French missionaries, both of whom lived with their flock and shared their lifestyle. A French navy officer described the scene:

> On the 17th [of October] I was present at the great banquet given in honour of our allied Indians who had come to receive the usual gift (valued at 4,000 francs) which the King's ship brings over from France every year. They camped near the government administration centre in those big cabins which they put up in a matter of hours: about 300 souls, including women and children. They were regaled with meats, wine, brandy and bread in the open air where they danced and sang the King's praises.

(in Whitehead 1991:91–92)

Toward the feast's end, the French commander handed them their annual presents "in the name of his Majesty" (Murdoch 1, 352).

MI'KMAQ MISSIONS AND FRENCH WARRIOR-PRIESTS

Dauntless men working in dangerous borderlands, French priests assigned to Indian missions saw themselves as crusaders against the British Protestants. Unlike parish priests who ministered to the French Acadians, they acted directly on behalf of the French Crown. Because missions had strategic value as barriers against British encroachments, the French government invested thousands of *livres* (enormous sums) provisioning missions with basic supplies and gifts to maintain Wabanaki women and children while their men fought on the front (PD 8:991, 994; Casgrain, 367).

One such missionary active among the Mi'kmaq was Father Antoine Gaulin. Belonging to the Order of the Foreign Missions, he played a highly dominant role as warrior-priest for about 30 years. First stationed among the Abenakis of the Penobscot River, Abbé Gaulin was transferred to Nova Scotia, where he served the region's Mi'kmaqs in particular. A French officer who met with the missionary in 1716 described him as follows: "[Gaulin] has embraced all [Indian] customs, officiates at their weddings, baptisms and burials, celebrates mass for them and conducts their prayers every day. He often eats meat and fish without bread, sleeps on the snow, suffers the extreme cold and has also adopted the [Indians'] footwear, which is made from seal skins" (in Whitehead 1991:92–93).

The influence that priests like Gaulin had on Indians was vital to French interests. After France lost control of Acadia from Canso to Penobscot, the Wabanaki became all the more crucial as a buffer against British expansionism. Unable to operate through its military officers during official peacetime, the French Crown depended on missionaries to spearhead Wabanaki aggression against the British. As the governor of Canada himself noted: "The English can have no room to [block] one missionary's visiting another, the treaty of peace not forbidding it, whereas, if a French officer was sent, they might complain that we sent French men into a country, which they [the English] pretend belongs to them, to excite the Indians to make war upon them" (Vaudreuil, 15 June 1721, in Hutchinson 2:198).

After 1713 the French made an unsuccessful effort to draw all Mi'kmaqs of Nova Scotia Peninsula to Cape Breton and consolidate them in a single mission town. Because the Mi'kmaqs refused to abandon their ancestral domains, in 1716 Abbé Gaulin proposed taking the mission to them and suggested Merigomish Island (in the district of Antigonish on Nova Scotia's north shore) as a site. Seeing the benefit of a native guerrilla movement operating within British-held territories, the French Crown supported Gaulin's idea, providing funds to purchase "seed, corn, tools, munitions, and arms" (Leger, 99). Funds were also appropriated to build a mission church to serve as a religious focal point for the regional tribespeople.

By 1722 Abbé Gaulin was serving about 150 Mi'kmaq families in British Nova Scotia. That year he founded another Mi'kmaq mission in Nova Scotia, this one on the banks of the Shubenacadie River. Strategically located in the interior woodlands, it was within reach of the French Acadian villages of Cobequid (Truro) and Minas. From this place, as the missionary noted,"we will be able more easily to deter [British] evil enterprises" (in Upton, 43). Unlike the mission towns founded among the horticultural Abenakis, the posts established for the migratory Mi'kmaqs north of them served more as places of resort for small bands ranging the districts. Usually, each site contained a small wooden Catholic church and a residence for the missionary. Surrounding the church was an encampment of little cabins and wikuoms, seasonally occupied by Mi'kmaq families. During the moose-hunting and raiding season, the settlement was mainly occupied by old people, women, and children. When the priest visited the mission, especially for religious celebrations and special holidays, even more families pitched their wikuoms in the mission village (Casgrain, 367).

During the next few decades, the French Crown would continue its twin strategy of entrenchment and harassment: Building fortifications on its remaining domains and employing Indian guerrillas to operate behind enemy lines. Mi'kmaqs and fellow Wabanakis complied, still hoping that with French support they could drive British intruders from their ancestral lands.

THE FOURTH ANGLO-WABANAKI WAR (1722–1726)

Unlike past and future Anglo-Wabanaki wars, the fourth one was not a spillover of British-French clashes in Europe. It was a local war rooted in Indian reactions to British intrusions.

When British settlers made inroads on their hunting territories, Wabanakis protested repeatedly. In 1721 Mi'kmaqs and Maliseets joined hundreds of local

Abenakis for a conference with the British on the Maine coast (PD 7:904). They drafted a letter to Massachusetts Governor Samuel Shute, stating:

> Thou seest from the peace treaty of which I am sending the copy that thou must live peacefully with me. Is it living peacefully with me to take my land away from me against my will? My land which I received from God alone, my land of which no king nor foreign power has been allowed, or is allowed to dispose against my will, which thou hast been doing none the less for several years, by establishing and fortifying thyself here against my wishes, as thou didst. . . . Consider, great captain that I have often told thee to withdraw from my land and that I am telling thee so again for the last time. My land is not thine either by right or conquest, or by grant or by purchase.

(PD 7:904–05)

The British governor responded that the entire region, including Maine and the Maritimes (minus Cape Breton and Prince Edward Island), had been given up by the French Crown and was now British colonial domain. In the summer of 1722 angry Wabanakis resumed their naval guerrilla war with new vigor. Within a few months, they had captured 25 fishing vessels, commandeering some of them as privateers (Upton, 43; Whitehead 1991:94–95). Stung by so many losses at once, the British outfitted two sloops, manned them with soldiers from the garrisons, and retook the stolen vessels within three weeks.

In June 1724, after their winter hunt in the woods, 60 Wabanaki warriors (both Mi'kmaqs and Maliseets) attacked the British fort at Annapolis (Port Royal), wounding and killing some of the troops. The British retaliated by shooting an Indian hostage whom they had held in the fort for two years (Upton, 43). Soon thereafter, Wabanakis captured two enemy schooners at Penobscot Bay (Baxter 10:289). Early in 1725 60 Mi'kmaqs and Abenakis destroyed two British fisheries buildings at Canso and killed six men. By June armed Wabanakis were again sailing the Atlantic coast and snatching fishing boats (Upton, 43), and by mid-summer New England volunteers arrived from New Hampshire to hunt "Indian pirets [pirates] cruising the gulf of Maine." This proved to be a daunting task. According to one account, the volunteers encountered "the Indian privateer . . . full of Indians, extraordinary well fitted, who chased them 3 hours & she takes all she can come up with, so that the fishermen don't go east of [Saco River] or scarce to sea" (in Baxter 10:212–13). Determined to put an end to these sea raiders, the British recruited three dozen Wampanoag warriors, expert seamen from Martha's Vineyard, and sent them aboard three whaleboats to terrorize Mi'kmaqs in the fisheries area (Upton, 43).

Wabanaki damage to British fisheries was considerable, but it had little far-reaching effect on the enemy, who continued to soar in number. By the 1720s about 40,000 New Englanders had settled along the Atlantic seaboard from Cape Cod eastward. Aware that they were now collectively outnumbered eight to one, some factions of the Wabanaki Confederacy (5000 people) were worn by warfare and sought peace with the British (NEHGR 20 [1866]:9; McLennan, 66–67).

On 15 December 1725, Abenaki tribal leaders signed the Dummer's Treaty, which was ratified six months later by Mi'kmaqs and Maliseets in Annapolis. It guaranteed them "the free liberty & privilege of hunting, fishing, and fowling" and the right to "peacefully enjoy all their lands which have not been by them conveyed and sold unto or possessed by the English" (CMeHSI/3:423). While the British agreed not to molest the Indians nor to interfere with their way of life, the Wabanaki promised to "submit" themselves (however they now understood this term) to King George I and recognized him as "the Rightful Possessor of the province [of Nova Scotia]." Dummer's Treaty became "the cornerstone of British Indian policy in Nova Scotia, and it was carefully renewed after every subsequent rupture as the definitive statement of the relationship between Indians and whites" (Upton, 43–44; see also Baxter 10:379–80, 385–87; PD 8:991).

Like most acts of accommodation, however, Dummer's Treaty was disputed among Indians (within the confederacy, within tribes, even within local bands), and, not surprisingly, the French greeted this Anglo-Wabanaki peace treaty as "an unexpected inconvenience" (in Upton, 44). Chiefs who favored peace with the British were repeatedly blocked by the pro-French faction, which was supported by resident missionaries. Obviously, when the king's gifts were distributed, the latter group stood to gain the most. With presents in hand, the French pressed for continued resistance by their Indian friends, hoping not only to derange the British fisheries but also even to regain control over Acadia.

Situated in his recently established mission at Shubenacadie, Abbé Gaulin began inciting Mi'kmaqs from his district in Nova Scotia and Wabanakis from the St. John River to continue the guerrilla war against the British. Sometimes French

In 1710, British troops finally captured Port Royal and renamed French Acadia's colonial capital Annapolis Royal. During the next few decades, Mi'kmaq warriors and their allies tried several times to retake the stronghold. A View (1751) by Thomas Chamberlain after a watercolor by J. H. Bastides.

Acadians joined the warriors in their sea raids. In the summer of 1726 Wabanakis captured five ketches and a Massachusetts schooner (Baxter 10:291, 303, 352–53). Later, the schooner's crew recaptured the vessel, killed several warriors, and took the others to Boston as prisoners. Found guilty as pirates, the warriors and some of their French companions were executed by hanging (Upton, 44–45).

In reprisal, 30 Indians seized a 70-ton schooner at Port-aux-Basques, Newfoundland, and sailed it to Cape Breton (in Whitehead, 94). And in the summer of 1727 a party of eight Mi'kmaqs from Cape Sable captured another English vessel, killed its crew, and sold the craft to the French at Cape Breton Island for 2,000 pounds (PD 8:989).

Despite such breaches, Dummer's Treaty did bring official closure to another violent Anglo-Wabanaki war.

UNEASY PEACE AND NEW MISSIONARIES

After more than 30 years as a warrior-priest among Mi'kmaqs, Abbé Gaulin became physically incapable of continuing his arduous work and retired to Quebec. In 1735 the Crown sent a new Foreign Missions priest, Pierre Maillard, to Cape Breton. This abbé's assignment was Malagawatch, a dormant island mission established in Bras d'Or Lake at Gaulin's suggestion in 1724. Abbé Maillard's district was large. He served 80 households (about 350 people) at Malagawatch, plus several families at Malpeque (on Prince Edward Island) and Antigonish (Nova Scotia), which had no resident missionary. In 1740 the bishop in Quebec appointed him vicar-general of Cape Breton. Typically, Maillard visited his mission post only during the summer, when Mi'kmaqs congregated there for religious and political purposes. He spent most of the year at the French garrison town of Louisbourg at Cape Breton's northeast coast and devoted considerable time to writing a Mi'kmaq dictionary and grammar "to help the missionaries who later will devote themselves to this mission" (Roger, 171). He developed a now-famous script of five thousand Mi'kmaq hieroglyphs (based, no doubt, on local Mi'kmaq expertise and, probably, Father LeClercq's earlier efforts). This was used primarily for hymns and other elements of religious services (Rogers, 171; cf. Schmidt 1993, Casgrain, 366, n.1). Maillard also authored an important treatise titled *An Account of the Customs and Manners of the Micmakis and Maricheets, Savage Nations,* later published by the British in London (1758).

Another Foreign Missions priest, Jean-Louis LeLoutre, arrived in Mi'kmaq country in 1738. Abbé LeLoutre's assignment was the mission post at Shubenacadie in central Nova Scotia. His was the largest in Mi'kmaq country, numbering 200 households (NYCD 10:17). Next largest was Miramichi (on the coast of present-day New Brunswick), where 195 Mi'kmaq households were served by a Recollet missionary. Another Recollet served the mission at Restigouche, which counted 60 Mi'kmaq households (NYCD 10:17). Collectively, these four Mi'kmaq mission districts counted almost 3,000 people in the mid-18th century. Compared to their number (2,000) fifty years earlier, this indicates that the Mi'kmaq, in spite or their tribulations, were experiencing a demographic rebound.

THE FIFTH ANGLO-WABANAKI WAR (1744–1748)

In 1744 France declared war on Britain (and Austria-Hungary). As usual, the conflict spilled over into northeast America, turning into a contest over Wabanaki ancestral domains. Most of the French Acadians in British Nova Scotia tried to maintain their neutrality, as did many Wabanakis. Because open war had been declared against its British neighbors in Nova Scotia, the French military command at Fort Louisbourg sent word to the four Mi'kmaq mission headquarters at Malagawatch, Shubenacadie, Miramichi, and Restigouche, asking the priests to muster support from warriors in their districts. Similar requests went out to missions at Meductic (on the St. John River), Panawamskek (on the Penobscot River), and beyond.

While French troops from Fort Louisbourg destroyed the British fort at Canso, 300–400 Wabanaki warriors (mostly Mi'kmaq, Maliseet and Abenaki) assembled at Shubenacadie in preparation for an attack on Annapolis. Joining the French military campaign, they were placed under command of Sieur de BelleIsle, a French officer who had married into the Abenaki tribe at Penobscot. Abbé LeLoutre served as chaplain. However, BelleIsle suddenly aborted their intended assault when he learned that British reinforcements from Boston had arrived at Annapolis (Upton, 46). Nonetheless, the British retaliated by officially declaring war on the eastern Wabanaki, calling them "rebels, traitors, and enemies to His Majesty's Crown." Recognizing that his fort had barely avoided siege, the British commander at Annapolis felt it was necessary "to set Indians against Indians, for tho' our men outdo them in bravery, yet, being unacquainted with their sculking way of fighting and scorning to fight under cover, expose themselves too much to the enemy's shot" (in Murdoch 2:39) Also, aware that scalp bounties made it easier to raise troops and gave incentive for a wide-range pursuit of enemies all along the coasts and throughout the interior woodlands, the British boosted premiums on Wabanaki scalps to an all-time high: 100 pounds for an adult male above 12 years of age, and 50 pounds for any Indian woman or child (Baxter 23:296; Murdoch 2:40). The top fee was 16 times the monthly wage of a colonial coast guard (Swanson 1991:99). Soon, under the command of captain John Gorham of Massachusetts, a mercenary force of 150 rangers (including Pigwacket Indians from the Saco River, Maine, and perhaps some Mohawk mercenaries) pillaged a small Mi'kmaq camp and massacred its occupants: "five women and three children, two of the women big with child." Shocked by the cruelty, Mi'kmaqs vowed revenge (Maillard, 63–64; Upton, 46). They, too, resumed scalping, "encouraged by the French to these desperate undertakings, by a reward" (in Whitehead 1991:106).

Before the year ended, British troops from Massachusetts retook Fort Canso and destroyed Port Toulouse—desecrating Mi'kmaq graves and breaking "all the crosses, planted on the graves . . . into a thousand pieces" (Maillard, 66). A British privateer hauled Mi'kmaq Chief Jacques Padanuques of Cape Breton and his entire family to Boston, where they were imprisoned as hostages (Maillard, 64). Hearing that the British planned "to destroy all the [French] inhabitants that had any Indian blood in them, and scalp them," in January 1745 French Acadians assured the British commander at Annapolis "of their intention to continue faithful subjects" (in Whitehead 1991:104).

As was typical in Wabanaki warfare, fighting halted during the fall and winter, only to flare up again the following spring. In May 1745, 600 Indians and French Canadians again laid siege to Annapolis. Most of the warriors were Mi'kmaqs and Maliseets, along with some Abenakis and French-speaking Hurons from the Lorette mission near Quebec. Maillard and LeLoutre, true to their warrior-priest vocation, came along as army chaplains. After three weeks they heard that a British fleet was en route from Boston to attack Fort Louisbourg, so they gave up the Annapolis siege to assist the French garrison at Cape Breton (Upton, 47). Despite their effort, the citadel of Louisbourg fell to the British. According to the terms of capitulation, 2,000 Frenchmen were transported back to France. Abbé LeLoutre was seized at high sea and held as prisoner for the remainder of the war. Abbé Maillard was detained on a British warship and taken to Europe. Now not a single stronghold on the Atlantic coast remained in French control.

Mi'kmaqs in Exile

With their missionaries Maillard and LeLoutre in British captivity, Mi'kmaqs were cut off from French supply lines. In the fall of 1745, fearing that they and other Wabanaki would strike a deal with the British, French authorities in Quebec sent them gifts and instructed the remaining missionaries in the region to relocate Wabanaki mission Indians beyond British reach. About 80 Mi'kmaq families vacated their lands at Cape Breton and went to the Miramichi, Restigouche, and St. John rivers (NYCD 10:17–18). Later they found temporary refuge in the St. Lawrence Valley near Quebec.

In the summer of 1746 the French launched a massive, but ill-fated, naval expedition from Europe to retake Fort Louisbourg. By the time this fleet of ships carrying 71,000 men anchored at Nova Scotia's Chebucto Harbor (Halifax), scurvy and smallpox had begun to take a "terrific toll" among the troops (Francis et al., a:114). Over 1,100 Frenchmen died and were buried there. Moreover, Mi'kmaqs "who flocked thither in great numbers for supplies of arms, ammunition and clothing, took the infection," which spread rapidly, killing perhaps 200 of them (in Whitehead 1991:108; cf. Baxter 11:345).

Determined to recapture the colony, the French military command instructed Wabanakis residing in refuge encampments to raid British settlements and vessels all along the coast from Maine to Nova Scotia. A large war party of about 300 warriors, including Mi'kmaqs, was sent in eight sloops from Quebec to Bay Verte on Nova Scotia's northwest shore with orders to "lie in a safe place there, and wait for Canadian reinforcements" (NYCD 10:42, 44–45, 51). Just south of them a French commander ranging through the Bay of Fundy oversaw 300 Canadian troops and an equal number of Catholic mission Indians made up of Mi'kmaqs from Miramichi, Restigouche, and Shubenacadie missions, plus some Hurons from the mission at Lorette (near Quebec), Maliseets from the St. John River mission at Meductic, and Abenakis from the Penobscot River mission at Panawamskek (Old Town) (NYCD 10: 17).

Although the British had captured all the French strongholds at Cape Breton, they found it more difficult to subdue the highly mobile Mi'kmaqs, who once again launched seaborne raids against British merchant vessels and New England fishermen. Other Wabanakis often joined in these assaults, and Hurons did, too—coming down the St. John River (Pote, 14–49, 59; Maillard, 63). While these war parties, sometimes reinforced by Canadians, attacked British in the region (Upton, 47; NYCD 10:153–54, 172), their families remained in exile, dependent upon the French in Canada for basic provisions.

Cease-Fire

In 1748 the French and British agreed upon a cease-fire in Europe and held peace treaty negotiations at Aix-la-Chapelle, France. The French knew that, even in peace times, if they did not possess Fort Louisbourg, their trading ships would be easy targets for British privateers. This would stop the flow of ammunition and other commodities that the French needed for their Indian trade in the interior of North America. Afraid that they would lose Canada if they did not regain Fort Louisbourg, the French sacrificed their conquests in the Dutch Republic as well as the city of Madras, India, in exchange for Cape Breton (Francis et al., a, 114–15). After the war between the French and British had stopped in Europe, the French government ordered its military commanders in Canada to "make the Indians cease all hostilities against the English" (in NYCD 10:176–78).

HALIFAX (1749) AND THE CHANGING POWER BALANCE IN NOVA SCOTIA

Having agreed to give Cape Breton back to France, the British began building up their presence next door in mainland Nova Scotia. In the summer of 1749 they

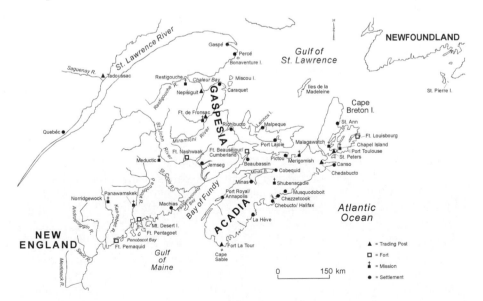

Mi'kmaq country in the colonial period.

founded Halifax at the place traditionally known as *Chebucto* ("at the biggest harbor"). Authorities offered free tracts of land to attract "officers and private men lately discharged from the Army and Navy" (Akins, 4). Then, transferring the seat of government from Annapolis to Halifax, they began fortifying the city to equal the strength of Louisbourg. Soon 2,400 settlers lived there (Francis et al., a:133).

Tired of turmoil and exile, the Wabanaki refugees in Canada were anxious to return to their ancestral domains. Learning of the peace treaty between their French father and the British Crown, the Mi'kmaq, Maliseet, and Abenaki convened for a Wabanaki Confederacy meeting at the Penobscot village of Panawamskek and agreed to make peace with New England. In 1749 several of their chiefs went to Halifax, where they renewed the 1726 Dummer's Treaty.

Wary of a British-Wabanaki alliance on its frontier, the French Crown continued its policies of giving gifts and relying upon missionaries as political agents of subversion. In the fall of 1749 Mi'kmaq chiefs and elders rendezvoused with their French allies at Port Toulouse. Receiving presents from the French king, they swore loyalty to "their old father" (Upton, 35, 37). When Abbé Maillard (who had made it back to Mi'kmaq country after his capture by the British) informed them that the British planned to "destroy" all of them, Mi'kmaqs sent a war declaration to the governor at Halifax—written in their own language (with Maillard's help):

> The place where you are, where you are building dwellings, where you are now building a fort, where you want, as it were, to enthrone yourself, this land of which you wish to make yourself now absolute master, this land belongs to me. I have come from it as certainly as the grass, it is the very place of my birth and of my dwelling, this land belongs to me, the Indian [literally, "to me, the human person"] yes I swear, it is God who has given it to me to be my country for ever. . . . Show me where I the Indian will lodge? you drive me out; where do you want me to take refuge? you have taken almost all this land in all its extent. Nothing remains to me except Kchibouktouk [Chebucto/Halifax]. You envy me even this morsel. . . . Your residence at Port Royal [Annapolis] does not cause me great anger because you see that I have left you there at peace for a long time, but now you force me to speak out by the great theft you have perpetrated against me.

> (in Upton, 201–02; Whitehead 1991:114)

In response, only a few months after the treaty signing in Halifax, the British renewed their scalp bounty offers, promising a high premium of "Ten Guineas [gold coins] for every Indian Killed or Taken Prisoner" (in Whitehead 1991:115).

Beginning in December 1749, Mi'kmaqs, Maliseets, and Abenakis, as well as Hurons, launched a series of raids against British settlers near Halifax. Applying a scorched earth policy, probably on the advice of Abbé LeLoutre (who, like Maillard, had returned from British captivity), they set fires to the vast woodlands around the new settlement. Encouraging such raids, LeLoutre distributed valued goods among Mi'kmaqs at Bay Verte in 1750: weapons and parts, table cloth, apparel (white linen shirts and cloaks), 85 sealskins (for moccasins?), 200 awls, 3,000 needles, 30 pounds of vermillion, 60 pounds of rope, and 100 copper kettles. Also among the gifts were drink and victuals—200 gallons of wine, 28 gallons of brandy, salt, 7,500 pounds of bacon, 418 pounds of hog's lard, some 50,000 pounds of flour, and about 100 gallons of molasses (in Murdoch 2:196).

Prompted by their priests and their own anger, Mi'kmaqs recommenced raiding British fishing stations all over Nova Scotia, capturing vessels and holding their crews for ransom. In 1751, eager for large numbers of new colonists, the British authorities invited 1,500 German Protestants to settle at Lunenburg, just south of Halifax. As Europe's wars had amply demonstrated, sharing religious beliefs was often more critical in forging solidarities than was sharing a language or territorial background. As such, the British felt secure in matching the Wabanaki-French Catholic alliance with an Anglo-German Protestant partnership. The influx of Protestant settlers, along with the construction of roads to the French Acadian settlements and the introduction of a large British garrison at Halifax, shifted the balance of power in what was left of French Acadia (Francis et al., a:133).

Desperate for new colonists, French authorities requested emigrants from France, noting that soldiers were preferred but that "some smugglers" would do, "and even some bad women . . . [and] sturdy beggars can also be added." In short, "nothing must be spared to strengthen these colonies against the English" (in NYCD 10:232).

Seeking a more strategic site for the Mi'kmaq mission at Cape Breton, Abbé Maillard removed his post from Malagawatch to Isle de Sainte Famille, a small island in Bras d'Or Lake only seven miles from Port Toulouse. At this site, later known as Chapel Island, a new wooden chapel and residence for the priest were built (Pacifique 1933:35; Rogers, 170).

TREATY OF 1752

In 1751 Abenakis at Penobscot notified the British that their Wabanaki allies, including Mi'kmaqs, wanted the peace of 1749 restored. But once again factionalism stirred within the Wabanaki Confederacy. While accommodationist sentiments gained the upper hand in villages more directly exposed to the British, resistance remained strong in mission villages closer to the French.

In autumn of 1752 Mi'kmaq Chief Jean-Baptiste Cope of Shubenacadie, who claimed that he "had about forty men under him," sailed to Halifax. Holding the French military rank of a major, he came to negotiate peace and ask that his people be compensated for the land the British were occupying in Mi'kmaq country. Receiving the chief at his residence, Nova Scotia Governor Peregrine Hopson replied:

> Friend, It is with pleasure that We see thee here to commune with us touching the burying of the hatchet between the British Children of his puissant Majesty King George and his Children the Mickmacks of this Country. We do assure you that he has declared unto us, that you are his Children. and that you have acknowledg'd him for your great Chief and father. He has ordered us to treat you as dear Brethren. . . . We will not suffer that you be hindered from Hunting or Fishing in this Country as you have been used to do, and if you shall think fit to settle your Wives & Children upon the River Shibenaccadie, no person shall hinder it, nor shall meddle with the lands where you are, and the Governour will put up a Truck House of Merchandize there, where you may have everything you stand in need of at a reasonable price, and where shall be given unto you to the full value for the peltries, feathers, or other things which you shall have to sell. . . . We wish you an

happy Return to your Friends and that the Sun and the Moon shall never see an
End of our Friendship—And for a more particular mark of our Sincerity, we have
given you a golden Belt, a laced Hat for your self, and another for your Son.

(in Whitehead 1991:124–25)

Despite these appeasing words, fighting continued. In October 1752 Wabanaki
delegates met with British commissioners from Massachusetts at St. George's Fort
on the central Maine coast. Colonel Louis Mascadoue, a Maliseet chieftain, explained why the raiding had continued:

. . . God hath planted us here God gave us this land, and we will keep it. God decreed all things; he decreed this land to us; therefore neither shall the French or
English possess it, but we will.

(CMeHS I/4 [1856]:174)

A month later, Chief Cope returned to Halifax to conclude a formal agreement
with the British. Once again confirming the 1726 treaty, all recent hostilities were
"buried in Oblivion with the Hatchet," and the British Crown guaranteed the Mi'kmaqs
that they were to enjoy "free Liberty of Hunting & Fishing as usual." Following
French custom, the British governor offered the chief's followers gifts, including
blankets, tobacco, gunpowder and shot (Upton, 54). He had the treaty printed and
widely distributed and put out notification that if other Mi'kmaq chiefs came, they
would be "flattered and showered with gifts . . ." (in Whitehead 1991:136–37).
    When the French commander at Fort Louisbourg found out about Chief Cope's
treaty with the British, he sent a dispatch to Paris denigrating the disloyal chieftain as
"a bad Mi'kmaq whose conduct has always been regarded as uncertain and suspect
by both nations." Aiming to reassure his superiors, he noted that Cope's treaty had
been "ratified by only ninety to a hundred Indians, men, women and children, all bad
subjects" (in Whitehead 1991:136–37)
    Having hunted and trapped all winter, the Mi'kmaqs returned to the coast with
their pelts and hides. When Chief Claude Gisigash of the La Hève band learned of
Cope's deal with the British, he went to Halifax and signed the same agreement in
early April 1753 (Akins, 40). However, unbeknownst to Chief Gisigash or Governor
Hopson, the treaty had already been violated. It happened that same spring, when the
crew of a British schooner anchoring at Jeddore on Nova Scotia's Atlantic coast
robbed local Mi'kmaqs of 40 barrels of government provisions. When this vessel
shipwrecked soon afterward, Mi'kmaqs rescued two sailors—who actually killed
and scalped their benefactors, six in all, then went to Halifax to collect bounty from
the government (in Whitehead 1991: 129–131). Considering the two sailors' normal
wages as seamen, these six scalps represented a considerable fortune: 60 guineas—
more than a man could earn in four years of full-time service with the British Royal
Navy (Swanson, 219)!
    Seeking vengeance for this treachery, Chief Cope's son requested the use of a
government ship to transport from Jeddore provisions given to the Indians (Upton,
55). When the sloop arrived the Mi'kmaqs immediately killed and scalped the entire
crew, with the exception of the pilot, who was French Acadian. After trimming the
scalps and fixing them into small round hoops, they dried them with hot stones and

painted them red (in Whitehead 1991:131). Then Cope "threw his copy of last year's treaty in the fire, telling [the pilot] that was the way they made Peace with the English" (in Upton, 55).

KEEPING ANGER ALIVE: FRANCE'S ONGOING NEED FOR INDIAN ALLIES

Although the Mi'kmaqs' 1752 treaty with the British was quickly broken, the French at Cape Breton still worried about losing Wabanaki support. The French governor at Quebec noted:

> Our Abenakis, Malachites [Maliseets] and Micmacks should never be permitted to conclude peace with the English. I consider that these Indians are the mainstay of the colony and in order to maintain this spirit of hatred and vengeance, they must be deprived of every opportunity to yield to corruption. The present position of Canada requires that those nations which are strongly allied should strike without delay, provided it does not appear that it was I who gave the order, for I have definite instruction to remain on the defensive.

> (in Whitehead 1991:140)

Missionaries remained vital components in the French Crown's strategy to keep the Wabanakis in their camp. From their respective headquarters, Abbé Maillard (at Fort Louisbourg), Abbé LeLoutre (at Fort Beauséjour), the Jesuit Father Charles Germain (at the mission village of Aukpaque in the St. John Valley), and Abbé Jean Manach (at the French Acadian settlement of Cobequid) guided or encouraged the Wabanakis in guerrilla raids against the British.

In August 1754 Abbé LeLoutre reported that Chief Cope had returned to the French fold. Along with Maliseet Chief Toubick of Meductic and a fellow Mi'kmaq who spoke French, Cope "undertook on Sunday last, after high mass, to inform all these [neutral French Acadian] refugees [at Fort Beauséjour], that, if any of them should be bold enough to return to the habitations which are now under English rule, they, the Indians, speaking in the name of the whole nation would look upon them as enemies, and would treat them as such" (in Whitehead 1991:139–40).

Meanwhile, within the Wabanaki Confederacy, accommodationists who favored peace were in conflict with hard-liners who still believed they could defeat the British through their alliance with the French. In December 1754 Penobscots, claiming to represent fellow Wabanakis, renewed peace negotiations with the British (Baxter 24:23). Two months later, Mi'kmaq chiefs Joseph L'kimu (or Algimouche) of Fort Gaspéreau (originally from Chignecto) and Paul Laurent (originally from La Have River) "set out from Beauséjour for Halifax to treat for peace" and to request a reservation "from Cobequid to Canso" (in Akins, 45–47). L'kimu fell ill at Cobequid, but Chief Laurent (who, having been a captive in Boston, spoke English) appeared before the British with a formal plea "that the government will grant us a domain for hunting and fishing, that neither fort nor fortress shall be built upon it, that we shall be free to come and go wherever we please" (in Upton, 56). In essence, this petition matched a 1754 request presented by Abbé LeLoutre—a request that the British had dismissed as "too insolent and absurd to be answered" (Murdoch 2:236–37). Rebuffing the chief, the British governor complained about the "perfidious breaches of all former treaties on the part of the Indians . . ." (in Akins, 47). Negotiations ended, leaving the land question to be settled by force (Upton, 56).

THE SIXTH ANGLO-WABANAKI WAR (1755–1760)

In early 1755 ships arriving in Halifax from Europe brought bad news: The French and British were once again at war. Immediately, Mi'kmaq messengers carried the information to the Wabanaki villages. As usual, this conflict across the ocean had ramifications in colonial North America, intensifying the ongoing hostilities and skirmishes.

By this time the French population in New France had reached 55,000, the vast majority living in the St. Lawrence Valley. Although they had tripled since 1700, the French were outnumbered nearly 20:1 by the British, who counted 1 million in their North American colonies (Francis et al., a:117). Numbering about 13,000, most French Acadians inhabited the fertile coastal region of Bay of Fundy. About 400 lived in the coastal lands of New Brunswick's north shore, and a small number resided in the St. John Valley. Prince Edward Island, then known as Isle St. Jean, which was first settled by the French in 1720, now counted over 4,000 colonists, many of whom were fishermen and farmers. In addition to growing corn, they kept over 10,000 horned cattle and earned cash by shipping corn and beef to Quebec (Murdoch 2:348; Bird, 394).

In contrast to the rapidly growing French population in the region, Mi'kmaq numbers, while on the increase, fell behind. Counting at most 3,000 people in 1755, Mi'kmaqs now had become a small minority. The following numbers show their regional distribution and military strength. Reporting on the number of warriors in the region at this time, a Mi'kmaq informant at Fort Gaspéreau noted: "At the village of Tattemigougouche [Tatamagouche], there are 20 Indians fit to bear arms; at Pektou [Pictou], 50; at Chediak [Shediac], 20; at Richibouktou [Richibucto], 17; at Miramichi, 150; at Baye des Chaleurs, 120; at Remickik [Remsheg], near Baye des Chaleurs, 120; at Gaspéreau, 47; in all 449 [nota bene: 554] men or youths, not counting women and children" (in Whitehead 1991:141).

In the summer of 1755 British troops attacked and took over Fort Beauséjour. Located at the head of the Bay of Fundy, this key stronghold commanded the portage between the French-controlled St. Lawrence Gulf and the Bay of Fundy. In the clash, some 60 Frenchmen were killed, as were three Wabanaki, including "a Sachem of the Mickmac tribe,—a stout fellow, six feet and a half high, about 40 years old" (CMaHS IV/5:397). The British renamed the stronghold Fort Cumberland. They went on to take Fort Gaspéreau at Bay Verte, changing its name to Fort Monckton (NYCD 10:358).

Ethnic Cleansing: Expulsion of the French Acadians

The capture of Fort Beauséjour cleared the way for the British to attack the French at Cape Breton from Halifax and to expel the Acadians from mainland Nova Scotia

Mi'kmaq Wikuom Encampment. Anonymous Canadian, Nineteenth century.

(Francis et al., a:117). Choosing a policy of ethnic cleansing, British authorities ordered troops to round up these French "neutrals," forcing some 7,000 onto ships headed for Louisiana (NYHS, 1881:196). Several thousand Acadians escaped to Prince Edward Island, Miramichi, Chaleur Bay, and wherever else they could find refuge. Many died in this violent ousting. Mi'kmaqs also fell in the fury, and many who survived joined the exodus. Among the exiles, death by famine or pestilence was common (Cooney, 34–35; Murdoch 2:312–13).

Some Acadians who fled to the St. John River area joined a French and Wabanaki Indian resistance against the British organized by the French officer Sieur de Boishébert and the Jesuit missionary Germain. In 1756 British officials, declaring that the Acadians had ceased to be "neutrals" now that they were acting in "conjunction with the Indians," placed a bounty on French Acadian scalps matching that offered for Indian scalps: 20 pounds apiece—soon raised to 25 (Murdoch 2:307–08).

In early 1757 several Wabanaki warriors joined the large French army assembled at Lake Champlain, which counted 6,000 French soldiers and 2,000 Indian warriors representing 32 nations—including Abenakis, Maliseets, and even some Mi'kmaqs (NYCD 10:607–08). That summer this force captured British-held Fort William Henry at Lake St. George in New York. Meanwhile, bored British soldiers at Fort Monckton in Nova Scotia occasionally dropped their guard and ventured into the fields, where they fell prey to Mi'kmaq guerrillas, who scalped them (Ayer Ms. #304). As if the fighting had not caused enough suffering, a smallpox epidemic made "great ravages" in Mi'kmaq country this same year (Bougainville, 137). In

December 1757 the last Wabanaki raiding party left Fort Louisbourg for Halifax (Upton, 56).

Fall of French Canada (1758–1759)

After the fall of Beauséjour and Gaspéreau, a Wabanaki-Acadian force of 500 men under the command of French officers came to Fort Louisbourg, where more than 2,000 French troops were stationed. The Indian troops were "strong men, very tall, who had already fought with distinction in Canada" (in Dickason 1986:55). To French eyes, these warriors looked exotic: wearing laced jackets over shirts smeared with vermillion and carrying blankets appliqued with colorful ribbons (Roy, 1932:381). When the French navy arrived at this Atlantic citadel, an elaborate war council ensued. Lasting several days, it featured a combination of Wabanaki and French Catholic rituals, including war dances, endless speeches, feasting, and High Mass sung by Abbé Maillard, who was accompanied by a choir of Indians. At one point,

> The chiefs prostrated themselves at the feet of the naval squadron commander . . . who raised them up. A [Maliseet] chief advanced and placed at the [commander's] feet four scalps woven into a wampum collar, which the commander received, expressing the hope that there would be more to come. He added that the moment was near when the French would be counting on their allies' bravery and valor. The assembled warriors responded with their cry "heur." . . . [Then the governor of Fort Louisbourg invited them to] a feast, consisting of salt pork, raisins, wine and biscuits, which the warriors received with a restraint that impressed the naval officers; the warriors kept most of their food to take to their wives and children. More speeches were followed by war games and finally by a dance, which to the audience was characterized by the "singularity of [the dancers'] postures and cries, the strangeness of their accoutrements." Their war paint added to the colorfulness of the occasion.
>
> (Dickason 1986:55)

But the days of French colonial rule in northeast America were numbered. In 1758 the British stepped up the effort to conquer Canada, giving orders to the Royal Navy to blockade French harbors. Soon Fort Louisbourg's defenders were outnumbered three to one by 13,000 British naval troops poised to strike (Francis et al., a:118–19). Up to 200 Mi'kmaqs may have been involved in the ensuing battles over Louisbourg, including the renowned Mi'kmaq war leader, Chief Jeannot Piquidauduet of the band at Minas, who was among the many wounded (Hoffman 1955:546). After struggling to hold the British at bay, the French finally surrendered their Cape Breton citadel in August, seven weeks after the siege began. Many hundreds of French soldiers had been killed and the rest taken prisoner. British losses, in contrast, counted only about 200 men (Bougainville, 312).

After Cape Breton, the British took Isle St. Jean (Prince Edward Island) and launched a 4,000-troop invasion in the St. John Valley, where they built a new fort. En route to Quebec the British navy destroyed French strongholds and churches in the Chaleur Bay and Gaspé area. Successfully blockading Canada, the British deprived their opponents of any major outside assistance. In the summer of 1759 the French gathered an army of more than 12,000 men to defend Quebec. Once again, Indian auxiliaries, including Mi'kmaqs, joined the French regulars and Canadian militia (Roy, 90). But the odds were stacked against them by "nearly three to one in ships, four to one in soldiers, and ten to one in money" (Francis et al., a:119).

In September 1759 the British won the battle for Quebec on the Plains of Abraham. Both sides suffered about 650 casualties. Once again, in comparison to the European theater of war of that time, these figures are relatively small. (For instance, in 1760 Austrians lost nearly 40,000 soldiers in two battles against the Prussians!) The defeated French army retreated, still controlling all of the St. Lawrence Valley. Some French and Canadian troops and Indian warriors, including Mi'kmaqs and Maliseets, retreated to the Miramichi River and Restigouche or removed to the interior, unable to fight as they were now cut off from supplies. Their arrival caused friction with the local Mi'kmaqs (Murdoch 2:312–13). A British frigate then entered the Miramichi River, and troops began dismantling the French forts. In revenge for the ambush of a boat's crew, the commander put the Indian church to the flames. (The Mi'kmaq village was since that time called *Eskinuo'pitij,* or "Burnt Church.") (Gaynor, 55–57).

With the defeat of their French allies, who had supplied them with arms, trade goods, and military support, Mi'kmaqs were faced with a bitter choice: Continue a losing battle or surrender (Upton, 57–59). This given, during the winter of 1759–1760 Mi'kmaq chiefs (some accompanied by a missionary) trailed into Fort Cumberland at the Chignecto Isthmus (between New Brunswick and Nova Scotia) and surrendered to the local British commander (Murdoch 2:390, 396). That summer, one year after surrendering Quebec, 2,000 French troops confronted 17,000 British troops and New England militiamen at Montreal. Assaulted from three directions, the French army was forced to capitulate. On 8 September 1760 the British took possession of Montreal. Canada, like Acadia, had passed into British hands (Francis et al., a:122–23).

In 1761 about a dozen Mi'kmaq chiefs came to Halifax to sign a peace treaty with the British—once again a renewal of Dummer's Treaty of 1726. Abbé Maillard was instrumental in negotiating its terms.

With the French defeated and the British in control of aboriginal domains, the Mi'kmaq entered an entirely new phase in their colonial experience. The somewhat-symbiotic relationship they had with the French was about to be replaced with a relationship of subordination and domination.

11 / More Treaties and Broken Promises

The British defeat of the French in Canada in 1760 ended a scramble for empire that had brought epidemic scourges and relentless warfare to Mi'kmaq country. So far, following a flexible strategy that alternated between resistance and accommodation, the Mi'kmaq had managed to hold on to their autonomy. This was made possible, in part, by the unique colonial arrangement that the French had worked out with the Indians inhabiting the region claimed by them.

In contrast to the benign rule and symbiotic reciprocity of French colonialism, the British introduced a regime of political subordination. Their imperious policy was briefly interrupted by the American Revolution, which resulted in the independence of the United States. Like other Wabanakis, Mi'kmaqs joined in the uprising. France also sided against the British. Although the war did not win Mi'kmaqs any long-term liberty, it did provide them short-term benefits, such as gifts and trade subsidies. More important, it resulted in various treaties, which turned out to have great political significance many years later.

THE ROYAL PROCLAMATION OF 1763: DISPOSSESSION BY DEFAULT

As noted at the end of the previous chapter, in 1760–1761 Mi'kmaq chiefs and their men visited British forts to discuss terms of peace. Both parties once again confirmed the 1726 Dummer's Treaty, which recognized the Mi'kmaq claim to a large area in northern Nova Scotia "for the more especial purpose of hunting, fowling, and fishing" (in Upton, 59). Religion was also an issue, brought up in the summer of 1761 by tribal representatives of "the several Districts of the general Mickmack Nation of Indians," who met with Nova Scotia lieutenant-governor Jonathan Belcher near Halifax. With Abbé Maillard as interpreter, a Mi'kmaq chief from Cape Breton requested "the free Exercise of the Religion in which I have been instructed from my Cradle" (in Whitehead 1991:159). When the governor granted this in the name of King George III, he and the assembled chiefs ratified the treaty in an elaborate ceremony of peace and friendship. The event "concluded with dancing and singing and toasts to His Majesty's health. An honour guard fired three volleys to mark the joyful occasion . . ." (Upton, 58–59).

153

A year later Belcher issued an official proclamation "that His Majesty was determined to maintain the just rights of the Indians to all lands 'reserved or claimed'
by them." But where were these lands? Probably informed by Abbé Maillard, the
British Crown official agreed that the Mi'kmaq claims comprised "a Common right
to the Sea Coast from Cape Fronsac. . . . to Bay des Chaleurs, and the environs of
Canso, from thence to Mushkoodabroet [Muscoudabouet], and so along the
Coast . . . for the more especial purpose of hunting, fowling and fishing" (in Upton,
59) In other words, the Mi'kmaq claimed that part of their homeland that only recently had been relinquished by the French Crown, *plus* the northern Nova Scotia
peninsula. This latter region matched the area demanded in vain by Abbé LeLoutre
on behalf of Mi'kmaqs in 1754 and later by Mi'kmaq chiefs L'kimu and Laurent
(Murdoch 2:236–37; Upton, 56, 59).

Perhaps uneasy about the possible repercussions of his proclamation, Nova
Scotia's lieutenant-governor assured his superiors in London that the Mi'kmaq
claim did not invalidate British sovereign title over the colony "since the French
derived their Title from the Indians, and the French ceded their Title to the English
under the [1713] Treaty of Utrecht." Of course, Belcher must have known that
this was only half true. The British were well aware of the fact that the French had
based their colonial claims on the Principle of First Discovery. Not recognizing
aboriginal title, they had never signed treaties with the Mi'kmaq. Perhaps worried that his proclamation could lead to "extravagant and unwarrantable demands"
by the Mi'kmaqs, Belcher decided not to circulate his own official statement
(Upton, 59–60).

Whatever hopes the Mi'kmaqs may have had for a reversal of their fortunes,
their political undoing became definite when the Treaty of Paris was signed in 1763.
Conceding British title to northeast America, the French retained only two small offshore fishing islands in the Gulf of St. Lawrence—St. Pierre and Miquelon. Although the Mi'kmaqs' future was at stake, no one asked for their opinion on this
agreement.

Perhaps Mi'kmaqs put faith in the 1763 Royal Proclamation, issued by King
George III in an effort to centralize the management of Indian affairs. This decree
promised Indians in British North America that they would not be "molested or disturbed in the possessions of such parts of our dominions and territories [that were
not] ceded to or purchased by us [Great Britain]." By asserting the Crown's supreme
power in the colonies, the British government "required that extinguishment of aboriginal title be purchased by treaty, and reserves be set apart for the aboriginal population" (Bartlett, 581; Upton, 62).

However, the king's officials in Nova Scotia acted as if the proclamation did not
apply to their region. They conveniently presumed that all Mi'kmaq territory (as former French colonial domain) was legitimate Crown land and did not see any reason
why the government should invite the chiefs to formally surrender their aboriginal
title. Accordingly dispossessed by default, the Mi'kmaq received nothing in compensation for these lands (Upton, 98–99). When Mi'kmaq country was thus "magi-
cally" transformed into Crown land, it was as if a terrible curse had been put on its
indigenous inhabitants.

SETTLING MI'KMAQ LANDS

Soon thousands of white immigrants began pouring into Mi'kmaq country. They came from Scotland, Ireland, Germany, and New England, joining the French Acadians remaining in the region. Halifax grew rapidly to more than 6,000 inhabitants. Nearby, some 1,500 German Protestants settled in Lunenburg. Another 2,000 Ulstermen had come from northern Ireland and settled in Truro (formerly known as Cobequid). They were followed by 200 Scots, who founded Pictou, and a group of 30 families belonging to the MacDonald clan, who moved to Tracadie at Prince Edward Island. In addition, 750 Yorkshiremen from England settled at Chignectou, and 5,000 Yankees from New England settled at various other places in the region. Many others went to Cape Breton, which soon resembled a multicultural patchwork of Mi'kmaqs, Acadians, English, Irish, Scots, and Germans—like the rest of Nova Scotia. On the eve of the American Revolution, there were about 22,000 white settlers in Mi'kmaq country. Many were illiterate and quite a few given to frequent drunkenness (Allison, 45–51).

Having usurped Mi'kmaq country, the British Crown hired surveyors to measure out the newly won tribal territory. The lands were then divided into sections and lots to be auctioned off in London. As such, the sale of Mi'kmaq lands helped raise the revenues required to carry out British imperial policy. Large tracts were sold or granted under certain conditions to settlement companies, wealthy businessmen, Protestant missionary societies, speculators, and other interested parties. For instance, the Crown sold all of Prince Edward Island to a British investment company in 1767, leaving nothing to the Mi'kmaqs of this 1.4 million-acre domain they called *Epekwitk* ("lying in the water"). Although large expanses, such as Lennox Island, ended up in the hands of absentee landowners, much of the best land was taken up by Irish and Scotch immigrants (CNBHS III/9:485–89).

No one bothered to inform the Mi'kmaqs about the transfer of their hunting districts to newcomers, and the process was anything but orderly. Soon their favorite places were occupied by strangers who took without asking. Beyond helping themselves to Mi'kmaq land, fish, game, and timber, they cultivated crops such as wheat, rye, oats, and barley, as well as potatoes and cabbage. When Mi'kmaq hunters set up camp at their customary sites, they were reprimanded for trespassing and told to leave. Of course, this sometimes led to angry confrontations. Fearful that they would be entirely crowded out of their own ancient hunting domains by whites, some Mi'kmaq groups asked officials to set aside reserve lands for their exclusive use. For instance, a Cape Breton band asked a British surveyor in 1767 that "a Tract of Land along St. Patrick's Lake & Channel [would be] granted to them by His Majesty for the Conveniency of Hunting, & in which they might not be molested by any European Settlers" (Holland, 67–68).

About this time, ragged Mi'kmaqs began showing up in the streets of Halifax and other towns, begging for help. Noting that this was the first time that British records referred to "indigent Indians," Canadian historian Leslie Upton (71) observed: "This term involved an important new concept, for it fitted the native peoples into a recognized segment of white society: the very poor whose maintenance was traditionally a charge on the community. With Nova Scotia now a settled colony, the Mi'kmaqs would have to learn to accept their new status."

Greatly troubled by these affairs Mi'kmaqs turned to their Indian allies. Meeting at the Penobscot village of Panawamskek in 1767, Wabanaki Confederacy delegates discussed their common anxiety about British hunters and settlers moving up their rivers. Some suggested taking up arms to halt the encroachment (Baxter 13:343–44, 24:149–52). In what must have appeared a miraculous reversal of political fortune, their opportunity came soon enough.

THE AMERICAN REVOLUTION (1775–1783)

In April 1775 Massachusetts militiamen exchanged fire with British soldiers. This clash, rooted in a disagreement about taxes on imported goods, ignited the revolt that became popularly known as a revolutionary war for "the defense of American liberty." Calling themselves Patriots, many colonists joined the rebellion against what they considered to be tyranny. Others sided with the British as Loyalists, while most remained more or less neutral. By May, when Patriot troops captured the British strongholds of Fort Ticonderoga and Crown Point (at Lake Champlain), the American Revolution had begun in earnest. In June, George Washington was picked as commander-in-chief of the revolutionary forces. Because Boston was then under British siege, he immediately moved his headquarters to nearby Cambridge, across the Charles River.

Wabanakis Join the Revolution

Apprehensive about the potential danger of Indian warriors siding with their enemies, both parties sought their support, or, minimally, tried to convince them to stay out of the fray (Washburn, 1975:151). Sending letters to the Mi'kmaq and other Wabanakis, Washington invited them to join the American cause. Although uncertain about the motives of this fratricidal war, the Indians generally welcomed the breach within their old enemy's ranks. Did the battle cry for "American liberty" also apply to their own freedom struggle?

In June, a few days after the Battle of Bunker Hill near Boston, Penobscot Chief Joseph Orono declared his support for the American Patriots. In return, he gained the promise that further encroachment of his tribe's domains would be stopped (Leger, 116–17). Because the Wabanaki Confederacy still functioned and convened on a regular basis, the Penobscot decision was probably not made without informing their allies. As one Maliseet chief explained: "We are all Brothers and Cousins—we are of the same Flesh & blood and can't make War or be attacked separately" (in Baxter 24:180).

Several months later, a delegation of tribal diplomats representing the Maliseet and Mi'kmaq met with leaders of the revolution in Massachusetts and formally declared that they would "stand together and oppose [those] that are endeavouring to take yours and our lands and Libertys from us" (in Kidder, 55). In recognition of their pledge of loyalty to the cause, the delegates were given some presents.

Because Nova Scotia had only recently been settled by the British, few colonists there openly supported the American Revolution. The British garrison in Nova Scotia had been reduced to almost nothing, counting only 36 troops. News that Mi'kmaqs and other Wabanakis were once again on the warpath kindled old fears among Loyalists there—and beyond (Upton, 30, 71, 75). Although mostly armed with "old, large, long Dutch muskets" (Seume, 175), the 11 Mi'kmaq bands could jointly raise at least five hundred armed men. Moreover, the Maliseet, Penobscot, and Passamaquoddy could field about sixty warriors each (Baxter 24: 183). In addition, the western Abenaki in the borderlands between Quebec and northern New England were estimated to count another 220 fighting men (Calloway, 215; Day, 65). In sum, with a combined force of some 900 men capable of bearing arms, the Wabanaki Confederacy was still a military force to reckon with. As such, both the Patriots and the Loyalists sought to gain its favor.

Treaty of Watertown (1776)

In March 1776 the besieged British army was forced to give up Boston, still North America's largest port at the time. Four months later, probably encouraged by this news, six Mi'kmaq delegates sailed from Machias to Boston. Joined by some Maliseets, they met with Massachusetts Governor James Bowdoin in nearby Watertown and announced that 85 warriors were ready to join the American forces. Pleased, the governor read them the newly issued Declaration of Independence and pronounced them "brothers." He then presented a treaty of alliance and friendship and proclaimed, "The United States now form a long and strong chain, and it is made longer and stronger by our brethren of the [Maliseet] and Micmac Tribes joining with us; and may the Almighty God never suffer the Chain to be broken." Offering a toast to the new bond, he expressed his wish "that the friendship now established might continue as long as the Sun and Moon shall endure," and this was "pledged by the Indians" (in Baxter 24:181, 187–93). Signed 19 July 1776, just 15 days after the Declaration of Independence, the Treaty of Watertown was the first Indian treaty made on behalf of the new republic of the United States.

Immediately, three Mi'kmaq warriors joined Patriot troops in New York, while the other delegates returned to their villages in the northeast. That same summer, western Abenakis also formally declared their support for the United States (Baxter 24:193–95). Meanwhile, most Iroquois (with the exception of the Oneida) decided to bet on the opposite side and supported the British Loyalists. In the southern colonies, the Cherokees and other tribal nations followed suit and dispatched their warriors to destroy the recently founded white settlements in the borderlands. A cruel guerrilla war ensued, with American scouting companies sometimes fighting in Indian disguise.

Warriors at Machias (1777–1780)

During the Revolutionary war, the coastal town of Machias in eastern Maine acquired strategic importance as the easternmost Patriot stronghold. Of course, the British called it "a nest of pirates and rebels" (Davies, 13:115). Founded in 1763 by settlers from Massachusetts, it could be supplied by vessels from Boston and beyond and offered ready access to the Wabanaki villages, in particular the Passamaquoddy tribal headquarters at Pleasant Point, less than 30 miles away. The Patriot force at Machias numbered about 150 troops, consisting of an infantry company, a small artillery company, and about 60 Wabanaki warriors, sometimes many more (Williamson, 164–65).

Warriors were paid the same wages as the white soldiers, namely "forty shillings p[e]r month, equal to Six Dollars & two thirds, and each of the Indians to be allowed a Rifle Shirt such as the Rifle men have, a Blankit, Shoes & Buckles or Morgasons [moccasins]," as well as free provisions "while in the service" of the United States. Moreover, each would be paid one dollar for his own gun "and in case the Gun shall be lost in the service shall be paid the value of it" (in Baxter 24:180–181, 191). Their war chiefs were commissioned as captains and lieutenants. They received silver medals and a small sword "in behalf of the Commander in chief [Washington] to Defend their rights & Liberty . . ." (in Kidder, 247–48; see also Prins 1989). In military maneuvers against the British during the Revolutionary War, Wabanaki fighters would clash not only with English-speaking soldiers, but also with German-speaking Hessian mercenaries, as well as Celtic-speaking Scottish Highlanders—dressed in tartan kilts, their traditional battle fatigue (Williamson, 164–66).

As provided by the Treaty of Watertown, a trading post was opened at Machias, where Wabanakis could sell furs, hides, feathers, and seal oil for "the same price they will fetch in Boston" (Baxter 24:175). A local blacksmith would repair their guns and other broken hardware. Inventory records show the store was well-stocked with foodstuffs—500 bushels of corn, 15 tubs of hog's lard, 30 barrels of flour, 20 of pork, and three of molasses, plus 20 barrels of cider, two of rum, and two of wine. Also stored for the Indian trade were 30 blue strouds (blankets), six white blankets, two pieces of fine drab (brownish woollen cloth), two fine scarlet drab, seven dozen ordinary shirts, three dozen fine ruffle (fancy) shirts, and thread. Moreover, stock included hardware—50 guns, 10,000 pounds of musket balls, 150,000 pounds of shot, thousands of gun flints, 400 hatchets, hundreds of scalping knives, as well as steel beaver traps. Among luxury items were silk, lace, ribbons, felt hats, mirrors, camp kettles, combs, soap, sugar, rice, raisins, chocolate, snuff boxes, tobacco, and small clay pipes, plus bags of vermillion and, most expensive of all, wampum beads (Baxter 24:182; Mass. Acts and Resolves 20, 112; Mass. Archives 150:213, 323).

In the fall of 1776, raids against British positions began with a campaign to capture Fort Cumberland, at the head of the Bay of Fundy. A force of 150 Patriots, joined by Maliseet and Mi'kmaq warriors, sailed northward to its target—but the assault failed. The following spring, when Maliseets and Mi'kmaqs returned to the St. John River Valley from their winter hunting grounds, they found themselves in vulnerable territory. Encouraged by American Patriot officers at Machias, some 500 Maliseets and a few dozen Mi'kmaqs evacuated the St. John Valley and removed to the woodlands near Machias.

The British, aiming to contain the American rebels at Machias, built Fort Howe at the mouth of the St. John River. They also allowed a French Acadian priest to return to the St. John Valley. "Authorized by the Bishop of Quebec to excommunicate all those who acted against the constituted [British] authorities of Nova Scotia, [the priest told Mi'kmaqs and Maliseets] that loyalty was a condition of their receiving the sacraments of the church" (Upton, 76–77). He convinced a good number of the region's Indians to restore their ties with the British. Such strategic moves were effective because they created a split within the Wabanaki communities. While many continued to side with the United States, 14 Maliseet and 12 Mi'kmaq chieftains came to Fort Howe, and, in the company of their new missionary, signed an oath of allegiance to the British king (Murdoch 2:595–96). Among the many presents offered by the British on this occasion were gold-plated and silver-plated crucifixes, each "with the figure of our Saviour on it" (CNBHS I/3:320). In return, the Wabanaki leaders offered strings of wampum "as their Seal of approbation and agreement." Before their departure, a Maliseet war chief "began a Song and Dance in honor of the Conference," followed by a Mi'kmaq captain (CNBHS I/3:317).

In October 1778, a month after the Treaty of Fort Howe, the political landscape shifted once again: A French navy squadron sailed into Boston Harbor, and its admiral, the Count d'Estaing, proclaimed that the French king supported the Americans in their war of independence. When Mi'kmaqs heard that their "old father" had declared war against the British king, they sent three wampum strings to the American commander at Machias: "one from the Civil Chiefs, one from the Warriors to the U.S., and one for the King of France welcoming him into this Country and as an Ally of America,—they declared their Zeal & attachment [and were] ready when called upon to take up the Hatchet . . ." (in Baxter 17:64). British authorities worried that as soon as the Mi'kmaqs would actually see French warships off their coasts, they would rise up in arms and "throw the whole colony into the utmost confusion and distress" (in Davies 17:174–75).

British colonist visits Mi'kmaq camp.

Julian's Treaty (1779)

The message from the French admiral in Boston had an enormous impact on the Wabanakis. At Miramichi, a large Mi'kmaq fighting force assembled and launched raids against British shipping and trading posts. When the warriors saw a warship sailing up the Miramichi River and flying the French flag, they were elated. The ship's crew put out a longboat under American colors, and the Mi'kmaq quickly prepared themselves to welcome their French and American brothers. Sixteen chiefs and ranking warriors "came on board in silk stockings, etc. dressed like Frenchmen" (Davies, 17:209). Great was their outrage when they discovered that they had been tricked into boarding a British ship, appropriately named the *Viper.* A bloody skirmish claimed the lives of three Mi'kmaqs, and the others were captured. One of the men, an immensely strong Mi'kmaq named Pierre Martin, made a particularly valiant effort to avoid capture. Two British marines "were unable to bind him, and he nearly strangled two others with whom he was engaged" (Gesner, 48–49). While the Mi'kmaq hostages were kept aboard in chains, the British captain met with tribesmen on shore. He reproached them for their behavior and accused the Miramichi River chief of treason against the British king, forcing the chief to flee. Then he appointed another high-ranking Mi'kmaq, John Julian, to assume the place of "first chief" of the Miramichi Indians and declared Julian's younger brother Francis to be "second chief." After getting them to sign a peace treaty, the *Viper's* captain lifted anchor and set sail for Quebec—with the Mi'kmaq hostages still on board, clamped in irons (Hamilton, 1984:7; Davies, 16:173). Because there was "no proper gaol [jail] there for rebel prisoners" (Davies, 17:209), they were taken to jail in Halifax. To find out what the British intended to do with their prisoners, the newly appointed Miramichi chief, along with the chief of Richibucto and several other ranking Mi'kmaqs, traveled to Halifax. Blamed for the hostilities at Miramichi, they were summoned to sign another treaty. In exchange, the British promised not to harm the hostages, who stayed in jail. However, of the 13 imprisoned Mi'kmaqs, only six ever came home again (Upton, 77–78; Gesner, 48–49).

More than 100 years after this encounter, Mi'kmaqs continued to talk about it, weaving it into a story that echoed the confusion and distrust their ancestors felt in dealing with Europeans and that endowed those ancestors with the sort of superhuman physical and mental powers that might have turned the tables. In the early 1900s, Peter Ginnish, an old Mi'kmaq at Eskinuo'pitij (Burnt Church), recounted the event, which occurred when his grandfather was just 19 years old. In his narrative, we meet one of several *kinap* characters (warriors with supernatural strength) appearing in Mi'kmaq legends. He is Kaqtukwaq ("Thunder"), also known by his Indianized French name Duneil (from "tonnerre"):

> When, one evening, a war vessel arrived . . . all were frightened. It sent a shell, which burst and scattered fire over the entire island. The Indians went to Duneil and asked him what they should do. He said, "They will do no harm. Go home and sleep." That night, he cut a stick two or three fathoms long, stuck it into the war vessel, and carried the vessel onto a hill in the woods. Next morning, the crew found that they were in the woods. They thought that all of them would be killed. . . . Duneil came, looked at them, asked the captain who they were, and what they intended to do. . . . The captain came, shook Duneil's hand, and said,

"My friend, I did not come here to injure anyone. I came merely to cruise about and see the place. Now we are done for. I suppose we shall lose our lives." "No, you will not lose your lives. If you are not trying to injure us, we shall not hurt you. I will put your vessel back into the water." . . . Duneil told the captain to get on board; then, with his stick, lifted the ship, and put it in the water. . . . Later a ship came, and the King was on board. Two Indians asked who it was. The King came ashore. Julian, one of these two Indians, would not shake hands with him, but Ginnish [the narrator's grandfather], the other Indian, did so. Julian said, "I must kill that King and all the men on this war vessel." But Julian could not carry out this threat while Ginnish was there. . . . The [treaty] terms suggested by Ginnish did not suit. Julian said, "Go back, and come again tomorrow." The King went back, and next day came again. Ginnish asked, "Is your mind right?" The treaty was not yet made. He sent the King away again, and told him to come the follow- ing day. . . . [Then came two vessels,] a French King on one, and an English on the other. Next day, when these two came ashore, they said, "This is our final proposal. We will not come again." The [English] King said to Ginnish, "This is the last time I shall come ashore with my proposal. As long as the sun shines, the tide rises and falls, and the grass grows, I will support you. I shall give you your living: food and clothes. If you die, it will not be because of any fault of mine; if I die, it will not be because of any fault of yours." The Indians said, "All right." They dug a grave four feet deep. The Indians said, "Put your bayonet in first, the French bayonet on it, and the Indian will put his battle-axe on them. You see me put them in. I shall never take one out. If I do take mine out, I promise you that I will finish you. But I will never take it out, unless it is through your fault." The grave is there to this day.

(in Wallis and Wallis 1955:461–63)

Diplomatic Betrayal: The Treaty of Paris (1783)

In the summer of 1779 British troops defeated an American naval force sailing up the Penobscot River. Effectively controlling the central Maine coast, the British were also able to block the supply route of Machias. No longer receiving vitally important goods from Boston, the Wabanakis encamped near Machias became discouraged and difficult to handle (Baxter 17:421).

In June 1780 a large delegation representing the Ottawa, Huron, Algonkin, and Abenaki, as well as other tribal nations in Canada, visited the Maliseet head village at Aukpaque in the St. John Valley, "where about 300 fighting men, besides 600 women and children, were assembled." They "required the [Mi'kmaq and fellow Wabanakis] to withdraw from the Americans, and to remain quiet, for that they had declared war against them, and consequently should treat all Indians found among the Americans as enemies. Upon this declaration, the Indians almost all withdrew from Machias and its neighbourhood" (in Murdoch 2:610–11).

By 1782, when it became clear that the British could not turn the military tide in the territories south of Penobscot Bay, Loyalists from Maine to Georgia understood that their cause had been lost. Without a future in the United States, about 80,000 Loyalists (and their Iroquois allies) evacuated to domains still under British com- mand (Wright, 1983:249). Of these Loyalists, some 32,000 went to Nova Scotia, while another 15,000 settled in the St. John River Valley (Davies 21:226). More than tripling the regional population, this sudden influx overwhelmed the Wabanakis, turning them instantly into a small minority of just 5 percent, with enemies as neighbors. Beyond the effective reach of the United States, and never a French warship in sight, the Mi'kmaq saw their final opportunity to regain their liberty vanish.

In 1783 diplomats representing the three great powers convened in France for peace talks. The future of the Wabanaki Indian nations was not on their agenda. Signing the Treaty of Paris, Great Britain and the United States agreed on a new international boundary. Slicing right through Wabanaki territories, it assigned the woodlands west of the upper St. John and St. Croix rivers to the United States and left the northern and eastern parts to Great Britain, which also maintained control over former French Canada.

A few months after the ceremonies in Paris, Mi'kmaqs and other Wabanakis heard about the terms of the peace. Greatly disturbed, they convened at Passamaquoddy Bay, asking the U.S. military commander of Machias to join them. Holding a wampum belt, the great Maliseet war chief Nicholas Hawawes spoke for his own tribe and the Mi'kmaq:

> A number of [white] people have come among us whom we don't know and taken our lands and streams. You say it is peace . . . but we don't hear anything is done for us, no mention is made of the Indians in this country. We have been fighting for you and secured for America all the lands on this eastward country to the River St. Croix and always been ready to take up the hatchet when you call. You promised to secure for us our hunting grounds. . . How must we live now, we know nothing but hunting, you white men can live other ways. . . . Brother, the [wampum] belt we have delivered you is for the great council [Congress] of America as a token of our love and friendship. We desire that they may look upon us as their brothers, that they will support us in our rights.

(Papers of the Continental Congress, Rolls Nr: 71, 58, 59)

INTERNATIONAL BORDER-CROSSING RIGHTS: JAY TREATY (1794)

For the next several years, Mi'kmaqs and Maliseets continued to meet with their Wabanaki allies at the Passamaquoddy headquarters. Meanwhile, the U.S. federal government began to assert its sovereign power over its vast domains. Adopting the Trade and Non-Intercourse Act in 1790, it extended official protection of all unceded lands to all Indian tribes in the United States and prohibited state or private purchases of Indian lands without federal intervention or approval. In New England, however, no attention was paid to this federal law. In Maine, for instance, Indian lands continued to be taken or purchased without even asking, let alone receiving, congressional approval.*

Reduced to "extreme poverty" and still deprived of Catholic priests despite promises to the contrary, the destitute Wabanakis turned to the American authorities and asked for justice. In 1792 they sent the following petition to Boston, signed by four Mi'kmaq, five Maliseet, and three Passamaquoddy chiefs:

---

*This neglect came to haunt the state of Maine in 1972 when the Passamaquoddy (later joined by Penobscots and Maliseets) in Maine filed suit, claiming two-thirds of the state. Eight years later the case was settled out of court for $81.5 million (see Prins 1994c, d).

Since Peace, we have been wandering from place to place. Those spots of ground, which were wont to be our abode, are taken up on the American as British side, and when our Familys attempt to encamp thereon are threatened with every insult, so that our women & children are in continual fear—It is to you therefore, we look as our Chiefs . . . It is in this Country we wish to make our home—We ask from you to fulfill those promises made in War. . . We have given no trouble, nor any expence arose on our parts since Peace. We expect you will answer this, with friendship. . . .

(in Banks, 1972: 34–35)

During the next few years, tribes of the Wabanaki Confederacy continued to meet at Passamaquoddy Bay and elsewhere. Like other border tribes, they complained bitterly about the new international boundary that severed their lands. In 1794 the United States and Britain signed the Jay Treaty, which offered legal resolution of the problem of border crossing: Article III states that the Indians were "to be perfectly free and unmolested in their Trade and hunting grounds and to pass and repass freely undisturbed to trade with whom they please" (USLR, 5).

Still, the Mi'kmaq and other tribal nations on the Atlantic seaboard were painfully aware that the old times were over. By then they had heard the tragic news that their "old father" in France had lost his head on the guillotine. His wife, Queen Marie Antoinette, and thousands of French aristocrats had also been put to death. What did the future have in store for the Mi'kmaq?

THE DEMOGRAPHICS OF DISPOSSESSION

Immediately after the American Revolution, the British decided to divide the enormous province of Nova Scotia. While the eastern part retained its old name, the other part became known as the province of New Brunswick. Pretending that the Mi'kmaq and Maliseets inhabiting this area possessed no aboriginal rights to their ancestral domains, the administration applied the legal fiction that the Crown possessed full title. Petitioning the provincial governments for land grants, immigrants settled on land that they could legally claim as their own. Others settled on tracts that had been purchased or otherwise acquired by companies, churches, or other organizations.

Each year thousands of landless Scots, Irish, and other poor immigrants arrived from Europe, drawn by the promise of 100 acres of free land. For instance, about 40,000 Scots came to Nova Scotia between 1815 and 1838. Often coming in clans, most of them were Highlanders, many of whom had recently been dispossessed themselves. They settled as farmers, fishermen, and boat-builders, especially at Cape Breton (Francis et al., a:301). New Brunswick attracted tens of thousands of Irish peasants desperate to escape beggary or starvation on their own overpopulated island across the ocean. During the potato blight of 1847, when many lost their major source of subsistence, some 17,000 poverty-stricken Irish embarked for New Brunswick (Francis et al., a:302)! Others sought a new life across the ocean to escape ruthless conditions in British factories, where common laborers were often obliged to work 15 or 16 hours a day for hunger wages.

Although Mi'kmaq country was settled mainly by white newcomers, there were also numerous people of African descent. Among the first was a handful of black slaves employed in Halifax since about 1750. About 1,500 "freed Negroes" settled in Shelburne in 1784. Twenty years later, Halifax counted almost 750 blacks. Moreover, there were 500 "Maroons" (runaway slaves) who had been deported from Jamaica. After a few years in Nova Scotia, many were taken to Sierra Leone. In 1814–1815, when the British fleet bombarded Washington and Baltimore, about 2,000 American blacks were settled on Crown land near Halifax (Marston, 230–31; Oliver, 293; Winks, 456).

By the 1860s this demographic surge had dwarfed the Mi'kmaqs into political irrelevance. The following figures are indicative of their utter powerlessness. There were only 1,400 Mi'kmaqs in Nova Scotia, where the total population had mushroomed to 400,000. Because they formed small bands, the largest of which counted only 169 people, their numbers seemed even less. A similar situation existed in New Brunswick, where perhaps 1,200 Mi'kmaqs were surrounded by nearly 300,000 descendants of American Loyalists, French Acadians, and Irish immigrants. It was the same story in other territories still frequented by Mi'kmaqs. For instance, there were about 250 Mi'kmaqs at Prince Edward Island, which counted in total 94,000 people. Just a few hundred Mi'kmaq lived in Newfoundland, where the total population was 150,000. Fewer than 700 Mi'kmaqs resided in Quebec province, which counted in

Mi'kmaq encampment at Halifax Harbor; on opposite side, the bustling port city.   Etching by R. Petley (1837).

total about 1 million people. Finally, a few dozen straggling Mi'kmaqs could be found across the border in Maine, where the general population had mushroomed to about 650,000 (Francis et al., b:2–3; Abbott, 542; Murdoch, 3:ix).

Reduced to a mere fraction (less than 0.5 percent) of the total population, the Mi'kmaqs were at best regarded as exotic survivors of a wild and savage past. Indeed, many expected them soon to become extinct. Already in 1786 a British observer predicted:

> Their numbers, once so formidable, are now reduced as to forebode the entire anni-
> hilation of the race; and it has often been observed, with the strict truth, that they
> are continually degenerating and decreasing. . . .

(Hollingworth, 47–48)

Outnumbered by hordes of poor immigrants running from cruel exploitation and squalor in Europe, Mi'kmaqs found themselves pressured into misery. Ranging through their former domains, they saw gangs of white loggers destroying their woods and felt the pain of hunger when the game was gone. Great was their anger when aggressive newcomers refused them access to their ancient fishing sites or chased them from their favorite camping grounds. Even firewood was denied them. By the 1830s Mi'kmaqs were "all in as depraved a condition as it was possible for human beings to be" (Upton, 115). Many were reduced to peddling baskets, broomsticks, porcupine quillwork, and birch-bark toys or went begging in the streets. Ten years later Chief Louis-Benjamin Peminuit of mainland Nova Scotia wrote in desperation to Queen Victoria:

> Madame . . . My people are poor. No Hunting Grounds—No Beaver—no Otter—
> no nothing. Indians poor—poor forever. No Store—no Chest—no Clothes. . . . Let
> us not perish.

(in Whitehead 1991:218–19)

Having served as chief since 1814, the aged tribal leader did not exaggerate his people's suffering. As a government official observed in 1844, "the very sanctuaries of their dead, are in some instances desecrated and ploughed over" (Howe, 92). Four years later the Indian commissioner in Nova Scotia reported to the Provincial Legislature in Halifax:

> Almost the whole Micmac population are now vagrants, who wander from place to
> place, and door to door, seeking alms. The aged and infirm are supplied with written
> briefs upon which they place much reliance. They are clad in filthy rags. Necessity
> often compels them to consume putrid and unwholesome food. . . . The [white] in-
> habitants in general are kind to the Indians; but the wigwam is seldom visited ex-
> cept for curiosity, and little is known of the misery existing there. The half
> famished mother with her squalid infant and naked children, the emaciated bodies
> of the aged, and frightful distortions of the infirm, with the unrelieved sufferings of
> the sick, concealed in the forest beneath a few pieces of bark or a thin shelter of
> boughs, have a real but almost an unknown existence.

(in Whitehead 1991:237)

CONCLUSION

Left without space that they could "legally" claim as their own, the dispossessed Mi'kmaq had become squatters on their own lands and poachers of their own game. Earlier devastated by wars and diseases, they were now threatened by starvation. Whatever their misgivings, they were forced to humiliate themselves and petition the British colonial administration for relief. Moreover, they were told to apply for parcels of the rapidly shrinking amount of available "Crown land." Without an official permit, they could not reside on the lands that they had occupied since time immemorial.

12 / Survival under Internal Colonialism

Mi'kmaqs were accustomed to dramatic changes, but the massive numbers of incoming settlers overwhelmed them. Most remained socially distant from these newcomers. Intermarriage was very limited, in part because of the different religious beliefs and the racist attitudes of the British. In many respects, Mi'kmaqs resembled French Acadians. Both minorities held tenaciously to their ancestral language and heritage.

Too insignificant to pose a real threat, Mi'kmaqs were seen as a "backward race" to be pitied rather than feared. Few outside observers expected them to survive as a cultural group, because the British colonial regime seemed to offer only two alternatives: assimilation or extinction. Subjecting Mi'kmaqs to social policies that swung between paternalism and indifference, the British cultural offensive involved forced transition from "savagery" to "civilization" (in European terms). These policies insulted the Mi'kmaqs' human dignity and wreaked havoc on their traditional culture. But, remarkably, they were not crushed.

With so few resources to fall back on, how did the Mi'kmaq endure the intimidating pressures of assimilation and persist as a people? Two key factors came into play: They secured a fraction of their ancestral territory, and, like other subordinated groups, they engaged in cultural resistance.

Mi'kmaqs were coerced into a political system of internal colonialism. Structurally, this system operates on the basis of reservations—called reserves in Canada. These small tracts of Crown land were set apart for the exclusive use of the Mi'kmaq. Although inadequate as a subsistence base, these reserves provided a measure of protection against brutal outside forces. They also offered Mi'kmaqs space and time in which to work out innovative cultural resistance strategies that accommodated dominant white society without fully abandoning Mi'kmaq ancestral heritage.

For Mi'kmaqs, cultural resistance included holding on to their mobility, their ancestral language, their spiritual beliefs, and elements of their distinctive dress. They mastered just enough English to get by, but commitment to their own language held outsiders at arm's length and provided a shield against insults and cultural imposition. The Roman Catholic Church, with its wealth of symbols and rituals, strengthened the Mi'kmaqs' psychological resolve to defend their cultural heritage against British Protestant hegemony. Since the late 1700s, the St. Anne devotion played a vital role in Mi'kmaq efforts to distinguish themselves from the British, as did their strong adherence to sacred texts written in hieroglyphs that only a few could read.

Last but not least, Mi'kmaqs found mental shelter in the realm of their collective imagination. Fantastic stories about *kinap,* brave ancestors with magic powers, came to the fore, along with folktales about heroic tricksters (Scott, 162–66). Perhaps not surprisingly, it is during this period that the figure of *Klu'skap,* the great Wabanaki culture hero, first appears in written records.

BIRTH OF THE RESERVATION

Throughout the 19th century, incoming settlers founded dozens of towns, which were connected by trails, bridges, ferries, and unpaved post roads. Towns situated at the coast were easily reached by boat and usually featured a shipyard. Most had shops, a church, school, post office, and newspaper printing office, as well as saw- and gristmills. Some of the larger settlements had a courthouse, jail, hospital, and hotel. Town outskirts were scattered with farmsteads that raised livestock and crops (wheat, rye, oats, potatoes, and pulse). Beyond were vast forests and temporary log- ging camps. In exchange for timber, fish, oysters, and some hides and furs, settlers imported manufactured goods from Europe, molasses and rum from the West Indies, and other valuables from abroad.

Generally, unlike white immigrants, including illiterate Scotch and Irish peas- ants, Mi'kmaqs could not get title to land. Instead, they were granted "licenses of oc- cupation during pleasure." In other words, certain areas *owned by the Crown* were *reserved* for exclusive use by a particular Indian band (Upton, 70, 82).

In Nova Scotia, a few Mi'kmaq bands received their first licenses of occupation in the 1780s. Typically, these permits applied to riverine and coastal sites that were seasonally favored by them and their ancestors. For instance, in 1782 the La Hève band acquired rights to a 550-acre tract at St. Margaret's Bay and soon thereafter an- other 11,500 acres nearby (Upton, 83). A year later, in a (mostly futile) attempt to suppress the Mi'kmaqs' migratory ways, the British decreed that "every Indian shall be obliged to Stay at his Respective place or River and Not be Running from one Place to an Other." Mi'kmaqs were told to quit hunting, fishing, and gathering and to settle down as farmers or as wage laborers in the fisheries or lumber industry.

Beginning in the 1790s, a London-based Protestant missionary society, known as the New England Company, offered to buy land for Indians who agreed to give up the "wandering existence of their forefathers" and to "send their children daily to school" (in Fingard, 30–31). In 1817 one such tract was purchased at Shubenacadie (the site where Abbé LeLoutre's Catholic mission once stood). Concerned about their "most wretched and deplorable" condition, a Methodist minister named Walter Bromley attracted 24 Mi'kmaq families to this agricultural settlement (Murdoch 3:397; Upton, 165).

Two years later the provincial government of Nova Scotia made formal provisions for establishing Indian reserves and issued instructions that "lands should be immediately laid off in each county" near sites frequented by Mi'kmaq families (in Hutton, 77). But this prompted little action among local officials. In fact, Mi'kmaqs had to push to regain a toehold on their ancestral territory. Eager to secure a tract of land for his band at Bear River in southwest Nova Scotia, Chief Adelah (Andrew Meuse) traveled all the way to London in 1825. A British visitor to his camp wrote later:

> His country, he said, was getting very poor, and the soil almost all taken up by people who came to it, which made him wish to raise some produce from the land, and see his Indians, with their families, in better circumstances. "I go," he remarked, "once more [after an earlier visit to England in 1811] about the grant, may be they think I come too often, perhaps turn their back, then I turn my back, and never ask again."

(West, 246)

Chief Adelah's petition bore fruit. Instructed to implement the grant, the provincial government ordered the district supervisor of Indian affairs to reserve 1,000 acres for an agricultural settlement at Bear River. With the assistance of Abbé Sigoigne, a French Catholic priest at a nearby Acadian settlement, the land was divided into 30-acre lots, each given to a Mi'kmaq family. This priest knew something of the Mi'kmaq language from studying Abbé Maillard's writings (Gilpin, 117–18).

Throughout Mi'kmaq country, bands pushed for and frequently received reserves. But by no means did they always get the land of their choosing, and even when they did there were problems. Some allocations were useless barren tracts, far removed from river and coastline. Better sites were subject to encroachments by neighboring settlers. Some reserves were only won through patience and persistence. For example, in 1831 Chief Louis Francis Algimou (L'kimu) and four other Mi'kmaq leaders appeared at the Legislative Assembly of Prince Edward Island to plead for land. Chief Algimou delivered the following speech:

> Fathers: Before the white men crossed the great waters, our Woods offered us food and clothes in plenty—the waters gave us fish—and the woods game—our fathers were hardy, brave and free—we knew no want—we were the only owners of the Land. Fathers: When the French came to us they asked for land to set up their Wigwam we gave it freely—in return they taught us new arts—protected and cherished us—sent holy men amongst our fathers—who taught us Christianity—who made books for us—and taught us to read them—that was good and we were grateful. Fathers: When your fathers came and drove away our French Fathers—we were left alone—our people were sorry, but they were brave—they raised the war cry—and took up the tomahawk against your fathers.—Then your fathers spoke to us—they said, put up the axe—we will protect you—we will become your Fathers. Our fathers and your fathers had long talks around the Council fire—the hatchets were buried and we became friends. Fathers: They promised to leave us some of our land—but they did not—they drove us from place to place like wild beasts—that was not just . . . Fathers: Our tribe in Nova Scotia, Canada [Quebec], New Brunswick and Cape Breton, have land on which their Families are happy.—We ask of you, Fathers, to give us part of that land once our fathers'—whereon we may raise our wigwams without disturbance—and plough and sow—that we may live, and our children also—else, Fathers, you may soon see not one drop of Indian blood in this Island,

once our own—where is now our land?—we have none. Fathers, we are poor—do not forsake us—remember the promises your fathers made to ours.

(in Whitehead 1991:207–08)

It took 27 years and many more attempts before authorities responded to Chief Algimou's request—with a mere 204-acre reserve. After another 12 years, the London-based Aborigines' Protection Society purchased nearby Lennox Island (almost 1,400 acres) for the exclusive use of Mi'kmaqs of Prince Edward Island (Upton, 122). In addition to its rich fisheries and large oyster beds, Lennox Island offered farming opportunities.

By this time (1871), dozens of small reserves had been established throughout the Mi'kmaqs' former domains. The lots varied enormously in size, from ten to 16,000 acres. Because many Mi'kmaqs still tried to hold on to their traditional mode of subsistence as migratory hunters, fishers, and foragers, most reserves were seasonally abandoned. Others, inconvenient or useless, were left vacant altogether.

SPIRITUAL RESORT: RETURN OF CATHOLIC PRIESTS

Although the British replaced the French political establishment in Canada, they did not evict its 80,000 inhabitants. Because almost all French Canadians—like Acadians, Mi'kmaqs, and other Indians in the colony—were Roman Catholics, the new government also permitted religious freedom. Local parish priests could go on with their duties, and the religious hierarchy was left in place. However, unlike the French, the British government did not financially underwrite the Roman Catholic Church. Religious subsidies were the privilege of the newly established Protestant Church of England (Francis et al., a:163–65).

Politically decapitated by the British, French Catholics, Mi'kmaqs, and other Indians in the region turned to their religious institutions for moral support in their attempt to retain their cultural identities. Soon the social functions of Catholic symbols and ceremonies expanded well beyond their original religious significance. Especially shrines and sacred images of patron saints, as well as devotion rituals honoring these heavenly guardians, became highly significant as popular expressions of cultural identity among the faithful.

The British colonial regime was cautious about the political ramifications of these religious devotions, recalling the harm done by French warrior-priests such as Maillard and LeLoutre. Wary that the Mi'kmaq were still secretly loyal to the French, British officials repeatedly ignored their requests for Catholic missionaries. After many years without a missionary to marry, baptize, confirm, or confess them, Mi'kmaqs at Cape Breton complained bitterly to the Bishop of Quebec when he visited them in 1812: "We live like dogs, left to die without sacraments. Our children are ignorant of religion. No priest speaks our language. Our old people have not heard a sermon in fifty years. What have we done that we should be abandoned in this way?" (Plessis, 170).

Having no priests of their own, Mi'kmaqs periodically attended church in French settlements. Moreover, they relied heavily on their own *keptins* (captains) for religious guidance. Acting as catechists, these Mi'kmaq prayer leaders read from hieroglyphic texts handwritten on thin sheets of birch bark. Using Maillard's system, they read from what they called "the book," teaching their children the Lord's Prayer, some hymns, psalms, and segments of the Bible. In general, Mi'kmaqs still knew the magic incantations (hymns and prayers), practiced the sacred rituals (crossing, kneeling, and praying), and possessed their "medicine" (rosaries and crucifixes). From the French they obtained what the British called "superstitious baubles." Some of these items were quite peculiar. For instance, some devout Mi'kmaqs had "copies of a letter written by Jesus Christ to the Bishop of Lucca [in Italy] threatening eternal damnation to those who failed in any point of the Catholic faith and promising eternal bliss to those who shunned protestantism." Holding these words sacred, they hid these copies in a medicine pouch worn close to the heart (Upton, 65–67).

Mi'kmaq resistance to British efforts to convert them to Protestantism was strong. For instance, when a group of Mi'kmaqs suspected that their chief had become a Methodist, they threatened to kill him. He was spared after publicly denouncing the Protestant faith as "worthless" and convincing his accusers that he was still a loyal Catholic (in Whitehead 1991:192).

The Lord's Prayer in Mi'kmaq hieroglyphics, as developed by Father LeClercq and Abbé Maillard.

In the course of the 19th century Mi'kmaq communities once again gained the service of their own Catholic priests, some of whom learned the Mi'kmaq language. Like their predecessors, these priests faced the challenge of trying to assemble the entire congregation of migratory Mi'kmaqs.

SAINT ANNE: MI'KMAQ PATRON SAINT

St. Anne, the Virgin Mary's mother, was the original patron saint of New France and became the patroness of converted Wabanaki Indians, including the Mi'kmaq. From the mid-1700s onward, the St. Anne worship grew in magnitude and replaced local devotions honoring St. Mary, St. Peter, St. Louis, and other patron saints who historically were venerated in Mi'kmaq country. Mi'kmaqs embraced the "Blessed Lady" as their spiritual interlocutor in heaven, soliciting through her divine intervention blessings such as good health and relief from misery.

St. Anne's 26 July feast day fell at a convenient time when widely scattered Mi'kmaq families traditionally came together. Mi'kmaqs, like French Acadians and other Catholics in the region, began congregating annually at churches, chapels, or shrines to celebrate St. Anne's Day. For instance, when a French priest visited the French Acadian village church at Chezzetcook in 1817, about 200 tribespeople came to church and joined the local Catholics for the feast of St. Anne. After evening prayers and hymn singing, the visiting Mi'kmaqs "made a bonfire, and while the wood burned they fired off guns and danced around the fire, clapping their hands in imitation of musical instruments" (in Whitehead 1991:191–93).

Fearing that Mi'kmaqs would succumb to Protestant proselytizing or lapse into paganism, the Catholic Church began to offer special religious services for them. Selecting a few convenient sites throughout the region, the church hoped to attract dispersed Mi'kmaq family groups for at least a few days each year—usually during the feast of St. Anne. The religious rites of Easter were deferred to that date, making the gathering all the more elaborate. Soon several hundred tribespeople ranging within each district could be found camping midsummer at places with shrines in honor of St. Anne. Some of these places were former mission sites and emerged as religious centers for Mi'kmaqs: Chapel Island (Cape Breton), Merigomish Island (Nova Scotia mainland), Burnt Church (New Brunswick), Lennox Island (Prince Edward Island), and Restigouche (Quebec) became important from the early 1800s onward (Upton, 157–58).

As a modern continuation of the Mi'kmaqs' traditional summer gatherings, St. Anne's Day turned into a grand ritual of religious celebration and cultural affirmation. Typically, each family set up its own birch-bark wikuom for a stay of several days or even weeks. During this time, people not only attended daily religious services in the chapel or church, but also visited with each other. St. Anne's was (and is) also a time for fun and business: playing games, matchmaking young people, discussing communal affairs, resolving disputes, electing chiefs, and dealing with economic matters, such as dividing collective income from rental fees for reserve lands or fishing grounds (cf. Gould and Semple, 63). Moreover, the priest attending the ceremonies gave Mass, heard confessions, and consecrated marriages—which were collectively celebrated (Upton, 157). Describing his visit to Chapel Island (Cape Breton) to celebrate St. Anne's, Father Vincent de Paul wrote in about 1830:

> [When] we approached to the island two canoes were sent ahead to announce to the [chief] that we would arrive immediately. The [chief] had all his braves armed, for they all have guns, and the moment we landed he commanded them to fire, after which he formed them into lines and made them kneel to receive our benediction. They then arose and we passed among them. They accompanied us to the church where we chanted the "Te Deum."

(in Whitehead 1991:206–07)

Soon a tribal folklore developed around *Se'ta'n* (St. Anne), who was usually portrayed as an Indian woman who "was not born here, but somewhere else . . . . three or four hundred years ago, when the French first came" (Ginnish 1911, in Wallis and Wallis 1955:399). Se'ta'n was married to an Indian named Suasin (Joachim) and had a daughter *Ma'li* (Mary), the mother of *Niskam* (Jesus, originally "spirit" or "sun"). In their prayers to St. Anne, Mi'kmaqs usually addressed her as *nukumijinen* ("our grandmother"). Many credited her with giving special assistance to sick

Father Pacifique of Restigouche, Big Peter Paul, Catherine Sack Maloney, Judge Christopher Paul (with formal top hat), Mary Jeremy Jadis (seated), Stephen John (in fashionable head-dress), and fellow Mi'k-maqs at St. Anne's Celebration, Shubenacadie, Nova Scotia, Ca, 1905.

pilgrims, ailing mothers, and newborn children. Today, St. Anne's Day remains the most important date on the Mi'kmaq calendar.

MI'KMAQ CHIEFS: POLITICAL ORGANIZATION AND INDIRECT RULE

Reduced to an insignificant minority, Mi'kmaqs realized that their survival depended on representation by individuals who were able to negotiate tolerable arrangements with the British government. They turned to their chiefs. Some chiefs proved to be incompetent or selfish, but many stood up as judicious leaders. Beyond settling internal disputes, they mediated in conflicts with neighboring settlements and officially represented their bands when dealing with outside authorities. This was not easy. The government tried to manipulate them, making them responsible for wrongs committed by their followers. It also tried to use them as agents to accomplish its political agenda. When a chief refused to comply, he risked punishment or removal from office.

Forcing the Mi'kmaq into a system of internal colonialism, the British initially followed a political strategy known as indirect rule. Common throughout much of their empire, this practice involved using tribal leaders to control indigenous subjects. But, as noted in earlier chapters, Mi'kmaq chiefs traditionally possessed only limited power. As migratory foragers, each kin-group relied primarily on its own abilities and made its own decisions. A saqmaw was only a "first among equals."

Although the title was not strictly hereditary, Mi'kmaq saqmaws were usually selected from a distinguished family that historically produced respected individuals known for courage and wisdom. Typically, they held their leadership position for life. Elections usually took place during the summer, when Mi'kmaq families convened for religious ceremonies and social celebrations.

Functioning within the British colonial order, newly elected chiefs had to be confirmed by high-ranking British administrators or officers. Granting honorific titles, British leaders commissioned each elected saqmaw as "captain," "first chief," "grand chief," or even "king." They also bestowed gifts, such as silver medals embossed with the British monarch's bust, silver-laced high hats, and other impressive insignia of office. Such symbolic aggrandizement suited the British colonial policy of indirect rule.

Operating from a concept of hierarchical and authoritarian leadership British government officials and Roman Catholic clergymen helped undermine the democratic principles of traditional Mi'kmaq political organization—boosting the status of Mi'kmaq officeholders by a process of external validation. (Today many Mi'kmaqs have come to accept the elevated political position of their chiefs as an indigenous practice rather than a post-European contact practice.)

Although the chiefs were more than colonial figureheads, their political power remained limited. After all, they were in duty bound to both the British Crown and the Catholic Church. This subordinated position within the British system of indirect rule is well illustrated by the following ceremony involving Chief Peminuit of Shubenacadie. After his election as grand chief or "king" of Mi'kmaqs in mainland

Nova Scotia in 1814, his position needed to be confirmed by Nova Scotia's lieutenant governor, Sir John Sherbrooke:

> . . . relying upon the Loyalty, Zeal, Sobriety, and good character of you, the said
> Louis-Benjamin Peminuit, I do ratify and confirm the choice which the said Tribe
> has made and do hereby appoint you Chief of the Micmac Tribe of Indians in this
> Province. You are therefore to use your utmost endeavours to keep all persons be-
> longing to said Tribe, Loyal, Industrious, and Sober, and to render them good Sub-
> jects and Christians, and the said Tribe are thereby required to obey you as their
> Chief.

(in Whitehead 1991:190)

On special occasions, Mi'kmaq chiefs were invited to parade in festive pageants
staged by the British colonial elite. For instance, in 1840 old Chief Peminuit and his
followers joined the citizenry of Halifax in celebrating British Queen Victoria's marriage. He and his wife rode in an elegant carriage, which was decked with evergreens
and pulled by a horse "decorated with blue and white ribbons." He was attired "in
royal Indian style," reported a writer for *The Nova Scotian,* the Halifax newspaper.
She, like other Mi'kmaq women at the event, wore a "picturesque costume, [a] high
peaked [cap], and many coloured spensers, overlaid with beads, bugles and various
ornaments." Mi'kmaq boys marched "with bows and arrows and badges . . ." When
the procession "made the circuit of the [dock] yard, the artillery fired a salute, [and]
three cheers were given." On the Parade Ground, tables were spread—the officers
and wardens of the Philantropic Society, also in festive dress "and their Indian guests
sat down to a repast. This consisted in an abundance of fish, fish pies, bread, butter,
cheese, cake, and porter. (The day being Friday, and the Indians of the R. Catholic
persuasion, meat was not provided. . . .") (in Whitehead 1991:216–17). After this
grand dinner and music performance by the military band of the Royal Welsh
Fusiliers playing "Even as the Sun goes down," the gala was concluded with "an Indian dance." It had been an occasion of "melancholy mixed with pleasure," reported
The Nova Scotian with romantic sensitivity: "The Chief and his poor followers, a
remnant of his tribe, reminded one of the captives which the Romans led in their tri-
umphs, and which told the conquests of the masters of the soil" (in Upton, 136).

Roman Catholic clergy also participated in the investiture of Mi'kmaq chiefs.
Performing religious rituals originating in Europe, they offered newly appointed
Mi'kmaq chiefs a sacred blessing. Moreover, they gave them a gilt medallion as a
papal gift intended to encourage them to keep up the Catholic faith. Church influence
is evident in the following description, penned by a British missionary after the
death of 82-year-old Grand Chief Peminuit in 1844:

> [Two rival leaders vied for Peminuit's position.] It was agreed to lay their respec-
> tive claims before the Catholic Bishop resident in Halifax. The decision was made
> before the altar; the interference of the Bishop was satisfactory; the right of the de-
> cision was unquestioned, being received with unqualified submission; the newly
> elected chief [the old chief's younger brother] was then invested with the insignia
> of office, homage was tendered to him by every Indian present; and a procession
> was afterwards formed, which wended its ways to Government House, when the
> whole party presented their chief; tendered their respects to their "great mother's"

Mi'kmaq Chiefs meeting the Marquis of Lorne, governor general of Canada, 1878–83.

[Queen Victoria's] representative, and concluded their visit to the Governor, Lord
Falkland, with the native dance.

(Churchill, 188)

These ordaining rituals bestowed a divinely authorized status on the political position
of Mi'kmaq chiefs. Not infrequently, priests had a direct hand in the political elections.
Because British authorities did not tolerate such power mongering, priests operated behind the scenes. This excerpt from an 1823 letter by Abbé Painchaud of Restigouche to
his Bishop in Quebec reveals that manipulation could be considerable:

A squad of Micmacs are on their way to Quebec to submit their claims [against a
white landowner], having at their head Thomas Barnaby. . . . I take it on myself to rec-
ommend this latter to your Grace to make him second chief, for the following reasons:
first because the poor Francois Condo (of my creation) lives no longer at Restigouche
where his drunkenness . . . made him lose all consideration; second, that the insignificant Jacques Ganong wishes to resign in favour of a grandson yet more insignificant
than him . . . ; third, that the said Thomas Barnaby, with sense and firmness, has further the advantage of being able to express himself in English. . . . His sobriety and
honesty . . . have merited him the confidence of the Whites as of ourselves.

(in Pacifique 1926:167)

MI'KMAQ DISTRICTS

Until the late 19th century, Mi'kmaq country appears to have been politically divided
into four major districts, each of which comprised several regional bands. This quarterly

division corresponds to the four Indian missions once served by French priests. A *kji-saqmaw* (grand chief) headed each of these districts, residing in the major village, typically the site of a Catholic church or chapel. Periodically, usually during the time of St. Anne's mission, the region's band chiefs convened in the major villages to discuss communal affairs. Outranking all his peers, the grand chief of Cape Breton became recognized as the preeminent leader of the Mi'kmaq nation. Presumably, this renown traces to the mid-1700s, when a Cape Breton war chief was honored by the king of France for his valor in the war against the British (Speck 1922:108). His glorified status was apparently passed on to his successors (*The Cape-Bretonian*, 01–25–1834, in Whitehead 1991:209). The leadership breakdown in Mi'kmaq country looked like this at the time:

District	Head Village	Chiefly Lineage
Cape Breton	Eskasoni	Denny/Googoo
Nova Scotia	Shubenacadie	Peminuit (Paul)
Miramichi	Burnt Church	Julian
Chaleur Bay	Restigouche	Ganong/Condeau

Relying primarily on 19th-century documentation, many Mi'kmaqs today accept the idea that Mi'kmaq country was originally divided into seven districts. Because the grand chief of Cape Breton ranked above his peers, his district, called *Unama'kik,* was recognized as the head district. The remaining six districts were geographically grouped into a "right hand" (*Kespe'kewaq, Sikniktewaq,* and *Piktukewaq/Epekwitk*) and a "left hand" (*Eski'kewaq, Sipekne'katikik,* and *Kespukwitk*). Each of these districts once had its own head chief, who had a measure of influence over local band chiefs and whose settlement served as a district meeting place (Anderson, 45; Speck 1922:94–95, 107). Many are satisfied that this sevenfold political division is indigenous—even though some scholars suggest that it may not be older than the 18th century (see also Hoffman, 1955: 517; Nietfeld, 418, 458; see also Fig. 1.1).

CHANGING SUBSISTENCE STRATEGIES

After the early 1800s, Mi'kmaqs could no longer depend on the diminishing wildlife of the forest, and much-needed remunerations for military support had become a thing of the past. Many Mi'kmaqs became demoralized, drowned their misery in alcohol, and turned into paupers, begging for food and clothing from town to town.

As a migratory people, most resisted the idea of being tied to a small piece of land that required clearing, plowing, seeding, weeding, and harvesting in a never-ending cycle of hard work. Still, although it is true that Mi'kmaqs in some areas never settled down as farmers, others did begin cultivating crops and keeping livestock. One of the first Mi'kmaq villages to make this transition was Restigouche, which became relatively prosperous—even more so than some neighboring French Acadian villages. An 1832 chronicler described Restigouche like this:

Mission Point [is] an exceedingly rich tract of land, comprising upwards of 1,200 acres, and owned by the Micmacs, to Two Hundred of whom, it offers a permanent residence. This settlement consists of a Chapel, capable of containing 300 persons, together with a Mission House, a Burying ground, and 24 dwelling houses. The houses are constructed of logs, covered with shingles or boards; they are all provided with chimneys and stoves; and some of them have even chairs, bedsteads, tables, and similar other conveniences. Most of the householders own Live Stock, consisting of oxen, swine, &c. some of them have horses; one of them owns a small schooner of 25 tons; and other have small Fishing Boats. The Indians residing here [are] contributing much to their own respectability and comfort, by annually raising a small stock of Indian corn [maize], beans, potatoes, &c.

(Cooney, 216–17)

Mi'kmaqs at some other reserves also took up farming. But, like those at Restigouche, they continued to do some hunting, trapping, and fishing. Among these were Mi'kmaqs at Bear River on mainland Nova Scotia and at Whycocomagh on Cape Breton. Whycocomagh Mi'kmaqs lived in frame houses by the 1880s and grew hay for their horses and cattle. Their most important food crop was potatoes, followed by wheat, oats, peas, and beans. Each winter they hunted fox, mink, muskrat, rabbit, and sometimes seal. And they were active as coopers, making wooden barrels and casks to sell to neighboring farmers and fishermen (McIsaac, 32).

Not all reserves were on fertile land, and quite a few contained leached and acidic soil that made farming nearly impossible. But some barren reserves offered good fisheries, and in these places Mi'kmaqs often specialized as market fishers. For instance, reserve communities on New Brunswick's coast earned much of their income from deep-sea fisheries, faring "quite as well as their white neighbours engaged in the business" (Carter, 50–52). During the summer, the men sailed in small schooners or other boats, fishing with nets, hook, and line. In the winter they caught smelts and oysters, and during the late spring and early summer they speared salmon, lobster, eels, and other fish from their canoes or trapped them in weirs. Typically, they sold their catch at the town market or ship wharves and used the cash to purchase flour, molasses, blankets, hardware, and a host of other products.

Other Mi'kmaqs turned to part-time wage labor, hired as cheap seasonal workers at white-owned farms, fisheries, or lumber camps. Whatever their new subsistence strategies, most Mi'kmaqs had no choice but to supplement their income by making and selling baskets, broomsticks, moccasins, porcupine quillwork, birchbark toys, and other crafts. Some, gifted with knowledge about healing diseases, became itinerant Indian "doctors" (or medicine men) and peddled medicinal herbs throughout the Northeast (see also Whitehead 1980; McBride and Prins 1990, 1996).

Beginning in the mid-1800s, quite a few Mi'kmaq men hired themselves out during the summer as guides to British or American sport hunting and fishing parties. Touched by the spirit of romanticism, these early tourists sought the natural wilderness as a temporary refuge from the pressures of the city and its commercialism. Arriving by steamship or train and being unfamiliar with birch-bark canoes and woodland survival, they hired Mi'kmaq guides—and paid them quite well for their services.

Mi'kmaq men who found seasonal work in the timber industry typically worked with large international crews, cutting trees in the winter and transporting the logs downriver to the sawmills during the spring. By the mid-1800s they were known as expert river drivers—as noted in this 1894 Indian agent report:

The Indians of Restigouche are sought after for making logs in the winter. Several camps are composed entirely of Indians under an Indian "boss." . . . The same Indians, that is to say, all the men who can leave the village, are employed in the spring taking rafts down the river, which affords them an important means of livelihood.

(SP 1895:33)

In 1876 railroad crews completed the Intercontinental Railway, linking the New Brunswick port at St. John with Quebec and Maine. This, along with the Canadian Pacific Railway and other lines established soon thereafter, fanned industrial development in the Northeast and greatly increased the Mi'kmaqs' already significant mobility. Traveling more extensively and more swiftly than ever before, Mi'kmaqs sought cash-earning opportunities as seasonal workers (Prins, 1996). They also increased their production of baskets and other "Indian" crafts, which they could now sell at railway stations or at lakeside and coastal resorts where tourism now flourished, thanks to trains (Whitehead 1980; McBride, 1995).

By the 1880s growing numbers also accepted work at the ship wharves, loading and unloading vessels. Others found employment at local sawmills, ironworks, stone quarries, or tanneries. After the turn of the century, many worked as potato pickers on northern Maine's farms each fall—and made the sturdy wood-splint baskets used to bring in the harvest (McBride 1990; Prins, 1996).

As market hunters Mi'kmaqs had discovered the precariousness of being overly dependent on a single commodity whose value was determined by distant markets. Now, even as they tried to diversify their subsistence activities, they found themselves increasingly exposed to the vicissitudes of international capitalism.

PORPOISE HUNTING IN THE BAY OF FUNDY (C. 1815–1895)

In the early 1800s Mi'kmaqs from Bear River in southwest Nova Scotia became specialized sea-mammal hunters. At the time, high-quality oil extracted from porpoise blubber was used as fuel for newly built lighthouses all along the Atlantic coast. It produced very good light, was unaffected by cold temperatures, and was neither smelly nor sticky. The oil was also valued for greasing machinery. For about 80 years, "porpos" hunting was a highly profitable enterprise, not only for Bear River Mi'kmaqs, but also for Passamaquoddies across the Bay of Fundy. Each summer during porpoise-hunting season, a cluster of Mi'kmaq families camped oceanside in a sheltered cove with access to fresh water (Leighton, 410). While women gathered berries, prepared meals, and fashioned baskets and other crafts to sell, hunters in pairs paddled and sailed their 24-foot birch-bark canoes across the cold open waters in pursuit of their prey. Usually they heard the animal blow air before seeing it and paddled toward the sound. While the man in the stern held the canoe steady with his paddle, the gunner at the bow stood up and aimed his long-barreled gun. Loaded with a heavy charge of very coarse "double B" shot, the weapon gave a kick so forceful that it could fracture a gunner's jaw or shoulder bone. Once hit, the porpoise (commonly six feet long and 250 pounds) was harpooned with an iron-tipped 12-foot spear and deftly hauled aboard. A typical day's catch was two animals, but hunters sometimes came back with six per canoe. On shore, they stripped the mammals of their thick layer of fat and whatever meat was desired. The blubber (up to 100 pounds on a good-sized porpoise) was cut into chunks and placed in huge iron pots placed over hot stones. As the blubber melted, a purified amber liquid surfaced. This was the precious oil. Skimmed off and cooled, the oil from a single porpoise was typically between one and two gallons. The oil was poured into rum kegs or tin cans for transport to the market in Digby. A skilled hunter could harvest about 150–200 porpoises a season, producing some 250 gallons of oil. But in the 1890s porpoise oil prices suddenly collapsed when petroleum-derived kerosene fuels and lubricants appeared on the market. In 1936* Matthew Pictou, an old Mi'kmaq from Bear River, recalled the final days of porpoise hunting:

> Them was great days, but they was hard days, too. Yes, boy, they was hard times. My uncle lost his life. He was out porpoisin' with a small boy and a shark come along and stuck his nose right through the bow of the canoe and tore a hole as big as that—[Matthew made an "O" with his arms]—The old man was so scared that he forgot himself and shot down on the shark through the canoe and she filled with water and turned over. The boy could swim a little and held on the canoe, but the old man sank and never was seen alive again. The boy was picked up by other canoes and he never seen no more of the shark. . . . Two years after the machine oil come in and we didn't go porpoisin' no more.

(Leighton, 458)

CHANGING MATERIAL CULTURE: FIXED DWELLINGS AND COMMON DRESS

Birch-bark wikuoms remained popular among some Mi'kmaq groups until well into the 1880s. By then, however, only a few families lived in them year-round. Others used them in the summer but during the rest of the year typically dwelled in frame "houses built of boards and logs, furnished like a backwoodsman's shanty" (Halleck, 430–31).

As long as Mi'kmaqs held on to their traditional life as hunters, fishers, and gatherers, they retained many elements of their distinctive dress, including leggings, tunics, robes, moccasins, and various ornaments. But as they took up farming or seasonal wage labor, they discarded their characteristic clothes in favor of a less conspicuous appearance.

Among the slowest to change were Cape Breton Mi'kmaqs, who were more isolated and conservative—as described in this 1860 chronicle:

> They do . . . still partly retain their dress of former years; consisting of a blue tunic, with the seams inlet with scarlet cloth and wings or epaulets upon the shoulder of the same colour. A leather strap . . . keeps his tunic close to the waist. A woolen sash of diverse colours is sometimes worn, or even often. An ordinary hat covers their head encircled by a coloured band of ribbon. Beads and tin ornaments usually decorate their breast,—and especially their moccasins or shoes, which are made of moose skin

---

*In the summer of 1936 anthropologist Alexander Leighton filmed a historical reenactment of porpoise hunting by Bear River Mi'kmaqs, titled *Porpoise Oil.*

and highly adorned with patterns and bead work. . . . They invariably smoke, and a
pouch containing a pipe and tobacco is almost always carried at the waist.

(Uniacke, 156)

Less dependent on outside employment, Mi'kmaq women in general were
slower to adjust their public image and held on to customary clothing longer than did
the men. Typically, these clothes consisted

of a coloured bed-gown and loose blanket thrown over the shoulders like a shawl;
with petticoats of various colours. The head dress is very peculiar being a high
pointed cap of blue or red cloth, with loose ends falling almost over the shoulders,—highly ornamented with beadwork of various patterns, and adorned with
ribbons. . . . [Beads are worn] in strings around the neck, and [are] often worked
into her jacket as well as cap, and upon the sides and front of her moccasins.

(Uniacke, 156)

In contrast to Mi'kmaqs in Cape Breton, those in Quebec, New Brunswick, and
mainland Nova Scotia started to give up their unique dress in the 1830s. By the mid-
1800s Mi'kmaq men at mainland Nova Scotia generally dressed "in ordinary
clothes, but usually affect a grey tunic and pantaloons, with shoes or high boots." In
addition, they wore the common round felt hat. Among the women, "hats and

Three Mi'kmaq women in Victorian dress, late nineteenth century.

feathers, veils, flounces and high laced boots," typical of the Victorian period, were "rapidly taking their place" (Gilpin, 111). Only at special festivities, such as St. Anne's Day, did they still dress "in their gay and ancient costume"—which was not always easy to come by (in Whitehead 1991:239). When the British crown prince visited Nova Scotia in 1860, a special committee of citizens in Halifax published "An Appeal for the Indians" in the local newspaper, asking for contributions to help Mi'kmaqs buy goods needed to make traditional clothes for themselves:

> The Indians are entirely destitute of suitable National Costume, and without the means to purchase material to make it, and they have been refused any public grant. . . . The Indian encampments have been visited [by the Committee], the men mustered and enrolled, a certain portion of them provided with cloths, beads, &c, and their canoes are being numbered and got in order. . . .

> (in Whitehead 1991:260–61)

By the end of the 19th century, the daily dress of most Mi'kmaq males matched that of any other workmen in the region—flannel shirt, woolen jacket and pants, and boots or shoes. Women generally "covered the head with tight scarfs, often of figured material, and with a shawl fastened and draped from the crown of the head." Not long afterward, traces of traditional dress disappeared on Mi'kmaqs of both sexes, except among some during a few major ceremonial occasions (Wallis and Wallis 1953:111).

POLITICAL PATERNALISM: INDIAN AGENTS

In the eyes of British colonials, Mi'kmaqs were primitive degenerates, unfit to handle their own affairs. Treating them like children or mental incompetents, the government assumed guardianship over Mi'kmaqs, appointing Indian agents to carry out its responsibilities. After agents were in place, Mi'kmaqs had to get their approval for almost every official transaction.

As described earlier, after Britain defeated France in Mi'kmaq country, many Mi'kmaqs found themselves pauperized, reduced to begging for food, clothing, and blankets. Some found relief through the charity of church organizations or private individuals. In 1800, troubled about these "restless, savage people," the Nova Scotia provincial government organized a special Committee for Indian Affairs, which issued a "Plan for the Relief of the Indians." Not much came of this early plan to alleviate distress and suffering, because the policy was incoherent and inconsistently applied. In 1807 the province of Nova Scotia was divided into twelve districts, and a part-time Indian agent was assigned to each. Agents provided provincial authorities with information about Mi'kmaqs, made note of their grievances, and handled relief efforts. Twelve years later they were instructed to mark out reserve tracts at or near sites still frequented by local Mi'kmaq hunting groups (Hutton, 70–77).

Agents seem to have done little to curb white encroachment on reserves. Even if they had wanted to stop trespassers, they would not have had much official support for the endeavor. As the Indian commissioner acknowledged in an 1845 report to the Nova Scotia Legislature: "It will not be easy for any Commissioner holding a seat in the Provincial Assembly . . . to do justice to the Indians, and to retain the goodwill of

Former Pictou Landing Chief Peter Wilmot in ceremonial dress at age 106, shortly before his death in 1932.

his [white, voting] constituents. . . ." Pandering to white constituents went so far that in 1859 the Committee for Indian Affairs "proposed that [Indian] lands which had been trespassed upon be sold to the violators at varying sums." Ignoring Mi'kmaq protests, the government put reserve land up for sale, retaining only about 50 acres for each Mi'kmaq family and professing that the money from sold land would pay for Mi'kmaq pauper relief (McGee, 58–62; cf. Upton, 102–08).

As far as the government was concerned, the best long-term solution to the "Indian problem" was to "civilize" Mi'kmaqs and settle them down as small-scale farmers. Toward this objective, Indian agents received funding to buy and distribute seeds and sometimes to buy or hire draft animals, such as oxen.

FEDERAL GUARDIANSHIP: THE INDIAN ACT (1876)

Until the mid-1860s British North America consisted of provinces, each administered by a Crown-appointed governor. But in 1867, under the British North America Act, the provinces were united under a common dominion government based in Ottawa, and the nation of Canada was founded. Under a new constitution, jurisdiction over Indian affairs was transferred from the provinces to the new federal government.

In 1876, nearly a decade after Britain's North American provinces were confederated as Canada, the federal government passed the Indian Act, which consolidated all laws pertaining to native inhabitants (1 percent of its total population). The act aimed at [helping] the Indian to raise himself from the condition of tutelage and dependence. The official name of this ethnocide was enfranchisement, which literally means "setting free." Free from what? From the ties of their ancestral culture! In essence, enfranchisement meant that Indians who "matured" to the standards of civilization (as defined by the government) were sufficiently assimilated to accept the benefits and burdens of ordinary citizenship.

To implement the Indian Act, the federal government created a Department of Indian Affairs. The department, in turn, appointed special Indian agents to enforce federal regulations, carry out directives, and keep the government apprised of reserve communities. To hasten the assimilation process, Christianity was actively promoted and whatever remained of native spiritual traditions was repressed. Indian children were forced to attend church-run boarding schools where English was taught and where speaking Mi'kmaq was forbidden.

The Indian Act brought change to the political system of indirect rule. Denying the quasi-sovereign status of tribal nations, it decreed that the minister of Indian affairs possessed managerial prerogatives over Indian reserves and resources (Bartlett, 603)—and over tribal membership. For the first time in their history, Mi'kmaqs could not decide for themselves who was or was not an Indian. Status was now defined by federal law, which declared that an Indian is someone "who pursuant of this Act is registered as an Indian, or is entitled to be registered as an Indian." Federal law defined an Indian band as "a body of Indians for whom the government has set aside lands for their common use and benefit; for whom the government is holding moneys for their common use and benefit; or which has been declared a band by the governor-in-council for the purposes of the Act." The law also defined a reserve: "a tract of land, the legal title of which is vested in the Crown, that has been set aside for the use of a band" (Dickason 1992:284). The idea behind these regulations was to turn the Indians into Canadian citizens and their reserves into rural municipalities, much the same as the population in surrounding townships (Bartlett, 603).

The political transition was confusing. Some scattered Mi'kmaq groups were not federally recognized as bands. Without official status, they were left to their own devices—free from control but blocked from rights, including reserves. The government also abolished the position of life chiefs and prescribed democratic elections for specific terms in office. Many bands resisted this until their traditional saqmaws died, but by 1900 most held regular elections. Also, because the federal government limited recognition to individual Mi'kmaq bands, it refused to deal with grand chiefs in charge of large districts—thereby diminishing the political power of these high-ranking tribal leaders (Bock, 1966:22).

Although the grand chiefs were no longer recognized by the government, the Catholic Church continued to back them for a time as spiritual leaders. For instance, when Peter Paul (Peminuit) of Shubenacadie was elected grand chief of mainland Nova Scotia in 1912, he traveled with some fellow Mi'kmaq leaders to the archbishop's residence in Halifax. Dressed in old homespun clothes, the 59-year-old chief knelt before the archbishop. Candles were lit, and he "received His Grace's blessing, was invested with the gilt medallion of the Pope which the late Chief [John] Noel had worn, was exhorted to perform his duties as chief in an upright, faithful manner, and to attend the services of the Roman Catholic Church and to tell his beads regularly even when unable to attend the chapel, etc." (in Whitehead 1991:297–98). He served for only a few years. By then, except at Cape Breton, the title and position of grand chief among the Mi'kmaq had become a thing of the past.

By 1900 Indian agents had gained considerable political power over reserve communities. When a Mi'kmaq band elected new leaders, its choice was not official until confirmed and ratified by the agent. Moreover, the Indian agent could remove a chief at any time for "dishonesty, intemperance [alcohol abuse], or immorality" (in Dickason 1992:285). Because the Department of Indian Affairs controlled band funds, an Indian agent also possessed the power of the purse and could economically reward Mi'kmaqs who supported his agenda and deprive favors to those who did not. Wary of manipulation, Mi'kmaqs tended to keep agents at a safe distance. Hostile feelings were usually masked, but not always (Bock 1966:61). One old Mi'kmaq woman revealed these bitter memories about the Indian agent at Eel Ground Reserve:

> There was an Indian woman on the reserve and she was a stepper. The Indian
> Agent used to come to her house and she gave him what he wanted. She had a
> baby from him, and he gave all kinds of favors to her. That wasn't right. Why
> didn't he look after all the others who were so poor?

(in McBride and Prins, 1983:4)

INDIAN RESIDENTIAL SCHOOL OF SHUBENACADIE

Among the various acculturation agencies in a modern state society, schools are perhaps most effective. In 1867 the Canadian government claimed responsibility for educating Indian children. Federal educational policy presumed that indigenous cultures "were unworthy of perpetuation," representing the denial or negation of basic Canadian values. Primary schools were established on reserves to provide Mi'kmaq children "with the same intellectual skills possessed by non-Indians, and equip them equally to lead socially responsible and useful lives." Basic reading, writing, and arithmetic were taught. Most of the teachers were non-Indian Catholic lay instructors, but after 1900 a good number of Mi'kmaqs were qualified to teach. Because they could speak the language of their pupils, they were quite effective—but many "ran afoul of the suspicions and demands of Indian agents, school inspectors, or federal officials . . ." (W. Hamilton, 1986:12–15).

Risking exposure to racism, quite a few Mi'kmaqs were educated at public schools. Others attended Indian residential schools such as the one at Shubenacadie, Nova Scotia. Built on a big hill, "Shubie" housed nearly 200 hundred children under the tutelage of the Sisters of Charity. In operation from 1929 to 1967 and conforming to Canada's official assimilation policies, it stripped some 2,000 youngsters of their cultural identity. Upon arrival most of the children could not speak English; barred from speaking their own language they soon learned English—and forgot Mi'kmaq. Some children entered Shubie at age five and did not leave until age 16. Many stayed

10 months per year, but quite a few remained year-round. The school was strictly segregated by sex, and teenage boys were put to work on the school's farm and woodlots, while the girls were tasked with the laundry.

Many who attended Shubie describe it as a prison where they "were constantly told they were no good, they were heathens, they were savages . . ." (Basque, in MN, June 1989). Typically, their memories are of a harsh regime that included beatings. One Mi'kmaq woman, a basketmaker, told me a few years ago:

> [My] father was a drifter too. He never stayed anywhere for a long time. My mom . . . died too early, when I was an infant. When she died I was taken care of by an aunt. . . . When I was old enough to go to school I went to the Residential School in Shubie, which was run by the nuns. I was six when I got in, and sixteen when I finally got out. It was a horrible place. We were brutalized at that Shubie school. The nuns beat us. We had a line-up for a beatin' and we was shivering in the cold. Oh my God we had some agony there. We got beatings for talking Indian. . . .

> (Betsy Paul, in McBride and Prins, 1983)

Shubie may not have been as brutal as described by some, but because of its unquestioned goal of assimilation and outright denunciation of Mi'kmaq traditions, it has become a symbol of cultural repression. This is evident even in more tempered commentaries on the school. A Mi'kmaq woman from northern Maine remembers that her father, a trapper from Eel Ground Reserve, brought all his children to the school following their mother's death. She was not yet five when she arrived and stayed until she was 14:

> [My father] wrote to us and sent us little gifts, money. But we didn't see him during those school years. All of us were Indians—orphans, abandoned, children of single parents who couldn't raise us. . . . The nuns told us little Indian stories . . . but we weren't allowed to speak the Mi'kmaq language. We were punished severely if we did—straps on the hand, sent to bed without supper. . . . Once I was in the convent [school], it wasn't long before I couldn't carry on a Mi'kmaq conversation.

> (Sarah Lund, in McBride and Prins, 1983)

Indeed, upon returning home after years at Shubie, Mi'kmaq teenagers found they could no longer communicate with their elders.

MAGIC HEROES IN THE ENCHANTED WORLD OF IMAGINATION

As among other subordinated groups, folktales about trickster figures became very popular among the impoverised Mi'kmaq. Surrounded and controlled by strangers, Mi'kmaqs relied on the world of their imagination for psychological "breathing space." They created a fabulous repertoire of stories in which the political reality of powerlessness and helplessness was mysteriously turned around or upside down. In this illusionary world, they generally triumphed as great heroes or cunning wizards over opponents portrayed as mean cowards or gullible weaklings. Colorful stories about their heroic past were especially welcome. They wanted to hear *kinap* stories about formidable chiefs and warriors such as L'kimu and Kaqtukwaq and tales about *puowins* (medicine men) who were capable of performing magic tricks.

Also fitting this genre are *pa'tlia's* (patriarch) stories about tonsured, bearded, celibate, and long-robed missionaries. For instance, Mi'kmaq elders often recounted the legendary exploits of *Mosi Mayal* ("Monsieur [Abbé] Maillard"), attributing to him qualities of a traditional *puowin*. Apparently inspired by the biblical story of the Israelite exodus from Egypt, this story (recorded in 1911) features the priest as a French Moses saving God's Indian children from hostile heretics:

> After the English came here and dispossessed the French, they used to shoot into the churches when the people were in them, and kill the priest and all who were inside. Finally, a priest and his congregation, thus attacked, ran to the woods. The priest was [Mosi Mayal]. The thorns and bushes tore his clothes to ribbons. The Indians made him clothes of skin. A long time after this attack the English again found them. The Indians were not frightened for themselves, but merely on account of the priest. They ran away. They came to a lake, and started to cross it on the ice and snow. When they were about halfway over, they saw the army of the English behind them. The priest began to pray for them. When he had finished praying, he rose, took his bow, and drew a long scratch on the ice, separating the Indians from the English. They then traveled on, over the snow and ice. When the English arrived at this long scratch on the ice, the ice, with a [loud noise] like a cannon, suddenly broke, and left a stretch of open water in front of the foe, who had to turn back.

> (in Wallis and Wallis 1955:470)

Such legends sustained the Mi'kmaq in these troubled times. The Mi'kmaq were also comforted by Klu'skap stories, which seem to have become especially popular in the 19th century. In Wabanaki legends, as noted in Chapters 2 and 3, Klu'skap is an immortal giant and mystical culture hero who once roamed their lands. He was not the Creator, but rather a mythological transformer of the natural landscape and its animal inhabitants. Significantly, his name is traditionally associated with tall tales and exaggeration. Indeed, old tribespeople usually translate the name Klu'skap as "the Liar." (Today this translation is no longer popular because it is seen as disrespectful of their heritage.)

CONCLUSION

Considering their poverty, sickness, and other calamities, it is remarkable that instead of slowly dying out, Mi'kmaqs began to increase during the 18th and 19th centuries. Demographic data based on estimates by Indian agents indicate that the Mi'kmaq population had climbed beyond 4,000 by 1900. Loosely organized, Mi'kmaq bands varied in size from less than a dozen individuals to just over 500. Nova Scotia, home to 2,018 Mi'kmaqs, counted 57 separate clusters. However, fluctuation in numbers continued to be a hallmark of these social units. For instance, the band at Annapolis numbered 94 in 1861, 68 in 1871, and 324 in 1883 (Prins 1988:227–29). All told, more than 60 widely scattered reserves had been set aside for Mi'kmaqs. Because quite a few of these were seldom or never inhabited, it is clear that many Mi'kmaqs avoided the restrictions of reserve life.

13 / Mi'kmaq Cultural Survival: A Tribal Nation in the Modern World

By the mid-1900s it seemed that the Mi'kmaq had finally reached their culture's end. But, as events described in this final chapter show, instead of disappearing as a culturally identifiable group, Mi'kmaqs are in the throes of a cultural and political renaissance. The turnaround began in the late 1960s as they realized that the last vestiges of their tribal heritage were slipping away. Revitalization was not orchestrated by anybody in particular. It was (and continues to be) a mostly improvised affair involving dozens of spontaneous initiatives by highly motivated individuals widely scattered throughout Mi'kmaq country. With so many involved in the process of cultural remaking, confusion and even conflict are inevitable. But, despite differing views on how to get there, the destination of cultural survival and self-determination is shared.

MI'KMAQ PERSONHOOD AND INDIAN "STATUS"

As members of a cross-border tribal nation, Mi'kmaqs have been confronted by a multiplicity of political and socioeconomic pressures within transnational, federal, provincial, and state spheres. Their legal status has been subject to repeated challenge and revision within each sphere. In fact, the political ramifications and incongruences of legislation concerning Mi'kmaqs are so confusing that it takes a specialist to decipher them.

In Canada, where the vast majority of Mi'kmaqs reside, they (like other Indians in that country) have been governed since 1876 according to the Indian Act as wards of the federal government. Until quite recently, Canadian laws banned Indians from voting in federal elections. Today individuals recognized as Indians by the government possess the rights and privileges of citizenship available to all other Canadians—plus aboriginal rights identified in the Constitution Act of 1982 as well as various (not always congruous) federal and provincial laws pertaining to Indians. This means that people with Indian status have a legal position different from all other Canadian citizens. Indian status is conferred upon someone who is registered with the Department of Indian Affairs (DIA) in Ottawa, is formally affiliated with an officially recognized band, and falls under the jurisdiction of the Indian Act. However, not everyone who asserts native identity has Indian status, even if his or her biological and cultural heritage is unquestionably Indian. For instance, because of a patrilineal bias reflecting Western values, Mi'kmaq women who married non-Indian men had no Indian status—nor did their children. And, in reverse, non-Indian women who married Mi'kmaq men gained full Indian status—and so did their children. Status Indians have certain entitlements, rooted in historical agreements and treaties with dominant society, that guaranteed the survival and protection of native groups in exchange for their surrender of control over much of their traditional territories. These entitlements include the right to live on a reserve, special benefits and services (health, justice, education, welfare, and housing subsidy), and some financial support for band administration, economic development, and cultural programs.

MI'KMAQ BANDS TODAY: FEDERAL HEGEMONY

Traditionally, Mi'kmaq bands were loose socioeconomic aggregates that fluctuated in size and composition as individuals and families joined or left the group—prompted by environmental or social factors.

As we have seen, band membership lost its flexibility after 1876, when Canada's Department of Indian Affairs (DIA) began to define and manage native lives. Practicing internal colonialism, the federal government assumed evermore direct control over Mi'kmaqs, making the very existence of their bands contingent on government recognition. According to DIA definition, "A band is an administratively defined group of Indians who are given the right to use specified Crown land, called reserves, and who are given money to administer their community" (Price, 217).

Mi'kmaq bands in Canada were redefined as corporate groups with membership determined by the provisions of the revised Canadian Indian Act of 1951. Reinforcing assimilation policy, the act (article 11, chapter 29, section 1) rewards Mi'kmaqs financially for surrendering band membership:

> Each individual registered as a Band member is considered to have an equal (per capita) share "of the capital and revenue moneys held by Her Majesty in behalf of the Band," to which [s/he] is entitled *should [s/he] cease to be a member of the Band.*

> (Bock 1966:31, emphasis added)

Currently, Mi'kmaqs are officially organized in 29 federally recognized bands. All but one, the Aroostook band in northern Maine, are headquartered on Canadian reserves. At this writing, Buctouche is the smallest band (75 members), and Eskasoni is the largest (2,900). In total, Canada has established over 60 Mi'kmaq reserves. Some bands have more than one reserve, and several reserves are shared by more than one band.

RESERVES: PLACES OF REFUGE AND GOVERNMENT DEPENDENCY

All of Canada's Mi'kmaq reserves are economically marginal, forcing many Mi'k-maqs to seek work elsewhere. Building on their tradition as a migratory people, they have used their reserves as base camps, leaving them frequently in pursuit of subsistence. Historically, many found seasonal rural jobs as loggers, river drivers, and harvesters. Others signed on as day laborers or went "working out" in big cities along the Atlantic seaboard—as domestic servants or as factory or high-rise construction workers. Today, still seeking income and adventure, as well as education and career opportunities, Mi'kmaqs continue to quit their reserves for a season, for years, or forever.

In the late 1960s almost half of all Nova Scotia Mi'kmaqs lived off-reserve, as did about one-third of Mi'kmaqs from other areas (Upton, 175). Today one-third of the reserves in Nova Scotia are uninhabited, while some are occupied by only a couple of families (MN March 1974:14, May 1984:19). Absences vary enormously per band and fluctuate in time. For instance, the Indian Brook Reserve near Shubenacadie shifted from 76 Mi'kmaqs in 1912 to 243 in 1916 to 105 in 1936. Then came a dramatic upswing from 200 in 1944 to 630 in 1949 (due to the government's effort to centralize Nova Scotia's Mi'kmaqs). Four years later, its population dropped again to 500. By 1984 it had doubled to about 1,100, and it had increased to almost 1,600 in 1991 (Wallis and Wallis 1953:106; MN May 1984:19).

Mi'kmaqs who depart and return seasonally are often unskilled or semiskilled laborers with little formal education. Until very recently, they comprised the vast majority of the Mi'kmaq population. Their options are few, and they usually alternate short-term off-reservation jobs with social welfare. The jobs they take provide low remuneration and no security, but they offer the virtue of flexibility. Not tied to a daily eight-to-five routine, these Mi'kmaqs are free to respond to unexpected opportunities for other jobs, adventure, or social life. As in the past, maintaining social relationships is essential to Mi'kmaq survival, because social ties provide insurance in times of need. Generally speaking, Mi'kmaqs have a distinctly open attitude when it comes to job hunting, often venturing great distances to follow a work lead.

Today about 3,000 Mi'kmaqs live and work in the Boston area. Several thousand more can be found along the Atlantic seaboard in cities from St. John down to Washington, D.C. Others are scattered throughout eastern Canada. Mi'kmaqs who leave the reserve for years at a time often return for visits and frequently move back home later in life.

With few exceptions, the reserve economies are based on welfare benefits, government-subsidized programs, or administrative salaries paid by the DIA. Moreover, under Canada's constitutional and statutory obligations (DIAND, 1990), status Indians are exempt from federal or provincial taxes on income earned on reserves. Although reserve resources are too sparse to sustain most families on an ongoing basis, they provide a vital subsistence backup. Whether slipping away from the reserve for a month or for years, Mi'kmaqs rely on its steady, if meager, resources.

Generally speaking, the most stable reserve population is comprised of the elderly and women with children. It is common for Mi'kmaq women with growing children to "return to the reserve where they can get a tax-free, rent-free house, medical services, and emergency relief, while the husband alternates between 'working out' and brief periods at home" (Bock 1966:77). For others, the reserve is a place to turn in times of ill health, empty pockets, or social crisis—"a haven in hard times and . . . a focus of sentiments." Most Mi'kmaqs have some extended family members keeping the home fires burning while they are away (Guillemin, 61, 82–83, 126–32).

MI'KMAQ MOBILITY AND THE TRIBAL NETWORK

Although tied to particular bands on a bureaucratic level, many Mi'kmaqs have maintained their traditional flexibility and mobility. Reflecting on her long life, one Mi'kmaq elder in northern Maine commented: "We count by seasons and jobs more than by years. . . . I get all mixed up about dates of things because I moved so darn many times in my life. . . . Thinking about it makes me dizzy" (Caroline Copage, in McBride and Prins, 1983).

Social bonding beyond the boundaries of one's local community is crucial in Mi'kmaq economic and cultural survival strategy. Given their migratory work habits, Mi'kmaqs often depend on having fellow tribespeople in other regions open their homes to them. Typically, they mutually oblige each other not only with lodging, but also with information, job leads, transportation, and sometimes cash. The debt that one incurs by accepting hospitality is an obligation to return the favor in the future. This makes social interaction as central to survival as work itself.

Because communication about jobs is always circulated through the network, it is common to find individual tribespeople joining *ad hoc* crews of kinfolk and friends (often members of different bands) to seek collective work opportunities, usually seasonal labor (potato harvesting, berry picking, lumbering) in northern New England as well as Canada. Often they make an effort to remain together, sharing room and board. New England's draw on the Canadian Maritimes for labor (especially during the first two-thirds of this century) has had an important effect on the tribal network, increasing interaction between individual Mi'kmaqs hailing from remote reserves. The international boundary between the United States and Canada has not inhibited their labor migrations, due in part to the 1794 Jay Treaty, which recognized their right to work on both sides of the border.

Every Mi'kmaq adult knows where to find other Mi'kmaq groups within their fragmented, far-flung nation. As individual Mi'kmaqs move about, visiting family and friends, seeking temporary employment or buyers for their basketry and other crafts, it is not uncommon for them to link up with a Mi'kmaq partner or even spouse. An important factor in this fluid social network is widespread intermarriage between the various bands—a common practice today, as in aboriginal and historical times.

By means of transient relatives and friends, scattered Mi'kmaq families and communities keep abreast of each other's weals and woes. This is what they sometimes jokingly refer to as the "moccasin telegraph." Individuals who do not form part of this informal network of kith and kin are effectively cut off from their social identity as Mi'kmaq Indians.

It would be a mistake to think that Mi'kmaqs travel only for economic opportunity. Some hit the road simply for the sake of variety or adventure. The experiences they gather on their journeys are fine fodder for good stories, which are like meal and housing vouchers in the Mi'kmaq network. Generally gregarious, they like to visit with each other and swap stories and are willing to travel far to do so on a fairly regular basis (Prins, 1996). The two oral histories that follow here are emblematic of the persistent migratory lifeways of Mi'kmaqs in general.

Caroline Sark Copage: Oral History

I was born in Rollo Bay, Prince Edward Island, on 13 February 1910. I grew up mostly in Scotchfort, not far from there. Before I was born my father went to Maine and didn't come back for four years. He worked around Houlton (Maine) and was stayin' there with some lady. My father was a smart man and worked pretty hard. Wasn't lazy like a lot of men.

So, living there in Scotchfort there was my mother, her father and stepmother, and my older sister, and me. For a long time I thought my grandfather was my father. He used to wake up early and make us porridge or something to eat, then he'd take his violin and make music and my sister and I danced. She used to do a Highland fling. Oh that was good! As long as I remember, Grandfather played violin. He used to walk ten to fifteen miles to go to a party and get paid for playin' for white folks. There was no good transportation back then. The roads weren't very good, and we used to go through the woods. . . .

Grandma used to make moccasins and decorate them with [dyed porcupine] quills and them little small beads she bought in town. In the summers, people from the U.S.—I can't remember the names of them people. . . . Oh, yes, *tourists*—they used to come over and buy moccasins from my grandma when we were staying in

Mi'kmaq camp at Prince Edward Island, 1905.

Rocky Point by Charlottetown. They'd get to Charlottetown by train or car and ferry boat. They were from all over the place [and] used to give us kids money—maybe twenty-five cents—and we felt rich.

My grandfather used to make birch-bark canoes and boxes, and like most Indians he moved around some to make a living. Sometimes all of us went. The first time I ever went blueberry picking was with my grandfather. We went to the harvest in Springhill, Nova Scotia. Mama, Grandma, my sister and Uncle Alec, mom's brother, went, too. Uncle Alec was with us a lot. He never married and was a lot older than Mama.

In 1914, Uncle Alec somehow knew he was gonna die, and he said he wanted Dad to come home before he was dead. He told Mom to write Father and tell him he wanted to see him again. Mom did that, and Dad left that Houlton lady and came back to home before Uncle Alec died. After that, Mom and Dad got back together—I say they got back together! They had seven more children!. . . .

Just a few steps below Grandma and Grandfather's place, which was up a little hill, Dad built our place. He used wood supplied by the government. To make a living, my father mostly made ax handles and baskets. But he also used to go to Nova Scotia to pick berries—in Springhill, Sackville, and Maccan—and we'd go with him. In the fall we picked potatoes behind a plow in Scotchfort. And often in the summer, fall, and spring we went in a sailboat my father built and sailed to places where we'd sell baskets and ax handles and whisk brooms. Dad would make a tar-paper shack along the coast, and we'd stay ashore for a week or so, making and selling baskets. People would hear we were there, and they'd come and bring food, blankets, and other things for us—and we'd trade or sell our baskets, brooms, and handles.

Behind our house in Scotchfort there was a little one-room country school house, with all ages and all kinds of kids, both Indian and white. I got far behind in school since we were moving around so much. We had to make a living, so except for wintertime, I was away a lot. I did second grade so many times, and third grade, too. In fact, the year before I got married I was still in third grade. My last winter in the third grade, one of the white kids' mothers complained that an Indian boy had lice. It was true. That boy's family didn't wash much—but that wasn't true about all of us. Well, after that, none of the Indian children were allowed in the school anymore. That was the end of my education. I was sorry about that. I'd a' liked to keep learnin'. . . .

I met my husband, Rufus Copage, at the St. Anne's Day celebration up to Lennox Island. He lived there. I used to go up there and shell the cooked lobsters during the celebration. All kinds of white folks used to come and buy it. Anyway, I met Rufus there, and he started writing to me when I went back to Scotchfort. He was a good writer, and I wrote back, just to satisfy him. Then he came to Scotchfort, stayed at my grandparents' house, and visited me. He told my grandmother he wanted to marry me. We couldn't get no time alone together, so we got married. I was seventeen, and he was eighteen. It was August 30th, 1927.

After Rufus and I got married, we moved around to make our living, but we had a little house we went back to, right above Mama's. Not a very big house. Just one room. My husband, my father, friends, anyone who happened along helped to build it. My husband couldn't support me alone. . . . So I helped him, and so did Dad. He used to go in the woods with Dad to get wood for baskets. Then he and I worked together, makin' baskets [and] picking berries, potatoes, and apples in different places. We'd go to Nova Scotia—to Cambridge pickin' apples and visiting

Rufus's father, or to stay and work a little in Hantsport. But not long. [We] never stayed long—had to move to follow the jobs.

More than anything, we was makin' our living with baskets. Like when I was a kid, we had to go and peddle baskets to get by, and it was always hard to sell 'em in the wintertime.

Even though we were on the road, I always came home to have my babies—first Mary Elizabeth in 1928, then Preston in '29, and Billy the next year. I had nine children altogether, and one stillborn, but only my three youngest are still living. . . . Mama brought my children into the world—all but two. . . .

Donald and Mary Sanipass: Oral History

[Donald] I was born in Shediac, (New Brunswick) . . . back in 1928. My mother died of pneumonia when I was seven. That fall I went to residential school in Shubenacadie. It was the Depression, and Dad couldn't look after us, so he sent us kids to Shubenacadie.

[Mary] I was born in Antigonish [Nova Scotia] in 1935 and went to Shubenacadie when I was eight [the year Donald left]. Both my parents got sick, so we kids left home a few at a time to go to Shubie. First Harold and Henry, then me. Three or four years later, Annie and John came. We had twelve nuns running the school. We weren't allowed to talk Indian. If we did we got put to bed early with a spanking. They shouldn't have beat us for that.

[Donald] Yeah, we were kinda puzzled about that. They were breaking me of Indian, but my English was broken, too. One thing we had was good meals, though. They got top honors in health for a school.

[Mary] I stayed at the school till I was sixteen. . . . As for visiting, it was up to the parents if they wanted to see you. Mine never came.

[Donald] I stayed there until I was fifteen. By then Dad had moved to St. John [New Brunswick]. He'd gone there to work dry dock construction. So I went to St. John too and worked in the war plant—building parts of the Mosquito bomber. . . . I was a scaler—measuring the thickness of veneer sheets coming off the lathe. . . . .

After [the war ended] I worked from construction job to construction job, all in St. John. That place was expanding into a big city. . . . I was living in the East End, on Prince Edward Street. A few Indians were living there, but it was real mixed. I was in the East End Gang—a gang based on location, not race. That's where I learned my boxing. A man named Fred Kennedy had a boxing club. . . . [I] walked in one day. . . . took a swing at a bag, and it came back and hit me in the nose so hard that it gave me a nosebleed. Kennedy saw me and came over and offered to give me some coaching. When I was seventeen I won the New Brunswick lightweight. . . . I was called Chief Donald Sanipass in the newspapers. . . .

I left St. John when I was twenty. Started going back and forth between New Brunswick and Maine. I went mainly because I found out Indians could go 'cross border without any problems. Started working for Bangor Hydro, which sets up lines in western Maine. But I'd come back to the St. John area sometimes [to see Indian friends and family]. . . .

A year and a half later, I met Mary in Gouldsboro [Maine]. By then I was living in a trailer during the workweek but usually came to Gouldsboro for the weekends and shared a place with [Mary's brothers] Harold and Henry. [My] Uncle Joe Daniel was living in Gouldsboro then. He'd gone there 'cause he'd heard about pulp cutting jobs from his [Mi'kmaq] friend Noel Phillips. Joe Daniel was cuttin' pulp part of the year, and in the spring he was harvesting trap poles—the young spruce limbs that could be bent to make lobster traps. He used to get five cents for a twenty-stick bundle. Anyway, Mary was in Gouldsboro that weekend, and I met her.

[Mary] I was working at Big Chief Sporting Camps, cooking and other things at the time. The place was run by "Chief" Stanwood. He wasn't an Indian. It was at Tunk Road in Sullivan, Maine. I lived right there in the camp but started coming down to visit Donald on the weekends in Gouldsboro. It was less than ten miles away from Sullivan.

[Donald] In 1952 I came to Aroostook [County] to pick potatoes for the first time. I came right up here to the State Road in Mapleton and worked for John Carter.

[Mary] I had picked for Carter the year before, in 1951. He had 400–500 acres, and there were lots of Indians around.

[Donald] Yeah. I'd heard of Carter through uncles and aunts, and through Mary's father. Mary and I both picked potatoes in 1952. There were Indians all over the place here—working for Turner, Gough, Carter, all kinds of farmers. Presque Isle was one wild place on the weekends during harvest time. [After a hard week of "stoop labor," many Mi'kmaqs were ready to party in town by the time Friday—payday—rolled around.]

[Mary] You bet it was wild. During harvest the jail was full every weekend.

[Donald] Well, after that fall, me and Mary wanted to get married, but her folks didn't like the idea of her marrying me when she was so young. So we sneaked away. . . . Got married at Holy Cross Cathedral in Boston. We eloped. Went by train from Presque Isle to Boston. . . . I found a job at the Statler Hilton after a couple of days. But after doing that job two days I [switched to] the Parker House. I acted as a runner for food and liquor. . . .

[Mary] I found a job in an embroidery house. . . . After I'd been there a month, I quit. I was having a baby and was too fat to reach my table!

After the baby was born [Marlene Rose, 9 February 1954], we went back to St. John, and Donald went back to construction work. We stayed with Don's dad. Then we stayed a month with [my brother] Harold. Then we decided we didn't fit in there, and we went to Fairvale [just east of St. John]. Indians had been living there for years. The landowner just let people build their camps and stay. There were four or five camps near each other. We stayed [with relatives] till we built our own place. Once we started, we built it in a day. At first we didn't have any tar paper, so on our first night we slept inside the frame . . . under the stars. We put the baby in the center, between us. Good thing it didn't rain!

While we lived in Fairvale, Don traveled by bus to work construction in St. John.

[Donald] That summer we started going blueberrying in Cherryfield [Maine]. During raking time Cherryfield was like Presque Isle during potato harvest. Lots of Indians, all kinds of [tribal] nationalities. . . . From then on it was blueberries in August, potatoes in the fall, then maybe back to Canada. But by the sixties we were staying in Maine during the winter and spring to work in potato houses— filling orders by loading 50–100-pound bags of potatoes onto trailers or railroad cars, or cutting seed. . . .

In 1962 . . . I was working in the potato house, and this [jobber] by the name of Rand Junkins . . . came up to me and asked if I wanted to cut pulp for him. So Mary and I worked for him three to four years till he died.

Mary Sanipass making ash-splint basket; Chapman, Maine, 1990.

A jobber [like Junkins] . . . might have a contract with a paper company for one thousand cords or so [of wood]. He goes around lookin' for woodlots, offers to buy stumpage from a farmer, and then hires laborers. . . . We used to get up at 5 A.M., feed the horse, have our own breakfast, and then head into the woods around 7 A.M. If the kids weren't in school, we'd take 'em with us. They'd ride into the woods on the horse. Wood horses are nice and gentle. Usually the jobber had the equipment—a Homelite power saw, axes, wedges, a horse. Most jobbers would buy the equipment on time from a bigger wood company.

. . . We cut rough pulp—spruce, fir. Although sometimes in the spring we cut hardwood and then peeled it before hauling it out. . . . After I cut down fifteen to twenty trees, Mary'd haul 'em with the horse to the "yard." That's what we called the main road. She'd fill the yard out, leaving the center of it open. Then she'd mark or scale the trees. Once the yard was full and marked, I'd come with the power saw and junk up four-foot lengths. Then Mary'd make one long row of 4-foot-high by 8-foot-long piles. Those are called cords. While she did that, I'd go back in and cut some more. . . .

[Mary] All together I worked fifteen years in the woods.

[Donald] . . . . After Rand Junkins died, we cut for other people . . . in Island Falls . . . , Patton . . . , Oakfield . . . , Mars Hill . . . . , [and] Cherryfield.

[Mary] Everywhere we moved, I guess we followed work.

[Donald] It's all mixed up. We count by seasons and jobs more than by years. There's so many places I moved. . . . Finally settled down here about fourteen to fifteen years ago. . . . [Of] course we still went blueberrying every year. But after 1969 we [stopped cutting pulp in the winters and] started working more regular in the potato houses [cutting seed and bagging].

[Mary] We started making baskets more regularly in 1970. We made a few back in the sixties, but nothing like we do today. . . . In the sixties we got just one to two dollars a basket. If we were hard up we got seventy-five cents. Isn't that awful? Today we get anywhere from five dollars up for our baskets. We make all kinds—pack, potato, fancy, hampers—but mostly potato.

[Donald] I quit potato work around 1978 because I got arthritis and potato houses are like fridges—the cold aggravates the arthritis.

[Mary] I still work during potato harvest season. I'm driving a harvester this year [1982].*

COUNTERCULTURE AND REVIVAL IN INDIAN COUNTRY

Many Mi'kmaqs who went through assimilation programs as Donald and Mary Sanipass did look back with bitterness at the educational institutions that degraded their native heritage. By the late 1960s, confronted with a great demise in native speakers and a dearth of tangible evidence of their "Indianness," many Mi'kmaqs feared they were part of a "dying culture" (MN 10 March 1974:15). They were not alone in their fears of culture loss. Political independence movements abroad had brought the colonial era to a close and challenged the inevitability of assimilation into Western culture. Meanwhile, rapid modernization in Western nations, where a postwar baby boom generation had come of age, caused internal pressures. In the United States, these pressures were intensified by the civil rights movement and exacerbated by the uproar over the Vietnam War. Collectively, these forces contributed to a widespread sense of crisis in Western "civilization" and spawned the counterculture movement. Suddenly, a significant number of the members of white dominant society openly questioned the morality of claims of cultural superiority.

Examining the widening cracks in the walls of Western hegemony, many Mi'kmaqs and other native peoples recognized that the time had come openly to resist domination, to protest repression, and to undo the distortion of their withering cultures.

In this century, as in the past, Mi'kmaq individuals and groups responded differently to confrontations with dominant white society. Some acquiesced to assimilation. Many became accommodationists, trying to fit into mainstream culture while holding on to parts of their past. A modest number stood firm as conservatives, staying aloof from white society, maintaining fluency in its ancestral tongue, and sheltering remnant traditions. Others took a confrontational approach. This latter group, often uprooted and alienated from their ancestral identity and angry about domination by white culture, has frequently been in the forefront of battles for native rights.

*Donald and Mary Sanipass are featured in the documentary film on Mi'kmaq basketmakers and potato pickers in northern Maine, titled *Our Lives in Our Hands,* shot in 1983 and 1984.

Whatever their divisions, Mi'kmaqs began to avert cultural demise and clear a path toward collective revitalization.

POLITICAL RESISTANCE: INDIAN UNIONS AND SELF-DETERMINATION

In 1965, aiming for more efficient communication and coordination of its policies and programs, Canada's DIA organized national and regional Indian advisory councils, comprised of representatives from every band across the country who met regularly with federal officials. Bringing far-flung Indians together had the unintended effect of helping to spawn a national Indian movement. That movement took off in 1969 in response to the federal government's *White Paper,* which detailed a five-year plan to repeal all federal legislation pertaining to Indians and to demolish the DIA. This plan would turn reserve communities into rural municipalities under provincial jurisdiction, negating the distinct position that Indians had as aboriginal peoples. Mi'kmaqs and their native peers were outraged. If their unique status (as defined under the Indian Act) were no longer guaranteed, they could lose their native rights (as guaranteed under the Act). Moreover, their efforts to gain recognition of aboriginal title to land would be jeopardized.

Confronted with a federal policy that tried to eradicate what was left of their indigenous heritage, the usually separate Mi'kmaq bands joined forces with each other and with bands of other Indian nations. They established provincial organizations such as the Union of Nova Scotia Indians, the Union of New Brunswick Indians, and the Indians of Quebec Association. Local band chiefs comprised the board of directors of these provincial unions and initially elected among themselves union officers, including a provincial leader known as president. The unions, in turn, formed the National Indian Brotherhood (NIB), with a representative from each of some 600 bands across Canada. This representative body helped bands coordinate their activities, in particular as an effective lobbying force.

In a historic meeting in 1970, NIB presented the Canadian government with a *Red Paper* demanding recognition of native rights. High on NIB's agenda were issues of treaty rights, aboriginal title, and self-determination. Faced with high unemployment rates, poor health conditions, and a host of other problems on the reserves, NIB also pressed for federal funding increases. Soon millions of dollars in federal grants for special Indian programs and services became available, opening the door for economic development projects, better health care, educational opportunities, housing improvement, and welfare. Next, for band members residing on reserves, the unions gained tax exemptions on gasoline diesel fuel, and stove oil, insurance, and store licenses. Although the general living conditions improved dramatically, high unemployment remained typical for Mi'kmaq reserves.

The unions also secured funding to employ legal advisors and ethnohistorians. With their help, Mi'kmaqs and other Indians in Canada gradually began to explore the legal jungle of native rights, including the historical underpinning of aboriginal title. Based on the idea that Canada's indigenous peoples are sovereign and, as such, possess an inherent right to control their own affairs within their own traditions, they restyled Indian bands as First Nations. In consequence, they reorganized NIB and formed the Assembly of First Nations in 1979.

Collaborating with other Indian groups in provincial and national organizations, Mi'kmaqs have made impressive gains on many fronts. Despite frequent rifts in their unity, Indians in Canada have effectively pressured the federal government into repudiating its long-held assimilation policies. National policy is now to form a multicultural society, which leaves some room for tribal nations such as the Mi'kmaq to move according to their own drumbeat.

RADICAL POLITICS: AIM AND THE KILLING OF ANNA MAE PICTOU

As with many American Indian groups, the arising of Mi'kmaq nationalism was inspired by the "red power" political activism of the late 1960s and early 1970s. In particular, the intertribal activism and fierce rhetoric of the American Indian Movement (AIM) helped define the political agendas of many North American tribes. In 1973 some three hundred AIM "warriors" occupied Wounded Knee (site of the 1890 Lakota Indian massacre by U.S. troops at Pine Ridge Reservation, South Dakota) to protest ongoing subjection to white paternalist control via the U.S. Bureau of Indian Affairs (BIA). Specifically, warriors aimed to draw attention to the Oglala Lakota traditionalists at Pine Ridge, who demanded restoration of their sovereignty as a tribal nation according to the terms of the Laramie Treaty of 1868. For more than seventy days, the group of lightly armed AIM people holed up at Wounded Knee— surrounded by 40 BIA police, 125 FBI agents, and 150 U.S. marshals. Most of the protesters were "volunteers from other tribes [in particular, urban Indians], and the intertribal spirit at Wounded Knee inspired a revival of Indian sovereignty claims all over the continent" (Matthiessen, 66).

Several Mi'kmaq tribal leaders in Canada were among those who voiced sympathy and political support for this protest. Sending a telegram to Wounded Knee, three senior officials of the Union of Nova Scotia Indians commended AIM for "the stage of ultimatum that you have attained," lauding the Wounded Knee occupation as a clear signal that "Indians are fighting for world awareness of broken treaties, promises and bungling of Government administrations. The whole world must see that if Indians are to be free again, then we must be allowed to govern our own affairs" (MN, March 1973:25).

A year later a similar event took place in Canada when a radical group known as the Ojibway Warriors Society occupied Anishinabe Park at Kenora, Ontario. Although this conflict was solved by negotiation, it contributed to the proliferation of tribal and regional warrior societies throughout North America. These societies generally share(d) a commitment to establish "a landbase for the Native nation in North America . . . [and] a revival of the old, traditional, spiritual ways, where alcohol and drugs have no part in our lives." They called upon Indians to "go back to living the way their ancestors did [because changes since the European invasion] have caused the loss of Indian religion, culture and language" (Vern Harper, in MN Feb. 1978:25).

In contrast to some Plains Indian tribes—such as the Lakota, whose warrior tradition had not yet been fully broken—most Mi'kmaqs preferred a less aggressive stance. But there were exceptions, as the tragic story of a young Mi'kmaq woman named Anna Mae Pictou illustrates. Born at Shubenacadie in 1946, when her father was at a logging camp in Maine's woods, she and her sisters were raised by her mother. The family moved to Pictou Landing in 1951, when Anna Mae's mother married a Mi'kmaq from that northern Nova Scotia reserve. He carved ax handles and pounded wood to make splints for her mother and other local basketweavers who peddled their crafts in nearby towns. Throughout Anna Mae's youth, her family depended on the Indian agent for their clothing and other needs. As a teenager, she joined the seasonal labor force in Maine's potato fields and, like so many other Mi'kmaqs, moved on to Boston, where she helped organize the Boston Indian Council in 1969. Peers described her as a young woman who "spoke of Indian rights, of pride and self-determination. Poverty, alcoholism, unemployment, despair: these were the enemies she saw." By 1970 she was carrying this message of Indian pride across the nation as a member of AIM (MN, May 1976:10). Two years later she and several other Mi'kmaqs marched in the Trail of Broken Treaties and joined the Indian occupation of the BIA headquarters in Washington, DC. In March 1973, hearing of AIM's occupation of Wounded Knee, she traveled to South Dakota. Slipping through a cordon of federal troops, she joined the besieged community and took part in its defense as a "female warrior." The following month, she married an Ojibway artist named Nogeeshik Aquash at Wounded Knee. When the siege ended in May, Anna Mae and her husband returned to Boston, where they tried to establish an AIM survival school. When this failed, they moved to Ottawa, where she began researching Mi'kmaq traditional culture. Her marriage ended in divorce, and after many complex twists and turns, in the winter of 1975–1976 Anna Mae ended up back at Pine Ridge. The reservation was in the throes of a violent conflict between its BIA-backed tribal government and traditionalists who rejected BIA control and had the support of AIM.

Anna Mae fell victim to the violence. In February 1976 she was found frozen in a roadside ditch. Given a bogus autopsy, she was declared a victim of exposure and buried in a local cemetery as an unknown, under the name "Jane Doe"—after a local pathologist cut off her hands and mailed them to the FBI for fingerprinting. Some time after determining Anna Mae's identity, the FBI notified her relatives in Nova Scotia. Disbelieving the official account of her death, they demanded that her body be exhumed for a second autopsy. Reexamination revealed that she had been executed: A bullet still lodged in her skull. A few days later Anna Mae's body was turned over to Lakota Indians, who reburied her near the white bluffs of the Badlands. In the company of a Lakota medicine man who offered traditional prayers, 100 mourners paid their last respects to Anna Mae (Matthiessen, 77, 255–62).

Her killing remaining a mystery, Anna Mae is remembered as "a brave-hearted woman." Soon after her death, Nova Scotia's tribal newspaper reprinted a story that had appeared in the Boston Indian Council's newsletter, titled "Anna Mae Lived and Died for All of Us" (MN, May 1976:37).

Although few Mi'kmaqs walked Anna Mae Pictou's dangerous road, AIM had the sympathy of many. Adopting its fiery rhetoric, some Mi'kmaqs denounced accommodationists as "Uncle Tomahawks" or "apples" (red on the outside, white within). Others worried about AIM's radical politics, exclaiming that they did not want "this damn thing on our reserves" (MN 7 May 1976:38). No matter one's opinion about politics, Mi'kmaqs still remember Anna Mae's tragic story.*

CULTURAL RENAISSANCE

As with many American Indian groups, the revival of Mi'kmaq culture has been influenced by the pan-Indian culture spawned by intertribal political activism. Publicly asserting their "Indian" identity, some Mi'kmaqs embraced romanticized Plains Indian customs that were the hallmark of pan-Indianism—decking themselves out in eagle feathers, braids, and beadwork and plastering their vehicles with generic Indian bumper stickers that told the world: "I am Indian and proud."

Yet, remarkably, some Mi'kmaqs had retained fragments of their particular cultural heritage, and a critical number still spoke the ancestral tongue. Moreover, most Mi'kmaqs had an undeniable sense of, and pride in "being Mi'kmaq," even though external acculturation made it difficult to define exactly what that meant. In time, many Mi'kmaqs began to rediscover and reclaim these pieces of aboriginal identity.

The Paradox of Imprisonment: Discovering Indianness in Jail

In contrast to the Indian boarding schools, which systematically aimed to destroy Indian identity, Canada's federal prisons have functioned as *ad hoc* reculturation agents. Typically, Mi'kmaq inmates are young adult males, often culturally uprooted, economically marginal, and alcohol or drug dependent. In Canada, native inmates are incarcerated at about six times the national average and represent 12 percent of the country's prison population. Although the statistics are lower in the Maritimes, they are as high as 60 percent in the western prairie provinces. Indian inmates in western penitentiaries formed the Native Brotherhood (NB) in the early 1970s. Locked up, they dedicated themselves to cultural emancipation through reinvigorating traditions. Because they had undergone contact and conquest centuries after Mi'kmaqs and other eastern groups, many of the western Indian cultures' traditional features were still within the reach of living memory. During the 1970s and 1980s, Indians in overcrowded western prisons were transferred to jails in New Brunswick and Nova Scotia, where they organized more NB chapters. As a result, quite a few young Mi'kmaq and Maliseet inmates were exposed to rituals traditionally associated with the Cree, Ojibway, Sioux, and other western groups—rituals such as drumming and sweetgrass burning. Participating in these essentially foreign ceremonies (as well as sacred pipe and sweat lodge rituals reminiscent of their own lost traditions), Mi'kmaq prisoners gained a sense of identity, self-worth, and community

---

*Anna Mae Pictou has become the subject of a detailed biography (Brand 1978) and a documentary film *Annie Mae: Brave Hearted Woman* (1989).

(Prins 1994e). Some became interested in learning their ancestral language for the first time, and Mi'kmaq elders began coming to the jails to teach them. After serving their time, many Mi'kmaqs returned to their reserve communities more traditional than when they left. Continuing their newly learned cultural practices outside the prison walls, some have avoided recidivism and overcome substance-abuse problems (MN Sept. 1988:26).

Sante' Mawio'mi and the Paradox of St. Anne

Many Mi'kmaqs consider the *Sante' Mawio'mi* (Grand Council) at Cape Breton as their oldest and most respected institution. Its Mi'kmaq name translates literally as "holy gathering," pointing to its primary function as a spiritual body. As described in the previous chapter, the Grand Council at Cape Breton was the most prominent of the four that existed in the 19th century. Today it is the only one that survives— although it is in a state of transition. Traditionally, Grand Council members (known as *keptins*/captains) are respected Catholic laymen known for their religious commitment. Their number is not fixed, but it is currently over a dozen. Appointed for life, the grand chief and keptins are entrusted with a spiritual guardianship over the Mi'kmaq people. In the absence of a priest, these leaders are still sometimes called to conduct church prayers at their reserves during feast days—and to comfort and help Mi'kmaqs in their parish communities through prayer.

Although they usually convene a few times a year, keptins always meet at Chapel Island during the annual mission of St. Anne. Heavily influenced by Roman Catholic custom, the council's governing structure mirrors that of the Vatican: Like cardinals electing a distinguished peer as pontiff, keptins choose one of their own as *kji saqmaw* (grand chief). The kji saqmaw serves as the ceremonial head. At least until recently, a parish priest served as the Grand Council's electoral officer. The current kji saqmaw, Ben Sylliboy of Whycocomagh, was elected in 1992. Sworn into office at Chapel Island on St. Anne's Day, the new grand chief and his council were then blessed by the bishop of Antigonish. Other ranking members in the Grand Council include the *kji keptin* (grand captain). The kji keptin functions as the executive of the council. Next is the *putu's* (orator), who traditionally negotiated peace treaties and safeguarded the wampum belts (see also Marshall et al., 76).

Although not strictly hereditary, these titled positions have circulated within certain Cape Breton lineages, in particular the Denny, Sylliboy, and Marshall families. The present kji saqmaw, Ben Sylliboy, was elected after the death of Grand Chief Donald Marshall of Membertou, who had followed Gabriel Sylliboy of Whycocomagh in 1964. The latter had succeeded John Denny of Eskasoni, whose paternal lineage had held this position for several generations.

Although the Grand Council has been a stronghold of Mi'kmaq conservatism, it was not in the vanguard of the cultural revitalization movement. Historically associated with the Roman Catholic Church, it favored a mixed strategy of cultural retrenchment and reluctant accommodation. As conservatives, the Grand Council and its supporters appeared uncomfortable with some of the radical rhetoric of more defiant Mi'kmaq activists, many of whom were bitterly opposed to Christianity. But, fearing being pushed into irrelevance, the Grand Council and its followers had little choice but to come aboard. Their entry point was St. Anne.

Grand Chief Donald Marshall and Roman Catholic clergy. St. Anne's Mission, 1990.

Serving as a focal point in Mi'kmaq culture, St. Anne's Day has been celebrated for about 200 years. By the early 1960s, however, the gathering had lost much of its rich ceremonial character. Even at Chapel Island, a Cape Breton bastion of Mi'kmaq conservatism, participants no longer wore the traditional costume for the occasion. Likewise, the customary men's dinner assembly, acclamation of chiefs, and war medicine dance were no longer held. And during the procession with the statue of St. Anne, the men no longer lined up along the path, firing their guns in an old ritual known as "scaring of the devil."

Vestiges of the past could be seen at St. Anne's among older Mi'kmaqs, who still used prayer books printed in the traditional hieroglyphic script and who sang hymns in their native tongue. And after the age-old procession in which the cross and the image of St. Anne were carried from the church to the great iron cross on the knoll, the grand chief still offered a sermon (Howard, 1965:9). But the "pow-wow" held after this scaled-down ceremony featured costumes and dances that were "largely modern Ojibwa in origin, with a strong Plains or Pan-Indian influence apparent in the war bonnets, bustles, and geometric-design beadwork" (Howard, 10).

Although many Mi'kmaqs saw St. Anne's as their "oldest tradition," its popularity was rapidly eroding. In 1974 some publicly blamed the Grand Council for this—accusing keptins of poor organization and complaining that they had allowed

Statue of Mi'kmaq patron saint Se'ta'n (St. Anne), holding her daughter Ma'li (Virgin Mary) in right arm and eagle feather as token of her Indianness in left hand. Chapel Island, 1990.

the construction of unsightly cottages on Chapel Island and had failed to have the garbage cleaned up, and so forth. Calling upon keptins as "our religious leaders," some Mi'kmaqs asked them to

> recreate some of the best traditions our ancestors once carried through with dignity and respect. Let's bring back the well organized old customs, the old Grand Council, the council's meeting house, the ten day mission, and especially the fine preparation that took place before the mission . . . Our older generation for centuries have gone to Chapel Island to seek help and to observe the respect that the Grand Council once had . . . Let's talk seriously of looking at the future. How long do we have before the entire island will lose all of its traditions?

> (MN, April 1974:2)

While the Grand Council accepted this challenge, some Mi'kmaqs began to question the role of St. Anne in their cultural revival, calling her an "alien saint." Because the keptins and other Mi'kmaq conservatives typically hold that Catholicism "is the intrinsic element" of their culture, they sought a way to demonstrate long-term ties between the Mi'kmaq and the church. In 1985, actively supported by the church, they organized an elaborate historical pageant commemorating Chief Membertou's 1610 baptism—now a recurrent cultural event.

Beyond helping Mi'kmaqs stage these public celebrations of Catholic-Indian solidarity, the church began emphasizing that Christianity was not incompatible with Indian traditions. In 1988 a Catholic priest from the St. Regis Mohawk reservation attended St. Anne's mission at Chapel Island. After greeting the assembled Mi'kmaqs "with peace from the Mohawk nation," he told them the story of Kateri Tekawitha, a young Indian woman who is seen as a saint by the Catholic Iroquois. Known as Lily of the Mohawks, she was said to have performed miracles after her baptism in 1676. Four years later she died after a brief life of prayer and service at the Jesuit mission village of Kahnawake. In 1953 the Vatican recognized her as the "venerable" Kateri. And in 1980 she was elevated to the status of "blessed" in a ceremony in Rome (which several Mi'kmaqs attended). Since then Jesuit priests and prominent Indian laypeople have tried to promote her for sainthood. Telling the Mi'kmaqs at Chapel Island about Kateri's life, the priest stressed that she was able to "lead a life in the Roman Catholic Faith and still maintain her Indianness. . . . Kateri never stopped being an Indian, she always maintained her traditions" (MN Aug. 1988:14–15).

Despite meaningful conversion stories such as that of Kateri Tekawitha, many Mi'kmaqs, including those who consider themselves to be Christians, now question the impact that missionaries had on their ancestors. For instance, Nigola Jeddore of Conne River, Newfoundland, contended: "One time, before they became Christians, Mi'kmaqs were strong. . . . But [when] they became Christian they turned into very weak people." Recalling Jeddore's words, another Mi'kmaq recently asserted: "Christianizing mission work became an important part of all European colonizing efforts in Canada. . . . Some powerful spiritualism however, has protected us these past three hundred years" (Joseph Jeddore, in MMNN March 1992:11).

But what is this "spiritualism"? Questioning Christian doctrine, many Mi'kmaqs have been wrestling with this problem. Rethinking the "cultural correctness" of their religious practices, some have protested that St. Anne is "foreign" to them and have advised fellow Mi'kmaqs to redirect their prayers to Klu'skap. They began referring to this culture hero of traditional myth as "the Great Spirit of our forefathers" (MN May 1976:16). Comparing him to the Christian messiah, they related that "the Great Spirit (God) has sent his son [Klu'skap] to his people, the Indians. . . . He did not die on the cross like Jesus, but sailed into the sunset, to return to the land of his Father (Heaven). He was a Prophet. He was the Divine, the Good, the Truth, the Beautiful" (MN Nov. 1976:9, 15; MN Dec. 1976:13).

Since the mid-1970s growing numbers of Mi'kmaqs have found inspiration in a cultural mélange of *ecospiritual* belief and ritual. This neotraditional mélange includes some pan-Indian elements, as well as "New Age" thought and what is sometimes called "born-again primitivism." Some of the most vital spiritual components, however, can be traced directly to western tribal cultures such as the Cree, Ojibway, and even Lakota (Sioux). They include adopted traditions (vision quests, sweetgrass burning, and drumming, etc.) as well as ceremonies similar to lost Mi'kmaq traditions (the sweat lodge and the sacred pipe). In recent years these neotraditional ceremonies have become quite popular among Mi'kmaqs and their Wabanaki neighbors. A few Mi'kmaqs have even embraced the Plains Indian ritual of the Sun Dance, stirring some controversy on their reserves (Prins 1994e).

St. Anne's Mission at Chapel Island, July 26, 1990. Behind the cross-bearer walk Grand Chief Donald Marshall and Grand Captain Alex Denny, followed by clergy, keptins, and Mi'kmaq faithful.

Challenged by Mi'kmaqs advocating a return to native spirituality, the Catholic church has initiated new efforts to be culturally relevant.* In 1992 Father Haskell, an Ojibway priest, was invited to celebrate Mass at Chapel Island during St. Anne's. Blending Catholic rituals with pan-Indian ceremonies of sweetgrass burning and peace pipe smoking, the priest pronounced at sunrise Mass: "I bless you from the grandfathers, the grandmother earth, and all our relatives" (MN Aug. 1992:1, 4, 29).

Language: Key to the Survival of Mi'kmaq Culture

The Mi'kmaq language is still common in daily conversation at some reserves. At quite a few, however, only English is used. But even where Mi'kmaq is spoken most, there is a growing trend toward bilingualism (MN Dec. 1985:7). In most Mi'kmaq-speaking households today, children understand but do not speak the ancestral tongue. If this continues, language replacement will take place. But there are efforts to halt this, because many Mi'kmaqs now recognize language as the key to cultural

---

*The quest for spiritual renewal among the Mi'kmaq and their neighbors is the subject of a documentary film titled *Wabanaki: A New Dawn* (1995).

survival. Commenting on the importance of language preservation, one Mi'kmaq educator stated recently: "We have lost our culture and our way of life but we are fortunate that the majority of our native people [at Cape Breton] speak the language. [Our] language makes us special because we can describe the world from a different point of view. . . . When we lose our language we lose our value systems too" (Murdena Marshall in MN March 1985:7).

In 1974 Nova Scotia's bands founded the Micmac Institute for Cultural Studies to spearhead "cultural revival" among Mi'kmaqs. The institute organized cultural conferences and sponsored numerous workshops on reserves. It offered native language classes and native spirituality lectures, as well as instruction in traditional handicrafts, dances, games, and songs. Soon individual Mi'kmaq bands applied for federal funding to develop their own Indian culture studies programs.

Aiming to counter the process of ethnocide brought on by institutions such as Shubenacadie Residential School, Indian bands throughout Canada demanded educational control on their reserves—and won it by the mid-1970s. Soon larger reserves, such as Eskasoni, featured new bilingual-bicultural schools, which fostered native literacy. Although many people still spoke Mi'kmaq, only a few could read and write it. A handful understood the hieroglyphs that Abbé Maillard had developed in the 1700s for religious instruction of Mi'kmaqs. Maillard's system was not the only one at hand. In the 1800s Baptist missionary Silas Rand developed a 22-character system in his effort to translate the Bible into Mi'kmaq. He also experimented with phonetic spelling. And in the early 1900s Father Pacifique of Restigouche devised a 13-letter system (based on French orthographic usage).

Working separately, native language teachers at Restigouche (Quebec), Big Cove (New Brunswick), and Cape Breton began teaching people how to read and write in Mi'kmaq. Influenced by the various writing systems and operating independently in regions with their own particular dialect, these Mi'kmaq linguists developed three distinctive orthographic modes. It is likely that they will ultimately settle on a unified system.

Meanwhile the new Mi'kmawey School at Chapel Island has opted for Mi'kmaq as the only language of instruction since its opening in 1982. By then a Mi'kmaq teachers program had been launched at the Nova Scotia Teachers College. In 1983 the first cohort of licensed Mi'kmaq teachers graduated with a mandate "to correct the imbalance between Indian and non-Indian history, to defend native culture, and to alleviate misunderstandings which exist today regarding land claims and aboriginal rights" (MN June 1983:9). That same year the Micmac-Maliseet Institute (M-MI) was founded at the University of New Brunswick. In 1985 M-MI and St. Thomas College started a joint Native Studies Program, offering Mi'kmaq and Maliseet language courses. A year later a Native Studies Program started at the University College of Cape Breton.

In the summer of 1986 more than 70 youngsters from Nova Scotia's reserves participated in a 10-day Mi'kmaq Cultural Camp at Chapel Island. Commenting on the camp's objective, one of the organizers explained: "We are trying to bring back the history of this island. . . . If they know their history they will value the importance of this island and their culture" (MN July 1986:14).

POLITICAL REVITALIZATION: MI'KMAQ NATIVE RIGHTS

A cultural awakening has taken place, and Mi'kmaq traditions—from religious practices to ceremonial dances—have been reevaluated and reintroduced. Wrapping themselves in traditional (and sometimes reforged) customs and identities, Mi'k-maqs have been strengthened in their struggle against repression and have made considerable strides in claiming their native rights.

But what are these native rights? This is a multiplex concept with many discrepant points. Because the stakes are high, in terms of both wealth and power, native rights are perpetually argued and contested in the courts and in the political domain. In the ever-changing context of domination and resistance, these rights take on different forms. Moreover, they do not flow from a single wellspring. Some originate from the doctrine of aboriginal title, which itself is based on a principle of international law known as "possessory title." This, in turn, flows from a simple moral precept that it is wrong to take away another people's right to hold on to what they have had for so long. About 2,000 years ago, Roman jurists regarded this idea as "a rule of natural law, which was immune from challenge" (Bennett, 618–20). Since then the principle has been fundamental to Western legal thinking.

Other native rights come from formally negotiated agreements, documented in treaties signed by Mi'kmaqs and foreign sovereign powers, such as the British Crown or the United States Congress. Also, there are native rights that are legislated by federal, provincial, or state governments in the United States and Canada. Last but not least, there is a bundle of native rights that has its origins in time-honored aboriginal ideas and tribal practice.

Mi'kmaqs and others in the Assembly of First Nations have learned to protest immediately and loudly whenever they fear that their interests are at stake. After much public posturing and effective political lobbying, they managed to bring pressure on the Canadian government when it legislated the Constitution Act of 1982. According to section 35 (1), the existing aboriginal and treaty rights of Canada's indigenous peoples are now constitutionally recognized. But the debates with federal and provincial authorities continue. In a string of court cases, Mi'kmaqs and other Indian groups in Canada try to define and safeguard these special rights. Indeed, they have taken their struggle for native rights into the international domain, including the United Nations in Geneva.

What follows is a brief look at several cases, illustrating Mi'kmaq vigilance in the political arena of native and civil rights. Like other internally colonized tribal nations, they understand that in the knowledge of their history lies the promise of their future.

Land Claims

In 1970 Mi'kmaqs in Nova Scotia and New Brunswick officially notified Canada's federal authorities that they still owned all of their ancestral lands. Their claim was based on the Royal Proclamation of 1763, which stipulated that Indian lands could be taken only by purchase or cession. Because they had never ceded their territories, nor received any compensation for losing them, they argued that they still possessed aboriginal title to these lands. At the same time, they began archival research into the history of their particular reserve lands, seeking documentation of encroachments and other damage contrary to law. In the course of the 1970s and early 1980s, Mi'k-maqs bombarded the DIA with well over 100 separate claims, pressing for the return of wrongfully alienated reserve lands. In numerous cases, they either secured the lost tracts or were compensated financially.

Treaty Rights: Hunting and Fishing

The issue of Mi'kmaq hunting and fishing rights is very complex, involving numerous controversial court cases during the past few decades. Among the most spectacular confrontations were the so-called salmon wars, in which Mi'kmaqs defended their fishing rights. Mi'kmaqs have always depended heavily on fish, including Atlantic salmon. This century, overharvesting by commercial and pleasure fishers, coupled with damage caused by dams, logging, and pollution, has greatly diminished stocks. Trying to avoid further depletion, government authorities have regulated fishing sea-sons and limited the catch permitted by law. From their vantage point, the restrictions applied to Mi'kmaqs and other Indians—whether fishing off or on their reserves. Reg-ulations became especially stringent and vigorously enforced in the 1970s—just when Mi'kmaqs began demanding respect for their native rights. Citing Governor Belcher's 1762 proclamation, which confirmed their "Common right to the Sea Coast from Cape Fronsac onwards for fishing without disturbance" (see Chapter 11), they defended their right to fish where and when they desired. During the next decade, Mi'kmaq fishers faced numerous arrests, court trials, and even armed raids. One of the hot spots was Restigouche, where local Mi'kmaqs have always depended on fish to supplement their subsistence. Like other bands, they refused to acknowledge provincial jurisdiction over their fisheries and ignored the regulations. In 1973 about 60 Quebec provincial police and conservation officers staged a raid on Mi'kmaq salmon fisheries. This time, vigilant Mi'kmaqs were able to turn them back. Blaming the decrease in Atlantic salmon on illegal and excessive fishing by Indians, the provincial authorities continued their pressure, arresting "poachers" and confiscating their gill nets. On 11 June 1981, three years after a similar major action against a Maliseet band, another police raid shocked the Mi'kmaqs at Restigouche. A large force of about 300 Quebec provincial police and 90 wardens of the Department of Fisheries placed roadblocks around the re-serve. Police helicopters hovered as armed troops invaded the Mi'kmaq settlement, de-stroying and confiscating fishing nets. Throughout Canada, Indian activists demonstrated their support for the Mi'kmaq. Nine days later the Quebec police launched another air and land attack, armed with rubber bullets and tear gas grenades. After the showdown, Mi'kmaq Chief Metallic declared that the provincial government must respect Mi'kmaq "territorial rights." Although the conflict was far from over, a major turnaround came in 1982, when Canada's new constitution recognized "exist-ing" aboriginal and treaty rights. Eight years later the country's Supreme Court con-firmed the constitutional protection afforded Indians to fish for food in their traditional habitat. Mi'kmaqs had finally prevailed in defense of their aboriginal right to fish for food in waters both on and off their reserves.

In 1988, during Cape Breton's "moose harvest," Mi'kmaqs tested the legal ramifications of a recent Supreme Court ruling on their treaty rights. The case involved a
Mi'kmaq from Shubenacadie, convicted in 1981 for unlawful possession of a hunting
rifle outside the reserve during closed season. His defense team, hired by the Union of
Nova Scotia Indians, appealed the conviction on grounds that the Treaty of 1752 (originally signed by Mi'kmaq Chief Cope of Shubenacadie) guaranteed Mi'kmaqs "free
liberty to hunt and fish as usual."* In 1985 the case reached the Supreme Court, which
overturned the conviction, noting that the Treaty of 1752 was "still valid, existing and
in force" (MN Dec. 1985:1, 5). The case has been described as "only the tip of the ice-
berg of a gigantic aboriginal rights case over traditional territory . . . and native rights
to self-determination" (MN April 1989:5; see also Chapter 2:13–15).

Challenging Sex Discrimination

Until recently, due to a male bias in the Indian Act, Indian women who married non-
Indian men lost their status, and they and their offspring were deprived of all native
rights and entitlements. Many hundreds of Mi'kmaq women were affected by this
discriminatory law. Fairly typical was what happened to a Mi'kmaq woman from
Millbrook Reserve (Nova Scotia). At 18, after some years in the Shubenacadie Residential School, she married a white man. A few months after her wedding in 1955,
she received a letter from the DIA, asking for her signature on a document that officially surrendered her Indian status. She later explained that she didn't think much
about the future when she signed the form: "I was so used to taking orders that I felt
when a government letter comes to you stating that you had to sign papers, I had to
sign." After her divorce, however, she discovered that she could not return home and
live on the reserve (MN Nov. 1981:5). Also, like others stricken from the federal register, she could no longer share in band funds and was not eligible for special benefits such as housing. If objections were raised, she could even be denied burial on the
reserve cemetery.

   Challenging the Indian Act, Canadian natives formed a group called Indian Rights
for Indian Women in 1971. A year later Indian women in Canada, including Mi'k-
maqs, organized provincial chapters of the Native Women's Association. Recommend-
ing that Indian women refuse to sign "enfranchisement" papers upon marriage to a
nonstatus person, they argued that "Band membership and the rights to live on the reserve and to participate in community life and activity should be the sole decision of
the Band made at the Band level" (MN June 1977:23). In 1982, after a complex series
of court cases, a federal government committee asked the Canadian Parliament to
eliminate sections of the Indian Act that discriminate against Indian women. Three
years later Parliament passed Bill C-31, removing the offensive provisions. The new
federal regulations allowed restoration of Indian rights to those who had lost them and,
for the first time, legally recognized the authority of Indian bands to control their own
membership. As a direct result of this amendment, many Mi'kmaq women have regained their Indian status and have seen their native rights restored to them.

   *The Mi'kmaq salmon war at Restigouche forms the subject of a documentary titled *Incident at
Restigouche* (1984), by Abenaki filmmaker Alanis Obomsawin.

Boston Indian Council: Resurrecting the 1776 Watertown Treaty

Since 1969 the Boston Indian Council (BIC) has served the needs of about 3,000 tribespeople residing in the greater Boston area. Founded by a cohort of off-reservation Mi'kmaqs, it has a constituency that includes individuals from other Wabanaki tribes, plus Wampanoags, Narragansetts, Mohawks, Senecas, Lakotas, and others. By far the largest Indian group in the city, Mi'kmaqs have generally controlled the organization (reorganized as the North American Indian Center of Boston in 1992).

A fair number of early BIC activists were war veterans who found themselves denied government services even though they had served in the U.S. Army. Among them was Will Basque of the Shubenacadie Reserve, heavily decorated as a Marine staff sergeant in the Vietnam War. He recalled that "upon returning to Boston after our time in the war, we wouldn't let ANYONE tell our people we were not allowed government services in Massachusetts. We were told that we were Canadians and had to establish permanent residence!" (MN Oct. 1981:8–9).

Basque, elected BIC president in the mid-1970s, and other BIC activists lobbied the government of Massachusetts for formal recognition. Citing the 1776 Treaty of Watertown, they reminded the governor's office of the historic relationship between the Wabanaki Confederacy and the United States, in particular Massachusetts. Commemorating the treaty's bicentennial in 1976, Governor Michael Dukakis agreed to issue an executive order recognizing the BIC as the official liaison between the state government and Wabanaki Indians. The order included the creation of the office of a commissioner of Indian affairs, making it possible for Indians to be represented on state commissions (MN Jan. 1977:20). With official recognition, the BIC became eligible for federal funds from the Bureau of Indian Affairs and other special Indian programs.

Rebirth of the Wabanaki Confederacy

Because of their subordinated political status, as described in previous chapters, the Mi'kmaq found it impossible to uphold meaningful diplomatic relationships with neighboring tribal nations. Ever since the "brothers" had been divided by an international boundary (with Mi'kmaqs, Maliseets, and Abenakis primarily in Canada and Penobscots and Passamaquoddies in Maine), the Wabanaki Confederacy had been disintegrating. About 1870, its last convention took place at the great council fire in Kahnawake (a Mohawk reserve near Montreal).

One hundred years later, Mi'kmaqs and their neighbors actively participated in creating new political openings. In their quest for native rights, they not only availed themselves of legal expertise but also called long-forgotten history into play. In 1978, together with Maine's Penobscots and Passamaquoddies (who had filed a lawsuit against the state, claiming about two-thirds of Maine—12.5 million acres), they resurrected the Wabanaki Confederacy. At a joint conference at the Penobscot tribal headquarters in Old Town (Maine), they discussed common issues such as land claims and border-crossing rights. Two years later, complex out-of-court negotiations with the state of Maine and the U.S. government led to the 1980 Maine Indian Claims Settlement Act (MICSA), which granted federal recognition and $81.5 million to the Penobscot and Passamaquoddy. While the settlement caused dispute among the Wabanakis, the Confederacy still convenes at alternating tribal headquarters on a regular basis.

Beating the Melting Pot: Federal Recognition of the Aroostook Band in Maine

For a century northern Maine has been home to a small landless community of a few hundred Mi'kmaqs. Because reserves for Mi'kmaqs are situated in Canada, these off-reservation tribespeople were generally regarded as Canadian Indians and had no formal status as Indians in the United States. If found to be without gainful employment, they could be picked up as vagrants, jailed, fined, and/or forced to leave the country and "return" to a reserve in Canada. Until recently they typically subsisted as basketmakers, harvesters, lumberjacks, or day laborers. Most lived (and still live) in a string of rural hamlets and small towns along the Canadian border, where they suffered dismal poverty and racial discrimination. Moreover, on their journeys to and from their relatives in Canada they were frequently harassed by immigration officials. In addition to Mi'kmaqs, the region counted an equal number of off-reservation Maliseets, as well as some Passamaquoddies, Penobscots, and small numbers of other tribespeople.

To improve their miserable social condition and win recognition of their native rights, a local Mi'kmaq college student named Tom Battiste, along with several other regional Indians, founded the Association of Aroostook Indians (AAI) in 1970. Three years later they won access to social services and emergency health care through Maine's Department of Indian Affairs, as well as Indian scholarships and free hunting and fishing licenses. In 1980, the Maliseet band within the AAI gained inclusion in MICSA, but Mi'kmaqs were left out because they had not yet gathered the ethnohistorical evidence necessary to substantiate their claim.

Soon after this momentous event I hired on as AAI's director of research and development. A year later, when the Mi'kmaqs quit AAI to reorganize as the Aroostook Micmac Council (AMC), I went with them. The next few years were devoted to producing detailed ethnohistorical documentation of Mi'kmaq presence in Maine since first contact with Europeans in the early 1600s. An exhaustive review of Wabanaki ethnicity and territoriality showed that the prevailing characterization of the Mi'kmaq and their traditional allies in Maine was too rigid and static. Contrary to the "river drainage theory" (Snow 1976, 1978), which had served as the operating model of the Maine Indian Land Claims case (1972–1980), new research demonstrated that the Wabanaki tribes did not form closed corporate groups, each exclusively occupying a stable territory precisely coterminous with a major river drainage. Instead, Mi'kmaqs ranged widely through territories that frequently overlapped those of their allied neighbors and that were jointly used throughout much of their past (Prins 1986, 1988). Documentation of their historical and ongoing presence in the St. John River watershed (of which Aroostook County forms part) provided the historical and anthropological evidence required for federal recognition. This was edified by an exploration of documents that shed light on Mi'kmaq participation in the American Revolution (including the 1776 Treaty of Watertown). I also worked with the AMC on a documentary film about their community (*Our Lives in Our Hands,* 1986), which aired on public television and was extensively used by tribal representatives to focus attention on their native rights effort. Soon afterward, Legal Services attorneys supporting AMC's effort gathered all research into a thick *Briefing Book,* which spelled out AMC's case. It stated that "along with other members of the Wabanaki Confederacy, the Micmac Nation jointly owned and occupied lands in Maine, which were never transferred or sold. Therefore, the Aroostook Band of Micmacs, as the 'modern successor in interest' of the Micmac Nation, could still assert aboriginal title to those lands . . ." Accordingly, the band requested "a remedy for the loss of its lands and related rights [and was] prepared to negotiate a settlement of its claims in return for federal recognition of its status as a tribe and sufficient funds to purchase a small land base in Aroostook County" (ABM Briefing Book, Tab. #1, n.p.). In 1991, after complex legal maneuvering and political lobbying (including congressional testimony by AMC's first female president, Mary Philbrook), we finally managed to persuade the federal government to pass the Aroostook Band of Micmacs Settlement Act. This act not only provided this Mi'kmaq community with acknowledgement of its tribal status in the United States, entitling enrolled members to certain federal services and benefits, but also gave the band a $900,000 land acquisition fund to purchase 5,000 acres as their shared land base (Prins, 1988, 1994a,b,c,d; cf. Heald, 1987; McBride, 1987).

MI'KMAQ SOVEREIGNTY

Much of the current native rights struggles in North America hinges on the sovereignty question—the right of tribal nations to govern themselves and to make their own decisions. Energized by a cultural awakening, Mi'kmaqs have made great gains in their quest for political sovereignty. Asserting that they are a "nation" rather than a "tribe," they have begun to refer to themselves as the *Mi'kmaq Nationimow.* Mi'kmaq bands in Canada have delegates in the Assembly of First Nations, which represents more than 300,000 treaty and status Indians. Inspired and guided by this national organization, they have formulated their tribal policy regarding aboriginal and treaty rights. As such, they subscribe to the *Declaration of First Nations* of 1980, which insists: "The Creator has given us the right to govern ourselves and the right to self-determination. The rights and responsibilities given to us by the Creator cannot be altered or taken away by any other nation" (MN Dec. 1980:3).

Sovereignty and the *Sante' Mawio'mi*

Considering the new political challenges, Mi'kmaqs have debated what the role of the Grand Council was in the past and what it should be in the future. Typically, Mi'kmaq conservatives (particularly at Cape Breton) hold the view that this council is the governing body for the entire Mi'kmaq nation and that the kji saqmaw at Cape Breton is its sovereign head. Seeking to historicize this political construct, they assert that Membertou, the Mi'kmaq chieftain at Port Royal in the early 1600s, was once the nation's grand chief (Christmas, 2–4; Marshall et al., 75–77). Some even argue that the Mi'kmaq once formed a true nation-state, which disintegrated after the European invasion.

Mi'kmaq girl in beautiful (neotraditional) moose-hide dress. Chapel Island, 1990.

In the early 1980s the Grand Council began to assert itself politically in the international arena. It sent diplomatic delegates to the *First Working Group on Indigenous Peoples* at the United Nations in Geneva, Switzerland, and during the 1982 St. Anne's mission at Chapel Island discussed its future role within the framework of the United Nations. Acting as a sovereign power, it lodged complaints against Canada with the *Human Rights Commission* of the United Nations—declaring that Canadian policies were racist and violated Mi'kmaq aboriginal rights to self-determination. Canada dismissed the complaints, stating that the Mi'kmaqs were "just another minority group" (MN Aug. 1982:9).

Many Mi'kmaqs are uncomfortable with such efforts to turn the Grand Council into a supreme political body. They seem to prefer a separation of powers between the council as a ceremonial body with spiritual custody and the democratically elected band chiefs responsible for political affairs.

In 1989 a large number of these elected Mi'kmaq band chiefs met to discuss their common struggle for self-determination. Until then divided into provincial unions, they now formed a national council representing every Mi'kmaq band in Canada. Noting that this event "will be recorded in history as the moment when Micmacs were reunited into a strong nation," they issued a Declaration of Sovereignty: "We will remain united for as long as the sun and moon will shine" (MN April 1989:4).

Although the future role of the *Sante' Mawio'mi* in this revitalized Mi'kmaq culture is still subject to discussion, tribal leaders know that without control over land and resources the ideal of national sovereignty must remain a figment of their collective imagination.

CONCLUSION

This book has chronicled almost 500 years of Mi'kmaq history—a remarkable story of cultural survival in the face of epidemics, intertribal and colonial warfare, and the relentless pressures of assimilation. The fact that Mi'kmaqs still exist as a people is evidence of a versatile survival strategy. Alternating between resistance and accommodation, they have maintained some of the indigenous strands in their cultural web and have added new ones when and where required. While the newly adopted or invented strands allowed them to respond creatively to fresh challenges and opportunities, those that they managed to pass on from generation to generation provided a vital link to their distinct heritage as Mi'kmaqs. Both sorts of strands were essential for their survival in the modern world: Without the first, they were condemned to the grave, and without the second they were doomed to the melting pot. Perpetually engaged in a complex process of collective self-fashioning, Mi'kmaqs have often changed indigenous traditions or blended them with new or foreign elements. The transitory product is a cultural composite, a unique amalgam that provides them with the flexibility needed for survival as a tribal nation in the modern world.

With the emergence of more detailed and specific historical knowledge about their past, Mi'kmaqs are replacing some facets of pan-Indianism (and expanding others) toward a more Mi'kmaq-specific cultural revitalization. Adopting, retrieving, and even inventing "neotraditions," Mi'kmaqs are the living proof that indigenous cultures can function as dynamic and open systems of adaptation.

Today more people identify themselves as Mi'kmaqs than ever before in recorded history. Beyond the bounds of probability, they still reside in small communities widely scattered along the northern Atlantic seaboard. After 500 years of turbulent history, the Mi'kmaq persist as a tribal nation. They have succeeded where many other indigenous peoples have failed. The Mi'kmaq determination to survive in their traditional homeland is echoed in this ancient legend, as told by an old Mi'kmaq hunter:

> Some time after Klu'skap left the land of the Mi'kmaqs seven men went in search of him, going towards the west until they came to a high mountain. Klu'skap was elated when he saw the seven Indians for he knew the way was long and dangerous, and that only those who believed in him could find a way over the mountain, through the narrow pass, and under the hanging cloud of mist. The seven sat with him and smoked his sweet-scented tobacco, and to each he offered to grant a wish. To one he gave a potent medicine, to another skill in hunting, to others charm and the grace of manner. At last there was but one Indian left. And when he was alone with Klu'skap he did not know how to ask for the thing he most desired. Klu'skap asked him, "What is your wish?" The man said, "Of all the lands I have seen there is one lovelier than all others. It is there I would live forever." Klu'skap asked,

"What is that land called that is lovelier than all others?" The man said, "It is called Mi'kma'kik—the land of the Mi'kmaqs." "Ah, Mi'kma'kik," murmered Klu'skap. "The good land of the Mi'kmaqs, the true red men. It is indeed a land of beauty, a land to live in forever."

(Stephen Hood, 1869; see Rand, 1894:232)

Glossary of Mi'kmaq Words

abutalvikasik: hieroglyph (lit.: "it is written with curves")
epek witk: lying in the water (Prince Edward Island)
eski'kewaq: skin-dressers land (Mi'kmaq district in northeast Nova Scotia)
eskinuo'pitij: Burnt Church (name of Mi'kmaq village)
keptin: captain
kespe'kewaq: the last land (district north of the Miramichi R.)
kinap: magic-doing warrior; warrior with supernatural strength
kji-keptin: grand captain
kji-saqmaw: grand chief
Klu'skap: mythic culture hero [also spelled Gluskap]
komqwejvikasik: hieroglyph (lit.: "it is written like [the marks in the sand as made by] a sucker [fish]"(?)
kopitek: beaver's home
kwetej: Mi'kmaq name for Iroquois, in particular Mohawk
kwitn: (birch-bark) canoe
l'nu'k: humans; people; Indian
lusknikn: white fry bread
maqtawe'kji'j: black robe, lit. "little black one." Mi'kmaq name for Jesuit priest
matawe'k: confluent
meniku: island
meski'k mkamlamun: great heart (name of honor)
Mi'kma'kik: land of the Mi'kmaq
Mi'kmaq Nationimow: Mi'kmaq Nation
mkisn: moccasin
mntu: spirit power (now also "devil")
mu alasutmaq: protestant (lit.: "he who does not pray")
mu'su'lk: moosehide canoe
napew: cock
nesakun: fish weir
nikmanen: our ally (plural—**nikamanaq:** our allies, our alliance)
nikmaw: my kin-friend (plural—**nikmaq:** my kin-friends. From this word comes the tribal name **Mi'kmaq;** also spelled **Micmac.**)
niskam: sun, or sun spirit, later used to refer to Jesus
niskamij: grandfather
ntio'ml: animal-spirit
nukumij: grandmother
nukumijinen: our grandmother (form of address for St. Anne)
pa'tlia's: patriarch (Roman Catholic priest)
piktukewaq: where the sound of [gas] explosions is made (Mi'kmaq district)
puowin: mystery or magic-doing person (shaman)
puowinuti: mystery bag (shaman's bag)
putu's: orator, wampum record keeper
putu'swaqn: convention council
Sante' Mawio'mi: Grand Council (Holy Gathering)
saqmaw: chief (plural—**saqmaq:** chiefs)

sesali'kewey: bare-feet (Mi'kmaq name for the besandaled Franciscan priests, especially
   Recollets and Capuchins)
Se'ta'n: St. Anne
sipaqn: passage
sipekne'katikik: ground nut place (Mi'kmaq district in central Nova Scotia)
sipu: river
tmi'kn: axe
toqejkwe'k: morally excellent man
unama'kik: foggy land (Mi'kmaq district of Cape Breton)
waqan: knife
wa'so'q: land of the souls (heaven)
wenuj: stranger
wi'katikn: book
wikuom: bark dwelling (wigwam)
wnikn: portage (overland route for carrying canoes)

Note: As explained in the text (p. 5, n. 1, p. 208), no uniform spelling system exists as
   of yet. The author recognizes the expertise of native language specialists such as
   Mrs. Mildred Milliae of Big Cove, who favors the traditional 13-letter alphabet used
   by Father Pacifique in the tribal newspaper *Micmac Messenger*. In more recent years,
   revisions have been introduced which have resulted in different orthographic styles.
   Whereas the system devised by Alphonse Metallic and linguist Albert DeBlois has
   been adopted in Restigouche, Nova Scotia bands seem to favor the spelling system
   developed by Bernard Francis and linguist Doug Smith. This is also the orthographic
   style adopted in this text. The author acknowledges the help he has received from Dr.
   David Schmidt who has corrected spelling errors in this glossary.

Bibliography

Abbott, John S. C. 1875. *The History of Maine, From the Earliest Discovery of the Region by Northmen until the Present Time.* Boston: B. B. Russell.

AN = Acadiensa Nova. 1935. Acadiensa Nova (1598–1770). *New and Unpublished Documents and other data relating to Acadia [etc.].* 2 vols. Collected and edited by William I. Morse. London: Bernard Quaritch, Ltd.

ARPMB = Acts and Resolves of the Province of Massachusetts Bay. 20 vols. Boston.

Adney, E. Tappan, and Howard I. Chapelle. 1964. *The Bark Canoes and Skin Boats of North America.* Washington, D.C.: Smithsonian Institution.

Agenutemagen. [Micmac-Maliseet monthly paper]. Fredericton, NB: The Union of New Brunswick Indians.

Akins, Thomas. 1805. *History of Halifax City.* Halifax: Nova Scotia Historical Society.

Allison, D. 1891. "Notes on a General Return of the Several Townships in the Province of Nova Scotia for [1767]." In *Collections of the Nova Scotia Historical Society,* Vol. 7, pp. 45–71.

Anderson, William P., ed. 1919. *Micmac Place-Names.* Ottawa: Surveyor General's Office.

Anonymous. 1634. "A [True] Relation Concerning the Estate of New England." In *NEHGR* (1886), Vol. 40, pp. 66–73.

Archer, Gabriel. 1602. "The Relation of Captain Gosnold's Voyage to the North Part of Virginia." In *CMaHS,* 3rd Series, Vol. 8, pp. 72–81.

Axtell, James. 1981. *The European and the Indian. Essays in the Ethnohistory of Colonial North America.* Oxford: Oxford University Press.

Bailey, Alfred G. 1969. *The Conflict of European and Eastern Algonquian Cultures, 1504–1700, A Study in Canadian Civilization.* Toronto: University of Toronto Press.

Bakker, Peter. 1988. "Basque Pidgin Vocabulary in European-Algonquian Trade Contacts." In *Papers of the 19th Algonquian Conference,* edited by William Cowan. Ottawa: Carleton University Press.

Banks, Ronald. 1972. "Survey of Massachusetts' Relationship with the Passamaquaddy Tribe." Unpublished Manuscript prepared for the state of Maine, (on file with author).

Barratt, Joseph. 1851. *The Indian of New England, and the North-Eastern Provinces; A Sketch of the Life of an Indian Hunter, Ancient Traditions Relating to the Etchemin Tribe, Their Modes of Life, Fishing, Hunting, etc. . . . derived from Nicola Tenesles.* Middleton, CT: C. H. Pelton.

Bartlett, Richard H. 1978. "The Indian Act of Canada." In *Buffalo Law Review,* Vol. 27 (4), pp. 581–616.

Battiste, Marie. 1977. "Cultural Transmission and Survival in Contemporary Micmac Society." In *The Indian Historian,* Vol. 10 (4), pp. 2–13.

Baudry, René. 1966. "Thury, Louis-Pierre." In *Dictionary of Canadian Biography, 1000 to 1700.* Vol. 1, p. 649. Toronto: University of Toronto Press.

Baxter, James P., ed. 1893. *Christopher Levett of York; the Pioneer Colonist in Casco Bay.* Portland: The Gorges Society.

———. 1889–1916. *Documentary History of the State of Maine, Containing the Baxter Manuscripts.* 24 vols. Portland: Maine Historical Society.

Beck, Horace P. 1959. *The American Indian as Sea-Fighter in Colonial Times.* Mystic, CT: Marine Historical Association.

Bennett, Gordon I. 1978. "Aboriginal Title in the Common Law: A Stony Path through Feudal Doctrine." In *Buffalo Law Review,* Vol. 27 (4), pp. 617–633.

Berkhofer, Robert F. 1978. *The White Man's Indian: Images of the American Indian from Columbus to the Present.* New York: Vintage Books.

Biggar, Henry P., ed. 1911. *The Precursors of Jacques Cartier, 1497–1534: A Collection of Documents Relating to the Early History of the Dominion of Canada.* Ottawa: Publications of the Public Archives of Canada, 5.

————. 1924. *The Voyages of Jacques Cartier.* Published from the Originals with Translations, Notes, and Appendices. Ottawa: Public Archives of Canada.

Biggar, Henry P. 1937. *The Early Trading Companies of New France: A Contribution to the History of Commerce and Discovery in North America.* Toronto: University of Toronto Library.

Bigot, Jacques. 1857. *Relation de ce qui passe de plus remarquable dans la Mission Abnaquise de Saint Joseph de Sillery, et dans l'Establissement de la Nouvelle Mission de Saint Francois de Sales, l'Année 1684 [1684].* New York: De la Presse Cramoisy de Jean Marie Shea.

Bird, J. Brian. 1955. "Settlement Patterns in Maritime Canada, 1678–1786." In *Geographical Review,* Vol. 45, pp. 385–404.

Blair, E. H., ed. 1911–12. *The Indian Tribes of the Upper Mississippi Valley and Region of the Great Lakes, as described by Nicholas Perrot, French Commandant in the Northwest; Bacqueville de la Potherie, army officer; and Thomas Forsyth, United States Agent at Fort Armstrong.* 2 vols. Cleveland: Arthur H. Clark.

Bock, Philip. 1966. "The Micmac Indians of Restigouche: History and Contemporary Description." National Museum of Canada, Bulletin, No. 213. Anthropological Series No. 77. Ottawa: Department of Mines.

————. 1978. "Micmac." In *Northeast,* edited by Bruce G. Trigger, pp. 109–122. Handbook of North American Indians, vol. 15, William G. Sturtevant, general editor. Washington, D.C.: Smithsonian Institution.

Bougainville, Louis Antoine, Comte de. 1964. *Adventure in the Wilderness, the American Journals of Louis Antoine de Bougainville.* Norman: University of Oklahoma Press.

Bourgeois, U. J. 1966. "Martin d'Aprendestiguy." In *Dictionary of Canadian Biography, 1000 to 1700.* Vol. 1, pp. 66–67. Toronto: University of Toronto Press.

Bourque, Bruce J., and Ruth H. Whitehead. 1985. "Tarrentines and the Introduction of European Trade Goods in the Gulf of Maine." In *Ethnohistory,* Vol. 32, pp. 327–341.

Bouton, Nathaniel, ed. 1867. *Documents and Records relating to the Province of New Hampshire (1623–1686).* Vol. 1. Concord: George E. Jenks.

Boxer, Charles R. 1965. *The Dutch Seaborne Empire, 1600–1800.* London: Hutchinson & Co.

Bradford, William. 1847. *The History of Plymouth Plantation (1606–1646).* Boston: Wright and Potter.

Bradley, Robert L., and Helen B. Camp. 1994. *The Forts of Pemaquid, Maine: An Archaeological and Historical Study.* Occasional Publications in Maine Archaeology, Number 10. Augusta, ME: The Maine Historic Preservation Commission.

Brand, Johanna. 1978. *The Life and Death of Anna Mae Aquash.* Toronto: James Lorimer.

Braudel, Fernand. 1981. *The Structures of Everyday Life: The Limits of the Possible. Civilization and Capitalism 15th–18th Century,* Vol. 1. New York: Harper & Row, Publishers.

————. 1982. *The Wheels of Commerce. Civilization and Capitalism 15th–18th Century,* Vol. 2. New York: Harper & Row, Publishers.

Brereton, John. 1602. *A Brief and True Relation of the Discovery of the North Virginia, etc., made this present year 1602, by Captain B. Gosnold, Capt. B. Gilbert, etc. by the Permission of the Hon. Knight, Sir W. Raleigh.* In *MaHSC,* 3rd series, vol. 8, pp. 83–123.

Bridgewater, William, and Elizabeth J. Sherwood. 1950. *The Columbia Encyclopedia in One Volume.* New York: Columbia University Press.

Butler, Eva L., and Wendell S. Hadlock. 1962. "A Prelimary Survey of the Munsungan-Allagash Waterways." Bar Harbor, ME: Robert Abbe Museum Bulletin, No. 8.

Cadillac, Antoine de la Mothe, Sieur de. 1930. "Memoir on Acadia [1692]." In W. F. Ganong, ed., "The Cadillac Memoir on Acadia of 1692." *Collections of the New Brunswick Historical Society,* No. 13, pp. 77–97.

CSP = Calendar of State Papers. 1860– 1939. Calendar of State Papers: Colonial Series. Preserved in the British Public Record Office. 40 vols. London: Longman, Green, Longman & Roberts.

Calloway, Colin G. 1990. *The Western Abenakis of Vermont, 1600–1800: War, Migration, and the Survival of an Indian People.* Norman: University of Oklahoma Press.

Cardoso de Oliveira, Roberto. 1964. "A Nao de 'Colonialismo Interno' na Etnologia." In *Tempo Brasileiro,* Vol. 4 (8), pp. 105–112.

Carter, W. D. 1897. "Annual Report Northeastern Division, Richibucto, N. B. to the Superintendent General of Indian Affairs, Ottawa." In SP 14, pp. 50–52.

Cartier, Jacques. 1993. *The Voyages of Jacques Cartier.* With an Introduction by Ramsay Cook. Toronto: University of Toronto Press.

Casgrain, Henri-Raymond. 1897. *Les Sulpiciens et les Prêtres des Missions-Étrangeres en Acadie (1676–1762).* Québec: Pruneau & Kirouac.

Champlain, Samuel de. 1922–1936. *Works.* Edited by H. P. Biggar. (6 vols.) Toronto: The Champlain Society.

Charlevoix, Pierre F. X. de. 1900. *History and General Description of New France.* 6 vols. New York: F. P. Harper.

Christmas, Peter. 1977. "Wejkwapniaq." Sydney, N.S.: Micmac Association of Cultural Studies.

Church, Benjamin. 1867. *The History of the Eastern Expeditions of 1689, 1690, 1692, 1696, and 1704 Against the Indians and French.* Introduction by H. M. Dexter. Boston: B. K. Wiggin and W. P. Lunt.

Churchill, Charles. 1845. *Memorials of a Missionary Life in Nova Scotia, etc.* London: Mason, Hamilton, Adams.

Clark, Andrew H. 1968. *Acadia: The Geography of Early Nova Scotia to 1760.* Madison: The University of Wisconsin Press.

Colby, Benjamin, and Pierre Van den Berghe. 1970. "Ladino-Indian Relationships in the Highlands of Chiapas, Mexico." In Pierre Van den Berghe, ed. *Race and Ethnicity: Essays in Comparative Sociology.* New York: Basic Books.

CMeHS = Collections of the Maine Historical Society. 1831–1887. (1st series, 9 vols.). Portland, ME: The Maine Historical Society.

———. 1869–1916. (2nd series, 24 vols.). Portland, ME.: The Maine Historical Society.

CMaHS = Collections of the Massachusetts Historical Society. 1792–   . (7 series, 10 vols. each). Boston, MA.

CNBHS = Collections of the New Brunswick Historical Society. 1894–1973. (21 vols.). St. John, NB.

CNHHS = Collections of the New Hampshire Historical Society. 1832–1866 (8 vols.). Concord, NH.

Cooney, Robert. 1832. *A Compendious History of the Northern Part of the Province of New Brunswick and of the District of Gaspe in Lower Canada.* Halifax: Joseph Howe.

Coquart, Claude-Godefroy, S. J. 1927. "Relation of 1751." In *JR* 69:80–126. Reprinted in Kenton, vol. 2.

Cronon, William. 1983. *Changes in the Land: Indians, Colonists, and the Ecology of New England.* New York: Hill and Wang.

Cushman, David Q. 1856. "Ancient Settlement of Sheepscot." In *CMeHS,* Vol. 4.

Davies, Kenneth G., ed. 1972–1981. *Documents of the American Revolution, 1770–1783.* Colonial Office Series. 21 vols. Shannon: Irish Univeristy Press.

Day, Gordon M. 1965. "The Identity of the Sokokis." In *Ethnohistory* vol. 12, no. 3, pp. 237–249.

———. 1981. "The Identity of the St. Francis Indians." Canadian Ethnology Service Paper no. 71. Ottawa: National Museums of Canada.

De la Varenne, Sieur. 1756. "A Letter from Louisbourg." In *Acadiensis,* Vol. 10(1), pp. 113–130.

Denieul-Cormier, Anne. 1969. *The Renaissance in France, 1488–1559.* London: Allen & Unwin.

Denys, Nicolas. 1908. *The Description and Natural History of the Coasts of North America (Acadia) [1672].* Edited and translated by W. F. Ganong. Toronto: The Champlain Society.

Denys, Richard. 1907. "A Memorial of Richard Denys describing his Settlements at Miramichi and Nepisiguit [1689]." Edited by William F. Ganong. In *Collections of the New Brunswick Historical Society,* Vol. 3(1), pp. 37–40.

Dickason, Olive P. 1986. "Amerindians Between French and English in Nova Scotia, 1713–1763." *American Indian Culture and Research Journal,* Vol. 20(4), pp. 31–56.

———. 1992. *Canada's First Nations: A History of Founding Peoples from Earliest Times.* Norman: University of Oklahoma Press.

Diereville, Sieur de. 1933. *Relation of the Voyages to Port Royal in Acadia or New France (1708).* Edited by J. C. Webster. Toronto: The Champlain Society.

Dragon, Antonio. 1973. *L'Acadie et ses 40 Robes Noires.* Montréal: Éditions Bellarmin.

Eckstorm, Fanny H. 1941. *Indian Place-Names of the Penobscot Valley and the Maine Coast.* Orono: University of Maine Press (reprint 1960).

Erskine, J. S. 1958. "Their Crowded Hour: The Micmac Cycle." In *The Dalhousie Review,* Vol. 38, pp. 443–452.

Felt, Joseph B. 1849. *Annals of Salem.* 3 vols., 2nd edition. Salem: W. & S. B. Ives.

Febvre, Lucien. 1977. *Life in Renaissance France.* Cambridge, MA: Harvard University Press.

Fingard, Judith. 1972. "The New England Company and the New Brunswick Indians." In *Acadiensis,* Vol. 1 (2), pp. 29–42.

———. 1973. "English Humanitarianism and the Colonial Mind: Walter Bromley in Nova Scotia, 1815–1825." In *Canadian Historical Review,* Vol. 54, pp. 123–151.

Fleras, Augie, and Jean L. Elliott. 1992. *The "Nations Within": Aboriginal-State Relations in Canada, the United States, and New Zealand.* Toronto: Oxford University Press.

Francis, R. Douglas, Richard Jones, Donald B. Smith. 1988a. *Origins: Canadian History to Confederation.* Toronto: Holt, Rinehart and Winston of Canada.

———. 1988b. *Destinies: Canadian History Since Confederation.* Toronto: Holt, Rinehart and Winston of Canada.

Ganong, William F. 1933. "Crucial Maps in the Early Cartography and Place Nomenclature of the Atlantic Coast of Canada, V: The Compiled, or Composite, Maps of 1526–1600." In *Transactions of the Royal Society of Canada,* series 3, vol. 27, sect. 2, pp. 149–195. Ottawa.

Gaynor, William C. 1907. "In the Days of the Pioneers." In *Collections of the New Brunswick Historical Society.* Vol. 3 (1), pp. 55–59.

Gesner, Abraham. 1847. *New Brunswick with Notes for Emigrants Comprehending the Early History, an Account of the Indians, Settlement. . . .* London: Simmonds and Ward.

Gilpin, J. Bernard. 1983. "Indians of Nova Scotia." In *Nova Scotian Institute of Science Proceedings and Transactions,* Vol. 4 (1875–1878), pp. 250–281. Reprinted in McGee 1983, ed., pp. 102–119.

Goddard, Ives. 1978. "Eastern Algonquian Languages." In *Northeast,* edited by Bruce G. Trigger, pp. 70–77. *Handbook of North American Indians,* vol. 15, William G. Sturtevant, general editor. Washington, D.C.: Smithsonian Institution.

Gonzalez, Ellice B. 1982. "An Ethnohistorical Analysis of Micmac Male and Female Economic Roles." In *Ethnohistory* 29 (2), pp. 117–129.

Gookin, Daniel. 1806. *Historical Collections of the Indians in New England (1674).* Boston: CMaHS, 1st series, vol. 1, pp. 141–229.

Gorges, Ferdinando. 1890. *A Briefe Narration of the Originall Undertakings of the Advancement of Plantations into the Parts of America, Especially, shewing the Beginning, Progress and Continuance of that of New England (1658).* Boston: Publications of the Prince Society. Vol. 2.

Gould, Gary P., and Alan J. Semple, eds. 1980. *Our Land: The Maritimes; The Basis of the Indian Claim in the Maritime Provinces of Canada.* Fredericton, N.B.: Saint Annes Point Press.

Grace, Henry. 1977. *The History of the Life and Sufferings of Henry Grace (1764).* In Wilcomb Washburn, ed., *The Garland Library of Narratives of North American Indian Captives,* Vol. 10. New York: Garland Publishing, Inc.

Grenier, F. 1966. "Mathieu d'Amours de Chauffours." In *Dictionary of Canadian Biography, 1000–1700.* Vol. 1, p. 245. Toronto: University of Toronto Press.

Guillemin, Jeanne. 1975. *Urban Renegades: The Cultural Strategy of American Indians.* New York: Columbia University Press.

Gyles, John. 1736. *Memoirs of Odd Adventures, Strange Deliverances, etc., in the Captivity of John Gyles, Esq. Written by himself.* Chicago: The Newberry Library.

Hagar, Stansbury. 1896. "Micmac Magic and Medicine." In *Journal of American Folk-Lore,* Vol. 9, pp. 170–177.

Hakluyt, Richard. 1589–1601. *The Principall Navigations, Voiages and Discoveries of the English Nation.* London: George Bishop and Ralph Newberrie.

Halleck, Charles. 1869. "The Restigouche." *Harper's New Monthly Magazine,* Vol. 36, pp. 424–443.

Hamilton, Milton W. 1964. *Henry Hudson and the Dutch in New York.* Albany: University of the State of New York Press.

Hamilton, William D. 1984. *The Julian Tribe.* Fredericton: Micmac-Maliseet Institute University of New Brunswick.

———. 1986. *The Federal Indian Day Schools of the Maritimes.* Fredericton: Micmac-Maliseet Institute, University of New Brunswick.

Hammond, Otis G., ed. 1863. *Collections of the New Hampshire Historical Society.* Vol. 8. Concord.

Hardy, Campbell. 1855. *Sporting Adventures in the New World; Days and Nights of Moose-hunting in the Pine Forests of Acadia.* 2 vols. London: Hurst and Blackett, Publishers.

Heald, Nan. 1987. "The Aroostook Band of Micmacs' Struggle for Federal Recognition." Pp. 272–276. In *Maine Bar Journal* (Sept.).

Hemming, John. 1978. *Red Gold: The Conquest of the Brazilian Indians.* Cambridge, MA: Harvard University Press.

HM = Historical Magazine. 1857–1875. (22 vols.). Boston, MA.

Hobsbawm, Eric, and Terrence Ranger, eds. 1983. *The Invention of Tradition.* Cambridge, Great Britain: Cambridge University Press.

Hoffman, Bernard G. 1955. "Historical Ethnography of the Micmac of the Sixteenth and Seventeenth Centuries" Unpublished Ph.D. Dissertation, Dept. of Anthropology, Berkeley: University of California.

———. 1961. *Cabot to Cartier: Sources for a Historical Ethnography of Northeastern North America, 1479–1550.* Toronto: University of Toronto Press.

Holland, Samuel. 1935. *Holland's Description of Cape Breton Island and Other Documents.* Compiled with an Introduction by D. C. Harvey, archivist. Halifax: Public Archives of Nova Scotia.

Hollingsworth, S. 1786. *An Account of the Present State of Nova Scotia.* Edinburgh: Creech.

Howard, James H. 1965. "St. Anne's Day Celebration of the Micmac Indians, 1962." In *Museum News,* South Dakota Museum, Vol. 26 (March–April), pp. 5–13.

Howe, John 1983. "Report on Indian Affairs [1844]." In Harold F. McGee, ed., pp. 90–101.

Hubbard, William. 1865. *The History of the Indian Wars in New England, from the First Settlement to the Termination of the War with King Philip 1677.* (1680) (2 vols.) Edited by S. G. Dranke. Roxbury, MA: W. Eliot Woodward.

Hutchinson, Thomas. 1936. *The History of the Colony and Province of Massachusetts Bay [1764]* Ed. by Lawrence S. Mayo. 3 vols. Cambridge, MA: Harvard University Press.

Hutton, Elizabeth A. 1963. "Indian Affairs in Nova Scotia, 1760–1834." In *Collections Nova Scotia Historical Society,* (1963). Reprinted in McGee 1983, pp. 63–80.

Innis, Harold A. 1930. "The Fur Trade in Canada: An Introduction to Canadian Economic History." New Haven: Yale University Press.

Jaenen, Cornelius J. 1974. "Amerindian Views of French Culture in the Seventeenth Century." In *Canadian Historical Review,* Vol. 55, pp. 261–291.

Jameson, J. Franklin, ed. 1909. *Narratives of New Netherland, 1609–1664.* New York: Charles Scribner's Sons.

Jennings, Francis. 1976., *The Invasion of America: Indians, Colonialism, and the Cant of Conquest.* New York: W. W. Norton & Company.

———. 1984. *The Ambiguous Iroquois Empire: The Covenant Chain Confederation of Indian Tribes with English Colonies from its Beginnings to the Lancaster Treaty of 1744.* W. W. Norton & Company.

Jennings, Jesse D. 1989. *Prehistory of North America.* Mountain View, CA: Mayfield Publishing Co.

JR = Jesuit Relations. 1896–1901. The Jesuit Relations and Allied Documents: Travels and Explorations of the Jesuit Missionaries in New France, 1610–1791. (73 vols.) Edited by Reuben G. Thwaites. Cleveland: Burrows Brothers.

Johnson, Frederick. 1943. "Notes on Micmac Shamanism." In *Primitive Man: Quarterly Bulletin of the Catholic Anthropological Conference,* Vol. 16 (3/4), pp. 53–80.

Josselyn, John. 1833. "An Account of Two Voyages to New England (1675)." In *CMaHS,* 3d series, vol. 3, pp. 211–396.

Kenton, Edna, ed. 1927. *The Indians of North America.* 2 vols. New York: Harcourt Brace.

Kidder, Frederic. 1867. *Military Operations in Eastern Maine and Nova Scotia during the Revolution chiefly compiled from the Journals and Letters of Colonel Allan, with notes and a Memoir of Col. John Allan.* Albany: Joel Munsell.

LaChasse, Pierre de. 1708. "Récensement Generale de Acadie." Unpublished manuscript. Ayer Collection." Chicago: The Newberry Library.

LaHontan, Louis-Armand de Lom d'Arce, Baron de. 1905. *New Voyages to North America by the Baron de Lahontan [1703].* 2 vols. Edited by Reuben G. Thwaites. Chicago: A. C. McClurg.

Leavitt, Robert M., and David A. Francis, eds. 1990. *Wapapi Akonutomkonol: The Wampum Records. Wabanaki Traditional Laws.* Fredericton, N.B.: Micmac-Maliseet Institute University of New Brunswick.

LeClercq, Chrestien. 1910. *New Relation of Gaspesia, with the customs and religion of the Gaspesian Indians.* Translated and edited by William F. Ganong. Toronto: The Champlain Society.

Leger, Mary C. 1929. *The Catholic Indian Missions of Maine, 1611–1820.* Washington, D.C.: Studies in American Church History 8.

Leighton, Alexander H. 1937. "The Twilight of the Indian Porpoise Hunters." In *Natural History,* Vol. 40, pp. 410–416, 458.

Lemaire, Ton. 1986. *De Indiaan in ons Bewustzijn: De Ontmoeting van de Oude met de Nieuwe Wereld.* Baarn, The Netherlands: AMBO.

Lenhart, John. 1916. "The Capuchins in Acadia and Northern Maine (1632–1655)." In *Records of the American Catholic Historical Society,* Vol. 28 (3), pp. 191–229, 300–327.

Lescarbot, Marc. 1911–1914. *The History of New France (1609–1612).* (3 vols). Toronto: The Champlain Society.

Levett, Christopher. In Baxter 1893.

Levett, Christopher. 1847. "Voyage into New England, begun in 1623, and ended in 1624. (1628)." In *CMeHS,* 1st series, vol. 2, pp. 73–110.

MacBeath, George B. 1966. "Saint-Étienne de La Tour, Charles." In *Dictionary of Canadian Biography, 1000 to 1700.* Vol. 1, pp. 592–596. Toronto: Univeristy of Toronto Press.

———. 1969. "Damours (d'Amours) de Chauffours, Louis." In *Dictionary of Canadian Biography, 1701–1740.* Vol. 2, pp. 166–167. Toronto: University of Toronto Press.

Machias Truck House Accounts [1776–1780]. Unpublished on microfilm. In Massachusetts Archives, vol. 147. Boston.

MeHSSP = Maine Historical Society, Selections and Proceedings, 2nd. series, vols. 1–10 (1890–1899). Portland, ME.

Maillard, Pierre (Antoine-Simon). 1758. *An Account of Customs and Manners of the Mickmakis and Maricheets, Savage Nations, Now Dependent on the Government of Cape Breton [1751/1755].* London: S. Hooper and A. Morley.

————. 1863. Lettre [á Madame de Drucourt] de M. L'Abbé Maillard sur les missions de l'Acadie et particulierement sur les missions Micmaques [c. 1754]. In *Les Soirées Canadiennes,* Vol. 3, pp. 289–426.

Mandrou, Robert. 1975. *Introduction to Modern France, 1500–1648: An Essay in Historical Psychology.* London: Edward Arnold.

Marcus, George E., and Michael M. J. Fischer. 1986. *Anthropology as Cultural Critique: An Experimental Moment in the Human Sciences.* Chicago: University of Chicago Press.

Marshall, Donald, Sr., Alexander Denny, Simon Marshall. 1989. "The Covenant Chain [of the Mi'kmaq]." Pp. 71–104, in *Drumbeat: Anger and Renewal in Indian Country.* Edited by Boyce Richardson. Toronto: Summerhill Press.

Marston, Benjamin. 1784. Letter to Israel Mauduit. In William O. Raymond, "The Founding of Shelburne: Benj. Marston at Halifax, Shelburne, and Miramichi." In *CNBHS,* No. 8 (1909), pp. 204–293.

Martijn, Charles. 1986. *Les Micmacs et la Mer.* Montréal: Récherches Amérindiennes au Québec.

Martin, Calvin L. 1978. *Keepers of the Game: Indian-Animal Relationships and the Fur Trade.* Berkeley: University of California Press.

Massachusetts Archives. 242 vols. and additional unnumbered volumes. Archives Division, State House, Boston.

Massachusetts Acts and Resolves. 1869–1922. Acts and Resolves, Public and Private, of the Province of Massachusetts Bay. With Historical and Explanatory Notes, and an Appendix. 21 vols. Boston: Wright & Potter Printing Co.

MaBCR = Massachusetts Bay Colonial Records, see Shurtleff.

MaHSC = See CMaHS.

Mather, Cotton. 1853. *Magnalia Christi Americana; or, The Ecclesiastical History of New England (1702).* Introduction and Notes by T. Robbins. (2 vols.). Hartford: Silus Andrus & Son.

Mather, Increase. 1864. *Early History of New England: Being a Relation of Hostile Passages Between the Indians and European Voyagers and First Settlers.* With an Introduction and Notes by Samuel G. Drake. Albany, NY: J. Munsell.

Matthiessen, Peter. 1991. *In the Spirit of Crazy Horse.* With an Afterword by Martin Garbus. New York: Viking Penguin.

McBride, Bunny. 1987. "The Micmacs of Maine: A Continuing Struggle." Pp. 67–71. In *Rooted Like The Ash Trees: New England Indians and the Land.* Edited by Richard G. Carlson. Naugatuck, CT: Eagle Wing Press, Inc. (Originally published in the *Maine Times,* January 23).

McBride, Bunny. 1995. *Molly Spotted Elk: A Penobscot in Paris.* Norman: University of Oklahoma Press.

McBride, Bunny, ed. 1990. *Our Lives in Our Hands: Micmac Indian Basketmakers.* Gardiner, ME: Tilbury House, Publishers.

McBride, Bunny, and Harald E. L. Prins. 1983. *In Their Own Words: Oral Histories of Six Aroostook Micmac Families.* Report for the Aroostook Micmac Council, Presque Isle. On file with authors.

————.1990. "Aroostook Micmac and Split Basketry: Tradition, Adaptation and Survival." Pp. 1–23. In Bunny McBride, ed., *Our Lives in Our Hands: Micmac Indian Basketmakers.* Gardiner, ME: Tilbury House, Publishers.

————. 1996. "Walking the Medicine Line: Molly Ockett, a Pigwacket Doctor." In *Northeastern Indian Lives.* Edited by Robert Grumet. Amherst, MA: University of Massachusetts Press.

McGee, Harold F. 1974. "White Encroachment on Micmac Reserve Lands in Nova Scotia, 1830–1867." In *Man in the Northeast,* No. 8, pp. 57–64.

McGee, H. F., ed. 1983. *The Native Peoples of Canada: A History of Indian-European Relations.* Ottawa: Carleton University Press.

McIsaac, D. 1882. Annual Report Indian District No. 11, Inverness County, N.S., to the Superintendent General of Indian Affairs, Ottawa. In SP 6, p. 32.

McLennan, John S. 1918. *Louisbourg; from its Foundation to its Fall, 1713–1758.* London: Macmillan.

Micmac Briefing Book. 1987. Aroostook Band of Micmacs: Briefing Book. Prepared for the Mi'kmaq federal recognition and land claims case in Maine by Pine Tree Legal Assistance, Inc. for the Aroostook Micmac Council, Presque Isle, ME.

MN = Micmac News. [Union of Nova Scotia Indians monthly paper]. Sydney, NS: The Native Communications Society of Nova Scotia.

MMNN = Micmac-Maliseet Nations News. Monthly published by the Micmac-Maliseet Nation News Association. Truro, N.S.

Miller, Virginia P. 1976. "Aboriginal Micmac Population: A Review of the Evidence." In *Ethnohistory* 23 (2), pp. 117–127.

Mitchell, David J. 1981. *The Jesuits, a History.* New York: F. Watts.

Mooney, James. 1928. *The Aboriginal Population of America North of Mexico.* Smithsonian Miscellaneous Collections, 80, no. 7. Washington, D.C.: Smithsonian Institution.

Morison, Samuel E. 1971. *The European Discovery of America: The Northern Voyages,* A.D. *500–1600.* New York: Oxford University Press.

Morrison, Alvin H. 1990. "Dawnland Dog-Feast: Wabanaki Warfare, c. 1600–1760." Pp. 258–278. *Papers of the Twenty-First Algonquian Conference.* Edited by William Cowan. Ottawa: Carleton University Press.

Morrison, Alvin H., and Harald E. L. Prins. 1989. "Wabanaki Algonquian Ethnohistory Since Eckstorm." Paper presented at the Annual Meeting of the American Anthropological Association. Washington, D.C.

Morrison, Kenneth M. 1984. *The Embattled Northeast: The Elusive Ideal of Alliance in Abenaki-Euramerican Relations.* Berkeley: University of California Press.

Morton, Thomas. 1883. *The New English Canaan (1637).* Edited by C. F. Adams, Jr. Boston: The Prince Society.

Munro, William B., ed. 1908. *Documents Relating to the Seigniorial Tenure in Canada, 1598–1854.* Toronto: The Champlain Society.

Murdoch, Beamish. 1865. *A History of Nova Scotia.* 3 vols. Halifax: James Barn.

Nash, Ronald J., and Virginia P. Miller. 1987. "Model Building and the Case of the Micmac Economy." In *Man in the Northeast,* No. 34, pp. 41–56.

NEHGR = New England Historical and Geneological Register. 1847–1896 (50 vols.). Boston, MA.

NHPSP = New Hampshire Provincial and State Papers. 1867–19 (40 vols.). Concord, NH (etc.).

NYHS = New York Historical Society.

NYCD = New York Colonial Documents. 1849–1851. *Documents Relative to the Colonial History of the State of New York.* (15 vols.) Edited by E. B. Callaghan. Albany: Weed, Parsons.

Nicolar, Joseph. 1893. *The Life and Traditions of the Red Man.* Bangor, ME: C. H. Glass, printers.

Nietfeld, Patricia K. L. 1981. "Determinants of Aboriginal Political Structure." PhD thesis. The University of New Mexico.

Niles, Samuel A. M. 1860. "A Summary Historical Narrative of the War in New England with the French and English in the Several Parts of the Country [1760]." In *CMaHS,* 4th series, vol. 5, pp. 309–589.

Oliver, W. P. 1949. "Cultural Progress (of the) Negro in Nova Scotia." In *The Dalhousie Review,* Vol. 29, pp. 293–299.

Pacifique, Père [Henri Buisson de Valigny]. 1906. "Quelques Traits Caracteristiques de la Tribu des Micmacs." In *Proceedings of the International Congrès des Americanistes,* vol. 15, pp. 315–328.

———. 1926. "Ristigouche: Métropole des Micmacs, Théatre du Dernier Effort de la France au Canada." In *Bulletin de la Societé de Géographie de Québec,* Vol. 20, pp. 171–185.

———. 1933–34. "Le Pays des Micmacs." In *Études Historiques et Géographiques.* Vols. 10, 11, 14. Bonaventure.

Papers of the Continental Congress, Microfilm rolls 58, 59, 71, Washington, D.C.: National Archives.

PD = Paris Documents. (9 vols.). In *NYCD* 9 & 10.

Parkman, Francis. 1907. *Count Frontenac and New France under Louis XIV.* Boston: Little, Brown, and Company.

Penhallow, Samuel. 1859. *The History of the Wars of New-England with the Eastern Indians, or a Narrative of their Continued Perfidy and Cruelty [1726].* Cincinnati: For Wm. Dodge, by J. Harpel.

Pike, John. 1870. "Journal of the Rev. John Pike (1678–1709)." In *CNHHS,* Vol. 3, pp. 40–67.

Porter, Harry Culverwell. 1979. *The Inconstant Savage: England and the North American Indian, 1500–1660.* London: Duckworth.

Pote, William. 1896. *The Journal of Captain William Pote, Jr. During His Captivity in the French-Indian War from May , 1745 to August, 1747.* Edited by J. F. Hurst. New York: Dodd, Mead.

Price, John A. 1979. *Indians of Canada: Cultural Dynamics.* Salem, WI: Sheffield Publishing Company.

Prince, Thomas. 1755. *Annals of New England,* Vol. II, No. 1.

Prins, Harald E. L. 1985. "Een Wabanaki Renaissance?: Een Kritisch Overzicht van de Politieke Beweging bij Micmacs en Maliseets in Noordoostelijk Noord-Amerika." Pp. 108–144 in *Terugkeer van een Verdwijnend Volk: Indiaans en Inuit Activisme Nu.* Lemaire, T., and F. Wojcienchowski, eds. Nijmegen, The Netherlands: Katholieke Universiteit Nijmegen. Sociaal Anthropologische Cahiers No. XVI.

———. 1986. "Micmacs and Maliseets in the St. Lawrence Valley." In *Actes du 17e Congres des Algonquinistes,* edited by W. Cowan, pp. 263–278. Ottawa: Carleton University Press.

———. 1988. *Tribulations of a Border Tribe: A Discourse on the Political Ecology of the Aroostook Band of Micmacs (16th–20th Centuries).* Ann Arbor: University Microfilms International.

———. 1989. "Two George Washington Medals in the Chain of Friendship between the United States and the Wabanaki Confederacy." In *Maine Historical Society Quarterly* 28/4: 226–34.

———. 1992. "Cornfields at Meductic: Ethnic and Territorial Reconfigurations in Colonial Acadia." In *Man in the Northeast,* No. 44, pp. 55–72.

———. 1993. "To The Land of the Mistigoches: American Indians Traveling to Europe in the Age of Exploration." In *American Indian Culture and Research Journal,* vol. 17, no. 1, pp. 175–195.

———. 1994a. "Maliseet." P. 328. In *Native America in the Twentieth Century. An Encyclopedia.* Edited by Mary B. Davis. New York: Garland Publishing, Inc.

———. 1994b. "Micmac." Pp. 339–340. In *Native America in the Twentieth Century. An Encyclopedia.* Edited by Mary B. Davis. New York: Garland Publishing, Inc.

———. 1994c. "Passamaquoddy." Pp. 435–436. In *Native America in the Twentieth Century. An Encyclopedia.* Edited by Mary B. Davis. New York: Garland Publishing, Inc.

———. 1994d. "Penobscot." Pp. 441–442. In *Native America in the Twentieth Century. An Encyclopedia.* Edited by Mary B. Davis. New York: Garland Publishing, Inc.

———. 1994e. "Neo-Traditions in Native Communities: Sweat Lodge and Sun Dance among the Micmac Today." Pp. 383–394. In *Proceedings of the 25th Algonquian Conference,* edited by William Cowan. Ottawa: Carleton University Press.

———. 1994f. "The Children of Gluskap: Wabanaki Indians on the Eve of the European Invasion." Pp. 95–117. In *American Beginnings: Exploration, Culture, and Cartography in the Land of Norumbega.* Edited by Emerson W. Baker, Edwin A. Churchill, Richard S. d'Abate, Kristine L. Jones, Victor A. Konrad, and Harald E. L. Prins. Lincoln: University of Nebraska Press.

———. 1995. "Turmoil on the Wabanaki Frontier, 1524–1678." In *Maine: The Pine Tree State from Prehistory to the Present,* edited by R. Judd, et al. Pp. 97–119. Orono: University Press of Maine.

————. 1996. "Tribal Network and Migrant Labor: Mi'kmaq Indians as Seasonal Workers in Aroostook's Potato Fields, 1870–1980." Ch. 2 in *Native American Wage Labor: Ethnographic and Ethnohistorical Perspectives,* edited by Alice Littlefield and Martha Knack. Norman: University of Oklahoma Press.

Prins, Harald E. L., and Bunny McBride. 1992. "Discovering Europe, 1493." In *World Monitor* (November), pp. 56–62.

Prins, Harald E. L., and Ruth H. Whitehead. 1984. Early Sixteenth-Century Micmac-Portuguese Pidgin in the Gulf of St. Lawrence. Manuscript on file with authors.

PCRM = Province and Court Records of Maine. 1928–1931. Province and Court Records of Maine. Edited by C. T. Libby. (2 vols.) Boston, MA.

Purchas, Samuel. 1905–1907. *Hakluytus Posthumus or Purchas, His Pilgrimes, Contayning a History of the World in Sea Voyages and Lande Travells by Englishmen and Others [1625].* 4 vols. Glasgow: J. MacLehose & Sons.

Putnam, Donald F., editor. 1952. *Canadian Regions: A Geography of Canada.* New York: T. Y. Crowell.

ROM = Records of Massachusetts, see Shurtleff.

Rand, Silas T. 1850. *Short Statement of Facts Relating to the History, Manners, Customs, Language, and Literature of the Micmac Tribe of Indians, in Nova Scotia and P. E. Island.* Halifax: James Bowes & Son.

————. 1888. *Dictionary of the Language of the Micmac Indians.* Halifax, N.S.: Nova Scotia Printing Company.

————. 1894. *Legends of the Micmacs.* New York: Longmans, Green & Co.

Raymond, William O. 1910. *The River St. John, Its Physical Features, Legends, and History from 1604 to 1784.* Sackville, N.B.: The Tribune Press.

Reid, John G. 1981. *Acadia, Maine, and New Scotland, Marginal Colonies in the Seventeenth Century.* Toronto: University of Toronto Press.

Rink, Oliver A. 1986. *Holland on the Hudson: An Economic and Social History of Dutch New York.* Ithaca: Cornell University Press.

Robertson, Marion. 1969. *Red Earth: Tales of the Micmacs. With an Introduction to the Customs and Beliefs of the Micmac Indians.* Halifax: The Nova Scotia Museum.

Rogers, Norman M. 1926. "Apostle to the Micmacs." In *Dalhousie Review,* Vol. 6 (2), pp. 166–176.

Roy, Pierre-Georges. 1932. *Rapport de l'Archiviste de la Province de Québec,* Québec: Proulx.

Sagard-Theodat, Gabriel. 1939. *The Long Journey to the Country of the Hurons [1632].* Edited with Introduction and Notes by George M. Wrong, and translated into English by H. H. Langton. Toronto: The Champlain Society.

Sainsbury, William N., ed. 1860–1880. *Calendar of State Papers. Colonial Series (1574–1660).* Vols. 3–5. London: Longman, Green, Longman & Roberts.

Salwen, Bert. 1978. "Indians of Southern New England and Long Island: Early Period." In *Northeast,* edited by Bruce G. Trigger, pp. 160–176. *Handbook of North American Indians,* vol. 15, William G. Sturtevant, general editor. Washington, D.C.: Smithsonian Institution.

Sanger, David, ed. 1979. *Discovering Maine's Archaeological Heritage.* Augusta, ME: Maine Historic Preservation Commission.

Sauer, Carl O. 1972. *Sixteenth Century North America; the Land and People as seen by the Europeans.* Berekeley: University of California Press.

Schmidt, David L. 1993. "The Micmac Hieroglyphs: A Reassessment." In *Papers of the Twenty-Fourth Algonquian Conference.* Pp. 346–363. Edited by William Cowan. Ottawa: Carleton University Press.

Schmidt, David L., and Murdena Marshall, eds. In press. *The Micmac Hieroglyphs: Readings in North America's first indigenous writing system.* Halifax: Nimbus Publishing.

Scott, James C. 1990. *Domination and the Arts of Resistance: Hidden Transcripts.* New Haven: Yale University Press.

SP = Sessional Papers. 1867–1925. Sessional Papers of the Parliament of the Domination of Canada. Ottawa: C. H. Parmelee, etc. etc.

Seume, Johann G. 1887. "Adventures of a Hessian Recruit." [Letter written in Halifax 1782].
    In CMaHS, 2d series, vol. 4, pp. 8–11.
Sewall, Samuel. 1878–1882. *Diary of Samuel Sewall [1674–1729].* In *CMaHS,* 5th series,
    vols. 5, 6, and 7.
Shay, John G. 1861. "Micmac or Recollet Hieroglyphs." In *Historical Magazine,* Vol. 5 (10),
    pp. 289–292.
Shurtleff, Nathaniel B., ed. 1853–1854. *Records of the Governor and Company of the Massa-
    chusetts Bay in New England, 1628–1686.* 5 vols. in 6. Boston: William White.
Silverman, Kenneth. 1984. *The Life and Times of Cotton Mather.* New York: Harper
    & Row.
Smith, Titus. 1799–1801. *Diary of Titus Smith.* Manuscript Document, Vol. 380. Halifax: Pub-
    lic Archives of Nova Scotia.
Smith, John. 1898. "Description of New England (1616)." In *American Colonial Tracts
    Monthly,* Vol. 2 (1), pp. 1–39.
Snow, Dean R. 1968. "Wabanaki Family Hunting Territories." In *American Anthropologist,*
    Vol. 70 (6), pp. 1143–1151.
————. 1976. "The Ethnohistoric Baseline of the Esatern Abenaki." In *Ethnohistory,* Vol. 23
    (3), pp. 291–306.
————. 1978. "Late Prehistory of the East Coast." In *Northeast,* edited by Bruce G. Trigger,
    pp. 58–69. *Handbook of North American Indians,* vol. 15, William G. Sturtevant, general
    editor. Washington, D.C.: Smithsonian Institution.
————. 1980. *The Archaeology of New England.* New York: Academic Press.
Speck, Frank G. 1915a. "The Family Hunting Band as the Basis of Algonkin Social Organi-
    zation." In *American Anthropologist,* Vol. 17 (2), pp. 289–305.
————. 1915b. "Some Micmac Tales from Cape Breton Island." In *Journal of American
    Folk-Lore,* Vol. 28, pp. 59–69.
————. 1915c. "The Eastern Algonkian Wabanaki Confederacy." In *American Anthropolo-
    gist,* Vol. 17, pp. 492–508.
————. 1919. "The Functions of Wampum among the Eastern Algonkian." In *Memoirs of the
    American Anthropological Association,* Vol. 6, pp. 3–71.
————. 1922. "Beothuk and Micmac." In *Indian Notes and Monographs,* No. 22. New York:
    Museum of the American Indian-Heye Foundation.
————. 1935. "Penobscot Tales and Religious Beliefs." *Journal of American Folklore,* Vol.
    48, pp. 1–107.
————. 1940. *Penobscot Man: the Life History of a Forest Tribe in Maine.* Philadelphia: Uni-
    versity of Pennsylvania Press.
Spiess, Arthur E. and Bruce D. Spiess. 1987. "New England Pandemic of 1616–1622: Cause
    and Archaeological Implication." In *Man in the Northeast,* No. 34, pp. 71–83.
Steiner, Stan. 1968. *The New Indians.* New York: Dell Publishing Co.
Sullivan, James. 1804. "The History of the Penobscott Indians." In *CMaHS,* 1st Series, Vol. 9,
    pp. 207–232.
Swanson, Carl E. 1991. *Predators and Prizes: American Privateering and Imperial Warfare,
    1739–1748.* Columbia, S.C.: University of South Carolina Press.
Swanton, John R. 1952. *The Indian Tribes of North America.* Smithsonian Institution Bureau
    of American Ethnology Bulletin 145. Washington, D.C.: United States Printing Office.
Thayer, Henry O., ed. 1892. *The Sagadahock Colony, Comprising The Relation of a Voyage
    into New England.* Portland, ME: The Gorges Society.
Thury, Louis-Pierre. 1884. "Relation du Combat des Canibas [1689]." In *Collection de manu-
    scrits, contenant letters, mémoires, et autres documents historiques relatifs à la Nouvelle
    France,* Vol. 1, pp. 477–481. Quebec: A Cote.
Trigger, Bruce G. 1985. *Natives and Newcomers: Canada's "Heroic Age" Reconsidered.*
    Kingston and Montreal: McGill-Queen's University Press.
Trudel, Marcel. 1973. *The Beginnings of New France, 1524–1663.* Toronto: McClelland and
    Stewart Ltd.

Tuck, James A. 1978. "Regional Cultural Development, 3000 to 300 B.C." In *Northeast,* edited by Bruce G. Trigger, pp. 28–43. *Handbook of North American Indians,* vol. 15, William G. Sturtevant, general editor. Washington, D.C.: Smithsonian Institution.

UNSI = Union of Nova Scotia Indians. 1976. Nova Scotia Micmac Aboriginal Rights Position Paper. Sydney, N.S.: Union of Nova Scotia Indians.

Uniacke, Richard J. 1865. *Sketches of Cape Breton, and other papers relating to Cape Breton Island.* Edited with an Introduction and Notes by C. Bruce Fergusson. Halifax: Public Archives of Nova Scotia.

Upton, Leslie F. S. 1979. *Micmacs and Colonists: Indian-White Relations in the Maritimes, 1713–1867.* Vancouver: The University of British Columbia Press.

USLR = United States Legal Rights. n.d. United States Legal Rights of Native Americans Born in Canada. Boston: Office of the Indian Task Force, Federal Regional Council of New England.

Villebon, Joseph Robineau, Sieur de. 1690–1699. Journals, Letters, and Memoirs. In Webster 1934, pp. 22–140.

Vizenor, Gerald. 1990. *Crossbloods: Bone Courts, Bingo, and Other Reports.* Minneapolis: University of Minnesota Press.

Walker, Willard. Gregory Buesing, and Robert Conkling. 1977. "A Chronological Account of the Wabanaki Confederacy." Draft of unpublished manuscript. Wesleyan University, Middletown, CT.

Wallis, Wilson D., and Ruth S. Wallis. 1953. "Culture Loss and Culture Change among the Micmac of the Canadian Maritime Provinces, 1912–1950." In *Kroeber Anthropological Society Papers,* Vol. 8, pp. 100–129.

———. 1955. *The Micmac Indians of Eastern Canada.* Minneapolis: University of Minnesota Press.

Washburn, Wilcomb E. 1975. *The Indian in America.* New York: Harper & Row.

———. 1987. "Distinguishing History from Moral Philosophy and Public Advocacy." Pp. 91–97. In *The American Indian and the Problem of History.* Edited by Calvin Martin. New York: Oxford University Press.

Watson, Lawrence W. 1907. "The Origin of the Melicites." In *Journal of American Folk-Lore,* Vol. 20, pp. 160–162.

Wax, Murry L. 1971. *Indian Americans: Unity and Diversity.* Englewood Cliffs, NJ: Prentice-Hall, Inc.

Webster, John C. 1934. *Acadia at the End of the Seventeenth Century: Letters, Journals and Memoirs of Joseph Robineau de Villebon, Commandant in Acadia 1690–1700, and Other Contemporary Documents.* Monograph Series 1. Saint John, N.B.: The New Brunswick Museum.

West, John. 1827. *A Journal of a Mission to the Indians of the British Provinces, of New Brunswick and Nova Scotia, and the Mohawks on the Ouse or Grand River.* London: L. B. Seeley & Son.

Whitehead, Ruth H. 1980. *Elitekey: Micmac Material Culture from 1600 A.D. to the Present.* Halifax, N.S.: The Nova Scotia Museum.

———. 1987. "I Have Lived Here Since the World Began: Atlantic Coast Artistic Traditions." In *The Spirit Sings: Artistic Traditions of Canada's First Peoples.* Glenbow Museum Exhibit Catalogue. Toronto: McClelland and Stewart.

———. 1991. *The Old Man Told Us: Excerpts from Micmac History: 1500–1950.* Halifax, N.S.: Nimbus Publishing Ltd.

Whitehead, Ruth H., and Harold F. McGee. 1983. *The Micmac: How Their Ancestors Lived Five Hundred Years Ago.* Halifax, N.S.: Nimbus Publishing.

Williams, Roger. 1798. "A Key into the Language of the Indian of New England [1643]. Second part." Reprinted in *CMaHS,* 1st series, vol. 5, pp. 80–106.

Williamson, William D. 1874. "Annals of the City of Bangor, Maine." In *Historical Magazine* (February/March], pp. 86, 164–166.

Winks, Robin W. 1969. "Negroes in the Maritimes: An Introductory Survey." In *The Dalhousie Review,* Vol. 48 (4), pp. 453–471.

Winslow, Edward. 1832. "Good Newes from New England (1624)." In *CMaHS,* 2d Series, 9, pp. 74–99.

Winslow, John. 1883. "Journal of Colonel John Winslow of the Provincial Troops, while engaged in removing the French Acadian Inhabitants from Grand Pre, and the Neighboring Settlements, in the Autumn of the Year 1755." In *Report and Collections of the Nova Scotia Historical Society, For the Years 1882–1883.,* Vol. 3, pp. 71–208.

———. 1885. "Journal of Colonel John Winslow of the Provincial Troops, while engaged in the Siege of Fort Beausejour, in the summer and autumn of 1755." In *Collections of the Nova Scotia Historical Society, For the Year 1884.,* Vol. 4, pp. 113–246.

Winthrop, John. 1853. *The History of New England, from 1630 to 1649.* Edited by J. Savage. (2 vols.) Boston: Little, Brown and Company.

Wolf, Eric R. 1982. *Europe and the People without History.* Berkeley: University of California Press.

Wood, William. 1865. *New Englands Prospect (1634).* Boston: The Publications of the Prince Society.

Wright, Louis B., ed. 1965. *The Elizabethan's America: A Collection of Early Reports by Englishmen on the New World.* Cambridge, MA: Harvard University Press.

Wright, Esmond, ed. 1983. *The Fire of Liberty.* New York: St. Martin's Press.

YCR = York Colonial Records

YD = York Deeds. 1887–1910. York Deeds [1642–1737]. 18 vols. Portland, ME: John T. Hull.

Young, Alexander, ed. 1846. *Chronicles of the First Planters of the Colony of Massachusetts Bay, from 1623 to 1636.* Boston: Charles C. Little and James Brown.

Credits

1.1 Map by Karen L. Turnmire (p. 1).

1.2 Photo by Marlene Sanipass (p. 3).

2.1 Photo by the author (p. 8).

2.2 Photo by Brian Douglas Dezagiacomo (p. 16).

3.1 Photo by Brian Molyneaux. Courtesy of Parks Canada (p. 22).

3.2 Courtesy of National Archives of Canada, Ottawa (p. 26).

3.3 Figure by Karen L. Turnmire, based on Charles Martijn, 1986 (p. 28).

3.4 Map by Karen L. Turnmire (p. 38).

4.1 Courtesy of Bibliothèque Nationale, Paris (p. 50).

5.1 Reproduced from the Lavardière edition of Champlain's works. Courtesy of National Library of Canada, Ottawa (p. 60).

6.1 Photo by Ruth Whitehead. Courtesy of The Champlain Society, Toronto (p. 79).

6.2 Photo by Ruth Whitehead. Courtesy of The Champlain Society, Toronto (p. 86).

7.1 Courtesy of National Archives of Canada, Ottawa (p. 90).

8.1 Courtesy of The Champlain Society, Toronto (p. 113).

9.1 Courtesy of Rijksmuseum-Stichting, Amsterdam (p. 127).

10.1 Courtesy of National Archives of Canada, Toronto (p. 139).

10.2 Map by Karen L. Turnmire (p. 143).

10.3 Courtesy of National Gallery of Canada, Ottawa (p. 149).

11.1 Courtesy of Art Gallery of Nova Scotia, Halifax (p. 159).

11.2 Courtesy of National Archives of Canada, Ottawa (p. 164).

12.1 Translation by David L. Schmidt and Murdena Marshall (p. 171).

12.2 Courtesy of The Nova Scotia Museum, Halifax (p. 173).

12.3 Courtesy of National Archives of Canada, Ottawa (p. 176).

12.4 Courtesy of Public Archives of Nova Scotia (p. 182).

12.5 Courtesy of The Nova Scotia Museum, Halifax (p. 183).

13.1 Courtesy of the Prince Edward Island Public Archives and Records Office, Charlottetown (p. 193).

13.2 Photo by Donald Sanipass (p. 197).

13.3 Photo by the author (p. 204).

13.4 Photo by the author (p. 205).

13.5 Photo by the author (p. 207).

13.6 Photo by the author (p. 215).

Films on the Mi'kmaq: An Annotated List

Annie Mae: Brave-Hearted Woman (1989). Produced by Lan Brooks Ritz. 16 mm., 1/2" vt., Color, 79 min. Distr.: Brown Bird Productions, Hollywood, Cal.

Documenting the political oppression of American Indians, it focuses on the life and death of Mi'kmaq activist Anna Mae Pictou (Aquash). It chronicles her childhood in Nova Scotia, her role in the Boston Indian community, and her political involvement in the American Indian Movement, and follows her trail to occupied Wounded Knee in 1973. Three years later, she was found murdered in South Dakota.

The Boston Indian Community (1979). Director Russell Peters. Producer Glenn Suprenard, for WGBY-TV, Springfield, Mass., 3/4" vt, 1/2" vt. Color, 28 min. People of the First Light Series. Distr. Native American Public Broadcasting Consortium, Lincoln, Neb.

As this film shows, many Mi'kmaqs have migrated to big cities such as Boston. Facing common challenges, they have formed urban communities, which enable them to cope with the problems.

Incident at Restigouche (1984). Directed by Alanis Obomsowin. 1/2" vt., Color, 45 min. Distr.: National Film Board of Canada.

Documents the 1981 salmon war at Restigouche, with gripping footage of Quebec's provincial police and fish wardens raiding the Mi'kmaq reserve community.

The Invisible Man (1981–1983). Director Daniel Bertolino. Produced by Via le Monde, 16 mm., 3/4" vt, 1/2" vt., Color, 25 min. Mi'kmaq language with English narration. Indian Legends of Canada series. Distr. Thomas Howe Associates Ltd., Vancouver, B.C.

A miraculous young man brings the first rainbow to the people.

The Magic Box (1981–1983). Director Daniel Bertolino. Produced by Via le Monde, 16 mm., 3/4" vt, 1/2" vt. Color, 25 min. Mi'kmaq language with English narration. Indian Legends of Canada series. Distr. Thomas Howe Associates Ltd., Vancouver, B.C.

With the help of a magic box, a young man learns the meaning of love.

Megmuwesug, The Enchanting Spirit (1981–1983). Director Daniel Bertolino. Produced by Via le Monde, 16 mm., 3/4" vt, 1/2" vt. Color, 25 min. Mi'kmaq language with English narration. Indian Legends of Canada series. Distr. Thomas Howe Associates Ltd., Vancouver, B.C.

An impish spirit teaches the people that they must always help one another.

Micmac: The People and Their Culture (1980). 1/2" vt, Color. A filmstrip series in seven parts (Domestic Crafts and Skills, 7 min.; Fisheries, 8 min.; Pastimes and Recreation, 7 min.; Clothing, 9 min.; Structures, 11 min.; Transportation, 9 min.; Hunting Methods, 9 min.) Produced by the Education Media Services of the Nova Scotia Dept. of Education, Halifax, N.S.

This series was produced to supplement the Mi'kmaq videotape series.

Mi'kmaq (1980). Directed and produced by Robert Vandekieft. Co-production CBC: Halifax and Nova Scotia Dept. of Education in cooperation with the Micmac Association of Cultural Studies. 1/2" vt. Five parts, each 20–30 mins. Distr. Communications Services, Dept. of Indian and Inuit Affairs, Amherst, Nova Scotia.

Dramatization of Mi'kmaq daily life in 1400, a century before the arrival of Europeans. It comes in a Mi'kmaq-only version as well as in a Mi'kmaq with English or French overlay version.

Our Lives in Our Hands (1986). Producers Harald Prins and Karen Carter. Sponsored by the Aroostook Micmac Council, 16 mm., 3/4" vt., 1/2" vt. Color, 50 min., Distr.: Documentary Educational Resources, Watertown, Mass., and Northeast Historic Film, Bucksport, Maine.

Examines the traditional craft of splint ash basketmaking as a means of economic and cultural survival for Mi'kmaqs in northern Maine. Focusing on the Sanipass family, it features them as artisans and seasonal laborers and aims at breaking down stereotypical images of "Indians."

Porpoise Oil (1936). Produced and directed by Alexander H. Leighton (with Bear River Mi'kmaqs). 8 mm., 1/2" vt. Black and white, 14 min. Distr. Canadian Broadcasting Corporation, Halifax, N.S.

Also known as "Micmac Porpoise," this film documents a historical reenactment of 19th-century porpoise hunting in the Bay of Fundy. In addition to "porpoising," it depicts a summer camp of bark wikuoms, with people making baskets and canoes and playing games.

The Song Says It All (Ktapehagn Kaqui-Theik) (1988). Directed by Ray Whitley. Co-produced by the Micmac Association for Cultural Studies and the Nova Scotia Department of Education, Halifax, N.S.

Documents the life and work of Mi'kmaq poet Rita Joe of Cape Breton Island.

Wabanaki: A New Dawn (1995). Filmed by David Westphal and Dennis Kostyk for The Maine Indian Tribal-State Commission. Produced by Acadia Filmvideo. 1/2" vt., Color. 29 min. Distr.: The Maine Indian Tribal-State Commission, Hallowell, Maine.

Since the 1980s, the Mi'kmaq and other Wabanakis in Maine (Maliseet, Passamaquoddy, and Penobscot) have experienced a resurgence of native spirituality. In this cultural revitalization process, the sacred mountain of Katahdin plays a central role.

Index

Abenaki, 38, 40, 49, 60, 66, 72, 107, 108, 109, 110, 112, 113, 115, 123, 136, 138, 141, 142, 144, 147, 150, 161, 212

Abenaki: The Native People of Maine (film), 213

Aboriginal title, 57, 133–34, 154, 169, 209–11; asserted by Maliseets, 146; asserted by Mi'kmaqs, 144; British ignore Maliseet and Mi'kmaq assertions, 163; British and Dutch view of, 134; doctrine defined, 209; extinguishment to be purchased by treaty, 154; French view of, 57, 134, 154; Mi'kmaq dispossession by default, 154; threatened by Canadian government plan to demolish its Dept. of Indian Affairs, 199; Wabanakis do not concede loss of, 133–34, 138

Aborigines Protection Society, 170; *see also* Lennox Island

Acadia: ceded to British by French (1713), 131; defined as territory, 55, 59; French-Indian intermarriage in, 67, 69; seigneuries, 63–67; redefined for political reasons, 134

Accommodation, *see* Cultural reactions to Europeans

Acculturation, *see* Cultural reactions to Europeans

Actaudin (a.k.a. Paul, son of Membertou), 81

Adornment: aboriginal, 25, 26, 95; traditional, 175, 181, 202

African Americans ("Freed Negroes") in Nova Scotia, 164

Agriculture, *see* Cultivation

Albany, 98, 131

Alcohol abuse, 101, 175; destroys tribal nations, 104; effect on missionary efforts, 69, 77, 78, 83; by Europeans, 89, 103; impact of epidemics and death, 54, 103; fuels intertribal aggression, 106; by Mi'kmaqs, 103, 104; officials require chiefs to prevent, 175; positive effects of neotraditionalism on, 202–203

Alcohol gifts, 125, 136, 144; used to attract seal-hunting bands, 100; French commander supplies warriors, 125

Alcohol trade, 48, 60, 89, 94, 136, 158, 168; cheating by European merchants, 104; cost (brandy and rum), 97, 104; French authorities try to curb, 104; sold by Mi'kmaq, 104; sold by smugglers, 104

Alexander, Sir Willliam (Scottish colonial entrepreneur), 62

Algimou, Louis Francis (L'kimu) (Mi'kmaq chief), 169–70

Algonkin, 38, 52, 72, 75, 112, 113, 114, 115, 124, 161

Algonquian language family, 1, 22

Alliances, 32–35, 39; Bashaba and colonists in Maine coastal villages, 109; English-Indian in New England, 110; English-Iroquois, 117; English-Wabanaki, 128; French-Algonquian, 115; French-Mi'kmaq, 62, 82; French-Wabanaki, 120, 159; Iroquois nations, 112; Mi'kmaq-Abenaki, 108; Mi'kmaq and other Algonquians, 112–13; vital for Mi'kmaq survival, 118; Wabanaki Confederacy, 117–19

American Indian Movement (AIM), 200–202

American Revolution, 155–162; French support Patriots, 159; Patriots versus Loyalists, 156–157; Wabanaki role in, 156–62; Wabanaki and the Treaty of Watertown (1776), 157, 212–13; Wabanaki warrior wages, 158; Wabanaki withdraw support for Patriots due to Canadian Indian pressure, 161

Annapolis, Nova Scotia, 131, 144; attacked by Mi'kmaq and Maliseet, 138, 141–42; *see also* Port Royal

Annapolis (Mi'kmaq band), 187

Anne (British queen), 131

Annie Mae, Brave-Hearted Woman (film), 202

Anthropological theory: linguistic history, 22; Mi'kmaq origins, 20, 21, 23, 24; and native rights, 5, 213; "river drainage" model, critique, 213; tribal cultures as open systems of adaptation, 5, 56, 216; Wabanaki territoriality and joint use, 213

Anthropologists, 7, 9, 13, 22, 180

Antigonish, Nova Scotia, 140, 195

d'Aprendestiguy de Martignon, Martin (seigneur), 68

Aquash, Anna Mae, *see* Pictou, Anna Mae

Aquash, Nogeeshik (Ojibway artist), 201

Archaeology: evidence of Mi'kmaq origins, 21; life before European invasion, 22–23

Aroostook Band of Micmacs, 1, 12, 17, 190, 213–14; cultural revitalization, 12; native rights effort, 4, 7, 16, 17, 213–14

Aroostook Band of Micmacs Settlement Act (1991), 17, 213–14

Aroostook County, 196, 213

Assembly of First Nations, 200, 209, 214